RABBI
MAX
HELLER

JUDAIC STUDIES SERIES
Leon J. Weinberger
GENERAL EDITOR

RABBI MAX HELLER

❧❧❧

Reformer, Zionist, Southerner,
1860–1929

by

BOBBIE MALONE

The University of Alabama Press
Tuscaloosa and London

Arlene and Paul —
The family who makes
reunion synonymous
with celebration!
Love,
Bobbie

∞

The paper on which this book is printed
meets the minimum requirements
of American National Standard for
Information Science–Permanence of Paper
for Printed Library Materials, ANSI Z39.48-1984.

Library of Congress Cataloging-in-Publication Data

Malone, Bobbie, 1944–
Rabbi Max Heller : reformer, Zionist, southerner, 1860–1929 / by
Bobbie Malone.
p.   cm.—(Judaic studies series)
Includes bibliographical references and index.
ISBN 0-8173-0875-X (cloth : alk. paper)
1. Heller, Max, 1860–1929.   2. Rabbis—Louisiana—New Orleans
—Biography.   3. Jews—Louisiana—New Orleans—History.   4. Reform
Judaism—Louisiana—New Orleans—History.   5. Temple Sinai (New
Orleans, La.)   6. New Orleans (La.)—Ethnic relations.   I. Title.
II. Series: Judaic studies series (Unnumbered)
BM755.H319M35   1997
296.8'341'092—dc21   96-48359

British Library Cataloguing-in-Publication Data available

Cover jacket and frontispiece: Max Heller, late in his career, circa 1922.
Courtesy of the American Jewish Archives, Hebrew Union College–
Jewish Institute of Religion, Cincinnati.

For Bill

CONTENTS

ILLUSTRATIONS

ᔆᔆᔆ

PREFACE

❧

Max Heller was a man of both passionate conviction and inner contradiction. In his public life, he consistently sought center stage, sometimes as an agitator, at other times as a mediator. During his first two decades in the United States, Heller confronted the full panoply of social problems that dominated the late nineteenth century—emancipation and racism, nationalism and nativism, immigration and assimilation—issues that remain unresolved even today. In grappling with them, he sought to define himself.

During the early years of his tenure as rabbi of the South's largest Reform congregation, Heller assumed various guises, according to his evolving sense of integrity. By the turn of the century he was beginning to fashion the contours of his future role as a community leader. As an American-trained Reform rabbi, he had imbibed the principles of a rational, liberal, and universalist Judaism, but these principles no longer seemed adequate guidance in a world increasingly threatened by ethnic and racial nationalism. Earlier than most, Heller realized that such nationalism would ultimately cause European Jewry to be scapegoated. At the same time he recognized that the spiritual roots of his faith were embedded in traditions casually abandoned by the Jewish reformers who had come of age at midcentury. Their sanitized Judaism now appeared sterile. As the twentieth century dawned, local, regional, national, and international events impressed upon him the profound cultural as well as religious implications of the Jewish experience. Integrating his new conception of Judaism and its mission, he became an ardent Zionist and an ardent humanitarian, a risk-taker who championed social justice and defended the underdog.

His life experience, then, provides a distinct vantage point from which to view the confluence of cultures—European, American, southern, and Jewish—that shaped him. Although Heller's ideas were substantially ahead of their time, they also were rooted in and reflected the particular intellectual and social climate in which he lived. For Max Heller was no revolutionary thinker or actor but a consummate Progressive. His career reveals the limits of his vision as much as it illuminates the ideals that he embraced.

When I taught in Tyler, Texas, one of my primary responsibilities was encouraging my gifted elementary students to choose and pursue a research topic and design a product that they could share with their schoolmates beyond the gifted program. I continue to believe that my students' enthusiasm convinced me to pursue a research topic of my own. Because I wanted to explore the roots of southern Jewish identity, I returned to Tulane University to study southern Jewish history.

During my first semester, Clarence Mohr recommended that I examine everything that had been written on Jews in New Orleans. In the process, I found Max Heller's *Jubilee Souvenir of Temple Sinai, 1872–1922.* This slender booklet intrigued me because it offered so much more than its title suggested. Heller's scholarship and emphasis on events beyond the history of the congregation stimulated my curiosity. Who was this turn-of-the-century Reform rabbi who revealed his passion for Zionism and respect for Orthodox Jews as he chronicled the history of the Crescent City's Jewish citizens? In Patrick Maney's research seminar the following spring, I decided to find out more about the author of the *Jubilee Souvenir,* and that initial seminar paper grew into my master's thesis. In a seminar on race relations under Lawrence Powell, I wrote a paper that eventually developed into the sixth chapter of the biography.

Clarence Mohr, Patrick Maney, and Lawrence Powell formed my dissertation committee. Their rigorous critiques, questions, and encouragement helped me find more in Max Heller than I had ever anticipated. Clarence Mohr became my dissertation adviser because he believed in my scholarship from the beginning and was the first professor able to accept a longtime friend as a fellow historian. Larry Powell generously helped me transform the dissertation into a biography.

Max Heller's papers are housed at the American Jewish Archives at Hebrew Union College–Jewish Institute of Religion in Cincinnati, the loveliest place imaginable to sift through primary documents. Through Helen Mervis and Buddy Jacobs, the New Orleans Jewish Endowment Foundation provided me with an initial research grant and two Willy and Erna Wolff Scholarships, the first ever given to someone pursuing an academic degree in American history. René Lehmann went beyond the duties of chairman of the scholarship fund in helping with a German translation.

After spending two weeks at the American Jewish Archives during the summer of 1989, I realized that I had only begun to uncover gems in Max

Heller's papers, and I had not yet looked at any of the other materials in the AJA's extensive collection. Twice awarded a Loewenstein-Wiener Fellowship in American Jewish Studies, in 1990–91 and in 1993–94, by the American Jewish Archives, I began to feel that the Hebrew Union College campus was my home away from home. The entire AJA organization, from director Abraham Peck to archivist Kevin Proffitt, and the world's most supportive staff—Ruth Kreimer, Eleanor Lawhorn, Elise Nienaber, Camille Servizzi, Kathy Spray, and Tammy Topper—did their best to make research in their superb collections a real pleasure.

Fanny Zelcer, since retired as archivist, was also extremely generous. She put me in touch with Hilda Weltman, whose sensitive translations of several of the German letters in Max Heller's papers proved indispensable in helping me to shape my interpretation of Heller's life. The New Orleans Jewish Endowment Foundation funded her contributions. Back in New Orleans, Rose Karpel also helped with a translation.

Working at the AJA, I also met several scholars who offered suggestions and support. Gary Zola shared much from his own research on Max Heller; Michael A. Meyer asked me provocative questions; and Jonathan D. Sarna, now at Brandeis University, became an unofficial adviser on all aspects of research, providing me with bibliographic and historiographic suggestions and reading and critiquing all my work in American Jewish history. His guidelines for revising my dissertation were immensely helpful. Others who worked at the AJA pursuing their own research helped me come to terms with mine, and our common research interests evolved into friendships. Leah Hagedorn, Marianne Sanua, Karla Goldman, Juliet George, Joan Nathan, and Peggy Pearlstein, especially, made the AJA experience memorable.

Like all other American Jewish historians, I owe a particular debt of gratitude to the late director Jacob Rader Marcus. When we met, he was in his late nineties, and he could not have been more gracious or genial. I interviewed him on each visit and gained much firsthand information about Hebrew Union College and the conflict between Zionists and anti-Zionists there before and in the aftermath of World War I. Whenever Dr. Marcus came across a reference to Max Heller, he mailed it along with a charming note. I cherish the memory of his extraordinary perspective, unfailing generosity, buoyant spirit, and intellectual stamina.

The staff in various parts of the Howard-Tilton Library at Tulane were exceptionally helpful, especially those in Interlibrary Loan, Special Collections, and the Louisiana Collection. Kevin Fontenot, a fellow graduate student, always alerted me to materials that I might find useful, while Bruce Raeburn, curator of the William R. Hogan Jazz Archives, allowed me to use the *Mascot* microfilm at my leisure. Joe Logsdon and Harriet Stern told me about local paths to pursue. Sally Stassi at the Historic New Orleans Collection searched for photographs of Temple Sinai for me after I had moved to Madison.

My dear friend Ruth Dreyfous, whom Heller confirmed at Temple Sinai in 1914, helped me understand what it was like to be a Reform Jew in New Orleans earlier in this century, while another dear mentor, Rosalie Cohen, shared her memories of Heller's relationship to the Orthodox community in the city. Moise Steeg, the late Hélène Godchaux, Mary Anna Feibelman, her late mother, Alice Fellman, and the late Mike Brener all filled me in with their memories of Max Heller, the rabbi they all claimed "looked like God."

Alan Avery-Peck and Mark K. Bauman read versions of the manuscript and furthered my understanding of American Judaism at the turn of the century. Mark continues to share insights from his own related research, which have proved invaluable. Marcie Cohen Ferris, past director of the Museum of the Southern Jewish Experience, and I have discussed southern Jewry far beyond Max Heller. Ann Hanaw first introduced me to the Southern Jewish Historical Society, an organization providing a supportive network for anyone interested in the Southland's Jews.

The University of Alabama Press has stayed the course. Director Emeritus Malcolm M. MacDonald and current director Nicole Mitchell contacted me before I had completed my master's thesis. They continued to cheer me on until I sent them my manuscript. Kathy Swain, assistant managing editor, and Marcia Brubeck, copyeditor, gently shepherded me through the seemingly never-ending series of steps between a revised manuscript and a full-fledged biography. Their welcome confidence in my work bolstered my resolve to complete the task.

Publication of this book has been supported in part by grants and donations from the Betty and Theo Heller Fund, Edward M. Heller, Cecile C. Burfeind, and the Southern Jewish Historical Society.

The descendants of Max Heller, his late daughter-in-law, Mildred Heller, and her two sons, Theo and Edward, and their families have been extremely encouraging, sharing with me their insights, documents, photographs, and unique perspective. My former father-in-law, the late Maurice B. Sontheimer, Jr., saw the scholar in me before I had finished my undergraduate degree. He maintained his interest in my work until his death.

I grew up in San Antonio, Texas, surrounded by a close family and friends, whose Judaism radiated from the core of their American identity. My godparents, Esther and Harold Vexler, and my father's dearest friend, the late Irving Frank, formed part of the cocoon of Jewish pride that enveloped me. My late father, Sheppard Scharlack, expressed his Judaism by healing all that ailed his friends and family with his chicken soup and his Jewish humor. My mother, Sylvia Goldinger Sugerman, has always delighted in whatever I have accomplished and is glad that she could finally *kvel* about her daughter's becoming "Dr. Malone" at fifty. In New Orleans, the friendship, prayers, and wisdom of Gussie Woodest helped deliver me to this point, especially the midnight calls many years ago during which she whispered, "He may not be there when you want Him, but He's always on time."

After years of making art and teaching elementary school, it would have been impossible for me to become a historian without the constant intellectual and emotional sustenance and nurturing of my husband, Bill, who lovingly encourages each new exploration. To paraphrase a line from a traditional country music song that expresses all that makes me grateful for our partnership: he gives my heart ease.

To all of them, to my children, Benjamin and Matthew Sontheimer, and to my daughter-in-law, Myra, who I hope find aspects of Judaism that enrich their lives; to my parents, who inadvertently kindled my curiosity about southern Jews by rearing me in Temple Beth-El; to the gifted elementary students whose questions stimulated me to ask my own; to friends made through Tulane's history program—especially Lee Farrow, Leslie Lovett Kohn, and Leslie Parr—with whom I have grown intellectually, I express my deep appreciation and gratitude.

RABBI
MAX
HELLER

CHAPTER I

❧

From Jewish Prague to Chicago, 1860–1879

On Sunday afternoon, 13 February 1887, the Board of Directors of the prestigious Temple Sinai in New Orleans called for a general membership meeting to select a new rabbi to lead the congregation. One hundred male heads of household came to discuss the candidacy of the young Max Heller, who had addressed the congregation earlier that month, and after a vote of 91–9, they offered him the position. The *Daily Picayune* described the new rabbi as "a fine Hebraic scholar, a man of deep thought and broad principles, a graceful and effective speaker" with "no trace of his Bohemian birth in the parity [purity] of his English."[1] Thus Max Heller began forty years of service to Temple Sinai, a career that encompassed the end of one century and the beginning of another.

It was a time of significant upheavals for both American Reform Judaism and the New Orleans Jewish community. Jews in New Orleans confronted problems of immigration and acculturation. Despite its cosmopolitan diversity, the city hardly escaped the fever of racism and nativism that infected "old stock" Americans around the turn of the century. The growing intolerance exacerbated conflicts within the American Jewish community, which did not know exactly how to cope with the massive wave of East European immigrants. The national debate touched a raw nerve among Jews in New Orleans, who felt that racial animosity threatened local patterns of acceptance and assimilation.[2] Heller's response to this crisis and others that were similar embodied the main currents of American Jewish thought. He worked to build support within the Reform Jewish community locally and nationally and sought to broaden its responsiveness. His experience as an immigrant combined with his American Jewish background to shape the Reform Zionist and urban Progressive stance that became the hallmark of his later career.

Heller learned to adapt while maintaining a basic sense of integrity and purpose during his years in the complex ethnic atmosphere of

Prague, his native city and the political and cultural capital of Bohemia. Born on 31 January 1860, the only son among the five children of Mathilde Kassowitz and Simon Heller, Max grew up in an intensely patriarchal Jewish milieu that placed a premium on male religious scholarship. Both sides of the family claimed a distinguished lineage of talmudic scholars and rabbis. The advent of a son meant that the family heritage could be transmitted to another generation.[3]

The year of Heller's birth marked the beginning of an especially propitious time for the Jewish community of Prague. The mythical *golem* who, according to popular Jewish legend, had earlier protected Prague's medieval Jews, seemed once again to hover over the city.[4] After centuries of ghettoization, Prague's Jews were becoming socially mobile. At the same time, German-speaking Bohemians, who enjoyed power as the beneficiaries of the Habsburg empire, faced a challenge from Czechs, themselves stirred by incipient feelings of nationalism. While neither group sought to win over the Jews, the Czech-German struggle defined the social and political framework in which Jews sought to legitimize their participation in civil society. In spite of the ethnic tensions, the promise of social and political equality filled Jewish Bohemians with optimism during the nineteen years of Max Heller's growth to manhood.[5]

The integration of Prague's Jewish community in the second half of the nineteenth century reflected social, political, and economic changes in Bohemia that the Enlightenment had wrought 100 years earlier. At that time Joseph II began liberalizing the restrictions placed on Jewish life. His object was to render Jews " 'more useful' to the state" by eliminating the differences between them and their neighbors. He hoped that the "Jewish problem" would disappear with the Jews' assimilation into the larger society. To this end, Joseph II established German as the official language. "Germanization" permitted the unification of diverse ethnic elements within the empire. Germanization also transformed the curriculum of Jewish schools, which had to expand beyond sacred studies. For the first time, Jews gained access to universities and other institutions of higher education.[6]

In response, Jews actively pursued Germanization. They modified their own cultural orientation to accommodate their expectations of improved civil status. As they adopted the German language, they embraced the whole of Western secular civilization. Centuries-old traditions of the static ghetto lost their social relevance, and the Jewish communal structure changed radically. Eventually the modernizers within the new Jewish social order created a more liberal and flexible Judaism that they hoped would preserve Jewish identity while facilitating Jews' survival in an assimilationist world.[7]

Jews throughout Western Europe took an active role in the constitutional movements that heralded the 1848 revolutions. They saw a direct link between their support of liberal governmental reforms and their prospects for securing civil rights. In Central Europe, however, the hopes and actions of Frenchmen inspired an illiberal nationalism that proved inimical to ethnic and religious tolerance. Anti-Jewish riots erupted as a consequence of a larger upsurge of Czech-German hostilities. Many disillusioned Jews, like other disappointed "Forty-eighters," left for America.[8]

In spite of the immediate reaction, 1848 initiated a new era for the Jews of Central Europe. Further reforms facilitating social integration followed, including civil equality with Christians and full political emancipation. Prior to 1852, most of Prague's more than 10,000 Jews still lived in the ghetto, the *Judenstadt,* then the city's most squalid, least attractive neighborhood. After liberation the area became the fifth borough of the city. Before Max's birth, the Hellers had been able to move from the Judenstadt into a home on a "quiet, tree-lined street." Bohemian Jews were grateful to the monarchy for their freedom. For the remaining decades of the Habsburg empire, they were a devoted and loyal national group that made important economic and cultural contributions to Austrian and Hungarian life. But such devotion bred complications.[9]

While emancipation in the West allowed Jews to participate in the national culture of the country in which they were liberated, in Bohemia and Moravia, Jews had to identify with one of the competing nationalistic interests—either Germans or Czechs. Paradoxically, just at the moment when the half century of Germanization assured Jewish allegiance to the Habsburg kingdom, the balance of power in Bohemia began to shift. As the thoroughly Germanized Jews emerged from the Judenstadt, they began to sense that their identification with German nationalism did not guarantee them political security.[10]

Class considerations reinforced linguistic preference; the German-speaking citizens of Prague, Jewish and non-Jewish, constituted the bourgeoisie. Prague's central Bohemian location on the Moldau River made it an ideal trading center. German speakers controlled most of the commerce and manufacturing as well as the city's administrative and cultural positions. Prague's prominence as a mercantile center affected both the social and the economic profile of its Jewish community.[11]

The Simon Hellers belonged to the stratum of the Jewish community in transit from a well-codified ghetto existence to a modern commercial world. Marriage helped consolidate social and economic gains. The Kassowitz family had a daughter, Mathilde. By securing a traditionally eligible mate, a Hebrew scholar such as Simon, she could bring the prominent family even greater distinction. And to help their daughter attract such a bachelor, the Kassowitzes were willing and able to include with the dowry a men's fabric business, purchased to give the young couple a livelihood. As expected, Mathilde worked alongside her husband so that Simon, "who had never had to engage in anything so mundane as the earning of a dollar," had time enough to study Jewish law.[12]

In the 1860s the Bohemian school system separated into two parts, one Czech and the other German. Jews overwhelmingly continued to support the German schools. As in other parts of Europe, Jews in Bohemia enrolled in secondary schools more frequently than did non-Jews. Max Heller enrolled in the Neustadter Gymnasium, where he prepared for a career in medicine. Like many other Jews, he continued to use the German language less for the sake of national identity than to help him succeed in the larger cultural mosaic of Habsburg society. Prague Jews often participated in German voluntary associations as well. Despite such survival strategies, the Jewish community remained separate socially, feeling no pressure to convert and no desire to intermarry to gain acceptance.[13]

Years later, when Heller was asked to compare Jewish and Czech nationalist aspirations, he replied that he could not. During his upbringing in Prague, he had completely dismissed Czech culture. He recalled being completely uninterested, "occupying as I did, a snobbish disdainful attitude in common with the German milieu in which I was reared." The young Heller considered the Bohemian language a "servant-language in which I could see no merit." Although he harbored no "unkind feelings towards the Czechs," he saw himself "too ardent a lover of German literature" to demonstrate any curiosity in, "much less sympathy with, the Czech struggles." Heller admitted that he had never envisioned "any parallel whatever between rising Czechdom and a reborn Israel."[14]

The Judaism of postemancipation Prague had evolved with the dissolution of the Judenstadt. To conform to the secular world that they were entering, the city's Jews wanted their Judaism to become less ethnic and to retain only ritual and religious aspects that would not interfere with their new position in society. Redefining Judaism as a "religion" allowed them to identify with the larger German community. Not surprisingly, elite and middle-class Jews formed the vanguard of the reform movement. Thus the driving force for many of the changes in Jewish worship came not from the rabbis but from the well-to-do members of the community, whose attachment to Judaism was more superficial than philosophical.[15]

The Heller home, with a traditional Jewish scholar at its head, retained its allegiance to Orthodoxy. Young Max grew up with one foot in the world of Hebraic scholarship and the other in that of German culture. For many neighboring households, assimilation and acculturation gradually led to a marked religious indifference. The Hellers, however, met the new social reality head-on without denying the significance of the religious obligations of the past. They undoubtedly admired the city's rabbis, now *Doktorrabbiner* (rabbis with doctoral degrees), who could discourse knowledgeably on a variety of topics beyond the Talmud and the Torah. The professionalization of the rabbinate and other traditionally dominant intellectual vocations mirrored the Jewish community's aspirations to upward economic mobility.[16]

Vienna's Jewish bourgeoisie set the standard for both Prague and Budapest. Vienna's well-ordered "world without haste," graphically portrayed by authors Stefan Zweig and George Clare, was also the Prague of Max Heller's generation. Heller himself described a nostalgic scene from his Prague Jewish childhood in an article he published thirty years after coming to America. In "The Chanukkah of My Boyhood," he wrote of walking through the streets of the old Prague ghetto with "my sainted father" on the eighth and final evening of the minor holiday. Heller recalled the "cheering and inspiring sight . . . [of] lit-up window fronts" in the Jewish homes where Chanukkah menorahs had been placed. He saw the display as the "public celebration of an episode in our own national history." Jews subscribed to "the primacy of the German middle class in a centralized Austria" while insisting "on respect for their identity as members of a distinct religious group." The latter helped save them from becoming "craven suppliants for status in Gentile society," that is, from emulating Christians without regard for Jewish distinctiveness.[17]

Jewish family life also reinforced the Victorian dictates of the period. The father was the patriarch, "the independent sheik of the house," in the words of Isaac Mayer Wise. Both Clare and James Heller, Wise's biographer, referred to the abuses of privilege, the "petty tyranny," of the father as despot. On the other hand, the rigid hierarchical familial structure imparted a reassuring sense of permanence, order, and stability. Both parents worked hard. Jewish women, like Mathilde Heller, often assisted their husbands in business as well as bearing household responsibilities. Children respected their parents' authority and values; parents encouraged their children's achievements by emphasizing education and material success. As late as 1848, economic pressure caused most children to be on their own after they reached thirteen, the age of Bar Mitzvah, when the male Jew was accepted into the adult community. Before the end of the century, however, parents in the Jewish community were financially able to send their children not only to secondary school but also to the university. A Jewish intelligentsia absorbed current liberal and secular trends in the Prague community just as Viennese Jews did in their capital.

Although Simon Heller was willing to prepare his son for the ever-widening opportunities that Prague society offered, he shrank from personally confronting the secular world and remained devoted to traditional Jewish scholarship. Unable to adapt to the hustle of the bourgeois world, he struggled to support his family in the increasingly competitive environment. His daughters remembered their father's annoyance when a customer entered the store and diverted his attention from a sacred volume. The elder Kassowitzes' plan when they provided a shop for their daughter and son-in-law was rapidly failing: the son-in-law showed no interest in making the venture succeed. In 1877, an uncle borrowed and lost the remnants of Mathilde's dowry. Simon's customers "almost completely stopped interfering" with his studies and took their business elsewhere. Hoping to improve their financial prospects, the Hellers sold their home and moved to Chicago, where relatives and friends had preceded them. The education of their only son was too important to interrupt, however. Accordingly, they arranged for seventeen-year-old Max to remain in Prague. He boarded at the home of a family friend. In this way he was able to complete his studies at the Neustadter Gymnasium with plans to continue as a medical student.[18]

Educationally Max could take advantage of both the Jewish and the German worlds of Prague. After his parents and siblings had emigrated, however, he was obliged to balance his studies with work to support them. While Simon Heller had acquainted his son with classic Hebrew scholarship, the Neustadter Gymnasium taught religion in addition to the fundamentals of a classic liberal education. Heller studied Greek and Latin, earning higher scores in Greek. During his final semester, he took both of these languages and, in addition, German, physics, mathematics, geography and history, and an introductory course in philosophy. In the winter and spring semesters of 1878–1879, he rose from twelfth to eighth in his class of thirty-four. The effort required a discipline that he evidently found difficult to maintain, however. After the family departed for America, Anna, his older sister, wrote him teasingly, "Always think I stand behind you and say: 'Max, study.' Or rather, don't think that, because as usual, when I said that, you didn't do it." Whatever his misgiv-

1. *Max Heller as a gymnasium student in Prague, circa 1879.*
Courtesy of the American Jewish Archives, Hebrew Union
College–Jewish Institute of Religion, Cincinnati.

ings about his own study habits, Max helped support himself by tutoring. Still, his father wrote, urging him not to "overburden yourself with giving lessons . . . never do we ask that you work at the expense of your health or your studies. . . . even if morally it is not condoned, 'be selfish and skeptical.' The sad experiences we had in every respect in the last years . . . [make it necessary] to give you a guide which we ourselves don't follow . . . , imposed upon us by the world around us."[19]

Simon Heller's words were more significant than he realized when he wrote them. He had left for America before his wife and daughters to find a suitable place for them to live. A Prague friend then warned Mathilde not to carry too much money along on the voyage across the Atlantic. Instead, the friend urged Mathilde to leave the funds safely in her keeping until reaching Chicago, when the friend would send them directly to her. Mathilde agreed, and the mother and daughters traveled in typical immigrant style, steerage class, encountering storms, filth, and seasickness before reaching Philadelphia, where Simon met them. Friends and relatives who were already settled in the new land often helped ease the arrival of newly arrived immigrants. Friends in Chicago invited the Hellers to stay temporarily in their crowded apartment. As soon as the money arrived from Prague, the Hellers could move into their new home and purchase a new shop. But the money never came. From cousins the Hellers learned that the Prague friends' business had gone bankrupt and had destroyed the Hellers' savings in the process.[20]

Hopes of using the nest egg to gain a measure of financial independence in America vanished immediately. Vestiges of the depression of 1873 still scarred the American economic landscape. While 1877 may have been a good year to invest in a business, inasmuch as prices were still deflated, it was not a propitious time to lack funds, language fluency, and job skills in a city full of immigrants. The family settled in a small tenement apartment. The floor served as a bed, and packing crates functioned as furniture. Simon Heller proved no more helpful in Chicago than he had been in Prague, but now his "great pride" became a further burden to his hungry family. He forced his family to give away food that they needed. His daughters later remembered that he allowed no one to touch baskets of food sent by friends because he refused to accept charity. Not surprisingly, he also remained emotionally and psychologically incapable of supporting his family. Religious scholarship was not in demand in the Southside Chicago Jewish neighborhood where the family settled. Because Simon Heller's pride allowed him to do nothing else, he earned only "an occasional pittance teaching in a Talmud Torah, from the day of his arrival in America until the day of his death."[21]

The difficulties that confronted the Heller family were common among those who arrived at the tail end of the depression. Mathilde and her four daughters made sacrifices for both father and son, who alone could take refuge in scholarship. Simon's pride and Max's studies shielded the men from the harsher realities known to the women of the household. Bearing most of the burden of support, Heller's wife and daughters engaged in peddling and factory work because no other jobs were available to them. The Heller children were able to find work when their mother could not, because immigrant children could be hired for less and acquired English more quickly than did their parents. Such facts of economic life undermined traditional family roles. Mathilde and Simon, like other immigrant parents, could no longer function as role models for the younger generation. Children became acculturated more quickly than did the adults and thus attained a stature in the household unknown in their country of origin.[22] But as granddaughter Ruth Heller Steiner observed, the physical strain endured by Mathilde and the girls "permanently ruined the health of some of them and probably blotted out the life of one of them." The two younger daughters, Ernestine and Louise, worked on looms in factories. Sabina, the sister immediately older than Max, died. Anna spent her days on a treadmill, "pushing primitive wine machinery around in an endless circle" and also helped her mother peddle whiskey door to door. Both later developed tuberculosis from peddling outdoors in cold winters. Despite the need to support himself and the distance from his family, Max had time to acquire an education that protected him from a similar fate.[23]

Max remained undeniably the most valued of Simon's children. Upon receiving a term report Max had sent, Simon wrote with elation, "I don't think that a calligraphic picture executed by the greatest artist would have pleased us more. What are the pictures of a Raphael compared to those thrown down with a dull pen but merited splendidly?" Simon addressed his son as "dearly-beloved Max . . . My shining light in the sun." His son's health afforded Simon the opportunity both to express his love and to offer parental advice. Repeatedly Simon entreated Max not to "overburden" himself, to "regard your health as your greatest capital on which you must not skimp," comments that take on a special poignancy when we remember the specter of illness and death that haunted the family in Chicago. Max internalized these admonitions and later became obsessively concerned with his own health.[24]

Despite Max's prodigious efforts and the "enthusiasm of his professors of logic, history, prose composition and universal literature," he could not stay in Prague after completing his studies at the Gymnasium, and he had to abandon his dream of becoming a physician. It remains unclear whether Max left Prague because of his concern for the welfare of his family and his desire to be near them or because no funds existed to support his medical education abroad. Simon, however, did his best to steer his son away from medicine—and toward America. The year before Max completed his studies at the gymnasium, his father casually but point-edly mentioned that if Max intended to become a physician, then Simon hoped that he had "overcome the disgust at injuries." The father told his son that he did not have to remain in Prague for his training but could study medicine or pharmacology in America and be closer to his family. Simon assured him that the family wanted only the best for him "but would only be too happy to have you with us before our strength fails." A possibly apocryphal story, related by one of his sisters, suggests that Max's departure may have occurred in response to parental urging. Sup-posedly a small boy was playing with a ball one day in the Hellers' Chi-cago apartment. While throwing the ball at the wall, he accidentally hit a picture of "the cherished only son, smashing the glass and arousing in his mother a superstitious conviction that if he stayed in Germany [Bo-hemia] something dreadful would happen to him."[25]

Simon urged his son to reconsider medical training abroad and de-tailed the advantages of the American rabbinate. He then complimented Max on his skill in composing school reports and lectures, a talent that would serve him in good stead during rabbinical training. Simon's state-ments were calculated to induce guilt. Max corresponded with his family erratically, and now Simon warned, "Mother cannot bear it to be sepa-rated from you any longer." She seemed to be aging "noticeably." Simon was aware that a new seminary had recently been established in Cincin-nati to train American rabbis. Now he suggested that Max could attend Hebrew Union College. If he did so, he would be separated from the fam-ily "by only a night's travel." The college, anxious for students, had pa-trons that defrayed the cost of room and board. As a further inducement, Simon reminded Max that, if he remained in Prague, he would be eligible for military duty. In America, he would be exempt. Financial prospects served as the final temptation that Simon dangled before his son. The father reported that physicians in America made less than preachers and that ministers commanded more respect from the American public.[26]

Max graduated in June 1879 and made plans to leave for America in July. Shortly before his departure he wrote his father that he was an athe-ist. Shocked and bewildered, Simon told Max that the postcard forced him "to revoke all my former letters concerning your profession and to give you my consent for the continuation of your studies in Prague." Max's confession made the rabbinate an unlikely career choice. That Max did not wish to be a rabbi was not the problem, Simon insisted. His son's "blasphemy," however, caused the father great distress. Simon wondered where he had gone wrong as a parent. "Where are all the religious im-pressions which I tried to give you since childhood when all observances were still holy for you?" he queried. Had Max thrown them all over-board? Simon had sought not to make his son an Orthodox or talmudic Jew, he protested, but only to place a "veil around a precious core," around that "sheltering, guiding and incomprehensible spirit" in hopes that, when doubts later arose, the sacred centerpiece of religious faith would remain firm. Now his son had mercilessly torn "all the magic of my dreams out of my soul."[27]

In the next paragraph, Simon regained control of his emotions. He attempted to convince the young skeptic that the father was no intellectual innocent. Simon was familiar with the methods of a variety of Western thinkers, from Spinoza and Kant to Leibnitz, and had perused Darwin's *Origin of the Species.* But having read them all, he still found himself speaking Faust's lines, "Here I stand, poor fool, and am as wise as before." Could science really replace faith? he asked rhetorically. Only a handful of "blasphemers" remained skeptics in their final hours. Wisely, Simon did not deny Max his doubts but told him frankly that he would rather count himself among those "honest enough to say: we believe because we cannot know anything" rather than with "heretics who insist that they know, and they don't know anything." What could science offer those beset by the "storms of life?" Simon begged Heller to abandon the arrogance of atheism, to "build up God within you—in whichever spiritual direction"—and not to forsake the heritage of a religion that allowed its followers a "free search" in searching for a "higher Ruler of fate."[28]

Max Heller replied by leaving for America. He never again alluded to the atheism he professed before leaving Prague. Probably it was a ruse of an adolescent eager to assert his independence from his father, but Simon reaffirmed his paternal authority when he instructed Max about the long journey to Chicago.

Simon gave his son precise travel instructions. Certain that the Atlantic passage was fraught with dangers, Simon armed him with suggestions and contingency plans to deal with any difficulty that might arise, from changing money and managing luggage to catching the proper train. He instructed Max to travel by train from Prague to Antwerp after sending most luggage ahead. Ships departing for the United States sailed to New York or to Philadelphia. "You should take the one to Philadelphia which saves you hours between New York and Philadelphia," advised Simon, since the cost of the steerage ticket included a train ticket from Philadelphia to New York. This ticket could then be sold in Philadelphia for $1.50, provided that Max would have let it be known in Antwerp that, although booked on a Philadelphia-bound ship, New York was his destination. The father carefully spelled out other such intricate cost-saving techniques.

Family members' past problems with money undoubtedly accentuated his concern. "Never take out any money, just have a few Mark [*sic*] handy to take care of an emergency. . . . it would be best if you had a vest made with a good pocket which you would wear during your trip." Perhaps Max's forthcoming transatlantic passage was the occasion for his photograph, which was apparently part of his identification papers. It shows a handsome and serious young man, wearing a vest beneath his jacket.[29]

Young Heller arrived late in the summer of 1879, equipped with a fine secular and religious education but no command of the English language. Although he had given up on becoming a physician, another means of service to others opened to him. He already shared his father's reverence for history and tradition, for protecting and perpetuating a Jewish cultural heritage. He had also acquired the tools of science and a measure of his mother's practical resilience. The education that he had so painstakingly attained in Europe conferred upon him certain advantages. Once in Chicago, Max surveyed the situation and immediately chose to prepare himself for the American Reform rabbinate. In so doing he undoubtedly enjoyed his father's blessings.

CHAPTER II

❧❧❧

Acquiring the Tools of Americanization,
1879–1884

Max Heller had resisted abandoning his dreams of becoming a European-educated physician and had not wanted to relinquish the independence he had enjoyed a continent away from his family. Within a month of his arrival in Chicago he moved quickly to regain his freedom. He enrolled as a rabbinical student in Hebrew Union College in Cincinnati, the first permanent Jewish seminary in the United States. Rabbi Isaac Mayer Wise, also Bohemian born, had founded Hebrew Union College several years earlier. The college represented the culmination of some three decades of struggle between the traditionalists and the reformers in the American Jewish community. Ironically, while Max had been seeking psychological distance from his biological father, his move to Cincinnati brought him directly under the influence of the father of American Reform Judaism, to whom the rabbinical students were like sons. Max quickly embraced both the man and the message.

Wise dreamed of creating a structure that could unify Jews all over the country—particularly those who resided far from major Jewish population centers along the eastern seaboard. He had found predominantly German Cincinnati particularly congenial to his vision. At midcentury, the "Queen City of the West" had become a thriving commercial center with a Jewish population second in size only to that of New York. Between 1860 and 1880, a national German Jewish business elite had emerged in the United States. It was dominated by clothing manufacturers, investment bankers, and meat-processing moguls, many of whom hailed from Cincinnati. The city was a major distribution center for Jewish wholesalers and manufacturers supplying Jewish peddlers in the West and in the South whose Jewish communities naturally looked to Cincinnati for religious as well as commercial leadership. Cincinnati bore some resemblance to Prague—with its strongly Germanic elite culture, comfortable German Jewish bourgeoisie, and beautiful hills situated on a major river.[1]

Wise believed that the Protestant American environment stimulated the development of a singularly American Judaism capable of adapting to the desires of rapidly acculturating Jews. Identifying with Moses, his biblical hero, he articulated his own "manifest destiny" in his bid for leadership of the American Jewish community. Neither a scholar hampered by precedent nor an intellectual craving rational justification, Wise essentially acted as an activist and publicist. He readily envisioned the goal of creating an organized American Jewry. Responding even in Bohemia to the fiction of James Fenimore Cooper, which he knew first through the tales of Natty Bumppo and later from "Porkopolis," Wise saw America as both the stronghold of freedom and an unlimited frontier. He incorporated these ideals into the institutions he built.[2]

Wise possessed essential qualities for success, and Cincinnati provided "a sort of paradise for the Hebrews," as one contemporary historian put it. The social and economic climate was just what was needed to accommodate Wise's dreams. Max Heller called Wise "the most tolerant of all aggressive partisans." As Heller observed, "unlike the writers, thinkers, preachers of the Atlantic coast [who] never abandoned their German ideas . . . , Dr. Wise, the pioneer, was a Daniel Boone of American Judaism." In building his panoramic vision, Wise, like many reformers of post–Civil War America, cared more about order, organization, and support than he did about doctrinal consistency. The reforms in ritual that he advocated reinforced a sense of decorum and respectability rather than suggesting a fundamental restructuring. Wise's genius lay in his ability to persuade the Americanizing Jews that his vision united the ideals of the young nation with the ethical essentials of a Judaism shorn of its ghetto rituals. He offered his coreligionists an American Judaism fully compatible with life in an open environment. To promulgate his ideas, Wise therefore edited and published two weekly newspapers, the *Israelite* (later the *American Israelite*) and *Die Deborah,* a German-language sheet. Later, Heller too found journalism the most effective way to put his ideas before a broad audience.[3]

Wise did not act in a vacuum. The impulse to Americanize Judaism responded to the will of the people. Wise, as Heller astutely observed, was *"in touch with the people."* The lay leaders of individual congregations, mostly from the South and the West, needed a central Cincinnati-based association that would allow them to work together. In 1873, their efforts led to the founding of the first enduring national Jewish congregational organization, the Union of American Hebrew Congregations (UAHC), an institution whose purposes and mission Wise quickly incorporated into his vision. Invoking the frontier spirit of his adopted country, he advocated the creation of an American-trained rabbinate capable of assuring Jewish survival in a pluralistic and voluntaristic society. As Heller noted, Wise wanted not an erudite "ministry of scholars" but "sensible, practical American men" in touch with the congregations they served and ready to "inculcate Jewish thoughts and enthusiasm." Two years later Wise established a seminary, Hebrew Union College (HUC) under the auspices of the UAHC, which could both underwrite the cost of such a facility and supply young men for the rabbinate.[4]

Although Wise invested immense energy in founding the college and anticipated a great future for it, its beginnings were modest at best. His original hope was to start a Jewish college that would teach secular as well as sacred subjects, but practical Jewish businessmen showed little interest in the institution. Wise responded by creating an eight-year curriculum with two alternative tracks, the first complementing a public high school education, the second leading to ordination in conjunction with an undergraduate degree at the McMicken University, which just a few years later became the University of Cincinnati. Neither course of study appealed to the sons of affluent German-Jewish businessmen. Instead they attracted poor German Jews or orphans and wards of Jewish communities who were seeking an education for their charges. Notwithstanding Simon Heller's confident declarations to his son, rabbis in America did not enjoy the status that they held in Europe. Moreover, the rabbinate had little financial appeal for young men contemplating America's legendary prospect of unlimited opportunity.[5]

Beginning with a group of fourteen first-year students in a single class, Wise added a new class to the college each year. Not all the students who met in the dimly lit basement of the Mound Street Synagogue from four until six in the afternoon had the dedication or the ability to remain the entire eight years. By September 1879, when Max Heller wrote to Wise inquiring about entrance to the seminary, HUC was just embarking on its fifth year and the first year that also included course work at the University of Cincinnati. On 22 September, Wise informed Heller that "nothing stands in your way . . . if you apply immediately for the examination." Since Heller was not yet enrolled at HUC, however, Wise could offer no immediate financial support. The rabbi counseled him first to become a student and then to apply for a stipend. "Arrange . . . the means [of support] for yourself for one or two months and I will try to help you." In a second note written a day later, Wise clarified the situation and urged Max to make up his mind. "I forgot to write yesterday that, in any case, you have first to come here and be admitted to the university before you can obtain a stipend. You should therefore come next week since the course started today."[6]

Max enrolled at Hebrew Union College and the University of Cincinnati under the conditions that Wise offered. Wise remained true to his word. By the end of November, Max's financial situation had improved enough to allow him to send money to his family in Chicago. HUC assumed a personal and familial role not simply in the education of its students but in their complete physical, psychological, and social welfare. The Board of Governors supplied students with clothing, books, and room and board in addition to a stipend. Future rabbis lived in a tightly regimented boardinghouse or boarded with selected Jewish families. Students often had the opportunity to supplement their stipends by tutoring children in the family. Hebrew Union College itself assumed the role of surrogate family, since a member of the board declared himself legal guardian for each out-of-town student during his stay at the school. According to one historian of the college, students needing new clothing were sent to a member of the Board of Governors who was a dry goods wholesaler. When the businessman saw the student, he invariably complained, "What again?" As Heller analyzed the HUC experience years later, he recalled that students tended to respond "with all the ambiguities of love and rebellion that characterize such a relationship."[7]

Wise tried to appeal to a broad audience. He therefore did not stress Reform ideology when he recruited students, but he did seek to establish a rabbinate that was trained to meet the needs of a distinctly American Jewry. At the start of the 1882 academic year, he announced, "Whatever has been advanced in the form of scientific or frivolous criticism to invalidate the authority of Moses or the genuineness of the Law is insufficient to unsettle our case." In any event, Simon Heller, although a traditionalist in Europe, would not have been opposed to the Reform character of the HUC program. Like many Jewish immigrants, he did not even try to keep the dietary laws once he had crossed the Atlantic. In fact, according to his granddaughter, Ruth Heller Steiner, the elder Heller viewed Judaism as "a living, changing, developing religion" apropos of an age that "demanded change." The father's definition of Judaism indelibly shaped the son's perspective, for Max eventually came to view his faith and culture as a continuum and Judaism as a process responsive to the changing needs of a historic people. Wise's ideas understandably struck a responsive chord with his new student.[8]

Moreover, as Wise had happily discovered, America's pluralistic religious environment, which valued pragmatic change over time-honored tradition, accelerated the modernization that he had witnessed in Europe.[9] His insistence that an American rabbinate should receive both a secular and a rabbinical education presumed that Jews would live openly among gentiles in a dynamic and mobile society. Wise therefore based his school's curriculum on a European model albeit one only recently conceived.

The traditional European education of a rabbi took place in a yeshivah where those seeking knowledge studied the complex, densely woven, and legalistic Talmud. Once a yeshivah student had mastered the practical aspects of the Jewish legal code and wished to serve as a communal rabbi, he sought a recognized rabbinical authority who could confer upon him *semikhah,* or ordination. In the self-contained ghetto world, the rabbi became the interpreter of Jewish law for his community. He nevertheless did not assume ministerial duties by giving sermons, visiting the sick, encouraging affiliation with the synagogue, or educating the young. When the ghetto walls fell, eroding the traditional power and stature of the European rabbinate, Protestant ministers offered new models for Jewish religious leadership. The fluid American environment, where German Jews had scattered across the continent, encouraged even greater "Protestantization." Where Jews were widely dispersed, identifying themselves as a distinct religious community provided an easily portable and accessible avenue for Jewish survival.[10]

The idea for an institution to prepare rabbis for broader duties in a modern world dates back only as far as nineteenth-century Jewish emancipation, when German proponents of the *Wissenschaft des Judentums,* the "science of Judaism," emphasized Jewish culture in a comprehensive context and subjected Jewish texts to critical examination. That movement's ideas resonated among the German-born rabbis of the late nineteenth-century American Jewish community before waves of Eastern European immigrants radically transformed a hitherto almost completely homogeneous group.[11]

Being familiar with the needs of small Jewish enclaves in the South and the West, Wise knew that most of the rabbis he trained would be working in communities with a relatively small number of Jews. Heller quickly learned that the rabbi, acting as a minority religious leader and a de facto liaison with the larger society, needed to be well informed in secular matters. His training had to prepare him for a role similar to that of an American Protestant clergyman—educating children, ministering to his flock, preaching and conducting well-ordered services, and exemplifying patriotism. Intellectually, the Wissenschaft movement embodied a philosophy of progress and reform consistent with modernization. In Americanizing the model, Wise offered students coming to Cincinnati the opportunity to gain simultaneously a secular university degree and a seminary education, thereby adapting the Jewish past to American needs. That a rabbi should fit smoothly into the life of his congregation was of paramount importance to the lay leaders, who held the real power in American Jewish communities. Well-to-do businessmen and established professionals formed the boards of directors hiring rabbis for their congregations. These men wanted a rabbi who would endorse their assimilationist ideals and would make a "good modern impression." The training of the Reform rabbinate thus reflected trends that were conspicuous in the German Jewish community on both sides of the Atlantic and were especially pronounced in the United States.[12]

With students Wise assumed a paternalistic role, both loving and demanding. Aspirants like Max regarded him as a "spiritual father" and became devoted disciples. In the first years of the college, when funds were scarce, Wise could afford only one salaried teacher, so he himself taught without compensation. By 1879 when the first college-level class started, Wise had managed to hire Moses Mielziner to teach the Talmud. Mielziner proved extremely able and communicative in preparing his students. Max, who began his HUC education that year, considered him a "pioneer in the field of modern Talmud teaching." Like others seeking entrance to the Collegiate Department, Max had to demonstrate familiarity with Jewish history, mastery of Hebrew and Aramaic grammar, and the ability to read from the Torah and other Jewish texts. His European training at the Gymnasium and his traditional Jewish upbringing prepared Max well for the secular and religious educational opportunities offered in Cincinnati.[13]

Although Wise had designed his collegiate curriculum to create a unified, universalistic, and thoroughly American religion, he remained sensitive to the needs of the many German speakers in American Jewish communities. He insisted that all graduates of HUC be able to deliver sermons in both German and English.[14] All classes at HUC, however, were conducted in English, the primary language of most of the seminary students who were American born. Max probably did not know English before he came to the United States, but he was already enrolled at the University of Cincinnati in the fall of 1879 when he was accepted for admission at HUC. His hard work and solid background in modern and ancient tongues allowed him to acquire the vocabulary, grammar, and syntax quickly enough to receive, in 1882, his bachelor of letters degree from the university and to be initiated into Phi Beta Kappa.[15]

Of the twelve graduates in 1882 from the university's academic depart-

ment, Max alone received the B.L. degree. He was also one of those selected to give a graduation address. It was entitled "The Psychological
Elements of Language." For financial reasons his parents could not be
present for his "day of honor," but he described it to them. Although he
had initially dreaded addressing so large an audience and the "terrible
excitement" of his first appearance in an auditorium, during rehearsal he
was thrilled to find that his voice "could fill the whole theater." Much to
his surprise, Heller felt completely relaxed during the ceremony. He presented his composition, which he had memorized, "without nervousness
but with warmth." Instead of glancing anxiously at his notes, he told his
family that he had looked "quietly at the audience." "Even those who
usually are slow to praise told me that I gave the best composition and
presented it so well." But the deepest pleasure came from I. M. Wise's
response. Wise, seated on the podium, had followed his disciple's delivery "with the greatest interest and with shining eyes." When Heller
finished speaking, Wise turned to one of the students and remarked that
he was particularly proud of Heller, strong praise indeed from his American mentor. Max passed "with distinction."[16]

The address was published the following year in *Academica,* a literary
magazine at the University of Cincinnati. In it the young immigrant
quoted Herder: "only through language has it been possible to embody
. . . all the forms of the heart and the soul which are our heritage from
the past."[17] On 16 June 1884, Heller received the master of letters degree
at the University of Cincinnati. That spring he also received Wise's blessing and forehead kiss of ordination. Looking back on his years in Cincinnati, Max remembered Wise as "my sainted teacher and friend" and
spoke of the "splendid staff of professors" at the University of Cincinnati,
where the "spirit which prevailed then was one of earnest work . . . , a
stimulating influence exercised upon the pupils which lasted far beyond
graduation."[18]

Max had to deal with strenuous and competing demands on his time
and intellectual ability during his college years, just as he had done in
1877–1879, when he remained in Prague studying at the Gymnasium. In
both situations, success required grueling self-discipline. "The rabbinical student who has two institutions to attend at one and the same time,"
he explained, "has, therefore, twice and often (when supporting himself
by teaching) three times the work of the average student to do." The regi-
men meant that he led "a secluded life" with "but little contact with the
people." Heller found his circumstances particularly frustrating and
feared that his isolation would leave him and other young rabbis "unprepared to meet the practical problems of life."[19] The demanding schedule

also drained his physical strength. Just as the financial pressures of the initial years of immigrant life had affected the stamina of his mother and his sisters, so too, the strain of the Cincinnati years permanently affected Max's health or at least fueled his overt concern with health issues. He became particularly vulnerable to upper respiratory and stomach problems.[20] His intellect thrived, however, as he wrote his master's thesis addressing contemporary philosophical issues.

Max enjoyed wrestling with conflicting ideas. His thesis topic, "Moses Maimonides and the Philosopher of Evolution," dealing with Herbert Spencer, offered such a challenge. Throughout his career, Max gravitated toward the center of ideological conflict that would allow him to play the role of interpreter and mediator. His thesis gave him an early opportunity to exercise this predilection. Given the preoccupation of liberal American Protestant theologians during the 1880s with the implications of Spencer's Social Darwinism, the topic was extremely timely. Moses Maimonides (1135–1204), in addition to practicing medicine during the Middle Ages, was the period's outstanding Jewish philosopher and an original reformulator of Jewish law. As perhaps the earliest exponent of a systematic, rational approach to Judaism, Maimonides applied Aristotle's principles to Jewish tradition. Heller must have identified with this great man who had had a dual career and had written works that, for centuries, exerted a profound impact on Christian and Jewish thought. In juxtaposing the contemporary British sociologist with the twelfth-century Aristotelian, Max attempted "to show the germs of living truth . . . still to be gleaned from Maimonides's writings." He chose to contrast his literary mentor with Spencer, because "not only is his philosophy the most recent, but it is inspired by tendencies the most opposite to those pursued by Maimonides; its inductive method diverges most widely from the deductions of the latter." The problem of finding "their points of agreement" therefore intrigued the young scholar all the more.[21]

Heller also integrated his thesis argument on a deeper, more psychologically satisfying level. A central focus of the Wissenschaft had been to justify Judaism's contemporary relevance and worth by proving its cultural significance. Using Maimonides as a vehicle to challenge the uniqueness of Spencerian assumptions, Heller in effect followed the principles of the Wissenschaft by trying to use Jewish scholarship to address the larger social issues of the day. He was intellectually comfortable employing the tools of scientific inquiry to mine Jewish tradition, allowing its eternal veracities to surface in a new context. By eliminating "all elements of a nature not strictly deductive or philosophical" from his consideration of Maimonides' and Spencer's writings, Heller showed that both philosophers judged science and religion not as mutually incompatible but as two aspects of a larger whole, with God remaining "the impenetrable mystery." Heller was already demonstrating an acute need to find a systematic means to reconcile aspects of Jewish philosophy with the intellectual currents of the day, an intellectual preoccupation that later permeated his professional life.

Heller maintained that Maimonides' "views still find defenders" and depicted Spencer as one of the "unconscious defenders." Maimonides, he argued, "must be looked upon as one of those who are 'of all times,' whose words and whose names partake of the immortality of all living, imperishable truth." True to the Wissenschaft legacy of rational self-justification, Heller grounded his religious, philosophical, and scientific attitudes in Jewish history, then used them to interpret the present. He found fault with the tendency of his day to recognize only the antiquarian merits of the past, and he criticized the lack of perspective in the "self-consciousness of superiority which characterizes many branches of modern research." The effort to reconcile eternal religious truths with reason and to affirm both the particular and the universal were central issues in the American Reform Jewish world of the 1880s. First-generation American Jews at the time were obsessively self-conscious in crafting their cultural responses to the rhetorical question "What does American culture say?" The maintenance of distinctively Jewish values and peoplehood, and the forging of an American Jewish identity, paradoxically demanded both separation from and assimilation into the broader American society.[22]

As a rabbinical student, Max capably handled intellectual and philosophical problems, but ordination abruptly brought into focus the practical aspects of pursuing a rabbinical career. Max undoubtedly shared his anxiety about the future with his family and with Joseph Stolz, a classmate at HUC. Stolz became his lifelong friend and his only real confidant beyond the family circle. James K. Gutheim, the venerated rabbi of Temple Sinai in New Orleans, delivered the baccalaureate sermon in honor of the four young rabbis who formed the second graduating class of Hebrew Union College. Wise did not surrender his claim upon students when he gave each his formal blessing and declared: "In the name of God and by the authority of the Governors and of the Union of American Hebrew Congregations, and in the name of all good men, I declare you to be rabbis of the Jewish faith, that you may preach the word of God to the people, that you may be patriots in America and standard-bearers of the people." He tried to help each student find a suitable pulpit, in the process fitting their careers into the framework he had skillfully devised when he established the Union of American Hebrew Congregations.

The placement process extended far beyond the ranks of trained rabbis. German-American Jews formed a tightly knit unit of interlocking families, congregations, lay leaders and professionals, all of whom functioned to further the careers, professional, commercial, and social, of their young. Max Heller's secular and rabbinical training formed the first stage in his Americanization. Now that his education was complete, Max was ready to move on.[23]

CHAPTER III

Initiating a Rabbinical Career
From Cincinnati to New Orleans, 1884–1887

The president of the Union of American Hebrew Congregations linked the accomplishments of Hebrew Union College's second graduating class with those of the first as he proudly told the guests at the 1884 ordination, "Nine teachers in Israel, fully equipped for their sphere of action, have been sent forth prepared to assume the functions of rabbis of our congregations."[1] The social networks of midwestern Jewish life were already operating smoothly to place these new rabbis when Max Heller began looking for an appropriate pulpit to launch his rabbinical career. His family was taking part in the process. Not long after the Hellers had settled in Chicago, their Jewish landlady had introduced Anna, the eldest daughter, to Samuel Stein, a wholesale wine dealer "of Bohemian descent." Shortly afterward the two married. According to Simon, "Anna made an excellent match which she would not have been able to make in Prague, even with a large dowry." Sam had begun in his uncle's liquor business. As he prospered, he brought his sisters and brothers over from Europe and incorporated them into the family economic domain.[2] Sam was prepared to assist his extended family as well. Although Max did not need a job distributing liquor, Sam paid close attention to any information that might help Max secure a pulpit in Chicago. Even before Max's ordination, Sam wrote to tell him, in strictest confidence, that Zion Congregation, on Chicago's West Side, was planning to hire an associate rabbi to assist sixty-two-year-old Bernhard Felsenthal.

Felsenthal, who had received his doctoral degree from the University of Munich, was a German intellectual, a major force in the American Reform movement, and a key figure in the midwestern Jewish world. True to the Wissenschaft spirit, he believed that Reform Judaism's integrity depended on German culture and the German language. He expressed the idea succinctly when he wrote, "That sun now stands in the German heavens and from there sends its beneficent light to all Jews and Jewish

communities among the modern cultured nations." In 1859, he had established the first Reform congregation in Chicago. Then, in 1864, when
Zion Congregation formed, he became its first rabbi. Felsenthal had originally opposed the establishment of HUC because he thought that America could not provide a "satisfactory foundation" for such an institution.
He had refused to teach there when he was invited to do so and only
reluctantly supported Wise. But once Wise proved his leadership, Felsenthal deferred to him and acknowledged his authority as "head of the College not only, but of all Israel in the United States." Felsenthal accepted
the reality that Wise now defined "the course in which Judaism in this
country has to run." By the time Max was ordained in 1884, the Chicago
rabbi was approaching retirement.[3]

An acquaintance of Sam's on Zion Congregation's Board of Directors
sought information from Sam about Max's status and prospects. Sam relayed that the congregation expected to pay $2,000 for the first year and
$3,000 the second, but he divulged to Max, "I told him that as an associate
you would not go and be subordinate to Felsenthal." After Sam met with
the congregational president, however, the position of associate rabbi appeared more attractive. Zion wanted to expand and to build a new sanctuary. Sam confided to his aspiring brother-in-law that, as "one of the old
timers . . . Felsenthal is not the man for their new Temple." Sam assured
Max that the growing congregation needed "a young man who would
work with them." Felsenthal retained his strong accent. Although he occasionally delivered a sermon in English, he never fully commanded the
language. In every way, his style was thoroughly "Germanized." The
board was looking for an "Americanized" rabbi. Sam advised Max that
the next time he visited Chicago, Max should give a lecture at the congregation's "Literary" [society] "to show them what you can do." Sam
believed that Max should consider becoming Felsenthal's assistant. "I am
talking for your future welfare and happiness," he reiterated. In addition,
by taking a position in a large city like Chicago, Max could easily advance. "In a small place you can not get very far," Sam warned.[4]

Wise agreed with Sam's reasoning. After the ordination, Wise mentioned two other congregational possibilities to Max, one in Philadelphia,
where the place of an "English lecturer" was available, and another in
Detroit. Wise assured Max that he should be "in no particular hurry" to
accept an offer but went on to say that "the Chicago place is the most
desirable."[5]

Max did choose to be Felsenthal's associate. He revealed his reasons to
Joe Stolz. The congregation offered him only $1,500, less than Sam had
anticipated. After being "unanimously elected" the day before, Max told

Joe that other circumstances swayed his decision to accept Zion's offer, including the "refinement" of the congregation's members. Among them one could find "the best Jewish legal talent of the city . . . , any number of high school and university graduates, of teachers male & fem. of enlightened & well educated businessmen, four or five bankers, many real est. & insurance agents & etc." To be placed as a leader among "intelligent and enthusiastic men" meant a great deal to the novice rabbi. He bragged, "So great is their opinion of me that at the cong. meeting last Sunday but one objection was heard of." Max also thought that, once he had proved himself, his financial outlook at Zion would improve. "The prospects of the place promise double salary in a year or 2 already," he declared. His workload did not appear burdensome; he would be expected only to preach "every other Saturday and lecture every next Sunday" and to read "alternately with Dr F." Heller showed astute awareness of the potential of such a position vis-à-vis Felsenthal, "This gentleman is my good & will soon be my useful friend," he claimed. During the high holidays, he added, "I shall preach but four times & then I have been given the most prominent occasions, Dr F. taking the rest." What better setting for a beginning rabbi than addressing probably "the largest holiday audience in Chicago"? "The Church that will be rented, seats 1650 persons," including "the young element . . . , the very best that can be found in this city." Heller enumerated the advantages of Zion's prestige in claiming Chicago's oldest Jewish literary society. More important, he noted, "By the rabbis I have been treated from the beginning with the evident conviction that I should soon be their colleague's colaborer." Heller assumed the position that very week and looked forward to a "lively social intercourse."[6]

Max was to stay at Zion Congregation less than two years. Although his relationship with Felsenthal was not always smooth, the latter proved instrumental in shaping Max's conception of the role of a congregational rabbi. Throughout his long, creative, and productive career, Felsenthal built and maintained his reputation as a strong leader who could, as the "conscience of his congregation," formulate an unpopular position without worrying about standing alone.[7] The combined experience of the four years with Wise at HUC and the two in Chicago with Felsenthal allowed Max to study two very different sorts of leaders. In his subsequent career, Max learned to synthesize the strengths of both and to use one or the other, depending on the situation.

In 1885, while under Felsenthal's tutelage, Max undoubtedly knew of the November conference that convened in Pittsburgh and changed the course of Reform Judaism by clarifying its ideological stance. The con-

2. *Max Heller as a young rabbi, circa 1885. Courtesy of the American Jewish Archives, Hebrew Union College–Jewish Institute of Religion.*

ference ushered in a period known as Classical Reform, the movement that tinted the next half century of American Reform with its radical hues. At the November conference, a watershed event, nineteen Reform rabbis developed and enunciated the Pittsburgh Platform,[8] a set of principles intended to define the American Reform movement. The conference sought to codify the precepts of American Reform and to recognize changes in ritual and practice that were already in process. The Pittsburgh Platform met with a mixed reception. The UAHC and the Conference of the Rabbis of Southern Congregations (CRSC) never formally adopted it.[9] Nevertheless, it stood as a defining moment in the evolution of American Reform Judaism. This reformulation of Jewish identity conceptualized Judaism as a "progressive religion, ever striving to be in accord with the postulates of reason"—an attenuated Judaism that corresponded to the middle-class aspirations of late nineteenth-century liberal Protestantism. It placed a Reform Jewish stamp on issues of moral suasion and imbued Judaism with social uplift similar to that being espoused by other liberal religious movements in late nineteenth-century America, such as the Ethical Culturalists and the Protestant proponents of the Social Gospel. In fact, by the turn of the century, prominent Social Gospel theologians like Walter Rauschenbusch and Lyman Abbott traced the social message of Jesus to the Hebrew prophets just as liberal Jews felt that the Social Gospel message resonated with their conception of prophetic Judaism.[10]

The Pittsburgh Platform confirmed certain ideas that Heller had embraced in his master's thesis, that "the modern discoveries of scientific researches . . . are not antagonistic to the doctrines of Judaism." Gone was the significance of ritual adherence, now replaced by a consciousness of responsibility to "moral Laws," to maintain only such "ceremonies as elevate and sanctify our lives." The eighth plank, closely identified with the Social Gospel movement, served as a renewed imperative to social action. Basing the stand on "Mosaic legislation" and its commitment to regulating "the relation between the rich and poor," the platform stated that one of the duties of American Reform Judaism was "to participate in the great task of modern times, to solve, on the basis of justice and righteousness, the problems presented by the contrasts and evils of the present organization of society." With or without the language of the Pittsburgh Platform, Heller certainly took the social action aspect of his Judaism seriously. It provided the best road map for his initial commitments as an activist.[11]

The harmony that Wise had achieved with his institution building of the 1870s proved ephemeral. The umbrella organization of the UAHC could not distance itself from the platform enough to avoid alienating some of the more traditional rabbis and congregations, who felt that the stance taken at Pittsburgh was a more radical departure from Jewish practices than they could tolerate. The platform was the last straw for many who had already been offended two years earlier by the disastrous "*trefa* banquet."[12] Those who had not abandoned ranks then deserted the UAHC now. The American Jewish community broke into two distinct camps. The traditionalists participated in the creation of Conservative Judaism, a sort of halfway house between Orthodoxy and Reform, while the radical element dominated the next fifty years of the Reform movement in spite of an active "traditionalist" minority within its own ranks.[13]

Felsenthal and Heller, who ultimately became friends as leaders of the traditionalists within the Reform movement, had a strained relationship at Zion. The tension was evidently intensified by the generational polarization of the congregation itself. Other factors exacerbated the situation. Both rabbis were brilliant and scholarly. Both were self-confident and competitive individuals with strong personalities and rigorous standards. Probably neither enjoyed sharing the role of leadership.[14]

Heller knew about Felsenthal's earlier clashes with Wise. Given Max's loyalty to his "spiritual father" and his recent ordination from HUC, the younger man undoubtedly strove especially hard to prove himself and to impress Felsenthal with the fruits of his education at HUC. Inevitably the two also clashed over mundane matters like the distribution of duties. From earlier correspondence with Sam, his brother-in-law, Max might have anticipated that Felsenthal would retire soon after Max became the associate rabbi, but apparently Felsenthal was in no hurry to do so.[15] Before Max resigned, however, a correspondent for the *American Israelite* who attended services at Zion described Max as a "splendid man. He is dignified, has an excellent voice, and philosophizes like Aristotle." Recently a student, Max was by nature rather formal and didactic and therefore easily shifted into the role of teacher, introducing a Sunday lecture course in which he surveyed Jewish history in a series of biographies of Jewish leaders. After his apprenticeship, Max was ready for a congregation of his own. When the pulpit of Houston's Temple Beth Israel became available, Max made his fateful move to the South.[16]

Again, the wheels of the career machinery, like the wheels of industrial America, were in full tilt. When Beth Israel, "the oldest congregation in Texas," offered him its pulpit, the chairman of the search committee wrote Max, "Here is a Congregation, in Texas, who never saw your face, or heard your voice, nay, who have never even seen a line from your pen, offering you the position of its minister." If Max were to reject the offer, the temple would take no one else. It would settle for an "itinerant minister" instead. Such endorsement of a neophyte was quite a bold stand for a small congregation to take. Although no member of the temple had met him, at least one member had corresponded with Max since the time of his ordination. Then, too, Jacob Voorsanger, Beth Israel's departing rabbi now on his way to Temple Emanuel in San Francisco, "suggested and recommended the Rev. Max Heller as the man whom he would like to succeed him." A classmate from HUC had also spoken highly of Max, so that, according to the congregation's spokesman, "taking the different versions of the two gentlemen named . . . , we have come to the conclusion that you are *just* the man we want!"[17]

Although Beth Israel could afford to offer Max only $2,000 as a beginning salary, the cost of living was much lower in Houston. The Beth Israel correspondent told Max not to be deterred by the "far off sound" of Texas, for "our community is as completely civilized . . . as many more pretentious localities." But he warned Heller about the laxity of Jewish observance. He told the young rabbi that he would be challenged to use his talents in "harmonizing and crystallizing an indifferent element of Israelites in our city." In a postscript he noted, "Beg to add that the duties of Sunday School Principal are included in the office of Minister." Evidently, Max had once again considered an alternative position before accepting the Beth Israel offer, because Wise wrote with helpful advice about improving the effectiveness of his speaking style, offering "hints" that would be especially useful if Max intended to go to Philadelphia. When he was unanimously elected by the Houston temple on 15 August 1886, however, Heller moved there in time to lead his own congregation for the high holidays the following month.[18]

The South, but not Houston, fulfilled Heller's destiny. Just a few months before he arrived in Texas, James Gutheim, the august speaker at Max's baccalaureate, died suddenly in New Orleans, leaving the pulpit of Temple Sinai vacant. Wise immediately interceded on his protégé's behalf. He probably understood that the New Orleans temple, like many of the Reform congregations at that time, was looking for a dynamic younger man who would attract new members. He let Max know that, according to his "informant in New Orleans," the rabbi of the Mobile congregation would not be offered the job at Temple Sinai because the congregations' close relationship might be imperiled if the larger synagogue hired the rabbi away from the smaller. "Therefore and therefore only I mentioned your name, and do decidedly think, if the position is offered to you, you may conscientiously accept it." Wise had never regarded Max's position in Houston as permanent. Just a month earlier he had remarked, "I hear . . . that you are satisfied with your present position; still I am trying to get you out of it, if I can."[19] By now, Wise had assumed multiple roles in Max's life. If before he acted as father figure, adviser, and career broker, he now became a colleague who poked fun at his younger disciple. And as editor of both the *American Israelite* and *Die Deborah*, Wise was in a position to advance Max's journalistic career, gaining him an audience far beyond that of a congregation. Already Wise had published Max's "German letter" in *Die Deborah* and had promised to publish some lectures that Max had sent from Chicago, perhaps those from the Sunday course he had given on Jewish historical figures. "As you know, good wine betters by age," he told Max.[20]

After moving to Houston, Max had offered to submit some lectures against card playing for publication. In response, Wise not only showed his keen sense of humor but also conveyed his particular sensitivity to the regional differences of Jewish communities. He told Max that there would be room for the articles in the spring and cautioned, "They may add by publication to your literary fame, which you hardly need, but they would not add to your popularity in the South, where every body plays cards, and considers it a social accomplishment to be an expert at cards." Earlier, when Max had been considering a pulpit in Philadelphia, Wise had advised him on a preaching style that would please the Reform Jews of that city. Now Wise helped his young friend understand that the southern Jews had their own values not dissimilar to those of the region in which they lived. If Max chose to live there, especially in New Orleans, and if he served in the largest and "most prominent" Southern pulpit, he should recognize that overweening moralizing would not further his cause.[21]

Max, no doubt, enjoyed the conviviality of Houston and the warmth of Beth Israel, but he could hardly pass up an opportunity to succeed Gutheim. In addition to Wise's strong support, Max had a champion within the New Orleans congregation to plead his cause. A few days before the congregational meeting voted on his candidacy, Edgar Cahn, the secretary of Temple Sinai's Board of Directors, sent an unofficial letter of reassurance to Max. "The comm. on pulpit met last night, & to them was referred the reply of the Presdt of the Chicago. Cong. where you were formerly minister. . . . You can hope for nothing but victory."[22]

Cahn also mentioned that such a recommendation from Chicago "knocked out the Leucht-men in one round . . . It destroyed their last resort, that of attacking your character." A contingent of Sinai members wanted Isaac L. Leucht, rabbi of Touro Synagogue, the other leading congregation in New Orleans, to succeed Gutheim. Leucht, several years Heller's senior, had emigrated from Darmstadt, Germany, in 1864, when Max was only a small child. In 1870, the year Temple Sinai was established, Leucht had come to New Orleans to serve as a reader at Gates of Mercy, the old "Deutsch shul" in New Orleans. Like most of the men of his generation who served congregations in America when few trained rabbis had immigrated, Leucht lacked both ordination and formal rabbinical training. He had moved from one New Orleans congregation to another, graduating from "Reader" to "Minister" or "Reverend," and was now called "Rabbi."[23]

Heller had locked horns with Leucht through an incident that had occurred just a few months earlier. This initial episode foreshadowed the antagonistic relationship that would later develop between the two. One of the functions that rabbis performed in their communities involved the dispensation of charity. American Jewish philanthropy often evolved through benevolent societies independent of any congregational affiliation. Elite lay leaders gained additional stature when they chaired the boards of these organizations, but people nonetheless looked to the community rabbis for at least symbolic assistance in dealing with the indigent or disfranchised temporarily within their domain. Leucht actually played an active role in distributing funds in New Orleans. His "scientific methods" in dealing with an itinerant Jew who wanted to travel to Schulenberg, Texas (about 100 miles west of Houston), had aggravated Heller.[24]

The New Orleans almoner believed that no Jewish community's charitable coffers should be overburdened. Accordingly, he wanted to give the man only enough money to reach Lake Charles, the next sizable Jewish community on his route west. Heller felt that Leucht could have provided the "old gentleman" with a ticket to his Texas destination. The ticket would have spared him the indignity of begging for funds from communities far less able to provide them than New Orleans. While Leucht rationally considered the extent to which the Jewish charitable institutions of his city could respond to such requests, Heller approached the situation from a different vantage point. Leucht's actions offended Heller's sense of social justice; his sympathies clearly lay with the itinerant. Heller's position reflected not only the traditional Jewish understanding that caring for the needy is the obligation (*mitzvah*) of the more fortunate—including the wealthier community—but also his own experiences as a more recent immigrant. The incident was the first in a catalog of charges that he compiled against Leucht over the next decade.[25]

Following Gutheim's death, Leucht functioned as the interim rabbi at Temple Sinai. His supporters (those Cahn had called the "Leucht-men") wanted him to secure the pulpit permanently. Knowing that Leucht was the other candidate could only have further intensified Max's interest in the position, for Temple Sinai was truly a plum for a young man less than three years in the pulpit. Cahn wrote Heller immediately after the membership meeting had given him its resounding, nearly unanimous approval. "The day is yours—the battle is won." Cahn promised to send clippings from the city's papers, the *Times-Democrat* and the *Picayune.* "The former journal," wrote Cahn, "says 'that if Leucht wanted the place, he could get it' or words to that effect. Well, let them temper the wind to the shorn lamb, but it's a li——, all the same."[26]

As Heller told the Houston congregation when he asked to be released from his contract, the offer from New Orleans was flattering "both to you and myself." On the same paper that bore a scratch copy of his letter of resignation to Beth Israel, Max scribbled the scratch copy of a thank you note to his congregants. They had already sent him congratulations on his election to New Orleans.[27]

Cahn was pleased that Heller would be able to leave Houston the following month and, as a former HUC student himself, added that he looked forward to the happy "prospect of your companionship." He explained that the eight " 'L-men' who voted against you showed a most obstinate spirit during the meeting" and prevented Heller from being elected by acclamation. Leucht, he observed, "might have worded it this way: I came, I saw, I was left.' " But Cahn warned Max, "It is absolutely necessary that no word or deed of yours should in any way betray your opinion of him." And Cahn reassured him that he could step into his new position "without the least difficulty, as everything is running first-class."[28]

Although this information did not mar the warm reception that Heller correctly anticipated, it undoubtedly put him on guard and may have contributed to the competitive defensiveness already apparent in his relationship with Felsenthal in Chicago. While the memory of James Gutheim, Sinai's founding rabbi, presented Heller with a challenge from the past, Leucht represented a challenge for leadership within the New Orleans Jewish community that was very much in the present. Heller had to carve out a career and make a place for himself despite the memory of one leader, the potential opposition of a minority of his congregation, and Leucht's presence in the other major Jewish pulpit in the city. Heller's abilities to defend his moderate views on racial issues and to promote Jewish nationalism proved great assets that served him well in the decades ahead. His success lay in the skillful manner in which he managed to resolve the conflicts and contradictions between his Jewish values and regional mores while retaining the loyalties of his congregation.

By March 1887, Heller had moved to the South's largest city and proudly filled the region's major Jewish pulpit at a salary of $3,000 for the first year. Heller's succession to Gutheim's place at Temple Sinai was an impressive feat for a twenty-seven-year-old immigrant less than a decade removed from the Old World. As he recalled thirty-five years later, he had come to New Orleans expecting the best. "The rabbi who feels, as I did almost from the beginning, that he is entering upon the field in which he is to spend his life . . . , will gather, with keen interest, all the information he can obtain as to the beginnings of the community . . . , for he wishes to know his community through the roots from which they sprang."[29]

CHAPTER IV

Southernization, Self-Righteousness, Nativism, and Social Reform
New Orleans, 1887–1891

New Orleans, culturally creole and Catholic, was relaxed in both attitude and style. The city had a reputation for religious tolerance and social accessibility. By the time Max Heller arrived, Jews there had been functioning as a community with established religious and benevolent institutions for about half a century. Many Jewish New Orleanians whose families had emigrated from France or Germany during the 1830s and 1840s enjoyed a considerable degree of social assimilation and financial success and were extremely lax in religious observance. Sephardic Jews had arrived in the city first, as they had on the eastern seaboard, and were considered at the apex of the elite. But so many of them had intermarried and virtually disappeared that, by the 1880s, members of the older German families had assumed leadership positions in the Jewish community. Since midcentury, Ashkenazic Jews who hailed from Central or Eastern Europe, including Russia, had begun arriving in New Orleans. In the mid-1880s their numbers were still negligible. Despite the similarity in their ritual, German Jews and Polish Jews brought to America the prejudices against each other that they had conceived in Europe. Elitism permeated every social situation, with the earlier arrivals from Alsace-Lorraine and southwestern Germany at the pinnacle of the Ashkenazic Jewish contingent and those from further east ranking below.[1]

The first permanent Jewish residents settled in New Orleans soon after the Louisiana Purchase established American control of the region. Mostly male, they tended to intermarry and thus felt no immediate need to establish the primary Jewish institutions of cemetery and congregation. Not until the late 1820s did New Orleans Jews begin to create a community infrastructure. In spite of the pervasive religious laxity, by 1860, four traditional congregations—three Ashkenazic (two German and one

Polish) and one Sephardic—served the city's culturally diverse Jewish population.[2]

After the Civil War, Reform Judaism seemed perfectly suited to the needs of the more acculturated and affluent New Orleans Jews. In 1870, some of the city's most successful Jewish professionals and business leaders left one of the two elite congregations, the Ashkenazic Gates of Mercy, to found Temple Sinai, the first Reform congregation in New Orleans. Although Dispersed of Judah, the Sephardic congregation, did not lose members to Temple Sinai, the older congregation remained essentially the same size during the postwar era. Under the circumstances, both Dispersed of Judah and Gates of Mercy found it increasingly difficult to continue functioning independently. About 1880, after several years in transition, they consolidated and formed Touro Synagogue. Both Touro and Sinai were located on Carondolet Street, immediately upriver from, or above, Canal Street in the central part of downtown.[3]

Further uptown on Jackson Avenue and third in prominence, Gates of Prayer, established at midcentury, was still conducting its services in German in the 1880s and thus appealed to the large contingent of recent German-speaking immigrants. In addition to these three institutions, there were two smaller and more traditional or Orthodox synagogues, Mikveh Israel and Congregation Tememi Derech (Congregation The Right Way) composed of Jews hailing from Eastern Europe. Both were in the vicinity of Touro and Sinai, an area known as the American quarter, which was then the city's most densely populated commercial sector and the neighborhood in New Orleans where most of the Jewish population lived and worked. The mixed residential and commercial character of the neighborhood replicated itself among the varying ethnic groups throughout the city. No single ethnic enclave dominated any given neighborhood, however, and integration and acculturation remained salient characteristics of the city's foreign-born populations.[4]

Given the close-knit nature of the American Reform community, Heller undoubtedly knew even before he moved to New Orleans of Temple Sinai's reputation as the most prestigious congregation in the South. His numerous contacts in New Orleans and the Gulf South, especially during his tenure in Houston, helped to pave a smooth transition. After Houston, even the sultry climate of New Orleans must have seemed familiar. Immediately after Heller accepted the position at the temple, a congregant suggested that he board with Mrs. Ellen Ullman at 227 Baronne—in the heart of the area where many Jews lived and worked—only two blocks above Canal Street and within walking distance of the temple. The congregant recommended Mrs. Ullman as a temple member of an "influential family" who "keeps a very *good* table" with "rooms [that] are splendid."[5]

By 1887, Temple Sinai's members, occupationally and socially, resembled both the bourgeois elite of the Prague German-speaking Jewish community of Max's youth and the German-Jewish communities of Cincinnati and Chicago. While Heller had encountered much that was familiar in Cincinnati, he soon discovered that New Orleans bore an even closer resemblance to his native Prague. Both cities had highly diverse ethnic compositions. In Prague, the mixture was principally Slavic, Czech, and German. In addition to its large African American population, New Orleans contained many creoles of French and Spanish descent, plus immigrants from France, Central America, the Caribbean, Germany, Ireland, and, more recently, Italy. Since both cities served as major river ports for predominantly agricultural areas, trade prevailed over industry. Just as Prague was home to most of Bohemia's Jewish population, so was New Orleans the domicile for Louisiana's. Both cities were mercantile centers where Jewish citizens experienced a high degree of assimilation and, often, social prominence. The majority of Temple Sinai's members lived at the upper end of the scale and, socially and economically, resembled the German-speaking Jews of Prague. Even their mercantile activities were similar, in that Jewish populations of both cities were concentrated in some form of agriculturally related industry or manufacturing or sales. Because the business-oriented Jews of Prague and New Orleans preferred an inconspicuous form of Judaism that would facilitate upward mobility, progressive or Reform Judaism took root in both cities.[6]

Temple Sinai's receptivity to the Americanized Reform movement underscored the patterns of acculturation and prosperity enjoyed by most of its membership. On the eve of Heller's arrival, approximately 58 percent owned or were partners in businesses that prominently featured their families' names. The cotton trade employed approximately one-fourth of the congregants as factors, commission merchants, buyers, or processors; nearly another third of the members dealt in dry goods, clothing, or furnishing goods, both wholesale and retail. By the turn of the century, over a third of Temple Sinai's members frequented the Harmony Club, a social gathering spot for Jewish business elites. Among those who left records of their occupations, only three of the 133 Temple Sinai members who appeared at a meeting two months before Heller's election worked as laborers, while 90 percent engaged in some form of commerce. New Orleans served as the hub of an intricate network of wholesale transactions between urban suppliers and peddlers or country store owners in sparsely populated Louisiana and Mississippi. Jewish merchants in New Orleans played leading roles as wholesalers, factors, or commission merchants, and Temple Sinai's members, active in all three areas, clustered their businesses in the heavily trafficked areas of the French Quarter and the central business and warehouse district close to the river.[7]

The 1880s stand out in retrospect as a transitional decade for New Orleans Jews. Much of the early Sephardic population had virtually disappeared through assimilation, and many Alsatian and German Jews still enjoyed a high level of social integration. With the onset of the Gilded Age, however, overt anti-Semitism began to increase in New Orleans as it did in other areas of the United States. According to some estimates, the Jewish population of the city, since 1860, had more than doubled. While the approximately 5,000 Jews living in New Orleans actually composed only 2 percent of the total population in the last two decades of the nineteenth century, Jewish affluence and Jewish philanthropy appeared disproportionately great. Judah Touro, the first Jewish resident in the city after 1800, was one of the greatest mid-nineteenth-century New Orleans philanthropists. He generously helped those outside the Jewish community before he supported institutions of his own heritage. Elite Jewish philanthropy in New Orleans continued to follow an outer-directed pattern, although Jewish organizations and institutions were not excluded from the largesse of successful coreligionists. While no other Jew in the nineteenth century could match Touro's record of munificence, in the 1890s, Isidore Newman, one of the city's leading philanthropists, came closest.[8]

Department stores owned by Jewish merchants dominated Canal Street, the heart of the downtown shopping district. Prominent Jewish families had begun building mansions along the lovely oak-lined thoroughfare of St. Charles Avenue as the city's residential area spread upriver. The rise of a significant number of Jews apparently threatened the previously more inclusive social elites. From the late 1880s, for example, cartoons and commentary reflecting a pronounced degree of social anti-Semitism began appearing in the *New Orleans Mascot*, a weekly newspaper of comment and satire. The city's most exclusive clubs, once open to elite Jews, now began closing their doors. Prestigious carnival organizations that paraded on Mardi Gras and had once included Jewish members also gradually restricted their memberships as anti-Semitism increased in the city. One *Mascot* cartoon depicted the stereotypical materialistic Jew—overdressed and hook nosed—groveling on his knees before distinguished men who were smirking at him. The caption reads "A

Recent Club Scene." In the 1890s, eight Jewish members (three of them from Sinai) still belonged to the Boston Club, and one religiously unaffiliated Jew kept up membership in the Pickwick Club. By the turn of the century, however, no new Jewish members were being admitted to either organization. Instead Jews joined the Harmony Club. Its 258 members threw the slight back at the gentile snobs by constructing, in the midst of a nationwide recession, a magnificent marble building at the corner of Jackson and St. Charles Avenues. In July 1896 the *Jewish Ledger* exulted, "To be in a position to erect so handsome an edifice at this time, when the cry of hard times is heard on all sides, and great stringency exists in the money market, speaks volumes for the management." Such financial audacity also spoke well for the bank accounts of the club's members.[9]

Well-connected Jews disturbed by the loss of social status who hoped to regain acceptance regarded non-Jewish opinions with special concern. And leaders in the congregation of Temple Sinai sought a rabbi who could conform to their social expectations, a spiritual leader who would please congregants while gaining respect in the community at large. Their temple, situated on Carondelet Street near Howard Avenue (illustration 3), was imposing with its high steps and twin turrets. Now it stood "redecorated like a bride" who "after deep mourning . . . appeared bedecked and ready to enter upon a new life." The distinguished new rabbi appeared equally poised to embrace his role. With his alluring combination of European charm and American training, Heller, handsomely erect in bearing and fastidious in dress, held sway in the "richly carpeted" Moorish interior, which was "as fine as that of any church . . . in the South." Moreover, his eloquent English and obvious intellectual prowess contributed to an altogether urbane image. Heller was just the kind of religious leader the circumstances demanded. He intuitively understood the situation that he was entering. Later, he himself perceptively noted, "whether the fashionable Jew likes it or not, his intelligence, his social standing, is measured among gentiles largely by the rabbi's scholarship and refinement."[10]

New Orleans and the state of Louisiana provided situations certain to test the mettle of an idealistic, slightly self-righteous, and intellectual rabbi who sought out personal challenges while attempting to win the confidence of the community. The path toward acceptance required Heller and other Jews to negotiate a terrain of community expectations, personal ambitions and antagonisms, and ambivalent attitudes if they were to secure social justice. In Louisiana during the Gilded Age, then in a sluggish economic recovery, election fraud, political violence, and ethnic and class conflict, not to mention racism, made the road all the rock-

3. *Old Temple Sinai. Courtesy of the Historic New Orleans Collection.*

ier.[11] New Orleans, which had been America's third largest city in the prosperous years before the Civil War, by 1880 had slipped to ninth place. Although it remained the largest city in the South until after World War II, its growth did not keep pace with that of emerging urban centers like Birmingham, Memphis, Houston, or Atlanta.[12]

Like their gentile counterparts, many business-oriented and civic-

minded upper-class Jews saw a connection between good government reform and economic growth. In 1880, partly in response to the city's economic woes and political corruption, they backed Joseph A. Shakspeare,
the reform mayoral candidate. His victory was a setback for the local conservative Democratic machine, an organization heavily supported by organized labor, immigrants, and working-class whites.[13] Shakspeare's
election also initiated a reform movement that marked the reentry of the
civic elite into local politics. The election thus heralded the beginning of
a tug-of-war between the local reform faction of the Democratic party
and the "regular" Democrats that colored all elections until the turn of
the century. At that point, the Democratic machine, under the auspices
of the Choctaw Club, built a solid power base that operated smoothly for
the next two decades. Sadly, neither the machine politicians nor the elite
reformers were willing to rise above their time and class to renounce
white supremacy, let alone entertain truly radical solutions to social and
economic problems.[14]

Heller clearly understood the implications of the social boundaries of
his position as Sinai's rabbi. During his initial years in New Orleans, the
temple's lay leaders aligned themselves politically with the same group
with which they were aligned economically—the Anglo-Protestant
elite—and Heller followed suit. From 1880 to 1900, many of the same
elites that commanded leadership roles in a succession of single-issue reform organizations were also prominent in the growing number of professional associations and exchanges that worked in concert to centralize
control of the city's commerce. In 1880 and later, the Reform Jewish community of the Gilded Age saw itself as part of the entrepreneurial and
civic establishment, interested in providing the healthiest possible economic and political climate for business and in winning a share of the
prosperity promised in the rhetoric of the New South. Several congregants served as board members in the city's banking and insurance establishments and consequently found it easy to rub shoulders with the
"better elements" among the business elite.[15]

The list of problems facing good government advocates was potentially daunting. Opposition to the Democratic machine alone was not
enough to address the issues that spoiled the political, social, and economic health of the city. Besides corruption, a host of festering urban ills,
from dilapidated wharves and inadequate drainage to stagnant canals
and other public health hazards, plagued the city and discouraged industrial development. Too often municipal improvements like street pav-
ing occurred only in the business and wealthy residential areas where

upper-class reformers worked and lived. Cosmetic changes masked but hardly addressed real social ills.[16]

By 1883, cotton receipts at the port of New Orleans finally matched those from the 1859 bumper crop. The Southern Pacific Railroad linking the city to the West Coast was completed, and the revival of business activity spurred a spirit of optimism that was celebrated by the city's cotton exposition the following year. But 1884 brought disappointment. The cotton exposition did not inaugurate the economic boom its promoters had promised, and the voters restored the city government to the hands of the Democratic-conservative machine. Four years later, however, the political pendulum swung back to the reformers when the newly formed Young Men's Democratic Association (YMDA), of which Temple Sinai's Felix Dreyfous was a member, helped reelect Shakspeare as mayor. Dreyfous himself was elected to serve in the 1888 state legislature.[17]

Heller marshaled the same spirit of bourgeois reform through Temple Sinai. Born and raised through adolescence in a city marked by political and ethnic coalition building, and schooled by Wise and Felsenthal in the nuances of enlisting local power, he lost no time establishing a working relationship with the congregational lay leadership, the assimilated Jewish community, and the larger gentile community. First, however, he bent his energies to enhancing the services that the synagogue offered. Almost immediately after his appointment, he asked board approval to update the temple facilities and rituals to conform to the ideals of American Reform espoused at HUC. In line with the Reform movement's emphasis on education and the inculcation of its progressive and universalist principles, Heller wanted to convert the basement into a Sabbath school to teach the congregation's children and prepare them for confirmation. As he wrote to a colleague in Mobile, "There is much to be done for Judaism, in the South and everywhere. Sabbath School and Confirmation instruction are both crude, there is no definite consciousness as to material and method, the text-books represent nothing." He complained that the rituals remained "characterless . . . even inconsistent!" while sermons "have not contact enough with the familiar occurrences of private and public life to bring . . . improvement," leaving "to the individual his undisturbed conceit of self-righteousness."[18] These criticisms hinted that Heller was already reaching for a Judaism that adherents would find more compelling. He insisted on hiring a cantor, for example, to chant or sing traditional prayers and hymns.

Heller had specific allies in the congregation to aid him, like Edgar Cahn and Julius Weis, but he had his detractors, too, probably the

"Leuchtmen," who had originally opposed his candidacy. Already well schooled in the dynamics of congregational politics, Heller rapidly proved very adept in his new position. As his friend Stolz appraised the situation when writing Heller, "with your abilities and your character, I feel confident that you will win triumphs even though following Gutheim . . . , [one of] few men [who] have ever been more beloved by their congregation." Gutheim had provided Sinai with strong rabbinic leadership. Likewise, on those occasions when the temple denied his successor's requests, the congregation acknowledged Heller's moral authority as spokesman.[19]

Heller thrived as a consummate strategist. He was well aware that Gutheim, his predecessor, had demonstrated support for the Confederacy by leaving New Orleans during the Union occupation of the city. By becoming an active member in the Conference of the Rabbis of Southern Congregations (CRSC), Heller gained further insights into the American Jewish South. While establishing his career in New Orleans, he was ever mindful of the importance of initiating new alliances to broaden his base of support. In his memorial address on the tenth anniversary of his predecessor's death, Heller wrote that Gutheim "placed before his people a shining example . . . by the conspicuousness and self sacrifice of his patriotism." He added that even though "we are glad today and thankful that the South was defeated and the Union preserved . . . , we shall honor as heroes . . . [those like] Mr. Gutheim, who clung with heart and soul to the cause of independence which their convictions and their loyalty had espoused." Even though Heller disagreed with the southern position, he well understood its sacredness.[20]

An astute observer of those around him, Heller realized that his success in the pulpit of Temple Sinai required respect both from those within the Jewish community and from those outside it. He quickly worked to establish himself as an insider with a viable "southern" identity. At the same time, he added to his prestige by drawing upon his journalistic skills to gain influence in the national Reform movement. Already familiar with the CRSC from his work in Houston, Heller soon began publishing sermons in the *Jewish Spectator*, a southern weekly edited by Memphis rabbi Max Samfield. In 1889, the Central Conference of American Rabbis (CCAR) was organized as a rabbinic association distinct from, but aligned with, the Union of American Hebrew Congregations. The UAHC, essentially a lay organization, tailored its membership rolls to congregations alone. The CCAR, on the other hand, consisted of rabbis of mainly UAHC congregations that, no doubt swayed by the same winds of professionalization that were then affecting the medical and legal communities, sought a centralized and national organization to clarify the shape and goals of the American Reform movement beyond the confines of the HUC. While promoting universal humanism and banishing all signs of Jewish parochialism, the CCAR rabbi was quickly expanding his traditional teaching role to include that of preacher, counselor, administrator, and ambassador to the gentile community—positions that Heller graciously assumed. Although he did not attend the first CCAR meeting in 1889, he became a charter member and served on the initial board of directors with his HUC friend Joseph Stolz.[21]

The year 1889 also witnessed the end of Heller's bachelorhood. Just as his father improved his social and economic status in Prague by marrying a Kassowitz, Heller consolidated his place in the New Orleans Jewish community by becoming engaged to the daughter of one of its largest and most prominent families. Ida Annie Marks (illustration 4) was a native of New Orleans. Like several prominent New Orleans Jewish families, her family had come to Louisiana from Columbia, South Carolina, where the Marks family had lived since the late eighteenth century. Not only was Ida Marks native born, but her American and southern lineage was so impeccable as to ensure future membership in the Daughters of the American Revolution.[22] Although Heller did not talk about the difference in their backgrounds, Anna, his sister, indirectly referred to it when she congratulated her brother on his engagement. This occasion prompted Anna to write to Max in English for the first time. She had used her new skill earlier in writing to her sisters, but she mentioned that she "didn't dare to use my yet very incomplete language" in letters to Max because she anticipated his upbraiding her about her mistakes. "Now I have made up my mind not to mind your criticism, for I want you to see first if my writing is good enough for your Dear bride, as I may write to her, if you want me to." As his sister knew, Heller demanded perfection not only of himself but of those around him, whether they were family members, congregants, or colleagues. His earlier dealings with I. L. Leucht had demonstrated both the fervor of his unflinching moralism and an impatience verging on contempt for conduct that he considered unjust or even incorrect.[23]

Heller's continual need to assert moral superiority increased the ongoing tension between him and Leucht. The friction became especially evident in cases related to the dispensation of aid to recently arrived "Russian" or "Polish" Jews, as all those from Eastern Europe were often classified by their already assimilated coreligionists.[24] Leucht was in charge of the funds controlled by Touro Infirmary and the Hebrew Benevolent Association (TIHBA), the New Orleans Reform Jewish commu-

4. *Ida Marks Heller, possibly an engagement photograph, circa 1889.*
Courtesy of Edward M. Heller and Theo M. Heller.

nity's largest charity. In accordance with the current tenets of "scientific charity," he rationalized the decision making when dealing with those he deemed among the deserving poor in the Jewish community. In 1881, New Orleans Jews had been among the first in America to offer aid to the thousands of immigrants arriving from Poland, Lithuania, Russia, and other countries of Eastern Europe. Gutheim spearheaded the local movement by founding an immigrant aid society and securing support from the general public. As with established Jewish communities elsewhere in America, however, pervasive ambivalence characterized the overall response by Jews in New Orleans toward Russian Jews. Fearing a rise in anti-Semitism and nativism, the "best men" in already established Jewish communities dispensed aid with a tinge of condescension. New Orleans was hardly inundated by the third wave of Eastern Europeans who transformed most Jewish communities elsewhere in America. In fact, the percentage of its foreign-born population actually began shrinking at the end of the decade. Unlike urban areas of the North, and in contrast even to other southern cities like Atlanta, which enjoyed late nineteenth-century growth, the city's periodic yellow fever epidemics and terrible drainage problems frightened new industry and new immigrants alike.[25]

In Louisiana, public facilities for poor relief were either overcrowded or nonexistent. The ongoing health and sanitation problems of New Orleans overtaxed the city's charitable institutions as they sought to cope with recurring crises in public health. Organizations like the Touro Infirmary–Hebrew Benevolent Association and the Jewish Home for Widows and Orphans received the bulk of Jewish funds,[26] but Jewish resources were limited. Leucht believed in helping only those applicants who were willing and able to help themselves after an initial boost from Jewish charitable monies. To Heller he complained that he had "refused to accede to the demands" of two men who had asked for work because they had neither proper identification papers nor a trade. "What do you propose to do? Shall I support them out of the funds of the Touro until the men find work?" Leucht turned down another individual's request for travel money, claiming that even if these applicants were given money, they would be in need again too soon. "I have never seen the tramp yet, who did not tell me, he was willing to work," he commented.[27]

Heller's attitude, on the other hand, seemed to have more to do with the urgency of an applicant's immediate need than with his potential for future usefulness to the community. The broadly inclusive humanitarianism implicit in Heller's stance on aid to paupers was not always endorsed by the German Jewish community, which had some members who lacked the immigrant rabbi's compassion and philosophical depth or had, like Leucht, been in the United States long enough to internalize Gilded Age sensibilities and to become insensitive to the pressures and disorientation felt by a recent arrival. Heller was less than a decade removed from his own experience as an immigrant. His father's inability to provide for the family remained a wound that Max tried to heal by sending his family money. He easily identified with the humiliation experienced by the city's needy Jews when they were forced to accept charity through the existing structure of organized Jewish communal funds. Transient and otherwise economically depressed Jews appealed to Heller to intercede on their behalf after Leucht turned them down. Heller used such occasions both to assert the authority of his ordination and to reaffirm his commitment to *tzedakah*, the Jewish equivalent of social justice.

He would certainly have been familiar with one of the traditional *Sayings of the Fathers* that tells Jews to "let the poor be members of thy household," to treat the poor as if they were in the family.[28]

But Jewish tradition alone did not motivate Heller's righteous indignation and relentless perfectionism. Like Wise, his mentor, Heller was driven by personal ambition to seek influence beyond a congregation, even one as prestigious as Temple Sinai. In 1888, just a year after becoming associate editor of the Memphis-based *Jewish Spectator*, Heller unceremoniously severed his ties with Max Samfield's struggling publication. "You deplore that the *Spectator* is not a better-looking paper," the editor angrily retorted, implying that Heller had made his decision for superficial reasons. Samfield, however, blamed the paper's shortcomings largely on the "indifference of the Southern rabbis who seem not to care whether the South has its own organ or not." In reality, Heller's ambition to be the editor of his own New Orleans–based paper probably contributed heavily to the rift, and the relationship between the two men deteriorated further when Heller did not call upon Samfield to officiate at his wedding. Heller, of course, had wanted Wise to conduct the ceremony, but the wedding of one of Wise's sons in Houston conflicted with the date set by Max and Ida. In Wise's stead Heller chose Rabbi Solomon Sonneschein of St. Louis, at the time a well-known Reform personality, rather than the less known Memphis rabbi and editor.[29]

For a short time in 1890, Heller actually did manage to establish the *Jewish Chronicle* in New Orleans, but he was unable to make the publication a financial success. When the *Chronicle* failed, Heller sent a circular to every subscriber, returning the amount of each "prepaid subscription." He explained that even though he was "in no wise responsible" for the paper's liabilities, he believed that "a large majority paid subscriptions, owing to my Editorship." Since they "trusted to it," he did not want them to lose their money. David Danziger was one of several who appreciated the circular that Heller sent with the returned check, but Danziger simply mailed it back to him with a note. He argued that Heller should not assume any responsibility "for the misdemeanor of others."[30]

At the same time that Ida and Max announced their engagement, the temple board voted Heller a salary increase of $1,000, raising his annual income to $4,000. The wedding at Temple Sinai took place on 6 March 1889 and was a major social affair. One of the local papers printed a sketch of the prominent and handsome groom in an article reporting, "Jews and gentiles of prominence . . . , even Christian divines . . . , attended." The temple's directors were undoubtedly pleased that the affair merited the attention of the community at large. This was clearly the perfect way to bind the promising young rabbi to his relatively new home. The newlyweds moved to an uptown apartment at Jackson Avenue and Coliseum Street, a fashionable residential address in the city's Garden District.[31] Ida and Max Heller were among those residents of the Crescent City who faced the future with great optimism. The following Thanksgiving the *American Israelite*'s correspondent in New Orleans noted that the sugar and rice harvest had been rich and that "many of the jobbing houses report greater prosperity than at any time since the War." The impact of such prosperity on the Jewish community was clear, he concluded, since "a large portion of the trade of this city [is] in Jewish hands."[32]

But in the fall of 1889, a series of crises that began in northern Louisiana cast an ominous shadow across the future. The ethnic and racial violence that plagued Louisiana during the 1890s affected Jews as well as Italians and blacks. First in late October, in the North Louisiana hamlet of Delhi, an armed mob, "recruited . . . both from town and the surrounding country," attacked three out of the four "Jew business houses" in town. The following month, the violence spread to Lake Providence, where "the lawless element singled out Jewish merchants" for their assaults. The *New Orleans Times-Democrat* decried the disorder that ranged from "the election row at Lafayette" to the "lynching of the Negro Keys at Carancro [and] the attempt to muzzle the press in Vermillion." The "latest outrage" affected the Jewish merchants in Lake Providence, East Carroll Parish. The editorial called for "boldness" in denouncing the illegal acts and "the greater boldness" of having "the perpetrators arrested and punished."[33]

The violence broke out again in January, and the message delivered by the "mob" was similar: Jews were not welcome. The "troublemakers" warned the Jewish merchants beforehand with anonymous letters demanding that "Christian clerks" be hired. In Delhi, lawbreakers "tacked up" a sign on the Blum store, threatening bloodshed unless "Stein, Blum, Hirsch and Pulver . . . discharge every Jew clerk they have and have their places filled by gentiles." Those making demands blatantly stated the cause of their grievance: "We do not propose that any one shall do business among us and the Jew take all the money." Gentiles must be hired by Jewish merchants, or the latter would have to go. There was only one exception to the racial animus: "Ben Stein, you may remain and will be unmolested." Even an angry rural mob shut out of the alluring promises of the New South seemed unwilling to condemn all Jews to a common fate. Obviously Ben Stein must have been considered part of the community in a way that set him apart from his coreligionists.[34]

Responding to the wave of disorder, Heller struck a moderate pose when he argued that "Antisemite" had been used by the daily papers "with . . . utter misunderstanding" of the significance of the name. He differentiated between the "Jew-hatred" of Germany based on "racial theories" and "this sort of lawless rowdyism." His optimism about the Jews' place in Louisiana remained strong in spite of the incidents. In the columns of one of the few surviving issues of the *Jewish Chronicle*, he wrote that those in "Northern Jewish circles" exaggerated the anti-Semitic content of the Delhi and Lake Providence disturbances. "How little these troubles mean as regards the general feeling in Louisiana towards the Jews ought to be patent even to outsiders." Heller carefully clipped and pasted in his scrapbook articles from various newspapers documenting atrocities of anti-Semitism in Russia occurring at the same time that the vigilante action, or "whitecapping," took place in northern Louisiana. The contrast undoubtedly contributed to Heller's perspective on the events. He cited the leadership positions that Jewish men had filled in the public life of the state as one instance of the distinction between events in Louisiana and in Eastern Europe. Heller praised the "perfect harmony prevailing between Jew and Gentile" when the sectarian press denounced the anti-Semitic acts in North Louisiana. The forcefulness of the press's "unanimous, unreserved and repeated" condemnations of the outbreaks, including even the *Morning Star and Catholic Messenger,* reassured him that such lawlessness remained an isolated aberration against Jews. He felt that only the region's African Americans were scapegoated with the virulence of European anti-Semitism.[35]

But 1890 brought more intense nativist attitudes to a head in New Orleans. Two years earlier, to the delight of reformers concerned with better law enforcement, Mayor Shakspeare had appointed David C. Hennessy chief of police. Hennessy had an outstanding record as a criminal detective and as a fighter against the Mafia. This outstanding record ultimately proved Hennessy's undoing, however. Misreading Sicilian attitudes toward law and order, he interfered in a battle between two families that he felt should be resolved in court. The families considered the disagreement a private matter, to be handled within the Sicilian community. Assassins, allegedly from one of the families involved in the controversy, gunned Hennessy down for his attempt at intervention.[36]

The entire Sicilian community bore the brunt of the outrage in New Orleans.[37] Two weeks later, the correspondent for the *American Israelite* in New Orleans noted that a committee of fifty, appointed by the mayor, had called a meeting to discuss the affair. The correspondent worried because "the eyes of the entire country are now upon this city. . . . whilst the murderers should be punished, innocent men should be let alone, and should not be assailed simply because they are Italians." The following March, jurors acquitted seven defendants and reached no verdict on another three. Angered by the outcome of the trial, prominent citizens led a mob to the jail, where it lynched eleven Italians, two of whom had not yet been tried. Similarly enraged by the verdict of acquittal, the *Times-Democrat* called the lynching "a supreme vindication of law and justice," since "desperate diseases require desperate remedies." Although the *American Israelite* mentioned that J. M. Seligmann, the foreman of the maligned jury, was Jewish, and the *Times-Democrat* accused him of being a friend of one of those on trial, Seligmann's Jewish identity passed without comment in the city's daily press. Perhaps because of Seligmann's role on the jury and the possibility of contaminating Jews with the public hatred that had attached to the Sicilians, Heller carefully avoided mention of the affair. His caution was probably well founded, belying the confidence he expressed in response to the Delhi threats about the Jew's place in Louisiana. His sister Ernestine wrote, "Mother says you should keep away from the Italians. . . . Was it that Mr. Seligman [*sic*] that was at the wedding at your house while we were there?" Rampant anti-Semitism seemed constantly on the horizon, only one inflammatory incident away.[38]

Discrimination against Jews, however underplayed by Heller and other journalists, still merited attention. The article in the *American Israelite* that reported the Hennessy assassination also promoted the campaign of General Adolph Meyer, a Confederate veteran and "an Israelite . . . of broad views . . . who will always maintain the dignity of his race," as the Democratic candidate for Congress from the First District. The First District, or the "American sector," was the "nerve center" of the city, the central business district, where the majority of Jews lived and worked.[39] Meyer seemed "certain of election" in spite of attacks on his candidacy by several newspapers "on the grounds of his being a Hebrew." The *New Orleans Daily States* supported General Meyer as a "fair representative of the energy, intelligence and public spirit of that historic race whose record in New Orleans is enriched by such statesmen as Judah P. Benjamin and B. F. Jonas" and attacked those who chose to vote against him "because he is a Jew." The next month Meyer won the election after a "campaign of great bitterness."[40]

It seems no mere coincidence that 1890 was a turning point in Heller's career, the year he created a truly public persona as an ally of the middle-class Protestants who were working for the moral rejuvenation of the state. Gutheim had set a local precedent for rabbinic participation in civic as well as Jewish communal affairs by serving as vice president, then president pro tem, of the New Orleans Board of Education shortly before his death. Emulating Gutheim, Heller sought to demonstrate that he too could be both a rabbi and a community spokesman. In 1890 he became involved in his first community-wide controversy as a strong opponent of the Louisiana Lottery along with many of the members of the Young Men's Democratic Association who also participated on the "Committee of Fifty." When appointed by the mayor in 1890, the Committee of Fifty included two Jewish men, Simon Hernsheim and M. J. Hart. But when reformers E. H. Farrar, George Denegre, John Parkerson, John Wickliffe, and other members of the Committee of Fifty led the mob to the jail for the nefarious lynching of the Sicilians the following March, Jewish names did not appear on the list of committee members responsible for galvanizing and leading the mob.[41] Historically, even assimilated Jews avoided violent confrontations, and those on the Committee of Fifty doubtless viewed a lynch mob as a cousin of European pogroms. Heller's anti-Lottery position gained him the respect of some of his congregants and the disdain of others, but the stand won the rabbi—as he undoubtedly meant it to—a degree of civic prominence beyond the confines of Temple Sinai and New Orleans Jewry.[42]

The Reconstruction legislature of 1868 originally granted the Louisiana State Lottery Company a charter to operate in the state without competition for the next twenty-five years as a private business for a $40,000 annual fee. The Lottery was connected with a variety of major businesses, had a large and secure financial base, and wielded tremendous political power—at least as long as the charter held. It controlled most of the state's newspapers, allied with several leading banks, and contributed directly to many politicians. During the 1880s, the Lottery reached its peak and controlled the New Orleans water works, a prominent cemetery, and cotton and sugar mills. Although the Lottery was based in New Orleans, where smaller daily drawings occurred, people all over the United States participated in its monthly drawings.[43]

The future of the Lottery became a politically volatile issue in 1890 when one of its owners applied to recharter the tax-exempt and extremely lucrative business. The owners' efforts to extend the Lottery's life by another twenty-five years stirred the reformist impulses of the good government supporters under the auspices of the YMDA. The group's dominant focus became opposing the rechartering of the Louisiana Lottery. Other ministers and lay leaders became active in the fight before Max Heller joined the cause, but he and the Reverend Benjamin Palmer, his Presbyterian mentor, soon became dominant figures in New Orleans, while Temple Sinai's Felix Dreyfous took a leading stand against the Lottery in the state legislature.[44]

The anti-Lottery issue attracted clergymen because it gave them an irresistible opportunity to campaign for moral uplift in the city and the state. Because the Lottery's control and capital benefited New Orleans and Louisiana financially even though gambling may have financially crippled many participating citizens, the Lottery question was not simple. Both pro- and anti-Lottery factions could be found among the state's leading citizens. When the legislature of 1866 originally permitted lottery vending, lawmakers stipulated that Charity Hospital in New Orleans would receive $50,000 in license fees. Since it gave less than 50 percent of its enormous income in prizes, the Lottery gleaned great profits, paying the state its annual fee and retaining the rest for its owners. In 1890, however, when the Lottery proposed to renew its charter, it agreed to raise its annual fee from $40,000 to $500,000, to be divided among public schools, levees, and charitable institutions. That same year tremendous floods badly damaged the state's levees, threatening to ruin many inhabitants. The Lottery sought to refurbish its image by offering to help fund emergency relief, but Governor Francis T. Nicholls turned down the money. When the Lottery suggested awarding funds directly to various levee districts, however, most of them accepted. After a local minister criticized Mayor Shakspeare for accepting $50,000 to protect New Orleans, the mayor replied that "sweet charity's treasure-box would be very empty" if money "stained with wine or crime" were eliminated.[45]

The Lottery cause, then, evoked strong feelings on both sides. New Orleans opponents argued, for example, that, if the Louisiana Lottery were rechartered, it would become "a monopolistic octopus which would strangle the state in bribery and corruption." In February 1890, New Orleans residents who opposed the Lottery organized the Anti-Lottery League and established the *New Delta*, the only newspaper in the city that was not in the Lottery's camp. It remained in print only during the two years of the anti-Lottery campaign. In June, when Dreyfous voted against the Lottery in the legislature, he stated that he did so because this form of gambling was responsible for "engulfing the savings of the working classes, making the poor poorer." His opposition to the Lottery, of course, drew criticism from the mainstream New Orleans press when the *Daily States* accused him of being a "political traitor."[46] Heller's stand resembled that of his congregant, but while Dreyfous angered those who disagreed with him, he was, after all, an elected state representative. "My concern is with the character of the individual," Dreyfous stated. In his own defense he sounded a maudlin note: "I think of the weak, the untutored before whom ruin and the loss of self are set in alluring pictures that they may sell their honor and happiness for an illusive hope." The New Orleans Jewish community opposed Heller because, as a *rabbi*, he had taken a political stand on a sensitive and controversial issue. As Ruth Heller Steiner recalled in a vivid memoir, her father had been "fearless" in his opposition to the Louisiana State Lottery "at a time when the president of his congregation was one of its leading officials." He had preached against it "all over the State in the face of threats against his life."[47]

Heller's foray against the Lottery not only aligned him with the elite reformers of the city but also put him on record as a religious leader unafraid to take on a contemporary secular issue in the larger community. His stand complied with the eighth plank of the Pittsburgh Platform, which targeted the "problems presented by the contrasts and evils of the present organization of society." The year 1890 marked the beginning of a decade when events increasingly strengthened Heller's commitment to social justice. His personal journey reflected a larger national trend in Reform Judaism. In the light of opposition from within his congregation and the lack of precedent for his political involvement, the Lottery provided a testing ground for addressing public controversy.[48]

Heller's fight for a more morally responsible means of financing state government also placed him in the company of Palmer and Catholic Archbishop Francis Janssens, the two most prominent Christian clergymen in New Orleans. By establishing himself as a partner in this triumvirate of religious leadership, Heller addressed the American Reform Jewish ideal of securing Judaism's place as one of the three great religions in the United States. Judaism's transformation from an isolated peoplehood to a religion integrated into the social fabric of America was the goal of the late nineteenth-century Reform movement. Although optimism colored the rationale for stressing the religious over the ethnic impulse, a degree of self-defensiveness accompanied the desire for assimilation. "We must persuade our fellow-citizens of other creeds that Judaism is a living . . . faith," Heller argued a decade later, "and we shall have removed the greater half of their unfounded suspicions."[49]

In April 1890, Heller's anti-Lottery stand gained him notoriety when the *Mascot* made him the centerpiece of a front-page editorial cartoon (illustration 5). The cartoon commentary criticized all who mixed "church with matters strictly political . . . , be he Roman Catholic, Protestant, or Jew." Referring to his participation in an Anti-Lottery League rally, the paper described Heller as "possibly the only man speaking at the meet-

5. *"Come Back to Temple Sinai": Heller's anti-Lottery stand as parodied by the* Mascot, *1890. Courtesy of the William R. Hogan Jazz Archives, Tulane University Library.*

ing who was evidently sincere." On the other hand, the article charged that he "based his opinion on the statements of others opposed to the lottery ... While his language was eloquent, his position [was] ... so apparently unstable that his arguments were the very essence of ridicule." The *Mascot's* criticism tacitly acknowledged the importance of both speaker and occasion, a view supported by the *New Delta*, which claimed that the rally, held in Coliseum Square, constituted the "largest political mass meeting ever held in New Orleans." Forty-two hundred people assembled there to hear Heller, the president of the Anti-Lottery League, speak "in his sincere and straightforward manner and with eloquence." While other men made a "secret of their views," the anti-Lottery press saw Heller and his colleagues vowing to stand "before the world on their righteousness." John H. Stone, the district attorney in Clinton, Louisiana, heard the unspoken message as well as the spoken one in Heller's speech. As he commented to Heller, "What a power for good, in the establishment of good government the Jews will be, if they but be directed by the lofty and righteous sentiments you uttered." Heller's "patriarchal counsel" impressed Stone, and Heller, in turn, appreciated Stone's recognition. Charles Parker of the *New Delta* requested a copy of Stone's letter, and Heller sent it along "to serve the cause of the Delta . . . , thankful . . . for any service in that connection" that "you may require of me."[50]

The following year, 1891, proved decisive in arousing the public's concern over the Lottery issue. Palmer and Heller took the lead in organizing support. A chronicler of the Lottery reported that without Palmer's address on 25 June at the Grand Opera House in New Orleans and Heller's in Shreveport on 13 August, the tide would not have turned in favor of their cause. Heller delivered his passionate speech in Shreveport under considerable stress, however. Two days earlier, he had received word from Edgar Cahn, then secretary of Temple Sinai, that the congregation's acting president refused to grant Heller permission to travel to Shreveport. The stated reason was that Rabbi Leucht of Touro Synagogue was also out of the city—a poor excuse, since other rabbis serving local Jews remained in New Orleans at the time, although none who served Reform congregations. Ida also opposed her husband's going to Shreveport. She wrote to him from Chicago where she was visiting his family: "It is all right if you speak at such a political meeting in your own home . . . , but for a minister of God to go away from home to ascend the public platform, I don't approve." She complained that he had done enough already "as a representative Jew." On the other hand, to go to a "*second rate* place to speak is a different matter, than even speaking at a little church in *New Orleans.*"[51]

Those close to Heller were not alone in registering their opposition to his actions. Less than a month after Heller's speech, the *New Orleans Item* carried a front-page series of articles documenting the protests of "Israelites" concerned about Heller's involvement with politics. According to the *Item,* some of the "prominent Hebrews" circulated a petition denying that Heller was their spokesman. One member of the Jewish community called Heller a "citizen of the North." An *Item* journalist claimed that Heller had not registered to vote in Louisiana, a statement retracted after the registrar of voters notified the paper otherwise. Heller, too, felt that a rabbi should not be involved in politics, but he made the anti-Lottery campaign an exception. The "battle of argument . . . rages around the great sanctuaries of man," he rationalized. The minister is a disgrace to his office "who will not light from the fires of love and faith the flaming torch of public appeal and scathing reproof."[52]

Heller's stand impressed the correspondent from the *American Israelite,* who defended Heller's journey to Shreveport. He argued that the rabbi had traveled to the city in response to "an invitation from the anti-

Lotteryites" there and "*not* as the rabbi of Temple Sinai." Heller instead had appropriately presented himself "as a minister of God going to perform what he thought was his bounden duty." A. Lewenthal, Jr., the mayor of Brookhaven, Mississippi, understood the full import of Heller's Anti-Lottery League activities. Having read the Shreveport speech, and noticing the "adverse criticism" that Heller's stumping had aroused, he told Heller that the speech "should dispel the oft-heard assertion that seven eighths of the Jews are among the opponents of every moral movement, the inseparable ally of the saloon and the supporter of every species of gambling." He applauded Heller's courage and added that he hoped to see "the revival of a truly Jewish religion, led by a fearless ministry who know the truth and dare to tell it, who comprehend their mission and dare follow it." A. Krauss, another Brookhaven Jew, commended Heller for organizing a relief committee to aid Russian refugees and congratulated him as well for his stand on the Lottery "as a moral teacher and representative of a great Jewish community."[53]

Even Ida changed her mind after the event. Heller received no written reprimand from the Temple Sinai Board of Directors, and when Ida realized that Max had not endangered his position, she expressed her relief and pride. "It is a gratification that you have done so much for the Jews and particularly when I was so afraid you would only harm yourself." Heller was not the only rabbi who risked his congregation's censure. Henry Cohen, rabbi in Galveston, wrote Heller that he, too, had experienced something akin to Heller's "lottery oeuvre." In a lecture that Cohen had delivered to the Galveston YMCA entitled "Practical Honesty," he had mentioned "the sin of lottery ticket buying." The next day he found that "our Jewish lottery-ticket sellers were panic-stricken; that I, a Rabbi, &c, &c, &c." had dared speak against their vocation. Cohen knew that Heller had heard more than enough of "their line of argument."[54]

Work on behalf of the Anti-Lottery League catapulted Heller into a larger sphere of influence, but another set of events during the same year ultimately did more for his evolving sense of social justice. In 1891 New Orleans received its first "wave" of Russian immigrants. In this connection the coincidence of several seemingly random occurrences allowed him to respond more authentically as—in the terms of Lewenthal's vision—a rabbi who comprehended and followed his mission.

CHAPTER V

༢༠༦

Dimensions of Leadership
Reformer, Traditionalist, Activist, and Dissenter, 1891–1897

Heller entered the 1890s armed for combat. With journalistic and oratorical skill, he sought recognition among both Jews and gentiles as a modern religious leader and advocate of middle-class civic activism. At the beginning of the decade, he felt relatively sure of himself and his place within the elite, reform-oriented audience that he was attracting. And while he recognized social injustice, he offered no original, radical, or compelling solutions to the long list of problems afflicting New Orleans and the South. Instead he emphasized the need for a heightened sense of spiritual zeal.

On Yom Kippur morning, 1889, he told his congregation that the "lack of real fervor and warm devotion" in the temple seemed "like a heavy chilling dampness on some cold, foggy morning . . . , dampening . . . and discouraging." His sermons continually chastised his congregants, urging them to shake off their middle-class complacency and materialism. Whether such appeals offended them or not, Heller apparently suited their needs. At the December 1890 annual meeting, Max Dinkelspiel moved that Heller's salary be increased from the $4,000 designated in the budget to $5,000. In his commendation, this Sinai stalwart alluded to the rabbi's learning, dignity, and education "in the Cincinnati college." The leading congregation in the "Southern States," he declared, "felt proud that their rabbi *was reared in an American institution,* and that they could point to him as the peer of any Jewish minister in the land." His American credentials served Heller well. A "ringing and enthusiastic vote" carried the day. His typical sermon, sedately cloaked in Victorian language, heartily condemned social injustice such as poverty, stressed the need to "eradicate *causes,*" and then urged mere "diligence, independence, stimulus" as a solution.[1]

During the Gilded Age, as labor unions gained power in New Orleans, they found political allies among the Regulars of the Democratic machine. Basing its electoral strength on control of patronage, concern for issues significant to the city's waterfront and other unions, and hostility to the "silk-stocking" Anglo-American elite, the Regulars had broad-based support from ethnic (mostly Irish and German) working-class interests and businessmen.[2] Heller was certainly not part of the machine, but neither did he wholly support the social conservatism of the silk-stocking element. Throughout the local events leading up to and continuing through the dockworkers' strike of 1892, for example, he remained silent on the labor question. Inasmuch as some of the community's leading capitalists were his congregation's lay leadership, even if he did sympathize with working-class needs, he undoubtedly would have felt reticent about taking an active position supporting organized labor against the economic interests of those who had hired him and who controlled his salary and tenure. He chose to align himself on most issues with the prominent reformers of the Anti-Lottery League who later formed the core of the Progressive movement in both the city and the state. Although they were genuinely concerned with social betterment, their extreme caution, elitism, and overt racism, as displayed in the action of the Committee of Fifty, marred the reformers' approach to any governmental or societal improvement. These flaws diminished the influence and effectiveness of both the Social Gospel movement and political progressivism in the South and defined the boundaries within which Heller could begin to work out more significant solutions to the problems around him.

Heller's stature and respectability allowed him to be outspoken on controversial topics, but his need for social acceptance and his sense of community allegiance, at all levels, meant that radical risk taking was not a political prerogative. He even had to deal with a major conservative impediment in the form of his father-in-law, an "unreconstructed rebel" who lived with him and his wife. Ruth, the youngest Heller, decades later recalled that her maternal grandfather used to drive Heller into "a red but firmly-controlled rage" when the older man expressed "such sentiments as 'show me a nigger and I'll show you a thief.' " She also remembered that her family went "along with all of white New Orleans," because they "accepted as a fact of life the unbelievably low estate of half of the city's population." Even though she considered her family "more conscious than most" of social injustice, "it impinged but seldom, and then only in the general terms of Father's conviction that the south was not doing its duty."[3]

Halting in his initial attempts at dealing with social activism, Heller soon became one of the first American rabbis to broaden his base of social involvement. Two of his contemporary but slightly younger southern colleagues, David Marx of Atlanta and Morris Newfield of Birmingham, remained cautious on sensitive issues throughout their careers. Like Heller, they saw themselves as ambassadors to the non-Jewish community, self-consciously attempting to personify the highest values of Jewish culture. Marx confined his activities to noncontroversial charities and philanthropies. Newfield's compassion eventually led him toward professional social work, but he remained silent on racial and labor issues prior to World War I. Neither rabbi played an active role as a reformer before the turn of the century.[4]

Later, in the 1890s, when Heller did express his sympathies with organized labor, he targeted events far removed from the New Orleans scene. He attacked the Pullman Company's callousness in the Debs strike. "This great leader of industry" admitted that it had never given the workers "the benefit of its own prosperity," justifying its policy with the excuse that "business is business." Heller condemned the "tyranny of the strong" as the "fundamental evil in every social injustice." Although inhibited from directly denouncing New Orleans business interests, he vehemently denounced the "frightful inequalities by which one man starves for want of bread while another pours away champagne." Where did he place the blame? He pointed a finger at the "selfishness of the gifted who claim every material award they can manage to grasp," and he decried the fact that "there is no one strong enough to force them to be fair."[5]

When Heller addressed the HUC commencement class of 1895, he used the occasion to explore the identity conflicts implicit in the role of religious leader in an age of increasing acculturation and accommodation. He described the role of the rabbi in outer-directed terms: "To the Gentile . . . [it] stands for the choicest of what Judaism has to give, as the model of Jewish manhood to place by the side of Christian ideals." But in portraying a rabbi's function in an open society, he also acknowledged the tensions involved in playing the role. "The rabbi of this free land [must] be an American in all that is . . . outward, and only the noble impulses of his heart . . . must proclaim him unmistakably a Jew."[6] The following year, as he discussed what he termed the "dual role" of religion, he stressed that "the Law and the Principle, the Precept and the Truth are ever upholding and again antagonizing one another." Whatever the underlying impulses and intent of such statements, they nevertheless referred to conflicts within Heller as the ideals of Judaism and the realities of a southern pulpit stretched him in two directions simultaneously. When he claimed that religion required "prophet and priest, the progressive and the conservative, the warrior to win new lands and the peaceful builder to make them habitable and secure," he tacitly acknowledged the compromise he was trying to achieve as he struggled to define his own sphere of activism. To survive successfully in New Orleans, he needed the respect and acceptance of his congregation and larger community, but he also needed to heed the call to stand for social justice. Understanding the need for accommodation, he suggested that "the rationale of all business prosperity and . . . professional success" involved "adaptation to prevailing conditions." Believing that a person gained in society only "in proportion with the degree of the need, the pleasure and the size of the public he is serving," Heller tried to carve out a relatively liberal position for himself.[7]

His ambivalence over the conflicting demands of social justice and civic responsibility shaped his attitudes toward the plight of Russian Jews. In 1881 a rise in popular anti-Semitism, together with the legal restrictions placed on Jews after the assassination of Czar Alexander II, prompted Jews en masse to flee from a fear of pogroms and economic devastation. The upwardly mobile yet socially insecure American Jewish community, still predominantly of German ancestry, felt ill equipped to handle the shiploads of Russian Jews who entered New York City. Unlike their geographically mobile German coreligionists, the newcomers were reluctant to disperse. I. M. Wise's remarks several years earlier indicate how unwilling the Americanized Jews were to acknowledge that they shared a heritage with the new immigrants: "It is next to an impossibility to associate or identify ourselves with that half-civilized orthodoxy. . . . We are Americans and they are not . . . we are Israelites of the nineteenth century and a free country, and they gnaw the dead bones of [the] past." Assimilated American "Israelites" or "Hebrews," as they liked to call themselves, were ever sensitive to the resurgence of nativism among the Anglo-Saxons they emulated. They worried about how non-Jews might react to the new wave of impoverished, Orthodox, Yiddish-speaking immigrants. Would reaction to the current influx bring about the exclusion of all Jews from full participation in American life? Heller chastised those who avoided calling themselves Jews. In December 1896, a humorous column, "The Picayune's Telephone," appeared in the *Daily Picayune* and included the following dialogue:

> "Say, Picayune, that was a fine sermon by Dr. Heller on 'Hebrew, Jew, Israelite.' But say, don't you think that this definition of the terms was not strictly accurate?"
> "No. How do you make it?"

"Well, I heard a gentleman talking about the sermon this morning. He said that the real definition was as follows: A 'Jew' is a poor 'Israelite,' an 'Israelite' is a rich 'Hebrew.' And the funniest thing about it was that the speaker was, according to his own dictum, an 'Israelite!' "[8]

Even as they tried to distance themselves from recent arrivals, established American Jews still felt responsible for their welfare. Believing that "as American Israelites we have a duty to the community in which we live, which forbids us to become parties to the infliction of permanent paupers upon our already overburdened cities," prominent American Jews organized the Hebrew Immigrant Aid Society (HIAS) for the purpose of centrally coordinating refugee assistance. In January 1890, the month that Jews in Delhi and Lake Providence felt the wrath of "white-capping" vigilantes, Heller concluded that a permanent bureau of immigration should be maintained by donations from Jewish communities across the country. Although most of the new arrivals were experienced textile workers who could move directly into jobs in New York City's booming garment industry, Heller and other prominent American Jews argued that concentrating Jews in that city would retard their assimilation. These leaders saw dispersal as the sole answer. Only after the refugee found "asylum in his new country," would the community come to his aid, supporting him as he acquired English-language skills. Although Heller initially found the newly arrived Russian immigrant "the most helpless creature under the sun," Heller believed that ignorance and degradation should prompt American Jewish philanthropies to maintain a permanent bureau of immigration to assist the newly arrived. He felt that the Jewish community's highest priority was to raise immigrants to the level of their new environment and prepare them to accept the "duties and responsibilities of citizenship."[9]

An editorial that appeared in the *New Orleans Daily States* just a few days before police chief Hennessy's assassination in the fall of 1890 seemed to validate Heller's view of Russian immigrants as candidates for gradual uplift and eventual assimilation. The paper assured its readers that America "could accommodate . . . thousands of immigrants from Russia. Hebrews, now perhaps one hundredth . . . of our population, might form a far greater proportion . . . with good results," since the Jewish people "fall into the customs of the people, build themselves up and become loyal, frugal and prosperous citizens." While a large and "indiscriminate" immigration should be avoided, "the American people will cheerfully afford asylum and refuge to the Jews fleeing . . . persecution."[10]

Shortly after the lynching of the Sicilians in March 1891, a new immigration bill was under consideration in Congress. The *Times-Democrat* now advocated a "more stringent" law that could check "certain classes of immigrants, especially from Poland, Russia, and the Slavic provinces of Austria." By this time, however, the Jewish community of New Orleans had a solid base of assimilated citizens who could afford to care for their own and undoubtedly felt under pressure to do so. According to the *American Israelite*, although the city claimed only "six thousand Israelites," it could boast of its large and "flourishing" congregations and its major charitable institutions. In addition, the correspondent bragged, "our people are always foremost in their contributions to public enterprises and charities," despite being "comparatively poor, with only a couple of millionaires among us." The following November, when Julius Weis, Heller's patron, friend, and newly elected president of Temple Sinai, received a letter from the American Committee for the Amelioration of the Conditions of Russian Immigrants, he called together representatives of various organizations within the Jewish community, including two Orthodox synagogues, to form a communitywide relief effort. This meeting became the first joint attempt to integrate all segments of the city's Jewish population.[11]

The *American Israelite* carried a weekly update of the local committee's activities and kept readers abreast of similar efforts in other parts of the nation. By the second meeting, Heller and Leucht predictably found themselves at odds over the structure of the local immigrant aid society. Rather than form a separate society, the majority of the group, including Leucht, decided that the Touro Infirmary and Hebrew Benevolent Association could handle all the arrangements for refugees through a special committee. Heller's minority report argued that New Orleans, like other Jewish communities throughout the country, should set up a special association with immigrant aid as its sole purpose. Six weeks later, the community notified New York that New Orleans—with employment promised by several local industries, including sugar refineries, foundries, bakeries, and tailor establishments—stood ready to receive twenty-five families. Not wishing to disturb the balance of labor or to perpetuate negative Jewish stereotypes, the Jewish community carefully avoided exacerbating resentment against the immigrants. The *Times-Democrat* praised the Jewish community's cautious approach. Since the city's few factories could not handle "an influx of refugees," the Jewish leaders were strongly opposed "to bringing immigrants here and making peddlers of them."[12]

In January 1892, the Jewish community of Opelousas, in St. Landry

Parish, informed the New Orleans Committee on Russian Immigration that the Louisiana town needed "six agriculturists, two tailors and two shoemakers." Leucht relayed word to New York. In February, the ship bearing the immigrants docked in New Orleans. Two children had died on board, but the immigrants, notwithstanding "traces of past suffering," seemed "strong, healthy, and determined to begin life anew." Most came from large cities "within the heart" of Russia. The Jewish community boarded the families until employment could be secured for the men, at which time families would be provided with homes near their workplaces. Several families went directly to Opelousas, while the children of those remaining were "taught English and given a primary education." Americanizing the new arrivals "as early as possible" formed the central objective of the plan. Spirits seemed high until the following week, when the New York office sent an additional thirty-five families. On the eve of the Hennessy assassination trial, Leucht informed the dailies that the New Orleans Jewish community did not intend "to bring down in great masses these Russian refugees and disturb the labor markets." He added emphatically, "We are only willing to help to a certain degree." The committee forwarded some of the new families to Opelousas and others upriver to Lutcher, in St. James Parish, where jobs were waiting. Locally, Heller took charge of education, while Leucht spoke to the elite members of the Ladies' Aid and Sewing Society, which kept Touro Infirmary supplied with linens. He solicited their help in "civilizing" the Russian refugees who remained in New Orleans, teaching them "to preserve cleanliness about themselves, their children and their homes" so that, "by the force of example," they might become Americanized. The Jewish community responded with the kind of efficiency that urban Progressives liked to see, and in less than a month, 167 Russians had been employed. Only 4 families still required help.[13]

Heller had a degree of personal expertise in immigrant education, not simply through his own experience at HUC, but more significantly, through the experiences in Chicago of his sisters, Louise and Ernestine. Both worked for the model program that Gabriel Bamberger had established at the Girls' Training School. There Louise taught sewing, and Ernestine managed the office, employing the typing skills she had recently acquired in a night school course (see illustrations 6 and 7). After receiving a letter from Louise describing her sewing classes and her students, Heller confided to her, "I really envy you, d. Louise you are getting a great deal more pleasure and satisfaction out of this Russian business than any of the rest of us." He wrote frankly about his in-fighting with Leucht "and his ring," which was hindering the organization of the kind

6. *Louise Heller, Chicago, circa 1885. Courtesy of the American Jewish Archives, Hebrew Union College–Jewish Institute of Religion, Cincinnati.*

of immigrant aid society he originally envisioned. He complained that the others "were bent upon having it all to manage themselves and playing the poor fellows as helpless victims into their hand." As Heller battled with Leucht, he was already shifting away from the smug and condescending tone of his editorial in the *Chronicle*. "How these people, the ring I mean, speak of the Russian Jew!" he complained, "Sometimes I feel

7. *Ernestine Heller, Chicago, circa 1885. Courtesy of the American Jewish Archives–Jewish Institute of Religion, Cincinnati.*

as if I would like to read such a letter as yours to a Touro [Infirmary] Board meeting." Then he promised to send a piece of sugarcane to Louise, in care of the Industrial School, so that her young charges might taste part of the American South. Manual training became a keystone in Heller's program for institutionalizing self-improvement, whether for immigrants or for those—both black and white—who had been educated in public schools.[14]

The practical concerns of children and educational settings interested him on all levels. In 1897, as Temple Sinai planned some physical improvements to its building, Heller lobbied for those immediately affecting children. He wanted funds allocated so that hooks could be installed for children's hats and clothes. He also stipulated that the path on the side of the temple where the students entered Sunday school should be widened so that they would not be forced to walk on the grass. Finally, he urged that the vestry rooms be furnished "with a sufficient number of chairs to permit the children [to] be seated together for weekly sermonettes."[15]

Heller's work with the Anti-Lottery League had truly won him a broader constituency. After the League-backed Murphy J. Foster became governor in 1892, he appointed Heller to the State Board of Education, a post previously belonging to Leucht. While Heller traveled in Europe that July to consult with doctors about his recurring stomach problems and to take the waters at some of the popular spas in Germany and Switzerland, his friend Edgar Cahn informed him of his appointment to the Board of Education. Cahn explained that many "antis" had been "left out in the cold by reason of the fact that there were not enough places to go around." "You can doubly congratulate yourself on your devotion to this post of honor," Cahn claimed, reminding Heller to write the governor "as soon as you receive this news." With this new appointment, Heller had the opportunity to expand his interest in education from work with religious school students and immigrants within the Jewish community to the wider field of public education in the state.[16]

By this time also, Max Heller was the father of two, Cecile and James Gutheim Heller, and Ida was expecting a third child, Isaac. Heller's interest in education thus took on a personal dimension. He delighted in watching his own children develop intellectually. He regarded all kinds of educational experiences as valid—formal and informal, at home or in class. He quickly criticized those he considered superficial, designed to instill obedience rather than to build analytical skills or aesthetic appreciation. At the end of the 1880s, Heller had told his congregants, "Your children study . . . not to understand or appreciate for themselves, but simply to be able to repeat like parrots . . . , all . . . to earn a harvest of applause." He warned that such fruitless effort only "leaves the soul barren." When Heller's children were growing up, he practiced what he had preached. In 1896, the birth of Ruth, a second daughter, completed the family. Looking back at her childhood years later, she recalled that "nobody else's Father—this we know—gave the things of the spirit as lavishly as did ours." He "had us stay up until all hours and watch when the night-blooming cereus plant, which flowers once a year, gradually opened the milky-white petals of its one large bulb," she wrote. Her father also "kept a butterfly cocoon in a leaf-filled jar on his desk, and called us in when the great insect emerged."[17]

Heller's fascination with and devotion to such experiences paralleled the intense interest in education for life that John Dewey and other Progressive educators were beginning to advocate. The intensity and diversity of his own academic career coupled with his interest in his two sisters' work at the Girls' Training School fueled his belief in the importance of education as a force for social change. Education, then, became a kind of intellectual bridge between Heller's own experiences as an immigrant and his experiences in the late nineteenth-century world. By actively engaging himself on this new front, Heller could simultaneously invest his energies in championing the causes of immigrants and in wrestling with problems that were crippling the South socially and economically.

Heller proudly told his family that Alcée Fortier, the other anti-Lottery Board of Education appointee from New Orleans, had been "sounding my praises everywhere," thus giving Heller entree to the local lecture circuit. During the four years of their tenure, Fortier and Heller developed a relationship as colleagues by working on such issues as textbook adoption and methods for textbook distribution to the needy. Afterward their friendship continued to grow. Heller forwarded Fortier the sermons that he thought might be of interest. In 1896, the two shared the same fate: neither was reappointed. "I suppose that Mr. Foster thought that you and I were too independent," wrote Fortier, "and did not admire the Ring sufficiently." After the defeat of the Lottery, Foster aligned himself with the New Orleans city machine, not the reform faction with which Heller and Fortier were associated. Fortier lamented that Heller's "eminent services have been lost to the cause of public education in Louisiana" and added that he would "always keep a most agreeable remembrance of our trips to Baton Rouge together."[18]

Despite the two men's friendship and their work together, Heller's opinions did not mirror Fortier's racism. Two editorial positions that appeared, unsigned, in the *Jewish Ledger* before Heller became editor very likely expressed his convictions. The first, in late April 1895, condemned Bible reading in schools on the grounds that "schools are a part of the state . . . and there is no reason why the church should so persistently interfere where it has no prerogative." The second appeared the following mid-July, decrying a recent school segregation decision in Florida and claiming that "it is impossible for such a law to receive the sanction of the higher courts, as it is not a question of separate schools for colored and white pupils based upon mutual preferences of the races or upon the grounds of temporary expediency, but seems to be a flagrant attempt to crystallize race prejudices into a permanent law." These sentiments contrast with those expressed by Fortier when he asked for Heller's ideas on distributing free books (donated by the Howard family of Louisiana Lottery fame). Fortier wrote that he "was thinking of asking the principals of the white schools in my district to use their judgment . . . and give the books to the children most in need."[19]

In 1894, Heller again tried to edit a local New Orleans Jewish weekly, the *Jewish Enquirer*. His financial backing again proved insufficient, and he was able to publish only one issue. The following year, however, A. Steeg, a Jewish printer in the city, began to publish the *Jewish Ledger* and in 1896 made Heller the editor. The periodical provided an attractive forum for his weekly sermons, or "causeries," which appeared on the front page. Heller used the editorial page to publicize his opinions on the issues of the day. The *Ledger* distributed papers throughout Louisiana and Mississippi and mailed courtesy copies to editors of other local or regional Jewish weeklies, thereby linking Heller to the Jewish journalism network of the South and West. While airing his views on a broad range of contemporary topics, Heller returned repeatedly to the subject of educational reform in his *Ledger* editorials.[20]

Even though education informed all Progressive thought, Heller was disturbed that primary education was "the last to respond to the voices of reform." Like other leading school critics of the 1890s, he deplored pedagogy that encouraged "the senseless memorizing of words . . . , the cramming of lessons for examinations," and the uncritical "storing of memory." Instead, he argued, the "highest function of a teacher" should be realized through "the awakening of independent thought, the spurring of a higher curiosity." Heller decried the lack of inspired teaching and the failure of schools to come to terms with "the needs of a complete education." Schools spent too much time dwelling on "flag and spread-eagle patriotism," he thought, and this "patriotism of the jingo" did not equip young minds to deal with solving the growing number of social and economic problems affecting their lives.[21]

During the mid-1890s, Heller equivocated or vacillated when the logic of his own arguments led him to conclusions that he suspected might offend the sensibilities of his readers. His swing from one end of the liberal-traditional spectrum to the other varied with the issues involved and reflected the tensions implicit in the roles he chose or was forced to play—whether those of immigrant, Reform rabbi, southern Progressive, Americanizer, repository of European conceits, standard-bearer of respect for religious freedom, or, as he himself put it, "priest and prophet." The warring impulses reflected both the internal contradictions of Heller's personality and the conflicting imperatives of his desire for social justice and civic respectability. He was not alone in having such experiences. As with so many other professions in the country, rabbis became "representative Jews" as the American Jewish rabbinate became more professionalized. Congregants wanted to believe that their rabbi was incorruptible, that he embodied the values American Jews held dear. Heller excelled at playing the part of ethnic entrepreneur in New Orleans, but when he tried to be a role model in various subcommunities, he felt himself under a great deal of personal stress.[22]

Heller's editorials and "musings" often revealed his internal conflicts. He attacked the American Protective Association (APA) for its "narrow Americanism which deifies the student of nativity" as it denounced Catholicism under the veil of the word " 'Protective.' " Then he quickly pointed to several planks in the APA platform that he endorsed himself, including "political equality for all races, creeds and parties in a faithful discharge of all civic duty." He also sympathized with the APA's emphasis on public education, its protection of American labor, and its call for "uniform and strict enforcement of proper naturalization laws . . . of a universally beneficial character." In an especially abstruse paragraph, Heller praised the APA's principles "to the extent of desiring that all children, without distinction of creed, rank, or color might mingle and associate in public schools." He would do nothing, however, to prevent "the wealthy or the religious" from establishing, "at their expense, separate schools for their children." This was no more than a tacit acknowledgment of the political power of New Orleans Catholics and the Protestant elite in a city marked by elite rule, privatism, and a Catholic majority. Establishing and enforcing a "proper standard" for all schools "in the interest of American citizenship" so that education might further the "process of assimilation" remained his chief concern.[23]

But two weeks later, Heller modified his statement "as far as the qualification 'color' is concerned," which was not intended to have "mischievous implications." Denying "the faintest prejudice against the colored race" as he bowed to community pressure, he now wrote that "our brothers of that race are entitled to every privilege which the white man enjoys, but we cannot deem close and equal association to be in the interest of the members of either race." In 1897, he pursued social justice only within well-defined boundaries of community consensus.[24]

The liberal Protestant leaders in the South included men like Benjamin Palmer, Heller's mentor, whose "dealings with the Jewish community," Heller felt, "deserve to stand . . . as shining examples of interreligious respect and sympathy." By including rabbis as colleagues, such ministers inspired their Jewish counterparts in late nineteenth-century southern pulpits. Together they attempted to address, more rhetorically than concretely, the social problems of the Gilded Age. The interfaith dialogue helped reinforce and deepen the already strong religious component within the social justice wing of southern progressivism. Some acts of mutuality, such as making Temple Sinai's facilities available after a fire destroyed St. Paul's Church, or the flowers that Sinai sent Palmer for his seventy-fifth birthday, required no bold innovation. But in 1893, when Heller invited Reverend Walter Pierce, "the eminent Unitarian divine," to speak at Sinai, it marked "the first time a Christian minister occupied the pulpit." Apparently, Heller knew his members well, because the *American Israelite* correspondent commented that "Dr. Heller's liberal views seem to be approved by the entire congregation." The following year Heller preached at the Unitarian Church while Dr. Pierce was at a conference. Sharing religious traditions helped to demystify Judaism in the eyes of non-Jews and to present the faith as a respectable American religion.[25] Inviting a Unitarian minister to the temple's pulpit satisfied, as well, the curiosity of religiously liberal New Orleans Jews at a time when the American Reform Jewish community as a whole worried about defections to liberal sects like the Ethical Culture movement, Christian Science, or Unitarianism. For Thanksgiving, 1896, Temple Sinai and the Unitarian Church of the Messiah, evidently emboldened by the success of the pulpit-sharing experiments, initiated celebration of the holiday with a joint service complete with one of Heller's "instructive and forcible sermons." Eventually including Congregation Gates of Prayer, the interfaith Thanksgiving service became a tradition that lasted until World War I.[26]

American Reform Judaism in the South deepened its regional roots by adopting a time-honored technique of southern evangelism, the use of itinerant clergymen. The Methodist Church, with its corps of circuit-riding preachers, reached out to southern rural believers and inadvertently supplied the southern Jewish urban dwellers a model for bringing religion to their rural coreligionists. The movement was not confined to the South. Since its 1873 national convention, the UAHC established a

Special Committee on Circuit Preaching to arrange and finance the use of circuit rabbis for congregations isolated from the Jewish mainstream. Because Jews continued to be widely scattered throughout the South, reaching them socially and encouraging them to identify with other Jews in the midst of intense Christian evangelizing became paramount concerns.[27]

The distribution of Jewish newspapers like the *Ledger* and the *American Israelite,* which brought local as well as international news, helped combat the isolation of some Jewish communities. For example, the *Ledger* carried information of Jewish settlements from as far west as Galveston and Jefferson, Texas, as far east as Mobile, and as far north as Shreveport and Jackson, Mississippi. In the mid-1890s, however, the Reform Jewish rabbinate considered introducing circuit-riding rabbis as a more direct method of ministering to the needs of the large number of Jews dwelling in southern hamlets. Heller became the first rabbi in the South who attempted to give people "in small country places where no regular synagogues exist an opportunity of hearing the word of God occasionally." As the *Southwestern Presbyterian* described Heller's mission, "It was not proposed to have traveling rabbis, but to induce the wealthier congregations to spare their pastors for work among the scattered and feeble Israelitish communities." In 1895, Heller began to travel for one week out of every month for seven months (see illustration 8). He preached in hamlets such as Summit and Brookhaven, Mississippi, tried to organize Sabbath schools in Jackson and Canton, Mississippi, and "took the existing classes at Brookhaven under his supervision." According to the *Southwestern Presbyterian,* "These congregations had no less than ten, nor more than thirty families; all, except one, had synagogues." The typical small-town Jews, although not wealthy, were "only in the most exceptional cases, objects of poverty."[28]

Administering to a community's needs and attending to the "spiritual welfare" of its congregants entailed more than a monthly Sabbath school class or a sermon, however. Families asked Heller to take the train to their town to marry a daughter or to bury a family member, both occasions that called for a traditional Jewish ritual even in a remote Louisiana or Mississippi hamlet. During such trips, Heller noted much of what he termed "interreligious peace," which reinforced his sense that the majority of Southerners embraced the Jewish citizens in their midst. "When a deliciously sleepy country town is to witness its first Jewish wedding," he recalled, "the city rabbi who has come on the local train observes with a kind of wistful wonder how busy the Gentile girl friends are 'fixing up' the floral arbor for which they have plundered their gardens." Also on

8. Handbill advertising a lecture by Max Heller, circuit-riding rabbi, in Canton, Mississippi, 1895. Courtesy of the American Jewish Archives–Jewish Institute of Religion, Cincinnati.

hand, working alongside Jewish women, he found "gentile housewives" displaying their "culinary art for the Jewish celebration." At a Jewish funeral, Heller saw "a great deal of genuine fellowship" as gentile friends helped cover the grave in the manner dictated by Jewish tradition, "each grasping the shovel in turn" in "unaffected brotherliness."[29]

Although he had written to the Temple Sinai Board of Directors that a rabbi's "deep allegiance to his congregation" should bind up "his heart-strings with the life, the joys and sorrows of every soul under his spiritual guidance," Heller felt obligated to represent Judaism to those "beyond his flock" who needed his services. If a conflict occurred while he was out of the city, another New Orleans rabbi could attend to the crisis. His own congregation should not cripple his "wider usefulness." But once away from the city, an emergency in New Orleans could call him back. One such occasion prompted an article in the *Summit Sentinel* praising Heller's resourcefulness. While preaching in Brookhaven he received a dispatch asking him to return to preside at the funeral of one of his congregants. Even for Reform Jews, Jewish law requires that a burial take place as soon as possible. All the passenger trains traveling south from Brookhaven had passed, forcing Heller to board a freight to Summit. From Summit he went to McComb, "secured a special train, and reached the city to perform the last sad rites over one of his flock." The act left quite an impression on the reporter. "There are not too many men wearing the livery of the Lord," he wrote, "that would have gone to all this trouble to fulfill the last wish of a member of their church, and it speaks well for his kindness and philanthropy." But the strain of performing in more than one arena soon became too great a burden for Heller to maintain. After less than a year, he had to abandon the monthly visits and limit his ministering to special needs.[30]

Just as Charles G. Finney and Dwight L. Moody had revitalized American Protestantism with their evangelical fervor, Heller was willing to Americanize his approach to the rabbinate by using an evangelical technique to spread Judaism. He, however, reacted against the "radical Reformers" who instigated the practice of observing Sabbath with services on Sunday instead of Saturday so that more Jews could participate.[31] Like Leucht and other southern Reform rabbis, Heller felt that Sunday services were inappropriate for Jewish Sabbath worship and represented a needless concession to modernity. As early as 1891, just five years after the Pittsburgh conference, he was already questioning the overemphasis on rationalism in the contemporary Jewish pulpit. In his sermon before the Central Conference of American Rabbis in Baltimore, he asked, "Which are the guiding purposes and laws of Jewish pulpit-teaching in these modern times? What can the Jewish pulpit do for Judaism?" He answered his own rhetorical question: "It is not knowledge we can give, but impulse, not the bare fact, but the strong personal enthusiasm." Heller believed that American Judaism, like American education, mistakenly "stores where it ought to stir."[32]

By the middle of the decade, Heller grew increasingly disillusioned with the sweeping changes that he feared would drain American Judaism of its vitality. "If the Jew retains, with miraculous obstinacy, every intensely vivid characteristic of the Oriental, is it 'practical,' is it acting in accordance with the teachings of educational psychology," he demanded, "to exclude in slavish obedience to fashion, whatever touches to life the secret springs stored up by the accumulated action of the centuries?" The debate over the propriety of Sunday services focused Heller's anger. "Would we do well to substitute an intellectual Sunday morning for a devotional Friday eve?" Reform had gone too far. Very little Hebrew remained in the service. Well-trained, paid non-Jewish voices filled the choir. Architecturally handsome, large, well-appointed temples with decorous services where congregation and rabbi read responsively in English had replaced small synagogues where pious men bowed and swayed in prayers that they themselves chanted at their own pace and rhythm. But the point of seeking change was not to ape the gentile. Was nostalgia for the piety he had known in the Old Country tugging at his heartstrings, or had Heller become, as he believed, a self-appointed spokesman for the "rising tide among thinking and loyal Jews of this country" who were appalled by the allegedly destructive impulses of reform? Although he felt that Reform Judaism had proven "an excellent cleaner of cobwebs," it did not address the emotional needs of its adherents. "After its fine house-cleaning," he asked, "where is the coziness of home-like possession?" With its bare walls, "the welcome is one of chill formality." Perhaps inspired by the piety and fervor of the southern Protestant pulpit, if not imbued with the message of Christianity, Heller hungered for a deeper religiousness, a faith "vivid in historic associations, rich in . . . symbols, strong in its clasp on life and supreme in its appeal for duty." The ceremonies Reform Judaism had obliterated left a shallowness, a "religious anemia." In fact, Heller began to find "an absence of nourishing heart-foods in all . . . sophisticated liberalisms." He grasped the significance of tradition in surprisingly modern terms. He did not call for blind adherence to outdated ceremony or a return to the "turbulent noises of impulsive orthodoxy." Rather he recognized that, with the newfound "freedom of formlessness," men still craved form. "Every new attempt to break with the forms of the past only tends to demonstrate our inexsuperable [inexorable] need for the past when the instincts of veneration are to be appealed to." Heller drew both praise and criticism for his "reactionary" stand.[33]

Heller's "instincts of veneration" inhibited his openness to change, especially when change confronted the traditional spheres occupied by men and women. Although Reform Judaism had taken a more democratic attitude toward women, allowing mixed seating and moving from male Bar Mitzvah to a Christianized mixed confirmation ceremony marking the completion of the Sabbath or Sunday School curriculum, the Reform Jewish community's position on women remained ambiguous and crisscrossed a liberal/traditional spectrum. In the mid-1890s, even as he witnessed the role of women evolving, Heller remained a steadfast traditionalist. He had himself been an only son, his family's "pearl" or "gold," adored and pampered by devoted mother and sisters, and the focus of his father's joy. The Central European upbringing had left indelible marks. The elaborate racial caste system of the American South idealized women, and its rhetoric spoke of the need to protect the purity of white womanhood. This attitude could only have reinforced Heller's already exaggerated desire to embody a "model of Jewish manhood."[34]

Heller's attitude toward women had both public and private consequences. The first convention of the National Council of Jewish Women (NCJW) in 1896 formed the subject of an editorial comment in the *Ledger*. Heller remarked that, of the 120 delegates who traveled to New York from "remote localities" such as Colorado or Oregon for the occasion, hardly any hailed from the South. Heller sensed that there were deep-seated reasons for "Southern indifference toward this essentially new movement." Women "in our latitude," he mused, showed "little enthusiasm for all mannish movements for so called emancipation." When the press reports of the meeting "pronounced a success," Heller remained unconvinced "that we are dealing here with anything more than a fad." Revising his view two weeks later, probably in response to criticism, he conceded that the "Woman's Council . . . bids to accomplish good and honest work." He admitted that he had expressed his "misgivings as to the usefulness of Women's Conventions" but avowed that he would "be the last to stand back from acknowledging any real good whenever and however accomplished." Despite a blanket endorsement of "every earnest well-directed enterprise that seeks to lift up Judaism," Heller remained a halfhearted convert who greeted with a "smile of amusement" what he considered to be exaggerated expectations concerning "a feminine 'salvation' of Judaism." Women, he felt, did have a "mission" to fulfill as Sabbath school teachers "who could function as 'country rabbis' in communities too small to pay a man's salary." This "new sphere," however, was not intended for the "aggressively forward woman who 'claims everything' " but, on the contrary, should be reserved for the "hard-working woman who is looking for usefulness and inward peace."[35]

Although patriarchal in structure and leadership throughout most of its history, Judaism is passed from generation to generation through the mother. The forgers of Jewish tradition recognized that culture resides in the food one eats and in the everyday habits of domestic life—the woman's sacred domain. Heller reflected the traditional perspective when he lamented that the "orthodoxies" have a "stronger hold on women in all faiths," since it is the "mothers . . . with whom are associated the most vivid religious impressions of early years." He believed that domestic training with its "monotonous duties" provided a woman with plentiful "opportunities for reflection." These character-building experiences, united with her "ready acceptance of authority," prepared her soul for the "teachings and stirrings of religion." Even as Heller sincerely, but with inevitable condescension, tried to temper his remarks, the movement to found a local chapter of the NCJW was underway. Leucht, one of the "prominent gentlemen" addressing the opening meeting, captured the moment. He recited the goals stated in the organization's constitution, which included "bringing together all those Jewish women who desire to be enlightened in regard to religious, educational and philanthropic subjects . . . , who wish to consider themselves a part of the great progressive movement of this age." He felt that "the time had come when there was something more demanded of the Jewish woman than that she should be wife and mother." Irma, his daughter, became the first secretary of the local chapter, while Rabbi Gutheim's widow served as the ex officio "presiding officer for Louisiana." The fifty-eight original members included an additional twenty-four wives or daughters of Temple Sinai congregants. Heller, who was sensitive to shifts in community power, must have been disappointed to lose the allegiance of the new organization to his nemesis. He was even more displeased to tell the family in Chicago of the "very disheartening trouble" he was currently experiencing with the "intrigues of L and Mrs. Gutheim who are now hand in glove." The promise of being a Sabbath school teacher in a hamlet like Brookhaven, Mississippi, scarcely seemed the sort of self-fulfillment that the young elite matrons who founded the NCJW were seeking.[36]

Heller's family also bore the brunt of his obsession with "manliness," which at times echoed his father's words to him while he was completing gymnasium training. But more often, the tone was one of self-importance, ambition, and excessive demands upon others. Ida, his wife, bore the brunt of his frustrations and perfectionism. For example, while Heller recuperated from his physical problems at Bad St. Moritz and learned of his appointment to the State Board of Education during the summer of 1892, Ida and the children visited his parents and maiden sisters, Louise and Ernestine, at their apartment in Chicago. Before Max departed, he had promised to write two letters for each one of hers. When several days passed without his receiving one from Ida, however, he became "thwarted and vexed . . . , deeply hurt that you should have failed . . . in so easy a promise," but "punish you by writing less I will not." With the children to tend, Chicago friends and relatives to entertain, and in-laws to please in close quarters, Ida complained that she had little time to write. Heller retorted that he had still less time, since it was difficult to concentrate on writing in a roomful of people at the spa. Excessively frugal, he complained that if he wrote in the solitude of his room, he would have to "burn expensive candles." How unpleasant it must have been for Ida, with her husband an ocean and two continents away, to be deluged with letter after letter filled with criticism! At one point Heller wrote patronizingly, "I must smile to see you writing about my 'new spirit of better . . . temper.' I do hope that my temper has improved. . . . It's really not my fault if my late letters have not shown it. I believe men with perfect nerves would have acted the same." But he insisted on maintaining his paternalistic imperative and expected the female members of the family to perform time-consuming tasks for him. He noted with pleasure that Ida had undertaken "working at the marriage ceremonies," and he assumed that some "ought to be quite familiar." He also hoped that "d. Ernestine will soon start at the diary copying [from his shorthand] as she will remember I told her, with an inside margin." Still, he could manage to close by promising "not to scold any more until we meet again," then sign "with love to you, babies, dear one, Your affectionate husband, Max." The only outward sign of affection was the word itself.[37]

Yet when he told his Chicago family about his children, Heller's observation of their development bespoke tenderness. "Cecile is getting to be quite a big girl . . . , not as talkative as James who always tells about what he sees, nor is she as congenial in getting up games, but she is more daring in exercise, rides his hobby horse of which he is almost afraid." Heller described several more of his children's activities, thrilled that "their greatest treat is [my] telling them a story." When he was away from the children, he expected his family to render their experiences in detail. "I know that cute sayings are hard to treasure or relate especially when children are not in the habit of uttering them often," he wrote, "but it should certainly have been of interest to me to hear how the children are taking to all of you." His own need to record impressions was so insistent that no adult could quite live up to his expectations.[38]

Four years later, Heller returned to Bad St. Moritz to take the waters and drowned poor Ida in another deluge of anger and criticism. "It seems to me you do not lay my letters before you when you answer them. I can remember a number of questions I asked which you never referred to." Another of her mistakes was in neglecting to address letters properly, "Having corresponded with me 4 years ago and read my diary you know that there are 2 St. Moritz: Bad & Dorf, yet you address your letters simply St. Moritz . . . , in consequence of which . . . your letters spent a day or two traveling around in Dorf." Although he promised "not to dwell upon it further," as was his style, he then drove the point home, "I do wish you would wake up, even if you have to put a loose pin somewhere to remind you occasionally of that necessity. It is one of the great duties of life to be awake."[39]

On the other hand, Ida was not spineless. Although she was self-effacing, she could respond to his abusive verbal barrage in a controlled, if not a confident, fashion. After Heller had written, she countered, "I will answer your letters first, but I shall *not* reply to what you still continue to sermonize about. I *might* have some arguments on my side, but I am tired of writing in such a spirit at such a time." She could also seek her own counsel on what to censor in letters home. On one occasion when the two were separated, Max had criticized something that happened in his parents' home during Ida's visit there. She was eager to gain her distance from his anger and glad that Max had "never referred to my opinions of the matter," which she had already expressed. Ida felt relieved, "As long as you did not scold *me* I suppose it was all right." She apparently not only understood the limits of her own tolerance but also seemed to accept the deficiencies of the marital relationship. "I could write and write to you, as if it were a sort of easing of my anxiety, etc. But *that* is a tabooed subject, for I am determined to write as cheerfully as I can, and am going to keep my ugly thoughts to myself." Ida submitted to Heller's entreaties, trying, as she told him, "to please you more in the future." She was, after all, the rabbi's wife. This additional burden to the already demanding role of southern lady, a role that strove to comply with the "domestic ideal" conceived during Victoria's reign, Ida accepted as her proper sphere. "What else have I to live for if it is not to do my duty by you and the children?" she wondered as she stoically managed the domestic world that sustained her husband in New Orleans. When the Temple Sinai Guild organized in 1900 "to serve as an auxiliary association to take charge of the furnishing and maintenance of the building," Ida was elected secretary of the organization, a post she held for nineteen years. An authentic partner in her husband's endeavors, she nevertheless maintained her own connections to other women and activities.[40]

In 1865, John Ruskin preached, "The true nature of home . . . is the place of Peace; the shelter, not only from all injury, but from terror, doubt, and division." Thirty years later, Ida and Max Heller, building their own home on Marengo Street (illustration 9), probably would have agreed. In March 1895, Isidore Hernsheim, a prominent member of Sinai, advanced Heller $8,000 to cover a mortgage.[41] As one of eight, Heller formed a "syndicate" with friends who purchased a square of land. For $1,905, he bought two of the lots on Marengo Street near Dryades, just a few blocks from fashionable St. Charles Avenue, where Hernsheim lived. After paying money to fill in the lot and put in a sidewalk, he calculated having some "$5600–5800 for building . . . an elegant home." Max, who was careful about finances, felt he could handle the house payments, "if Ida will economize as she promised me." He characterized the others "going in" as very "desirable neighbors," because they were "all considered among our first families, people in very comfortable circumstances, who will likely, build fine residences for themselves, much more expensive than mine."[42]

Heller hired the architectural firm of Toldano & Reusch to design a comfortable two-story house, in a modified Victorian style with a Doric-columned front porch that wrapped around one corner and balcony above. An ornamental carved swag decorated the main cornice between porch and balcony and further enlivened the facade. The overall design was both imposing and welcoming. In September, the *Ledger* reported that the Heller family had moved into their new residence, "a handsome and commodious structure, with all the modern conveniences . . . , a light and spacious study . . . fairly filled to the ceiling with hundreds of rare and valuable books that comprise the doctor's library." The family, which now included Isaac and Ruth, then still a baby, could claim its own "refuge" from the "hostile society of the outer world."[43]

Heller's own definition of Jewish identity included a strong sense of "duties to perform towards the present and future." Although the stately home on Marengo Street became his retreat, the world beyond the front porch beckoned. During the year when the Hellers built their home, he felt that the political situation, locally and nationally, demanded his attention. In 1895, reform once again dominated local politics, as did the same cast of citizens, men of "prominence and principle," who had organized the YMDA in the late 1880s and the Anti-Lottery League in 1890. They had now banded together to form the Citizens' League. Hernsheim

9. *Ida and Max Heller's home on Marengo Street, 1895. Courtesy of the American Jewish Archives, Hebrew Union College–Jewish Institute of Religion, Cincinnati.*

10. *Ida Heller and her children, from left to right: Cecile, James, Ruth, and Isaac, circa 1895. Courtesy of Edward M. Heller and Theo M. Heller.*

and Dreyfous played leading roles within the predominantly Protestant elite group, which was anxious to wrest city government from machine domination. According to the *American Israelite*, "Never within recent history has there been such a political uprising to uproot the cancer of corruption from within the confines of our state." Heller termed the reformers' battle one of the "greatest municipal struggles" ever to take place "in an American metropolis" but deplored the fact that the question of city autonomy and self-government "should have been obscured by so many side issues," including "race supremacy." He deemed it a "pity that the battle cannot be drawn clearly between the demagogues and their following . . . and those genuinely interested in the honest and capable administration of the city's trusts." Heller, however, straddled the fence on issues that linked corruption solely to the working class. While acknowledging that "maladministration of public funds . . . is frequently sought in the large number of foreigners which herd together in the principal centers," he believed that the root of the problem ran directly to "the example of the higher classes." He saw "corruption and bribery" emanating from "the capitalist's office" where such schemes are "planned and proposed," thereby creating "an opportunity for rings and their . . . exploitation."[44]

The New Orleans municipal election of April 1896 was the focus of the Citizens' League's campaign to replace John Fitzpatrick, the machine-backed incumbent, with Walter C. Flower, the conservative, well-heeled former president of the Cotton Exchange.[45] Flower's slate included Drey-fous, now president of the prestigious and powerful New Orleans Levee Board, as a candidate for councilman of the Tenth Ward. The city's especially mercurial political environment, with its compromises and ploys, aligned the elite and black voters against the white laboring classes and foreign born who supported the Ring. The *Daily Picayune* canvassed "leading ministers" to address the "Question of Citizenship and the Extent to Which the Pulpit Should Go in Upholding and Fostering Good Government." The clergy—Leucht, Palmer, and Heller among them—agreed on the issue. As Heller put it, politically, the minister needed to "speak for himself as a citizen and as a man, not for his congregation or faith, . . . and must lay no claim to any special respect for his cloth." He fully accepted the Progressive conceit that only the elite could provide disinterested service. Because he felt that city administration needed those from a "cultured leisure-class" to "furnish men willing and capable" of administering "the important trusts of a city corporation," he sang the praises of Dreyfous after his election to the city council. "As long as men of such integrity combined with a high order of executive talent will consent to give of their time to city affairs there is hope of bright things ahead," Heller averred.[46]

Heller's sentiments had little bearing on the steady growth of the Democratic political machine in the city. Immigrants and rising labor unions provided the new manpower. Established Jews expressed their insecurity about recent arrivals in their ranks who did not understand the importance of maintaining a low profile and blending into southern society. This association of the immigrant voters, including Jews, with the machine may have occasioned a letter to the editor of the *Ledger* opposing the organization of a "Hebrew political club," evidently composed of newcomers who were not part of the elite. The writer argued that Jews needed to "mingle with the people" in politics. He feared that such a political club could only create enmity, "deservedly so, against our people." In a separate column, the *Ledger* agreed, calling the method "detrimental and suicidal to our interests." The "Hebrew political club" threatened to pit the support of the new arrivals in the Jewish community against the interests of the established elite. Heller, too, addressed himself to the question of "how far and when it is . . . proper for the Jew to stand apart as a social unit" where religion is not the issue. Denouncing the idea of a "Hebrew vote," he felt that it was a "cause for congratulation (except where corruption and reform are arrayed against each other) to see the Jewish vote divided." Since the vulnerable Jew could easily be "victimized by prejudice," one should frown upon "any budding ward-boss who pretends to carry the Jewish vote in his pocket." The greatest danger lay in the "misapprehension furnished by the Hebrew Political Club which . . . conveys the idea as if the Jews had a distinct nationality to preserve from the encroachments of Americanism." He concluded with the ringing statement, "Let hyphenated nationalisms confine themselves to the emigrant generation . . . , and let them die a natural death with the native, no matter from whom descended."[47]

The intense conflicts between silverites and goldbugs in the 1896 presidential campaign caused Heller to take a stand that he carefully defined. He regretted that the debate, "wrapt up in so many technicalities of finance," had to be decided "on political grounds" and "expounded in the lurid light of the most vehement class oppositions." Calling forth the Darwinian imagery he favored, Heller criticized the "laggers in the race" for accepting the expedient and simplistic explanation of the silverites "which promises a presto change of top to bottom and bottom to top." While he explained that his sympathies tended to "embrace the party of the poor," Heller felt that the Populist solution would not cause a social revolution. The "well-posted broker" would still profit at the expense of the "uninformed workman." He did not deny the injustices inherent in the capitalist system but felt that they were "too deep for financial . . . [or] legislative remedies." Only "slow growth," not a "political cataclysm," could provide a "cure."[48]

As the election drew closer, Heller sadly feared that "liberalism may have seen its best days," because the emotionally and philosophically polarized nation had found its perennial scapegoat in the Jew. He deplored the stereotyping that paradoxically depicted the Jew as capitalist, the "Rothschild-Shylock who does the principal bloodletting," and, as proletarian, the " 'undesirable emigrant' who lowers wages." That he was witnessing the "temporary eclipse" of the liberalism that had fueled his highest dreams for America stung him. He felt an "ever rising" prejudice against the Jew, which he termed a "thermometer of hatreds." Although he still clung to the hope that "a hundred congenial influences under the surface of our century" would ultimately lead to the "gradual solution of the most urgent problems," Heller could no longer regard Americanization as a panacea.[49]

He had embarked upon the decade with great optimism in the ultimate triumph of universal enlightenment through progress and moral suasion, but now he found the vision dimming. In the first decade of his rabbinical career he had found satisfaction and a sense of community among the progressive leaders in his adopted home. Still, the conflicts and compromises inherent in accommodation were slowly becoming manifest to him. Despite the outward appearance of acceptance, America was turning more nativist, more racist, and more threatening. At the same time, rising national interests in Europe were exacerbating anti-Semitism. Heller watched as the light of reason and liberalism receded throughout the world, and he groped for an alternative vision in the gathering dark.

CHAPTER VI

"How Shall We Stand Unswayed in the Storm?"
Confronting the Rising Currents of Racialism

Heller's pessimistic appraisal of Jewish prospects in Eastern Europe and Russia tempered his optimism concerning Jewish life in the American South. The new outlook manifested itself in the New Orleans rabbi's passionate advocacy of the Jewish immigrants' cause and in his increasing concern for the welfare of the Jewish poor. During the late 1890s Heller emerged as a vocal champion of newly arrived Russian Jews. Abandoning his earlier commitment to assimilation, he also began to campaign as a Zionist for world Jewry and to concern himself with African Americans, the Southerners most in need of his energetic defense. That his dissenting positions on race and Zionism emerged at the same critical juncture was no mere coincidence.

The concept of ethnicity was unknown at the turn of the century. While some American Reform Jews argued that they were merely members of a religious group, European anti-Semites certainly regarded Jews as a race. Many non-Jews and Jews in this country accepted this view; the racial designation did not necessarily convey anti-Semitism. Theories regarding race at the time embodied concepts that we today place in separate categories, for example those of nationality, ethnicity, and peoplehood. Like many of his contemporaries, Heller was fascinated by discussions of "race," and he used the term interchangeably with "ethnicity."[1]

Unlike most southern liberals, however, Heller viewed the "Negro Question" as one aspect of an emerging global problem that turned upon the issue of "how the widely divergent races of the world are to cooperate peacefully in mutual and united unfolding."[2] Like his evolution as a Zionist, his growth as a southern racial liberal was gradual. It gained momentum as popular racial tolerance diminished between 1889 and 1915 and reached a low ebb by the time America entered World War I, a slough that continued through the subsequent decade. Southern racial extremism, with its insistence that "the future American society" had no place for the African American, made a belief in white supremacy the litmus test of regional loyalty and extinguished nearly all discussion of liberal or moderate alternatives to militant racialism.[3] Heller's statement linking the Negrophobia of the South with the anti-Semitism of Western Europe was unique. The solutions he proposed—for his European brethren seeking a haven elsewhere and for African Americans seeking justice in Heller's adopted home—illuminate the dimensions of a problem that still confronts the world today. As Heller surveyed the rising tide of racism here and abroad, he moved away from the optimistically assimilationist outlook of conventional Reform Judaism. In its place he substituted the concept of race as a major dynamic in human relationships and therefore in regional and national relationships. Like Theodor Herzl, father of modern political Zionism, on the one hand, and W. E. B. Du Bois, on the other, Heller attempted to invert the negative imperatives of racial thinking to reach a concept of political and cultural peoplehood that could reinvigorate both Jews and blacks.

Heller's sense of mission began to blossom when he championed the rights of poor Russian Jews. The compassion and social justice that he advocated were the silver lining of his darkening vision of the future of American Judaism. Wise, his mentor, still felt that the Russian immigrants were the UAHC's own "white man's burden" and that only the extensive Americanization that they resisted could help them become less obtrusive.[4] By 1897, Heller was embracing a very different strategy, that espoused by Bernhard Felsenthal, another mentor. Felsenthal may have been the first Reform Jew to see Russian Jews as presenting not a threat to the assimilated, but a spark to rekindle much of the religious flame beginning to sputter in an atmosphere choked by an overzealous liberalism that sought to eliminate the particularist thrust of Jewish history and culture. He early broke with colleagues who argued that Judaism in the modern world existed solely as a religious denomination. As Heller recalled, Felsenthal, radical reformer that he was, had always seen Judaism "in constant flux of development." Although Felsenthal had been reared "in the 1848 atmosphere of cosmopolitan humanity," his views continued to evolve as he witnessed the revolutionary changes wrought by the last decades of the nineteenth century. In 1895, he defined Judaism as "the sum of all the national-psychological peculiarities of the Jewish race," insisting that birth, not faith, makes the Jew. As his daughter noted, the phrase " 'the bond of race'—'*national verwandtschaftliche Bande*' " occurred frequently in his writings. This strong sense of Jewish peoplehood propelled him into the cause of Zionism shortly thereafter.[5]

Undoubtedly influenced by Felsenthal's 1895 assertion, Heller attacked an assimilationist rabbi in the North for attempting "to secularize your synagogues into literal temples" by stripping "your religious thoughts into bald philosophies, because your Unitarian colleague loves the dry mountain air of refined religious abstraction." Judaism, Heller claimed, was "a flesh-and-blood religion tied down to a living race, a race the most markedly typical and orientally intense-vivid that exists." American Reform rabbis were starving their congregants, making them "hungry after mystic spiritualism, occultism, Christian Science, anything that has color, body, poetry, character." In "The Future of the Jews in America," which Heller wrote for the *Jewish Gazette* two years later, he predicted an American Jewish "spiritual renaissance." Just as he had despaired of the crass materialism and the lack of religious sensitivity in members of Temple Sinai, Heller now pronounced the Russian Jew the "Hebrew of the Hebrews," for in him, the "radicalism of the race reaches . . . the pinnacle of absolute uncompromisingness." He envisioned a future spiritual renaissance in which the Russian Jew would become the "chief actor," closing "more firmly the bond of Jewish union."[6]

Heller's admiration of Russian Jews and concern for their plight reflected his anxiety about a pending congressional bill that proposed to limit immigration and to introduce literacy tests for immigrants. Heller rightly believed that such measures threatened to curtail the traditional "hospitality" that America had offered "to the oppressed of all races." Even though President Grover Cleveland vetoed the bill, the mere existence of restrictive proposals fueled Heller's growing apprehension and made him skeptical of the Americanization he had long espoused. Compounding that anxiety was a New Orleans lecture on "The Jehovah of the Jews," delivered by the Catholic prelate Cardinal James Gibbons, while the immigration bill was still before Congress. The speech, according to Heller, completely distorted the Jewish concept of God. In his reply to Gibbons, Heller stated, "We do not acknowledge Christianity as the foundation of modern culture, of nineteenth century humanity . . . , nor will we admit that Christianity lies at the basis of our American state policy, for we have studied the nature and the origin of our government." The next week he reiterated that when social reforms like temperance "are labeled 'Christian,' " an "insinuating exclusion" of Jews "is smuggled into the minds and consciences." Whenever such exclusion existed, Jews "should energetically knock for admittance."[7]

Heller's realization of the importance of Russian Jews to American Judaism caused him to lose patience with the methods of Touro Infirmary, and that impatience kindled a bolder activism. His tendency to equivocate when attempting to take a strong position evaporated when the simmering feud with Rabbi Leucht finally erupted. Although the tensions between the two had been mounting for a decade, more than a personal power struggle lay at the heart of the matter. Beyond jockeying with Leucht for personal and professional power, Heller had long resented the control Leucht wielded over charitable funds and his condescension toward itinerant or unemployed Jews. Leucht's and Heller's interpretations of social justice in dealing with the poor differed fundamentally. Leucht blamed the poor for their plight and sought to arrange minimal assistance for those who were willing to work; Heller blamed an unjust social order and tried to preserve the dignity of those who required help from the community. The melee that exploded in the spring of 1898 truly closed one era of Heller's career and opened another.

From the time Leucht began submitting annual reports as first vice president and chairman for the Committee on Charity and Relief in 1889, he had written disparagingly about those being helped. He was quick to condemn the "Jewish itinerant beggar" who was ostensibly drawn to New Orleans by the mild winter climate. Leucht's managerial style emphasized "practical charity" conducted "in a purely business way," with aid dispensed to "bring the best returns" in human improvement. Feeling that many other southern Jewish communities viewed New Orleans as a "general dumping ground" for their "resident poor," he claimed that the poor, in turn, viewed New Orleans as an " 'El Dorado' " for those like themselves, "shiftless, perambulating Hebrew[s]." During one Mardi Gras alone, he refused twenty-nine relief applications, preferring to help only those who appealed to his "sense of justice." Indeed, by "compelling the applicant to eat the bread of his own industry," Leucht believed that he had rescued at least one man "from a life of pauperism and dependence." Where Leucht believed his stringent rules would ultimately benefit the deserving poor who met them, Heller saw Leucht's policies as the tyranny of a "fussy despot" who "poisoned the hearts of the good pitying people towards their unhappy brothers."[8]

In the spring of 1896, the pressure between the two rabbis moved from private complaints to a public forum when the *Mascot* published a series of articles about the rabbis' feud. Charles Rosen, Leucht's future son-in-law, had evidently supplied the scandal sheet with the basic narrative. Airing the controversy outside the Jewish community naturally angered many on both sides of the debate. The *Mascot* stated that the daily papers, afraid of jeopardizing "the advertising given to them by the Hebrews," took "no cognizance of the rabbi's warfare," but the *Mascot*, eager for controversy, concluded that "both Rabbi Heller and Rabbi Leucht have evinced by their childishness that they are only men." Others on Leucht's side of TIHBA, like Sam Blum, secretary of the Committee on Charity and Relief, wrote Heller asking that he "desist in the future of interfering with the duties . . . [under] the province of the committee of charity and relief."[9]

The following year Heller penned an allegorical dialogue in the *Ledger* that mocked the basis of scientific charity that Leucht practiced unflinchingly. The protagonists were the Goddess of Truth and the Goddess of Charity, both spurned by the conceits of the Gilded Age. The Goddess of Charity lamented, "Can I congratulate myself that, through the magic battle-cry of 'organization,' thousands of the tender-hearted have been taught to turn the poor from their door, to deafen their ear to the painful pleading of the hopeless?" The following spring, the plight of Isaac Meyrowitz tipped the precariously balanced scale, and Heller could no longer contain his wrath.[10]

In February 1898, Heller had written to Reverend W. Willner, a colleague in Meridian, Mississippi, to inquire about "Rev." Meyrowitz, who was seeking funds in New Orleans. Willner described Meyrowitz as a displaced *maggid*,[11] a Yiddish term denoting a religious itinerant with a "smattering" of Jewish learning, who wandered from shtetl to shtetl, preaching and living on collections donated by members of the community. A maggid often became a beggar, or *schnorrer,* a role largely accepted in the European Jewish community. But in America, as Willner observed, "he finds this sort of thing won't do." Someone like Meyrowitz, not learned enough to be a rabbi but ill fitted to do anything but roam and preach, was totally out of place. Willner asked Heller, "What will you do with him? Tell him to work? How can he? Get a position? He had three of them, and both he and the congregations were extremely glad to sever connections. You can do nothing for him in your city, so you give him a few dimes, with which he goes to another city." Although Heller's father was no schnorrer, Heller certainly understood the weaknesses in a man of some learning, unfit for any kind of regular work, offering to exchange knowledge and talmudic anecdotes for a bit of money. Leucht, on the other hand, had no patience with Meyrowitz nor any others of his ilk that came begging of the New Orleans almoner.[12]

On a bitterly cold day at the end of February, Meyrowitz called on Leucht at home to ask for a ticket to Galveston. Leucht left him standing outside for over an hour, then rudely refused to give him any assistance. Like many before him, Meyrowitz complained to Heller, who, in turn, sent him to Julius Weis. Weis solicited funds "sufficient to send him on his way" from a few members of Touro Infirmary. Both Weis and Heller wanted the TIHBA office to move downtown, where Weis planned to donate an office in one of his buildings rent free. A more centrally located office would be easier to reach for those seeking help. Weis felt it would also facilitate processing complaints, because when someone objected to harsh treatment at Leucht's hands, "we could then go to that office and investigate as to the worthiness of the applicants, which we cannot do so long as the office is in Mr. Leucht's house."

Before the next TIHBA annual meeting, Weis met with Leucht's friends and associates and urged them to persuade Leucht to step down from his vice presidency in charge of charitable funds. Short of this answer, Weis hoped to offer a resolution establishing an office downtown, "with an advisory committee, which would avoid all friction between the ministers." All acknowledged that rumors about Leucht's ill treatment of the poor were widespread, and the contingency arrangement would protect both Leucht and the reputation of the TIHBA. At the meeting, however, Leucht evidently grew angry. He claimed that there had been a conspiracy against him. As if the Mafia itself were the enemy, he felt that he could plainly see " 'the fine Italian hand.' " After Leucht sat down, Heller arose and charged him with abusing those applying for charity by treating them as if they were criminals or impostors. "Members of the Association became very much excited, and a great deal of confusion ensued." Motions were made but not acted upon, and the meeting was adjourned.[13]

After another raucous meeting, the members agreed that a committee of five congregants of Temple Sinai should investigate Heller's charges, although Heller thought that the committee had too many close friends of Leucht to be disinterested judges. During the following two weeks, Heller and Leucht introduced witnesses and leveled claims and counterclaims. Heller mentioned making eighteen "specific charges"[14] against Leucht's directorship. The rabbi of Congregation Gates of Prayer supported Heller's contentions with witnesses of his own. But the committee ignored resolutions from two organizations of Russian Jews condemning Rabbi Leucht and refused to let Heller invite Russians to be present at the session when he testified on their behalf. Leucht was exonerated.[15]

Articles and letters to the editor peppered several Jewish newspapers both before and after the committee hearings, supporting one rabbi or the other. The *Ledger*, now out of Heller's hands, "regretted that such discord exists where concord should prevail." Although the committee dismissed Heller's charges, insinuating that his complaints were really nothing more than a personal vendetta against Leucht, supporters like Julius Weis remained faithful. The *American Israelite* reported that several prominent Sinai members, Weis among them, visited Heller to present him, "in an appropriate address, with $500. There was no popular collection, otherwise the amount would have been much larger; only a few volunteered to make up this sum," because "Dr. Heller has expended so much of his income for the needy who have been unable to find relief elsewhere." Moreover, the gift was a "demonstration on the part of those who support Max Heller in the position that he has taken in the recent controversy over the administration of the local Jewish charities."[16]

The *Chicago Israelite* carried a sympathetic account of Heller's actions, in which an anonymous writer admitted that "the way the Jewish poor are treated, as a rule, by the relief societies is all wrong." When the applicants were judged "suspicious characters" or "hardened offenders," it was understandable that an "honest man" should question "the right of such a custom." Even though "many look upon what is required to make a good supervisor of charity in a different way from what Rabbi Heller does," and "are as honest as he is in their views . . . , I and many others are of the opinion that Dr. Heller is right." He is not "the first man whose heart has bled at witnessing the treatment to which the Jewish poor are subjected by Hebrew relief authorities. But he is the first man of high standing who has had the courage to lift his voice against what is a widespread abuse," the *Israelite* concluded.[17]

The pitched battle was not a mere tempest in a teapot. Heller spoke out, made enemies, and achieved his ends, even though he lost support of some of the elite members of the Jewish community. When the Touro board met in June, it passed a resolution "by a unanimous vote" to open a relief office downtown, "on or before October 1st, engage a superintendent or clerk, etc." It must have been especially sweet to Heller to read that his allies considered the outcome "quite a victory and every one of us is satisfied, and hope it will meet with your approval also."[18]

Sweetest of all, however, was the increased respect and trust that Heller received from Russian Jews in New Orleans. He had prophesied that the "Hebrew of the Hebrews" would change American Jewry, a position untenable to most in the German Jewish Reform community, who were anxious to protect their own position of strength. Heller's encounter with Jewish peoplehood in many aspects runs parallel to that of Theodor Herzl. When many of the elite Western European Jews that he hoped to win to his idea of a Judenstat, or Jewish state, rejected the concept, he found his audience in the opposite camp of the Eastern European masses.[19] In challenging the established class-based organizational structure of the New Orleans Jewish community, Heller had not only found his own voice but had also gained a new audience beyond the elite and one that would figure significantly in his subsequent transition to Zionism. To this small band of local Russian Jews, Heller added an even less likely audience of African Americans whose plight he sought to address as he explored the way racial identity could reinforce individual self-worth. In the first decades of the twentieth century, Heller emerged as the most passionately outspoken of the American Reform Zionists[20] and one of the lonely white southern voices that remained fighting on behalf of black Americans.

Heller now had the inner strength to sustain inclinations and intentions that he had avoided confronting directly since the middle of the 1890s when he vacillated or temporized on issues involving blacks.[21] When George Washington Cable wrote *The Silent South* in 1888, he had tried to make his argument more palatable by drawing a distinction between civil rights and social equality. He stated that "the law that refuses to protect a civil right, construing it a social privilege, deserves no more regard than if it should declare some social privilege a civil right."[22] Heller may have based his equivocation on a similar premise. In castigating a northern rabbi for making disparaging comments in Atlanta about the treatment of blacks in the South, Heller assumed the typical guise of the southern apologist as he defended his region. "The Negro," he wrote in 1896, "is treated more humanely and considerately in the South than he is in the North," since neither lynchings nor "white-cap outrages" nor "social discrimination in school" are confined to the South. No, the black is no "toy of sentimentalism, but the playmate of childhood and the faithful servant of maturer years."[23] At that point, he sounded more like Gutheim's disciple than Felsenthal's, yet it is difficult to determine whether Heller's words were sincerely expressed or merely calculated to please. That same spring when he spoke as a civic reformer allied with the New Orleans Citizens' League, Heller deplored the fact that "so many side issues," including "race supremacy" obscured the serious questions in "municipal struggles." Heller's viewpoint on reform probably differed from that of many of the elite businessmen in the Citizens' League. In the same article, he noted that "corruption and bribery" emanated from "the capitalist's office" where such schemes were "planned and proposed."[24] As a man determined to be respected by his audience and to survive in a southern pulpit, he chose the rhetorical tools that a given situation demanded without making consistency of response a priority.

At the end of the decade, however, Heller began to take more controversial stands as he tried to reconcile his external roles and his private moral sensibilities. If Americanization characterized his first decade in this country and "southernization" characterized the next, "Zionization" was the process that marked his emergence as a mature leader. When Heller became a Zionist, he became a passionate spokesman for the rights of other groups as well. One event that may have initiated the shift toward Zionism—a form of separatist cultural and political national-ism—was the Dreyfus Affair. In December 1894, when Captain Alfred Dreyfus, a Jewish officer in the French army, was accused of espionage, anti-Semitism raged, and the case exploded into a cause célèbre. Heller felt certain that Dreyfus's innocence would be recognized, but he re-garded the experience of the nineteenth century as having taught a lesson that "national and racial prejudice undermines not only a nation's moral health, but endangers its very political existence."[25] The Dreyfus Affair had triggered Theodor Herzl's espousal of Jewish nationalism. The in-tensity of French anti-Semitism had shocked Herzl, at the time a sophis-ticated Viennese journalist in Paris. Although a thoroughly assimilated Jew, he now questioned the cultural and political foundations of Euro-pean liberalism. As he confronted his own assimilationist aspirations, he decided that the Jewish Question must be not just a "symptom of Euro-pean social malaise" but the raison d'être behind the creation of a Jewish state.[26]

On the other hand, Heller was not yet ready to accept Herzl's philoso-phy—or to speak out more forthrightly on southern racial issues. Ameri-can Reform Judaism espoused a universalistic position compatible with the rights and freedom of this country. Patriotic American Jews did not want to be accused of dual loyalties as American Catholics often were. The quest for a Jewish homeland, they felt, could only provoke such a reaction.[27] Still loyal to Isaac Mayer Wise, Heller was not immediately persuaded to dissent from the dominant American Reform anti-Zionist position. Yet his sympathies lay with the Zionists even before he was will-ing to speak as a Zionist himself. In 1897, four years before Heller de-clared himself a Jewish nationalist, he discussed the proposed Zionist Convention in Europe. He concurred with the *Jewish Messenger*'s compari-son of Zionist "agitation" and "our own Populism." Heller noted that the two movements shared "the credulity of the visionary" and that both were products of "gloomy times and of consequent restlessness." The two movements perhaps also shared a "vague consciousness of deep-seated wrong to which the wealthier classes are selfishly indifferent." He con-cluded that even though "Dr. Herzl's remedy is certainly at least as fan-tastic and impossible of execution as were the Populists' subtreasury schemes," a "more practicable plan" to solve the Jewish problem might possibly emerge from the Zionist Convention, just as one to remedy the small farmers' plight might result from the Populist crusade.[28]

Paradoxically, the repressive atmosphere in post-Populist Louisiana was as instrumental as his identification with the sufferings of European Jews in pushing Heller toward Zionism. After defrauding Louisiana

Populists in the elections of 1892 and 1896, the state's dominant Bourbon faction set about to change the voting rules to forestall future challenges to the Democratic establishment.[29] In 1898, as Heller was in the midst of his fight against Leucht and the TIHBA, a constitutional convention met in New Orleans determined to see that no class-based coalition of voters would ever overcome racial antipathies and threaten to overthrow the traditional state power structure. The Disfranchisement Convention was marked by irony. Ernest B. Kruttschnitt, a nephew of Louisiana's most illustrious Jewish politician, the former U.S. senator and Confederate cabinet official Judah P. Benjamin, had been elected to preside over the proceedings. Chairman of Louisiana's Democratic Party, Kruttschnitt, was unanimously elected president of the convention. Kruttschnitt's mother was Jewish, but he was not reared in the Jewish faith. A large man and a powerful attorney, Kruttschnitt also served as president of the local school board. In his acceptance speech, Kruttschnitt noted that "we have here none of the clash of faction . . . , no political antagonism." He was presiding over what he called "little more than a family meeting of the Democratic party of Louisiana." After being interrupted by much applause as he established the convention agenda, he concluded that in the very hall "where, thirty-two years ago, the negro first entered upon the unequal contest for supremacy," the convention, "through the evolution of our organic law," would reestablish "the relations between the races upon an everlasting foundation of right and justice." In other words, blacks would be stripped of the ballot, and many impoverished small farmers in areas of former Populist strength would be discouraged from voting. Kruttschnitt sent two invitations to Heller to appear at the convention in order to "open the proceedings with prayer." After the second invitation, Heller, like other prominent local ministers, complied.[30]

Heller's reaction to the wave of segregationist and disfranchisement activity that swept across Louisiana and other southern states after 1896 may be inferred from the content of sermons he delivered immediately prior to the 1898 Constitutional Convention. He was aware of the irony of the convention's timing: the proceedings coincided with Emile Zola's famous trial in Paris in connection with his support of Dreyfus. The *Times-Democrat* penned the headline: "The Dreyfus Case, Which Zola Is Mixed Up In, Treated by the Rabbi—Narrow Racial Prejudice Deprecated" for one of Heller's February 1898 sermons that was entitled "Modern Intolerance." In this sermon text he linked the Dreyfus Affair to the local constitutional deliberations and expressed his bitter disappointment with the failure of "the brazen machinery of our finely contrived social organizations" meant "to redeem mankind." He chided himself for his initial naive faith in the process of assimilation. In a century that had witnessed much "emancipating thought," including universal suffrage, freedom of the press, and the "deliverance of serfs and slaves," he had hoped that "the night-owl's shriek of intolerance would be heard no more." He asked his congregants, "Shall not . . . equality breed justice? Shall not republics be free from the taint of race hatred?" Sadly, Heller concluded, "widening opportunities have only embittered the clash. . . . even political enfranchisement . . . constitute[s] no safeguard whatever against those volcanic outbursts of blind injustice which vent the stored-up poison of decades." However veiled and hesitant, Heller's comments represented at least a preliminary probing of the hegemonic white supremacist position.[31] Along with the Dreyfus trial, events during that February in New Orleans allowed Heller to link Eastern European attacks on Jewish rights with the contemporary southern assault on African American liberties. Slowly and tentatively, he began to ponder some of the larger lessons suggested by the political demise of European Jews and southern blacks.

One of the lessons concerned the centrality of racial theorizing at the turn of the century. Contemporary European anti-Semitism seemed to grow in tandem with American Negrophobia, since both drew upon the same European racial theories. The noxious doctrines attracted supporters on either side of the Atlantic who were threatened by the changes posed by inclusion of those recently granted citizenship. Unhappily, Heller had come to recognize that, in spite of emancipation, European Jews were still considered "a plague-spot on the body politic," much as Cable had earlier argued against the accepted southern perception that "the man of color must always remain an alien."[32] In the United States academic sociologists like University of Chicago professor William I. Thomas affirmed a "scientific" basis of segregationist thought, viewing "race-prejudice" as too comprehensive and pervasive to disappear completely. It was, he explained, part of a more comprehensive "instinct of hate" originating in the "tribal stage of society, when solidarity in feeling and action were essential to the preservation of the group." Given its ancient history in human relations, race prejudice seemed unlikely ever to disappear completely. As a psychological phenomenon, prejudice could "neither be reasoned with nor legislated about very effectively, because it is connected with the affective, rather than the cognitive, process."[33]

Such voices intensified as segregationist legislation proliferated in the 1890s. They were echoed in the rise of racial anti-Semitism in Germany. Leaders like Felsenthal, Du Bois, and Heller had to leap the philosophical and psychological hurdle of squaring their universalistic humanism with the ever more scientifically respectable racialism that the era's great minds viewed, invoking Social Darwinism, as accounting for the successes and failures of the world's national and racial groups. Like his African American contemporary W. E. B. Du Bois, Heller was unwilling to abandon the concept of race. He turned to Zionism partly as a result of his quest for an intellectual and political alternative to the reactionary impulses of a race-conscious world.

At the same time, Heller championed a policy of self-help much like that of Booker T. Washington, who admired Jews for their hard work and willingness to help their coreligionists. He had argued in 1894 that African Americans should follow the example of a Jewish peddler (with all he owned "in a cheap and much-worn satchel") who had stopped overnight in a hamlet near Tuskegee, Alabama, and had then decided to stay. Four years later, after much hard work, he was making $50,000 annually. Washington felt that "the colored man's present great opportunity in the South is in the matter of business." Once he succeeded there he could then find "relief along other lines."[34] His reasoning can best be appreciated as a desperate strategy for securing at least an economic stake in a society that seemed bent upon excluding blacks from social and political recognition. In effect, Heller applied the Tuskegeean's philosophy to Russian Jewish transplants in America. Heller's embrace of Zionism initially arose from the same desperate attempt to deal with the inevitability of racial prejudice. Since Europeans would never accept Jews as equals, Jews who remained on the continent had to help themselves by working to build a state of their own in Palestine.

But Heller's initial proto-Zionist outlook also closely paralleled Du Bois's increasingly self-conscious emphasis upon the distinct cultural heritage of African Americans. Heller may have read Du Bois's 1897 *Atlantic Monthly* article, "Strivings of the Negro People," in which the black scholar described the African American as one "born with a veil," with a gift of "second-sight" or "double consciousness, this sense of always looking at one's self through the eyes of others." As a black American, he had the uncomfortable awareness of possessing "two unreconciled strivings" warring "in one dark body." Several years later, in "The Curse of Consciousness," Heller chose similar terms to describe Western Jewish alienation. "We are children that have been observed too much and made awkwardly conscious," he lamented, "conscious . . . in ways unknown to our fathers." As "strangers and sojourners," he looked at his fellow Jews "floundering about in the loose new clothes of modern culture . . . while the wounds of intolerance have as yet formed only a thin, new, sensitive skin." For southern blacks and for Russian Jews in America, however,

Heller embraced Washington's self-help philosophy as a means of building the social and economic power of each group.[35]

Like Felsenthal, Heller constantly sought to refine and clarify his
philosophical and religious ideas in the face of changing contemporary
realities. Like Felsenthal and Du Bois, Heller saw himself as both the intellectual heir of the Enlightenment and the witness of his people's recent
emancipation. These leaders painfully perceived the widening discrepancy between the powerful legacy of liberal thought and the increasingly
persistent grip of racism.[36] As European nationalism moved away from
its more inclusive liberal origins and focused increasingly on exclusive
*volk*ish concepts, it further marginalized Jews. European ideological anti-
Semitism grew apace. Fueled by "scientific" findings on race, it paralleled the growing anti-Negro sentiment in America that drew upon the
same European racial theories.[37]

Only a few white Southerners had dissented from the mounting racial
hostility in the region that resulted in the onslaught of legal segregation.
During the 1880s, dissenters like Atticus Haygood and Lewis Harvie
Blair promoted more equitable treatment for the region's African American citizens without challenging racial separation. These men were all
native-born, socially secure Southerners. Among them, George Washington Cable, from New Orleans, was by far the most outspoken and best-
known advocate for racial justice in the South. But in 1885, after receiving
a barrage of negative criticism in response to views expressed in *The
Freedman's Case in Equity* and *The Silent South,* the Crescent City's famous
author moved to the Northeast, abandoning both his home and the lonely
fight for civic equality for southern blacks.[38]

Heller arrived in New Orleans about the time that Cable departed, but
as a Jew, he viewed the South through different eyes. Unlike liberal gentiles, he perceived that the narrowing of civil liberties in Eastern Europe
and the growing outbreaks of violence there against the Jews had an ana-
log in the racial caste system of the American South. Although the parallels must have been evident from the beginning, he did not choose to explore them until the first years of the twentieth century.[39] In 1900, Heller
turned forty. Now a mature rabbi, well respected, if not loved by his congregants, he was ready to become his own person. After nearly two decades as an American citizen and a decade and a half as a Southerner, he
very likely felt secure enough to speak from his heart. He had earned the
trust of his congregation by responding to their emotional and intellectual needs and, in 1899, to their economic needs as well. Because Temple
Sinai was experiencing a fiscal crisis, Heller proposed a reduction in his
salary to eliminate his last $600 raise until "the finances of the congre-

gation will not require this sacrifice on my part."[40] Such unselfishness further bound him to the community. Then, too, changes in the larger political arena of racial politics obliged him, reluctantly, to take a more forceful stand on issues that concerned him deeply and challenged his sense of manhood. Having integrated these diverse impulses, Heller stood poised for the battles that awaited him. Goaded by the materialistic complacency of his congregants, the insensitivity of more established American Jews toward newly arriving Russian immigrants, intensifying anti-Semitism in Europe, and the disfranchisement of Louisiana's black citizens, he needed to take a stand.

Although Heller left no record of his reaction to the terrible New Orleans race riot in 1900,[41] the next year he became a passionate and outspoken Zionist and began increasingly to voice oblique criticism of the South's racial caste system.[42] For example, in his sermon on the eve of Yom Kippur, the solemn Jewish Day of Atonement, Heller began by telling his congregants that they had "not done their duty towards our brothers in Russia." In the middle of his speech he switched back to "our own Southland where we are so fond of declaiming about the white man's burden, of priding ourselves upon the condescending friendliness with which we treat the negro." He then asked, in words that echoed Georgia Methodist Bishop Atticus Haygood's *Our Brother in Black*, "If the negro is our weaker brother, where, indeed is our active sympathy, our energetic aid that shall lift him and with him the entire South, to higher levels of efficiency?" Haygood's views appealed to Heller as early as 1889, when his restless spiritual and intellectual quest for social justice had prompted him to correspond with George Washington Cable's Open Letter Club—a forum for discussing the "great moral, political and industrial revolution" then raging in the South. Heller's brief note commented favorably on Haygood's essay on southern race relations, which Cable had reprinted and distributed to the Club members.[43]

Heller had employed the "weaker brother" imagery earlier in 1901, when the *Jewish Daily News*, a New York periodical, asked "some of the leading thinkers in Jewry" to respond to the question "What should be done to bring about a greater community of interest between the Russian (Orthodox) and German (Reform) elements in American Jewry?" Describing the German Jew as "the elder brother so far as entrance upon modern civilization is concerned," Heller characterized the Reform Jew as feeling "bound by the closest ties with his Russian brother." He perceived that the German Jew's treatment of the Russian mirrored the way "he himself is treated by the Gentile" except that the German outlook involved "more liberality of pocket and less appreciation of intellect" than was true of gentiles. Heller reserved special contempt for the Reform Jewish "alms beadle," a quintessential hypocrite (like his nemesis, Leucht) who exuded "kindly sentiments" in public while privately scorning the "unfortunate *Shlemihls*" seeking aid. The prototypical almoner, Heller complained, reveals his duplicity when he metes out "starvation-doles" and then "prides himself in the annual report on his economy." Heller had even less patience with those German Jews who visited a Russian synagogue on Yom Kippur just as they might go to a "negro baptizing," in both cases "only mocking blindly at their own shameful ignorance." To Russian Jews here, and later to southern blacks, he delivered the same message, that each must learn to set aside the opinions of those hostile to them. Each Russian Jew or African American needed to redeem his "manliness of self-respect" by "standing by his colors as a man," by "know[ing] his own history," and by "uphold[ing] his own conventions, religious or otherwise."[44]

In the early spring of 1900, Edgar Gardner Murphy of Montgomery, Alabama, an Episcopalian minister, reformer, and racial moderate, organized a conference to be held that May in Montgomery, under the auspices of the Southern Society for the Promotion of the Study of Race Conditions and Problems in the South. Heller received an invitation to the meeting, although there is no record of his attendance.[45] It is possible that he even became a member of the society. Murphy and Heller may have had no direct contact, but the two held many views in common, especially their advocacy, as southern Progressives, of education as a key solution to solving social problems. They differed slightly, however, in their attitude toward white supremacy as an underlying tenet of racial separatism.[46]

Murphy had opposed disenfranchisement but accepted white supremacy "in the present stage of the development of the South" as affording the conditions "upon which the progress of the Negro is itself dependent." In a modification of Murphy's racial paternalism, Heller stressed his hope that "the benevolence of separation will appear in our efforts to lift the younger brother as speedily as possible to our own level."[47] He emphasized that "to recognize the backwardness of races must be also to acknowledge that they [eventually] may rise and become our equals." While Murphy felt that white supremacy must be maintained "until the Negro had acquired sufficient education and property to vote constructively," in 1904, Heller avoided open criticism of both disenfranchisement and segregation but warned that "much rankling bitterness and sad confusion" would occur before the reconciliation of "humanity with discrimination." He called upon the leaders of both races to exhibit "the utmost forbearance and mutual good will" to stem "the tide over the dangers of the transition."[48]

In *The Present South,* which appeared that year, Murphy devoted a chapter to "The South and the Negro" in which he classified the Negro Question as a regional problem that grew more complex when "this group is brought into contact with another." Heller, on the other hand, realized that the "Negro Question" had larger implications for an international situation in which increasing racism led directly to imperialism. As the U.S. crusade to aid beleaguered Cubans evolved into the Spanish-American War, Heller observed that the "white man's burden" had recently translated itself into the domestic use and export of Anglo-Saxon supremacy, which threatened any progress nonwhites could hope to make. Although he accepted many of the prevailing ideas of his time that all races were not inherently equal, Heller looked forward to a distant future when "all [racial] barriers may be safely superseded."[49]

But did he accept the "Southern solution" as a necessary evil for the present? A letter from Louis Marshall, a national secular Jewish leader, revealed the closest evidence of Heller's problematic attitude toward segregation. In evident response to a letter from Heller, Marshall wrote that he did not take "so hopeless a view of the future" as Heller, that he regarded "the idea of segregation and autonomy" as both "impracticable and contrary to the logic of historical development." After the convention of 1898, Heller's pessimism reflected his disappointment at finding that rational solutions to racial justice and civil rights could be nullified by a hostile white majority.[50]

Like Murphy and other southern moderates and liberals, Heller deplored lynching. In a memorial sermon delivered after the assassination of President McKinley in 1901, Heller decried many of the ills he had witnessed during the last decade, including "the drunken mob that kindles a pyre around a chained negro." He listed an incident of southern religious intolerance, "the night-gathering which tars and feathers a Mormon missionary," and referred to the "white-capping" vigilantes of the early 1890s in mentioning "the skull-and-bones notice to quit the town." Such "open anarchy" was not only "the despair of legal process" but also "an avowal of political incapacity which shames a whole people."[51] The argument struck a responsive chord in a fellow New Orleanian, who wrote praising the sermon's "inspiring tone of respect for and obedience to law and condemnation of lawlessness" and identified himself as "a member of the Negro race—a race persecuted and oppressed by lawlessness and *anarchy.*"[52] This letter was the first of several that Heller received in which the writer chose to disclose his racial identity as a person of color. It seems evident that southern blacks were actively reaching out to sympathetic allies in the white community, even as the walls between the two groups rose.

Although the white supremacist onslaught had effectively stifled racial dissent within the region, southern apologists continued to worry about national opinion. Theodore Roosevelt's reelection in 1904 generated fears that the president might dismantle the newly erected system of segregation. The New Orleans *Times-Democrat* called Roosevelt's dinner with Booker T. Washington at the White House three years earlier a "deliberate insult to every white man in the South." When a second editorial snorted at the idea of a "negro scholar" and "a negro gentleman," Heller found himself unable to sit by silently.[53] He penned a response to the *Times-Democrat,* reminding the paper of its larger public obligations. Since its editorial opinion was "very apt to be accepted universally as a good criterion of prevailing Southern thought," the rabbi pointed out, the paper should not "confuse the matter of social equality with the question of social mingling." He saw no reason why "esteem" must be withheld from the Negro scholar nor "respect" from the Negro gentleman. "The difference in color between races can not obliterate the intellectual and moral differences that may obtain between two individuals, irrespective of race," Heller added. "Why we should regard scholarship or gentlemanliness in the negro as something that does not or can not make him the superior of any white man altogether passes my poor understanding." He admonished the *Times-Democrat* editorial writers, "Let us not shut the door of advancement in the face of any backward race." When challenged on two separate occasions to defend his statement, Heller refused to back down. He even let the editors know that he agreed with literary critics who felt that Washington's autobiography makes "a very valuable contribution."[54]

Rabbi Heller's admiration of Washington was undoubtedly strengthened by the knowledge that Washington was a great admirer of Jews, among whom he numbered Tuskegee's major white supporters in Alabama. Not surprisingly, Washington felt that Jews were a people to be emulated. "The Jew," he wrote, once "in about the same position that the Negro is to-day," had achieved "complete recognition . . . because he has entwined himself about America in a business or industrial sense." He also saw Jews as people who had known suffering and had confronted it by clinging together, with "a certain amount of unity, pride, and love of race; and, as the years go on, they will be more and more influential in this country—a country where they were once despised. . . . It is largely because the Jewish race has had faith in itself."[55]

Manual training, a goal of Washington's Tuskegee plan, had its advocates among American Jews, including Heller and Leucht. Both of Heller's younger sisters had been educated by the Chicago Girls' Training School, a center for industrial education for Jewish immigrants, where they later taught. Both New Orleans rabbis had been in close contact with Gabriel Bamberger, the school's director, during the 1890s when the New Orleans Jewish community was exploring methods for training the orphans and wards of the Jewish Orphans' Home. Finally on 8 January 1905, through the generosity of local philanthropist Isidore Newman, the community proudly dedicated the Isidore Newman Manual Training School, "the first school of this character ever designed in this section of the country." As master of ceremonies at the dedication, Leucht recalled that fifteen years earlier he had proposed that something had to be done to enable our children to enter a useful career as mechanics . . . , reached by a thorough manual training, where the dormant faculties of our children may be developed, and a love of trade may be instilled." He deemed it "one of the most sacred aims" of the Home, not simply to care for its wards physically, "but to fit them for life and its struggles."[56] For once Heller and Leucht were in full agreement.

Respect for Washington also led Heller to challenge the conservative views of the New Orleans Jewish community. Assimilationist logic probably helped sweeten the bitter racism prevalent in the general community, making it palatable to some of the city's German Jews, as indicated in an unsigned editorial, "An Impudent Nigger," in the *Jewish Ledger*. Less than a year after the *Times-Democrat* had scorned the idea of a "negro gentleman," the *Ledger* berated the Tuskegee educator for comparing contemporary black tribulations to the erstwhile persecutions of the Jews, whose social solidarity and success in business, Washington believed, were worthy of black emulation. In its unsigned editorial, the *Ledger* blasted the black leader for suggesting the comparison and then quoted the racist novelist Thomas Dixon. "To compare the Jew, who occupies the highest pinnacle of human superiority and intellectual attainment," wrote Dixon, "with the Negro who forms the mud at its base, is something which only a Negro with more than the usual vanity and impudence of his race, could attempt."[57]

A year and a half later, Heller delivered a sermon that scolded those who forsook Judaism's best ethical traditions. In "How to Meet Prejudice," delivered in February 1907, Heller challenged his congregants to "pluck out from our own hearts whatever racial, national or religious prejudice may dwell there." He urged them to go further, "to champion . . . the cause of the oppressed and downtrodden of all races and climes," as he reminded them that "unreasoning racial antipathies" were particularly "ridiculous and absurd in the Jew, who must believe that all men are equally fashioned in God's own image . . . The Jew," he concluded, "ought, of all men, to have the widest horizon." The next year, on Yom Kippur Eve, Heller graphically argued that Judaism stressed equality before God, that since all mankind had been created in His image, all "the whites [sic] and the colored races descended from one pair of parents." Frances Joseph-Gaudet, founder and president of the Colored Industrial Home and School in New Orleans, wrote Heller that the sermon "was like a drink from the water of life refreshing and encouraging . . . to the Soul who hungers for righteousness." Although he identified himself as a "colored Methodist," Gaudet averred that "none of your hearers could have enjoyed the sermon more."[58]

Heller took comfort philosophically where he could find it, because even those at the pinnacle of the city's social and intellectual circles, which he frequented, did not support his racial liberalism. While spending the summer of 1905 in Colorado, for example, Heller wrote Stolz that he was reviewing *The Color Line,* a work by Tulane philosophy professor Benjamin Smith. Heller considered Smith one of the "broadest and deepest" scholars he had met, yet he never again mentioned the work, a sustained polemic for white supremacy. In his foreword, Smith stated clearly that he intended to prove the "assumed inferiority of both the Negro and Negroid" and to refute the notion that this inferiority was "merely cultural and removable by Education or other extra-organic means." Allegiances in New Orleans were complicated, and philosophical discrepancies did not displace friendships. Just as Heller and Fortier never let their different assumptions on race issues block their camaraderie, differences on the racial question did not prevent Heller from enjoying Smith's friendship. Heller taught Hebrew at Tulane, and the two were colleagues and corresponded on various academic topics over the years. When Smith retired in 1915, Heller chaired the resolution committee that paid tribute to his career.[59]

Although Heller often seemed to be a man completely dominated by the social and political currents that swirled around him, he sometimes adopted a surprisingly detached and prophetic perspective. For the centenary of Abraham Lincoln's birth, Heller devoted a column to reconsidering the former president's reputation while acknowledging that the first decade of the twentieth century was still too close to permit a "thorough and unbiased review of that controversial period." Not only were many Civil War veterans still alive, but the Reconstruction era in the South had not "quite reached its end." Especially during the past few years, Heller wrote, "the question of the negro's place and rights" had "become more acute than ever." Although Americans everywhere allegedly realized that the wartime president, by virtue of his "giant size," "towers above the quarrel of the sections," Heller predicted that it might not be until the centenary of Lincoln's death that "he will be canonized" and will be given "his abiding niche in the hall of American heroism and sainthood."[60]

The following Eve of Atonement, the religious service that traditionally draws the largest Jewish attendance, Heller again addressed the question of "the equality of all souls before God." He claimed even more forthrightly than before that equality was axiomatic for both "rich and the poor, the learned and the ignorant . . . , white and black," and, as such, lay "at the foundation of all our duties to our fellow men," a religious conviction that he believed the Jews were first to teach. "Why," he exclaimed, "today there are people, right around us, who are too stupid or too inhuman to understand that the negro has a soul, with the same rights as our own, to all of God's truth and beauty." He believed that the Jew functioned as "God's appointed preacher of spiritual democracy." Because the Jew was "the oldest and most unflinching victim of persecution," it was his obligation to "frown down every inhuman barrier that separates races, ranks, and creeds."[61]

In December 1909, just three months later, Heller's outspokenness drew bitter criticism from both Jews and non-Jews in the community. As the lead editorial writer for the *American Israelite,* he had chosen a mid-December issue to discuss the Christmas "confusions" that the holiday season delivers to American Jews. He enjoyed the "prevailing atmosphere of geniality" offered by the festivities but felt torn as a Jew. He noted wryly that the "most enthusiastic patrons" and generous contributors to the *Times-Democrat* Christmas Doll and Toy Fund were Jews "for whom the whole combination of childhood made happy . . . , of generosity from rich child to ragamuffin, has an irresistible fascination." If it were not travesty enough to question or poke fun at Jewish participation, he went on to impugn the fund itself for donating the gifts to white children only, making its success "a great fuss . . . over very little real substance." "The really nasty and revolting part," he continued, "is the drawing of the color line; either the colored child is not poor enough, the colored parent not mean enough, or the Christmas spirit not broad enough to obliterate that line; social distinctions," he mused, "must be upheld against the poor pickaninny; else white civilization would totter upon its throne."[62]

Obviously, the article was not written for a local New Orleans audience. But the *American Israelite* had subscribers in New Orleans, and

Heller certainly had enemies. One of them must have clipped the article and sent it to the *Times-Democrat,* which not only published it in its entirety but reprimanded Heller editorially. The editorialist argued that the existence of "race bitterness," even among tots, had precipitated drawing the color line. "Forced to choose, so to speak, between the elimination of the white children or the elimination of the black," "naturally" preference had been given to the former. "Dr. Heller is, we believe, the first white Orleanian to raise his voice in protest." The editors suggested that if Heller felt so strongly that the "children of the negro race should be provided for," he should organize a fund and conduct "an annual distribution for their benefit."[63]

Heller tried to explain away his criticism of Jewish confusion as "good-natured raillery." But on the deeper question of Negro racial discrimination, he minced no words in denouncing the "disdain and derision [with which] your paper has . . . both editorially and in other columns, treated the colored race." Often tempted "to come forward in defense of a broader social toleration," he realized that his criticism would lead only to "much futile spilling of ink." After pointing out that it was absurd to propose that a rabbi should "supervise a consistent carrying out of the Christmas teaching," he concluded that "each religion [should] attend to its lessons, always under the guidance of a humanity which beats responsive to human hearts, be the color of the skin whatever it may."[64]

Charles Rosen may have sent the "Christmas Confusions" clipping to the paper in the first place. Now he jumped into the fray, assuring the *Times-Democrat* that Heller's attitude "in no degree represents the attitude of the Jewish people of our community." As a consummate assimilationist, Rosen returned to earlier grievances and blasted Heller for his "protests against the occidentalization of our religion" and his desire for a "return of the Oriental spirit" and the ultimate "renationalization of his people," all of which stances, Rosen felt, denied a "liberal American spirit."[65] An editorial the same day encapsulated the paper's southern philosophy: "The *Times-Democrat* believes in white civilization and white supremacy, in the preservation of the integrity of the white race, in government by the white people, in the separation and the segregation of the races. . . . What has this paper done to the negroes," the editorialist wondered, "to cause Dr. Heller so much sorrow that he has with difficulty been unable to curb his desire to interfere?" A few days later, the *Times-Democrat* charged that "the rabbi's attack" was a strike against "the entire South." Functioning as "the mouthpiece of public opinion," the daily had advocated only southern racial policy, "so declared again and again." Unfortunately, "the learned rabbi had been most successful in stirring up religious and racial bitterness" without winning the sympathy or support "of the community, of his coreligionists, nor, we believe, of his congregation." The *Times-Democrat* was correct in its estimation of prevailing Jewish opinion; the *Jewish Ledger* roundly criticized Heller as well.[66]

Although Heller did not speak for most Jews or most southern whites, he was not alone. Others broke the South's silence by communicating with him. From Chicago, A. R. Perkins, an "old citizen of New Orleans," wrote on three separate occasions, claiming, among other things, that the "T D's explanation is lame & impotent,—there never was any distribution of toys to the colored children, and the colored line was always drawn." He mentioned that "the Jews of all people know what persecution means and I am glad that you have taken up the 'Lance' for the helpless & oppressed." J. W. Hawthorn, an attorney from Alexandria, Louisiana, had also followed the controversy in the newspaper. Although he was not a Jew, as he explained, he nevertheless approved of Heller's attitude. Hawthorn concurred: "Whatever may be the opinion of the South with reference to the race question, the cold fact remains that no one can be unjust without suffering the penalty." He concluded that since "We have not been just to the negro . . . , so long as that attitude remains, we will continue to suffer the penalty." Valcour [?] Chapman, a black Methodist Episcopal pastor in New Orleans, sent his appreciation to Heller for his "conviction" in showing "sympathy with the unfortunate, even a race which was the slave of an other race." Chapman vented his anger toward the *Times-Democrat*, averring that "it is the press which forms public sentiment and not public sentiments which form the press." He thought that the "T. D. is the 'Bible' of many of the Southern people. They think as it thinks and act as it directs." Movingly, he thanked Heller for his "manly stand" and hastened to mention that "no Negroes' letters would have been published as yours—and if they were, he would run the risk of being lynched."[67]

Still other brave souls wrote to the *Times-Democrat*. Dr. G. C. Boudousquie agreed that the headlines of the paper "have exhibited the negro man with contempt and derision." He posited a far distant future, "fifty years from now, when in all probability the negro man will advance to a higher plane and when the light of genius shall begin to burn for the negro, a copy of the *Times-Democrat* of the present time, will cause the exclamation 'could this have been possible?' " Another criticized the *Times-Democrat* for publishing its "double-column headlines for the criminal and his ways" instead of featuring "pictures of school children, church workers, etc." While the paper devoted space to "riots" and "mobs," it could focus attention on "accounts of kind treatment accorded the race by whites." Finally, the writer mentioned that "there is no danger of black supremacy," since "the line that separates the races is tightly drawn, so there needs be no fear in giving justice to all men."[68] That as relatively minor an event as Heller's criticism of the Doll and Toy Fund could have generated so much correspondence shows how heated the contest was over the limits of acceptable southern opinion.

When Julius Rosenwald, the philanthropist and president of Sears Roebuck, offered to donate $25,000 to any city in the United States that raised $75,000 to build a YMCA for African Americans, Heller praised his actions, although he recognized that such a "departure in Jewish philanthropy" would draw criticism from those who believed that Jews should give largely to their own people. In congratulating Rosenwald, he criticized his fellow Jews for avoiding "philanthropic work for the colored race," for neglecting their "elder-brother duty." He realized that although "the Jew does not like to hear himself compared with the negro," that "Jew, like negro, is slandered and abused as a 'race,' " that "Jew, like [the] negro, is made to suffer, the mass, for the sins of the individual" and that "race-prejudice" handicaps the individual in either group in "his ambition to advance." He reasoned that having been "steeled in the furnace of persecution," Jews should reach out to the black man, "be he ever so remote from us racially," since their sufferings united the two. In fact, he perceived this opportunity for uplift as a duty, one that he could appreciate more deeply as a "Southern rabbi . . . closer to the great negro problem, to its perplexities and heartaches" than were his northern colleagues. He concluded that southern Jews, "beyond others, are under indebtedness to the . . . humane foresight" that had "prompted" Rosenwald's "wise and timely charity."[69]

The following month, Heller's actions reinforced his words as he faced an African American audience for the first time at the Central Congregational Church, where Du Bois also spoke that year. Because of Heller's outspokenness, he was probably already a fairly familiar figure. His talk, "Manliness versus Prejudice," concerned breaking the "habit of indiscriminate prejudgment," which he found "everywhere to be on the increase." While he continued to believe, he said, in the ultimate goal of brotherhood, he felt it necessary to recognize "the direction of a current" that was indeed "changing the climate for us." The central question to confront was, he argued, "How shall we stand unswayed in the storm; how shall we hold our ground like men against whatever threatens to unsettle our self-respect and drag us down altogether?"[70]

Warming to the subject, Heller told the large audience that the problems of race conflict had "become active" only during the last few decades. The kind of prejudice that concerned him was that of the "civilized man who aspires to fair dealing," while indulging the "immoral habit of judging the individual by the mass." Speaking several years after the notorious Kishinev pogrom in Russia, Heller argued that injustice must be countered by arousing "a sense of solidarity by which each individual accepts responsibility for all the others." In line with his cultural Zionism, he also emphasized that "in the education of every race room must be made for teaching its noble traditions, for fostering its historic pride." The Negro child therefore should be taught "all the negro has done for this country," from the role played by Crispus Attucks as a leader in the Boston Massacre to "how invaluable negro labor has been to the development of the South," especially since Emancipation. "Instead of being crushed under injuries," he added, "manhood learns its loftiest lessons under the burdens of experience." Heller therefore urged blacks to work "against every misrepresentation of caricature and gossip." Still affirming the eventual triumph of righteousness, he concluded, "you have a right, and a duty, to confront the injustice of prejudice with the legitimate prepossessions of a strengthened loyalty."[71]

Two local newspapers covered the event. The *Daily Picayune*'s caption ran, "Rabbi Heller Analyzes Race Prejudice in a Special Sermon to Negroes," while the *Times-Democrat* piqued the interest of readers with the more sensational "Rabbi Would Stir Ambition in Negro."[72] "The church was packed with negroes," reported the *Times-Democrat*, "and the remarks of Rabbi Heller evidently made a strong impression upon them." Heller's appearance at Central Congregational Church practically coincided with the inception of a new movement, the interracial National Association for the Advancement of Colored People (NAACP). Moreover, the occasion of his address prompted a response from Du Bois, now editor of the recently established NAACP journal, the *Crisis*. In one of the journal's opening issues, Du Bois prefaced a lengthy quotation from Heller's talk, noting that the New Orleans rabbi had "defined race prejudice in a striking way." The American Missionary Association also published Heller's discourse in the association's journal, observing, by way of introduction, that many of the "Hebrew people" had recently shown sympathy toward the Negro. Because the Jews were "a people which has had many and long and hard lessons in the history of caste and prejudice," their experience "can speak with emphasis."[73]

In Heller's initial address to a black audience at Central Congregational Church, he had stressed that, in seeking to live meaningfully in a racially unjust world, the skillful survivor will "seek his brothers everywhere, especially among the persecuted and downtrodden." But he realized that high-minded idealism had its limits, that sometimes one had to deal with "difficult friendships." In an editorial that underscored the class bias inherent in Progressive reform, Heller admitted that it would be a "ceaseless struggle to keep one's idealities" in the many instances "in which our weaker brother, along every walk of life, makes it difficult to befriend him." The "weaker brother"—whether the African American or the Jewish schnorrer—unfortunately furnished "proof after proof for the arguments of those who trample on him, arraying our disappointments and irritations against our best willingness to be brotherly and helpful." Heller warned that "it requires the most determined reinforcement of your idealistic sentiments . . . not to break loose with vexation." In the case of the black man, he urged his listeners not to "wreak individual wrongs upon a . . . race of ex-slaves." The modern Jew, "in his own delectable private labyrinth of Jewish problems," needed the patience of the sage Hillel to see them through with resolve.[74]

The New Orleans rabbi's own quest for purpose and self-fulfillment had carried Heller from the ranks of elite reformers to the more precarious role of self-appointed spokesperson for blacks and Jews who lived beyond the fringes of middle-class life. Following his own advice, he now stood "unswayed" as he struggled to resolve the inherent tensions between the Zionist separatism he pursued on behalf of those fleeing Eastern European ghettos and the measure of racial justice he sought for his African American neighbors at home.

CHAPTER VII

❦

Zionism as "Our Salvation"

Heller announced his conversion to Zionism in a December 1901 article for the *Menorah* entitled "Our Salvation," a copy of which he promptly mailed to his friend and mentor Bernhard Felsenthal. By the time Felsenthal received the essay, he had read the published article, but he was flattered that Heller had mailed him an offprint. He let his younger protégé know that he basically agreed with Heller's "chain of thoughts," but Felsenthal worried about Heller's reputation among other rabbis in the Reform movement and predicted that he could expect "to hear bitter words" from some of them. Still, these slights should not diminish what Zionism offered. Felsenthal believed the movement more significant in "character . . . , aims . . . , and purposes" than any "which our history records." More important, he regarded the issue as essential to Jewish survival, truly "a question of life and death." As he welcomed Heller to the Zionist ranks, Felsenthal anticipated that "the logic of events" would eventually persuade other American rabbis who remained against the movement "to come over to your side, to our side."[1]

Heller wanted to make sure that his colleagues did not miss his "conversion." He sent offprints of his article to other Reform rabbis, including Jacob Raisin and David Philipson. Although Raisin was a Zionist, Philipson (1862–1949), remained antagonistic to Zionism throughout his career. He reacted just as Felsenthal had predicted, regretting Heller's "defection." Philipson was one of three Reform rabbis who had signed a resolution (subsequently adopted unanimously) at the 1898 UAHC meeting that declared in part: "We are opposed to political Zionism. The Jews are not a nation, but a religious community. Zion was a precious possession of the past. . . . as such it is a holy memory . . . , not our hope of the future. America is our Zion."[2]

Although Felsenthal died in 1908, he had defined the terms for Heller's major battles. Heller spent the lion's share of his later decades carrying on Felsenthal's work, fighting to demonstrate to Reform rabbis and others that the aims of Reform Judaism and Zionism could be reconciled. Reminiscing about Felsenthal more than a decade after his death, Heller claimed that his colleague had been a Zionist even before Herzl. Like Heller, Felsenthal had felt "utterly discouraged by the rapid fading out of Jewish religiousness and Jewish individuality." But Felsenthal turned to "national resurrection" for reasons beyond disillusionment. Felsenthal saw Judaism "as more than merely a religion, as a bundle of historic phenomena." Writing near the end of his own career, Heller acknowledged the affinities he still shared with one of his most influential mentors.[3]

By the time of his conversion, Heller fully believed that, given the dilemmas imposed by the modern world, Zionism offered the only key to unfettering the chains—even those of freedom—restricting Jewish survival. According to the Zionist goal, Jews would be able to live their Judaism freely in a totally Jewish environment, without constantly looking over their shoulders to ask, "What will the gentiles think?" Reform Jews in the early 1900s were particularly sensitive to charges of "dual loyalty." They were comfortable with a commitment to a solely religious Judaism but antagonistic to anything that hinted at what would later be called "peoplehood." As a "campaign for separate Jewish sovereignty," Zionism exacerbated the insecurities of most Reform Jews. Heller never developed this social neurosis but believed that Zionism would ultimately relieve American Jews of the social malaise that was sapping the strength and integrity of their historic legacy. He felt that, in a land free from racial prejudices, Zionism could offer a living example of a God-consecrated world where community superseded the individual. "Humanity can not be saved by individual righteousness," he wrote a decade later, but only the "righteousness of the social organism . . . will bring justice and salvation." Jews, as a "Messiah-people" dwelling in a "Messiah-state," would become "the social organism that shall redeem humanity and lead it thus united to the one God."[4]

Fears about dual loyalty increased in the years leading up to World War I, expressed in the shrill criticism against the so-called hyphenated American, the immigrant whose nationalistic loyalties might be divided. In October 1915, the *Literary Digest* called the problem of hyphenated Americans the hot topic of the day. That year also found the polar opposite articulated as American Jewish intellectual Horace Kallen introduced his celebrated doctrine of "cultural pluralism." The Harvard-educated immigrant believed that American democracy could flourish harmoniously only by providing "a multiplicity in a unity, an orchestration of mankind." Attempting to combat the antihyphen hysteria among his anxious coreligionists, Kallen also believed that Zionism could help

American Jews understand that *all* peoples have multiple loyalties and that the interwoven strands could make the fabric of American democracy more enduring.[5]

Heller had taken five years to overcome his initial perception of Zionism as a philosophy of despair, a period marked by profound changes in southern society. Certainly, the fact that the civil rights of African Americans could be so easily dismantled in a democratic society strongly affected him. The rising tide of nativism also disturbed him and made him doubt that European Jewry could look to the United States as its Zion. But he remained cautious about embracing Zionism as an alternative. In his sermon on Zionism delivered in 1899, Heller admitted that although he "often wished" for "conversion" by his Zionist friends, he still felt that the movement lacked "religious conviction" and that its foundations lay only in "sentiment and political motives."[6]

Stephen S. Wise, then a young Reform Zionist, responded to Heller's sermon by noting his appreciation of the significance of "the building of national ideals" in the nineteenth century. Wise asked him to follow the logic of his argument, "Why not Jewish [nationalism]?" Wise found an inherent contradiction in Heller's sermon. Heller felt that Zionism responded to a mood of desperation, yet noted that the movement, simultaneously, was "upborne by a wave of optimism." "We Zionists are pessimists, respecting the hope of securing justice from without," Wise explained, but "we are optimists in that we have the deepest faith in ourselves and our God-given powers to build up a country of our own." He chastised Heller for revealing his own despair in stating that "suffering and injustice should be the true Fatherland of the Jew," a sentiment that Wise considered "unworthy of any Jew, and most unworthy of you." Wise concluded by telling his reluctant colleague, "I somehow feel that we yet shall have your valued co-operation and support."[7]

Isaac Mayer Wise's death the following spring may have removed the final barrier to Heller's reticence, since he no longer had to worry about breaking with his major mentor and father figure on the topic. But the evidence suggesting that Wise's death may merely have coincided with Heller's change of heart is equally great. Heller was not above criticizing Wise even while the latter was alive. Gotthard Deutsch, a colleague whom Heller very much respected, told him that I. M. Wise was "a great man . . . , but for people who are independent he has no use." A few days later, Heller wrote his parents, "I had a letter from Prof. Deutsch in which he says he thought I would be chosen Dr. Wise's successor, but that Dr. W. did not want a strong man by his side." Later that month, Heller agreed with Deutsch. Far from believing Wise to be infallible, Heller likened him to many "great men" who sought to keep "the smaller fry at a distance, feeding them on smiles and other externalities." As a seminary student, Heller had often wished that there had been someone at HUC "to whom the students could have opened their hearts." After Wise's death, however, Heller's public writings mentioned none of the short-comings he had attributed to Wise earlier in his intimate correspon-dence.[8]

More than Wise's death, life in the American South undoubtedly dampened Heller's belief that the United States could become "Zion" for a despised minority. The severe race riot in New Orleans in 1900 was probably a more visceral reminder of the violent ends to which racial an-tagonism could lead, a close-at-hand version of the contemporaneous anti-Semitic pogroms in Eastern Europe. Inasmuch as Heller began to speak out on the unjust treatment of African Americans at the same time that he declared himself in favor of Jewish nationalist aspirations, his southern perspective may have been at least as instrumental as I. M. Wise's death in freeing him from the mental constraints that had earlier prevented him from accepting Zionist tenets.[9]

In December 1901, as Heller was formulating the ideas expressed in "Our Salvation," the *Times-Democrat* asked the Touro and Sinai rabbis for their views on Zionism. Leucht reaffirmed the current American Reform Jewish interpretation of dispersion. "The Jew can accomplish more by mingling with the peoples of every country," he told the reporter. The Jew's mission in the diaspora was to teach monotheism and eventually to bring "the whole world to the true religion of one God." Heller took the opportunity to share the recent changes in his own opinion. Al-though he still considered the movement "impracticable," his opposi-tion had "gradually receded." After witnessing the distinct rise in anti-Semitism and the equally "pernicious" rise in assimilation, he believed that what lay ahead was "a long and painful process of extinction." Heller felt that the "Jewish type" was not necessarily superior to any other, but Jewish "preservation" remained a real priority. While he still claimed that he was not "a fully accredited adherent," he now deemed Zionism "the only salvation of the Jew."[10]

Zionism answered Heller's deep psychological and intellectual need for a movement in which he could invest his commitment to Jewish pro-phetic idealism. While he could never reject the essence of the Reform movement in its attempts to adjust Judaism to the emancipated world of contemporary Western civilization, the dramatic turn of events in the last two decades of the nineteenth century profoundly altered his perspec-tive. Even though German Jews still claimed leadership of the American

Jewish community, their numerical preponderance was diminishing rapidly as massive numbers of their Eastern European brethren arrived an-
nually. Heller understood that Isaac M. Wise's dream of American Jewish
unity under the aegis of Reform Judaism was becoming increasingly
anachronistic. Although Heller was a committed Reform Jew, he realized
that Reform Judaism and the ideals of the Reform movement could no
longer hope to meet the needs of, or even seem relevant to, all American
Jews, much less address the needs of the majority of the world's Jews remaining in Eastern Europe. As he matured, Heller needed a Jewish identity that could accommodate his growing emphasis on self-respect and
self-worth as well as a deeper source of Jewish spirituality than he had
found in theology alone. He believed that, by ensuring Jewish survival,
Zionism's all-embracing Jewish nationalism completed the prophetic
ideal championed by Reform Judaism. With anti-Semitism on the rise in
Europe and anti-immigrationist and nativist sentiment on the rise in
America, Heller recognized that Jews everywhere were on the horns of a
real dilemma.

In "Our Salvation," he posed the alternative he now saw confronting
all Jews as a choice between "submergence or emergence." "Either we
must follow Bismarck's advice and mingle the precious Jewish drop with
the whole blood of Europe [or America] . . . , or we must withdraw to
where our individuality may have free play," Heller reasoned. He recognized Judaism as not only "religion preached by example" but also
"righteousness burning to nationalize itself, the patriotism of justice
dreaming of its final world-conquest." Unlike most other American Reform leaders, he did not share a belief in the uniqueness of the American
diaspora. As an immigrant, he could love his adopted country, but he
could never feel totally at home there. He projected this alienation onto
the entire experience of Jewish assimilation in the West. "Living in the
Christian world, and yet not of it," he claimed that the Jew would always
"feel himself an outsider." Something would always hold him back "from
throwing himself freely into the broad current so long as he has problems
of his own to solve." In a nation that perceived itself as Christian, "Christian tendencies to repel" the Jew would inevitably intervene.[11]

A decade later, Israel Zangwill, author of *The Melting Pot*, agreed with
Heller's diagnosis. In "The Jewish Race and Its Problems," a paper delivered in London in 1911 at the World's Congress of Races, Zangwill noted
that in the diaspora, anti-Semitism would always be "the shadow of
Semitism." Freed from the ghetto, the Jew brings "the unlike into the
heart of every milieu, and must thus defend a frontier-line as large as the
world." He averred that while civilization "is not called upon to save the

Jews, it *is* called upon to save itself." In its treatment of Jews, civilization was destroying itself. By 1911, Zangwill saw Jews reinstated in Palestine as a "bridge of civilization between the East and the West and a symbol of hope for the future of mankind." Interestingly, while Horace Kallen's cultural pluralism and Zangwill's melting pot metaphorically described differing views of American society, their images of Zionism complemented one another. In a 1918 essay, Kallen wrote that the continuity of Judaism as much more than a religious denomination depended upon a rich "Jewish community-complex" in which the individual could experience fully the traditions and history that sustained a "national life."[12]

Heller had discovered that Zionism, or the perception that the "spirit of Judaism" lived in a "national body," provided a tonic that could reinvigorate the modern Jewish spirit. As he experienced the powerfulness of his conversion, he wondered how any Jew could complacently consider "wiping his people from the slate of world-influences at a time when abstract truth and theoretical justice appear so weak, as against the reawakened greeds of commerce and diplomacy." Heller had won his struggle with existential despair. By fusing his belief in prophetic Judaism with his sense of Jewish nationality he was able to replenish what he termed his "soul-life," and he pushed his newly emerging energies in ever wider arcs.[13]

That Heller chose to make his formal announcement as a Zionist in a national publication is significant. He was redefining more than his stand on Zionism; he was announcing his intention to work for a fundamental reorientation of American Jewish life. Although he continued to be devoted to his congregants and to local progressive political issues, he intended to exert his influence on a larger nationalistic stage by becoming a leader of the mission to reconcile the aspirations of American Reform Judaism and Zionism[14]—a task to which he now pledged his considerable energies. In so doing, he consciously or unconsciously carried out the informal proposal that Gustav Gottheil had made after reading "Our Salvation." As rabbi of New York City's prestigious Temple Emanu-El, Gottheil had scandalized most of his congregants by embracing Zionism, but, since he was well respected and on the verge of retirement, his views were less threatening than they might otherwise have been.[15] Gottheil told his younger colleague that his article "summed up and laid bare the truth about our situation in the world as very few have done before you." Gottheil regretted that the constraints of the article did not allow Heller to elaborate and that few readers would be able to "grasp the importance of your statements and the cogency of your conclusion." He trusted that, in the future, Heller would avail himself of "ample opportunities" to make his "voice . . . heard far and wide . . . to bring in the final Salvation of Israel."[16]

Heller created or responded to these "ample opportunities" within the year, submitting occasional Zionist articles to the *Maccabaean*, the official organ of the Federation of American Zionists (FAZ) and writing the weekly lead editorial column for the *American Israelite*. As early as 1902, Jacob de Haas, the Federation secretary, wanted to take advantage of Heller's organizational skills and clout in the South in addition to his journalistic talents. De Haas proposed to travel there himself in the cooler months. He counted on Heller's "support in the convening in New Orleans of a conference of the Zionist societies of the South" because he needed Heller's "practical advice on matters and conditions in the South, which are practically unknown to me."[17]

In the winter of 1904, de Haas finally made the southern tour he had proposed. Describing it in the pages of the *Maccabaean*, he mentioned that he found the struggle in New Orleans "unusually hard." Although the small Orthodox community welcomed the Zionist appeal, de Haas wanted to speak to the unconverted, an idea that Heller supported. But de Haas claimed that "New Orleans is positively afraid of Zionism." While the non-Orthodox community may have contained some "Marrano Zionists," he was shocked that "not a Jewish institution would open its doors to the advocate of a Jewish movement." De Haas had discovered the level of assimilation that had driven Heller to Zionism with a vengeance. "The local Y.M.H.A. [Young Men's Hebrew Association] was broad enough to listen to Christian Science," de Haas noted, but the board of directors had a "standing injunction" against Zionism, making Heller's position "not the more comfortable in that he is an avowed exponent of the cause." This outsider's analysis of the Reform community's attitude makes Heller's achievements in maintaining his congregation's loyalty appear all the more remarkable.[18]

After I. M. Wise's death, Leo, his son, published the *Israelite*. Although he said he enjoyed featuring Heller's columns, Leo made it plain that the *Israelite* could not be used to showcase Zionist ideas. He warned Heller that the periodical would continue to convey I. M. Wise's teachings of the Jewish "religious mission . . . to carry . . . Monotheism to the utter ends of the earth." If Heller wished to "supplement" his work "in the pulpit and on the rostrum" with a column in the *Israelite*, he needed to keep Zionism from coloring his articles. Another journalist writing for an anti-Zionist Jewish newspaper expressed sympathy for Heller's predicament but nevertheless rejected his arguments on behalf of Zionism. Acknowledging Heller's integrity, the journalist commented, "Those who know

Dr. Heller personally know that he is incapable of saying one thing and meaning another." But as Felsenthal had predicted, Heller had a difficult time combining activities as a rising leader in the Reform movement's Central Conference of American Rabbis with his missionary efforts to bring others to Zionism. The journalist noted that Heller's "enthusiasm for Zionism and his honest desire to maintain his place as a Reformer" had caused him " 'to straddle the fence' in order to show the consistency of his own position." The editorial writer also feared that Heller would be distrusted by the Zionists who saw Reform Judaism as monolithically anti-Zionist. "Will Heller's interpretation of Zionism be accepted by the great majority of the Zionists?" he wondered.[19]

Heller's devotion to both positions constantly pushed him to refine and clarify his message. Although he complained about the obstacles and the difficulty of pursuing antagonistic paths, he enjoyed finding his balance between them. Years later, when Isaac, his younger son, was enrolled at Harvard Law School, Heller told him, "All my life I have always felt stimulated by the challenge of a really tough job." When Isaac wrote his father a warm, news-filled letter, Heller praised him, then told Isaac that such praise was more than Heller could ever have received from his own father. Analyzing his own cold, demanding upbringing, Heller decided that his father's stony demeanor and behavior had made the son "diffident for life." The unpleasant childhood experiences had made it difficult for Heller "to take praise gracefully." He realized, however, that his father's emotional aloofness may have "braced me to remain unmoved by praise or blame, to work on unpraised or to rise above unjust censure, to follow my own standards against the shallow world."[20]

Following his own lights certainly helped Heller, philosophically and psychologically, to deal with one of the significant disappointments of his professional career, namely his failure to be elected Gottheil's successor as rabbi of Temple Emanu-El. His failure to secure this post meant that he missed the opportunity to move to the center of American Jewish life. In the 1890s, Heller did not mention such a move, but prominent Jewish laymen in New York already had their eyes on the promising southern rabbi. As early as 1889, Emanu-El had invited him as a guest lecturer, while Ahavath Chesed, a second major New York congregation, had tried to court him for its pulpit. In 1894, Heller had replied to Ahavath Chesed that he could not leave New Orleans "to seek other spheres" because of his deep attachment to his "own people." He wrote, "Duty demands that I remain" in the city. At the turn of the century, Ahavath Chesed still maintained an interest in his candidacy. By this time Heller had become a more nationally recognized figure, and his feelings about remaining in the South had changed with the spread of lynching and racial hostilities in his region. Heller was willing to consider the pulpit, however, only if he was the sole rabbi asked; he refused to compete for the position. When he found that two of his colleagues were being interviewed, he decided to withdraw his name from consideration.[21]

But the chance to gain a New York pulpit increased in 1901 when Joseph Stolz, Heller's former HUC classmate and his closest friend in the rabbinate, spoke of Heller to his influential cousin, the attorney Louis Marshall. Marshall was one of the most prominent Jews in the country and was active in the affairs of Temple Emanu-El. He was also instrumental in seeking a new rabbi for the congregation when Rabbi Gottheil's health began deteriorating rapidly. In 1903, when Emanu-El had invited Heller to speak, he fully understood that the invitation was his one opportunity to interest the congregation in appointing him rabbi. When the potential New York pulpit was Emanu-El, Heller found himself able to tolerate competition. Stolz enthusiastically communicated once again with his cousin Marshall. He told Heller, however, that it was hard to predict what Emanu-El wanted in a rabbi. He hoped that Heller would "do himself the amplest justice" in his presentation to the congregation. Stolz also issued a veiled warning about Heller's outspokenness as a Zionist. Having recently returned from a conference at HUC that Heller did not attend, Stolz mentioned that David Philipson had been elected to the presidency. It was a position that Heller would certainly have been thrilled to accept, but Stolz told him that the Board of Governors had never seriously considered him. "Your Zionism must have stood in the way somewhat," Stolz explained.[22]

As Heller prepared for his forthcoming trip, the local New Orleans and national Jewish press speculated about his chances of acceptance.[23] He and Philip Cowen, editor and publisher of the *American Hebrew,* maintained a steady stream of correspondence, since Cowen was planning to publish the Emanu-El sermon after its delivery. Heller tried to keep expectations from escalating, begging Cowen not to think of him as someone simply seeking to gain a position "the nature of which I know very little." Instead, Heller claimed to be going to New York just "to measure myself agt. these opportunities & see whether I ought to make a change." Heller still insisted that he was not discontented in New Orleans, where he held "as many ties of love as any rabbi has anywhere" and "virtually a life tenure." He claimed that it was his "duty" to investigate an opportunity that afforded his family advantages—"climate, surroundings and education for my children"—that New Orleans could not offer. Just as Cowen counseled Heller to stress religion in his address, Stolz thought he made "a splendid dark horse" and advised him not to emphasize Zi-onism. "Those rich men look upon Zionism as a cranky whim," Stolz cautioned, and he opined that Heller would only risk an "explosion" that could "damage" his chances of being elected if he chose to focus on his "deep conviction." Stolz reiterated his belief that Marshall would support Heller's candidacy and advised Heller to bolster his self-confidence in the spirit of "veni, vidi, vici" and thereby win some other prominent men to his cause. The stakes grew still higher when Richard Gottheil—a pro-fessor at Columbia University, a Zionist leader, and the son of the dying rabbi—sent Heller a warm note, welcoming him to New York. Gottheil hoped that his father's pulpit would "be occupied temporarily and as I hope permanently, by one for whom my whole family has learned to have much esteem."[24]

On 3 May, when the long-awaited Friday night appearance at Temple Emanu-El arrived, Heller immediately sensed that, as he feared, he had failed to capture the hearts of his audience, although he felt that he did reach the minds of the intellectuals there. Marshall, millionaire Jacob Schiff, and Richard Gottheil were among those present. Solomon Schechter, the newly arrived British theologian who became the head of the Conservative movement's new Jewish Theological Seminary, also supported Heller. While the intellectuals conveyed their approval, the larger crowd of businessmen evidently received Heller coldly. Marshall initially supported Heller's candidacy before Emanu-El's Board of Direc-tors but withdrew the resolution when he saw that he had insufficient support.[25]

Heller begged Ida not to feel sorry for him. While he felt discouraged by "the discourteousness and cold-heartedness," he did not regret having made the effort. The trip had been worth it, he told her poignantly. It was enough to "have lived in Paradise 3 days" and to return knowing that "among scholars and thinkers my name is good enough." He realized that some of those at Temple Sinai would be "disappointed," but eventu-ally he could "live down" the "New Orleans effects of the fizzle." Grate-fully, he declared that he had "more than enough philosophy" to with-stand the defeat.[26]

Although Heller never spoke of the content of his Sabbath eve lecture, the following week's *Jewish Exponent* discussed his thesis thoroughly in an article that analyzed the problem of filling the pulpit at Temple Emanu-El. First, the congregation's sheer size limited potentially success-ful candidates to men gifted in oratory skills. The headline highlighted an even more conspicuous problem: "politics in a congregation." In his address, "Our Place Today," Heller had spoken in one breath of the "resounding clashes and glaring contrasts" that faced the Jews everywhere. The philosophical extremes of idealism and materialism provided basic contradictions to resolve. He proposed that the Jew was "best fitted by experience and teaching" to reconcile the two through the "mission of living [the] . . . faith." And when he rhetorically asked, "*how* Israel may start upon this loftiest rung of his varied career," he described Zionism, the "chief promise of this advance," as the answer. The *Jewish Exponent* contrasted Heller with one of the other candidates to address Emanu-El. While Rabbi Leon Harris had "indicated his disbelief in Zionism," Heller had "boldly pronounced himself a Zionist." Without naming Emanu-El specifically, but nonetheless clearly identifying it, the *American Hebrew* obliquely referred to Heller's candidacy in an editorial. If the congregation were seeking a rabbi whose "sensational sermons shall attract non-Jews to the Temple," this candidate (Heller) was not their man, but if they were looking for a "sincere man" with "a definite and strong grasp on the spirit of the Jewish religion," they need look no further. Heller had honored deep conviction above keen ambition. He was, however, unwilling to recast himself, to become the kind of rabbi who could win the pulpit. Henry Cohen, a rabbi and confidant of Heller's in Galveston, Texas, spoke comforting words the following year: "Let NY go! Some congregations do not deserve certain men. You would not be happy there."[27]

To Stolz, Heller conceded that he was "exceedingly eager to go to New York under almost any circumstances," for he was "heartily tired of New Orleans." He was glad he had enough pride to do "nothing in the matter that I shall have to be ashamed of afterwards." Months later, Stolz reported that one of Emanu-El's board members had spoken of Heller's "quarrelsome record in New Orleans." But Heller retorted that he was resigned and had temporarily retreated from contentious fights within the local Jewish community. At Leucht's birthday, a visiting rabbi had lectured against Zionism, interspersing his derogatory remarks "with negro talk," calling Zionists, "cowards, traitors, and Jew-haters." Heller told Stolz that he did not "deign a word" in reply. "That's how quarrelsome I am," he commented sarcastically. The search dragged on for some time, but Heller wrote Marshall the following February, effectively removing himself from the list of candidates. After receiving the letter, Marshall wrote Philip Cowen that Heller's modesty "impressed me much more than the presumption and self-seeking of other candidates for the pulpit."[28]

Heller, principles intact, had made a realistic assessment of his skills and needs and adjusted his ambition accordingly. Now he made himself content in New Orleans by continuing to reach beyond his congregation locally, broadening his influence nationally, and deepening his roots spiritually. According to an article in the *Jewish American* in 1903, Temple Sinai had an enviable record, because in its entire life, more than thirty years, the congregation had held only two elections for rabbi. "The confidence reposed in the occupant of the pulpit is of that lofty character that the bond of friendship becomes in the course of time so strong that the relationship between pulpit and pew is not only friendly, but of almost a familiar intimacy." In 1905, when another prominent New Orleans minister received a call to a pulpit in the North, the *Times-Democrat* compared his departure to Heller's decision the year before to stay in the South. While the minister was from New England, Heller had married a woman from New Orleans. His children had been born and reared in the city, the climate "suited him," and "he did not consider" leaving but "announced that he hoped his congregation would be pleased to permit him to remain with them to the end of his days."[29]

Although he had earned a reputation as a contentious dissenter in a number of causes, Heller had also crafted his interfaith alliances skillfully by championing mainstream reform issues with other prominent ministers. Having spent nearly two decades in New Orleans, Heller had clearly been embraced by the South as one of its own. Although disagreeing with his views on Zionism, Temple Sinai members could appreciate Heller's intellectual ability and the sense of personal integrity that had made him an effective force in respected circles in New Orleans. The traits that he had cultivated and the achievements that he had accumulated since first occupying the pulpit served him well. Community acceptance reinforced his self-acceptance as a southern rabbi. Inner security quelled his restlessness. He no longer sought to relocate if doing so meant forgoing the outspokenness that he was beginning to relish in himself. Rising to the forefront of the Reform movement as an opponent of a Reform radicalism that threatened to "dejudaize" Judaism, he sought a rapprochement with the Orthodox community mainly through Zionism—and he shrewdly did not espouse Zionism in any sermons but chose other, more suitable and less politically compromising venues in which to champion the cause.

Heller expressed his sense of inner conviction in editorials in Jewish periodicals and in deeds in the local Jewish community. While he could agree that Reform Judaism might theologically be closer to Unitarianism than to Jewish Orthodoxy, he nonetheless found Jews of every stripe far closer to one another than Reform Jews were to practitioners of another liberal religion. Religious orientation alone was insufficient to meet the demands of the modern Jewish experience. Heller feared that Reform's

universalist rhetoric had yielded only a community of "religious indif-
ferents in this indifferent day." The analytical framework of Reform Judaism and the currents of evolutionary and progressive thought provided him with enough detachment to recognize that, in its historical
development, Judaism was no system of "religious metaphysics." Instead,
he found it more appropriate to consider Judaism a "religion of conduct,"
a "progressive discipline" that embodied itself not so much in progressive thought as in the progressive development of the "race."[30]

The Reformers, Heller believed, had erred in stressing "abstract principles as against tender loyalties" and in toning down the "Oriental" elements that had traditionally endeared Judaism to Jews. Reform Judaism
in its intense Westernizing had failed to formulate a cohesive philosophy
sufficiently far-reaching to comprehend the paradoxes the new century
had brought to Jewish life. Current realities—from the sudden vicious-
ness of racial anti-Semitism abroad to social anti-Semitism at home—
hinted at the turbulence that Jews were encountering everywhere. In
January 1905, the *Times-Democrat* carried an article that chronicled Heller's participation at the UAHC biennial. The journalist mentioned a petition signed by prominent New York Jews like Marshall, Schiff, and
Adolph Ochs that condemned Melvil Dewey, then state librarian, for his
social anti-Semitism. As president of the Lake Placid Company, Dewey
had promoted policies that ensured social ostracism. Heller argued that
"when a gratuitous assumption of social superiority is exercised by a
public official . . . , it becomes our duty as men, first of all, as Americans
in the second line, and only in the last resort as Jews, to protest."[31]

Heller felt that the immigrants who arrived daily from Eastern Europe
and tightly clustered on New York's Lower East Side were also delegiti-
mizing and undermining the optimistic idealism of Classical Reform. In
trying to come to terms with the current combination of anti-Semitism
and nativism rampant in America, Heller contrasted the Scandinavian,
whom he termed "the pet of all the host of immigration philosophers,"
with the Jewish "alien." To the American capitalist, the Scandinavian exhibited many desirable characteristics. He did not "figure among the
multi-millionaires," nor did he "invade the sweat shops." Instead he remained contentedly among the "lower middle classes," from which he
rose "at most to moderate comfort." His reputation as a "steady, reliable
worker with little brilliancy, versatility or quickwittedness" diverged
greatly from Jewish restlessness and ambition. Where the Scandinavian
would "not lower wages by crowding the unskilled labor market," nor
"vex the millionaires with inconvenient commercial power," the Jew, the
"uncompromising radical in the history of thought," burning "with the

sense of indignation at injustice," was willing to "put up with . . . being "disliked." Even if "some shrewd psychologist might propose that we whittle ourselves over into a new semblance; the Jew is a protean creature outwardly; his inward temperament is of the primeval granite," and therefore he must be left alone to develop fully. Heller believed that Jewish ambition and genius inadvertently produced anti-Semitism in those with whom he competed. This conviction remained an integral part of his Zionist rationale—the need for a homeland where Jews would compete among themselves. On the other hand, Heller saw Jews not as exceptional but instead as the "embodiment of a pushing, restless, age." Their cause was that of "equal opportunity and universal justice."[32]

Like Horace Kallen, Heller now realized that Reform Judaism's message of religious mission, of Jewish dispersal as a means of propagating universalist faith to the nations, was wrongheaded. Assimilation had gone too far for him, and he wished to see Reform revitalized. A secularist, Kallen held that religion was merely "an item" in the larger "Jewish national life." He worried that cordoning off the religious aspects of Judaism denied its cultural dimensions and its viability in a culturally pluralistic American society. Heller essentially agreed with this analysis but considered the religious dimension of Judaism dynamic. He feared that the abstract and "sublimated" Judaism that Reform now offered would not hold the young. More than ever, Heller believed the Jewish "faith-mission" to be inseparable from Jewish "race-psychology." His Judaism represented an evolving consciousness that would continually respond to changing circumstances rather than merely echo the rational formulations of its religious mission. Changes in the nature of Jewish expression, therefore, reflected the deeper needs of the Jewish soul, while persistent occidentalizing only obscured the process. Heller maintained that Solomon Schechter had articulated one of the ironies facing contemporary Jewish life. "Aryans" had laid "claim to the name and heritage of Israel," while Jews, occidentalizing their religious heritage, aped the Occident in everything but its "admiration of Israel." Heller's understanding of the contemporary Jewish experience deepened and reinforced his commitment to Jewish nationalism. He intensified his efforts to reach out to Jews beyond the confines of the Reform community. Because the genius of the Reform movement recognized Judaism as an ongoing process, it encouraged innovation and adaptation. Heller believed that essential flexibility had inadvertently taught Jews "how to be Zionists in the full light of modern culture." In an article on Zionists within the Reform movement, Jacob de Haas quoted Heller's statement that he was "willing to let the world of Reform Judaism grow into Zionism as I have grown." De Haas felt that this declaration marked a "signal victory" for the strength of Zionist ideology.[33]

Like Theodor Herzl, Heller more readily sought Zionist converts among the enlightened Reformers. While he never abandoned the task of persuading Reform Jews of Zionism's compatibility with progressive Judaism, he found allies, locally and nationally, more immediately among the growing numbers of Orthodox coreligionists. Although New Orleans did not attract many of the newly arriving Eastern European Jews who flocked to northern and newer southern urban centers like Houston and Atlanta, the city's Orthodox population increased substantially at the turn of the century. Unlike other major metropolitan areas, however, New Orleans remained predominantly German-Jewish and Reform in character. The new arrivals in the city banded together in small congregations—divided by traditions and languages reflecting their countries of origin—in the Dryades Street area, where most of the immigrants lived. Heller helped the Orthodox community in any way he could. He participated in fund raising and officiated at synagogue dedication ceremonies. He also attended services in Orthodox congregations on those occasions when the Reform movement curtailed observance. Congregants recall his sitting modestly in the rear of the shul with the less prominent congregants, then visiting with Orthodox Zionist families on Shabbat afternoons. Seeking stability and a permanent home to replace rented rooms, some of the small, Orthodox enclaves chose to combine. Heller encouraged the consolidation just as he actively promoted more respect for the religious traditions of Russian Jews. "Just because we refuse to recognize the dogmatic authority of the Talmud," he editorialized, "we must be the more careful to honor its historic tradition."[34]

Heller berated the German Jews for dealing with Russian Jews in a manner reminiscent of the way gentiles treated the more established Reform Jews. Simultaneously, he counseled Russian Jews in the same language in which he addressed his African American neighbors. Both groups should demonstrate more self-respect if they wished to command favorable attention from those outside their own enclaves. He invoked the masculine ideal as he urged the Russian Jew to "resent insult," to demonstrate pride, to defend his fellow *landsmen,* to "stand by his colors as a man," and not to be ashamed to defend his convictions, religious and otherwise. Heller also insisted that self-respect went beyond individual responsibility. "We betray our vulgarity of heart," he noted sadly, "when we invite to our synagogue festivals and congregational anniversaries the Unitarian or even Presbyterian minister but not the Orthodox rabbi."[35]

In a heated discussion on "Reform Judaism and the Recent Jewish Immigrant" at the CCAR annual conference in Louisville in 1904, Heller proved a strong advocate on behalf of the cultural integrity of newly arriving Jews. One of his colleagues suggested that while Reform Judaism offered no appeal to the older generation, the children of these immigrants should be drawn into the Reform movement, ostensibly to be more fully Americanized, even if this action went against their parents. Heller vehemently disagreed, arguing that "the one pivotal point about the whole ghetto problem" was never to sever the moral and social ties binding the generations. To promote stability in the immigrant population and to ease the period of adjustment, the Reform community should work instead to assist in keeping "intact the link of reverence . . . and of obedience" that attaches child to parent. To denigrate Orthodoxy only exacerbated the misunderstanding between the two communities. He admonished the Conference that, when Reform Jews treated the Orthodox condescendingly, "we slander our ancestors and misunderstand our Torah."[36]

But Heller was not interested in a homogenized American Jewry. He felt that "reconciliation" between American Orthodoxy and Reform was "neither desirable nor feasible." Revealingly, he admitted that, even within himself, the two tendencies were not reconciled, that each "continues, within the same mind, to criticise the other." Because he valued the separate strengths and understood the limitations of each—the stubborn clinging to tradition in Orthodoxy, the persistent rationalism and accommodationism in Reform—he insisted that recriminations of one against the other should stop. He deplored the "coarse invectives and abuse" and proposed instead "peaceable co-operation." In arguing for interdenominational harmony, he believed that his experiences as a southern rabbi were instructive. He noted that, especially in the South, a smaller Jewish population made it imperative for Reform and Orthodox to support each other. Heller's observations and the examples of mutual support he chose were tinged with the noblesse oblige of progressivism and echoed the "elder brother" rhetoric of his advice to southern African Americans. Typically Reform rabbis preached in Orthodox synagogues on "second holidays." When the Orthodox community lacked educational facilities for its children, Orthodox parents often sent their youngsters to Reform Sunday schools. Heller believed that these collaborative efforts would inevitably lead from "kindly toleration and Jewish brotherliness" to the "reality of a Judaism unqualified by partisan adjectives."[37]

At the 1908 CCAR convention, Heller delivered a scholarly paper to commemorate the centennial of the birth of Samson Raphael Hirsch, who was widely viewed as a main promulgator of the modern Orthodox movement. Heller felt that Hirsch should be revered as a "born religious leader" with strength that derived from his "forceful . . . personality." By giving a modern Orthodox pioneer serious consideration before a body of Reform rabbis, Heller clearly intended to engender increased respect for the Orthodox movement. The commonalities of a Jewish identity and communal need should prevail, he insisted, no matter what the divisions, and he held up Zionism as one important means for achieving unity. Zionism, however, served to divide before it served to unify.[38]

Heller's activities as a Reform Zionist propagandist in New Orleans were comparable to Zionist initiatives undertaken throughout Jewish America. In the pre–World War I era, the Federation of American Zionists loosely held together a variety of local Zionist organizations. In New Orleans, Ohavei Zion became the institutional center of Zionism.[39] In December 1903, the Orthodox congregational rooms in the Dryades Street neighborhood hosted the group, with Heller as the principal speaker. This occasion marked Heller's debut as a Zionist spokesperson at a public meeting in the city. He reiterated the positions he had taken in essays and articles carried by what the *Times-Democrat* called "Eastern papers." Even while New Orleans Jews lived "with comparatively little prejudice," Jewish prohibitions against intermarriage posed problems for total integration into American, or any other majority, culture. Faced with "nationalization or dereligionization," Jewish survival depended on Zionism, since, gradually, assimilation would claim those who chose to remain in this country. While Heller believed that a country "where they could be themselves" provided the ultimate solution to the Jewish Problem in the contemporary world, he did not speculate on whether Jewish nationalism could be achieved in his lifetime. He mentioned, however, that the sixth Zionist Congress held in Basel the previous summer brought new impetus to the movement, with Herzl dangling before the delegates the prospect of England's granting Jews territory in Uganda in East Africa. Although this proposition was widely criticized and quickly proved untenable, Heller briefly embraced it with enthusiasm. If Jews refused to accept Uganda, he believed, it might be a long time before they received another "favorable" offer.[40]

The following year, even while Heller claimed not to be "daunted one whit" by the practical "obstacles" to attaining the dream of Zionism, he faced small-scale but unpleasant obstructions closer to home. The local YMHA had granted him permission to use the lodge room of its large facility, the Atheneum, for a lecture. When the chairman of the YMHA's house committee discovered that Zionism was the subject of the lecture, however, he withdrew his offer. He told Heller that he could not afford to hold himself "responsible for the results that will accrue to me individually and officially" for allowing the "rooms to be used for any purposes . . . opposed by a considerable number of our members and the Jewish Community at large." Since the YMHA was dominated by members of the Reform community, including many from Temple Sinai, Heller was probably not surprised.[41]

While Heller conducted his initial and passionate forays on behalf of Zionism, he did not neglect his congregation, nor did he cease to maintain a high profile as a Progressive in the greater community. In 1902, he decided that at least some of his sermons belonged in print, and a short-lived series was published under the name the *Temple Sinai Pulpit*. Several of these sermons dealt with Progressive themes, such as "The Minister and the Business Man" (7 November 1902) and "The Elements of Business Morality" (14 November 1902). In a congregation dominated by merchants, his addresses went straight to the heart of his concerns for the ethics of those he served.[42]

Although he generally did not promote Zionism from the pulpit, at times he obliquely pushed his message there. In a 1906 Passover sermon, for example, Heller linked Zionism with progressivism, first noting that "Zion . . . is no mere slogan for hidebound nationalism" but a "cry of weariness from all injustice." He then cataloged the current illustrations of how the strong were "trampling upon the weak." In concluding, he retreated to Reform's universalism and prayed that the time might come soon when "all races and climes" would "dwell . . . in the Jerusalem of prophecy." Issues of social justice loomed large in his sermonizing. He asked his congregation, "You, manufacturers, are you just to the laboring men and women that toil for you; just, I ask, not merely kind?" He wanted to know whether employees were being treated as fellow human beings or were being dismissed as a "kind of machine . . . replaced without cost." He also promoted democratization of Reform ceremonies and demonstrated a keen psychological understanding of the problems that adolescents face. At the CCAR conference in 1907, he argued for confirming thirteen- and fourteen-year-olds rather than delaying the ceremony until a year or two later, when the confirmands would be more mature intellectually. He maintained that the younger ages were the last "in which you can teach in the same class the rich man's child that still goes to school, and the poor man's child that has to work." Thirteen or fourteen represented, as well, the pivotal age standing between "childhood and adolescence," the last where "a girl and boy feel they are still of the same age." He believed that the benefit of the confirmation process was the "intimate association" of the students that crucial year, and the feeling of community that the study and culminating ceremony engendered. The memory of that year would remain strong enough throughout the confirmands' lives to promote a sense of belonging, a sense of allegiance to one another. The question of social justice gained prominence in the Reform movement at the 1908 CCAR Convention. Heller served on Stolz's committee, which recommended that the CCAR support all movements against child labor and those that advanced the "proper development of child life through education and recreation.[43]

For Heller, Zionism served as an antidote, not just to assimilation, but to the empty materialism that he witnessed rampant around him, a vacuousness that threatened his sense of purpose, even though membership at Temple Sinai continued to rise gradually from 290 members in 1895 to 356 a decade later. The Religious School at Temple Sinai also benefited from Heller's commitment to education. When he arrived in New Orleans in 1887, he found that no provision for classrooms existed in the temple but only "partition-stands between classes, shutting out sight but not sound." To help students learn, rooms were constructed immediately, and more were added fifteen years later. At first, he divided the school into four classes and taught these on Saturdays and Sundays. By 1905–1906, a more formal normal school prevailed, with a principal and an assistant. About that time, the harvest festival of Sukkot began to reclaim some prominence in the institutional life of the temple, and the congregation constructed a Sukkah for the first time. The trend toward the more traditional, which Heller championed in New Orleans and in the CCAR, was beginning to be reflected in other congregations throughout the country. As rewarding as this response must have been, when the Temple Sinai board voted Heller a salary raise in 1909, Stolz agreed with his friend's frustrations. While congratulating him, Stolz remarked sympathetically, "How much better it would be if our congregations were half as solicitous about the Rabbi's heart-satisfaction as they are to gratify his material needs."[44]

But the controversies that Zionism stirred, locally and nationally, kept Heller constantly on his toes as he tried to maintain the delicate balance between provocation and acceptability in both the Zionist and Reform camps. While Zionist and national Reform leaders pressured him to exercise his prolific pen and to proselytize energetically on their behalf, each desired his exclusive devotion. In the fall of 1907, FAZ secretary Judah Magnes urged Heller to organize the "Zionistic rabbis of the South," who could travel to various southern cities on a propagandistic campaign. Earlier that year, Leo Wise had told Heller, "I am sorry that you . . . take your Zionism so seriously," and had charged that Zionism was "the prime cause" of recent difficulties at HUC. That spring, Max Margolis, along with two other Zionist professors at the college, tendered his resignation. Thanking Heller for his support and sympathy, Margolis indicated that David Philipson, a real power in Cincinnati behind HUC president Kaufman Kohler, was to blame for the anti-Zionist commotion. While Margolis did not refer to Philipson by name, he told Heller that the unnamed party, "unable to secure the Presidency for himself, is interested in keeping—*you* out of it." Margolis assured Heller that "we Zionists," though dwelling in the diaspora, realized that dispersion was no "ultimate aim." Like Heller, he believed that with "great principles at stake," they must be "fought out manfully, courageously." Charles S. Levy thanked Heller for loyally trying to "save the College from the disastrous consequences" in the wake of Margolis's resignation. Outlining the situation for Heller, Levy mentioned that while Kohler did not "demand" that Margolis resign, once the resignation had been submitted, Kohler "exerted all his influence for having it accepted, on the plea that Zionism and Reform Judaism are incompatible."[45]

Meanwhile, Leo Wise continued to berate Heller. He suggested that it would be regrettable for Heller to apologize or propagandize for Zionism in another journal, since such action was "inconsistent with the general policy of the 'Israelite.' " And "in our own columns," Wise reiterated, "it is out of the question." He regarded the "Zionistic scandal" at the college as exaggerated and believed that personal antagonisms lay at the center of the controversy. When Heller did express his concerns about the future of the college in the *Israelite*, Magnes confided to Heller his pessimism about the long-term institutional consequences of an anti-Zionist atmosphere, and he proposed alternative scenarios. "Either the College remains what it was, a liberal institution, devoted to Jewish learning and to the training of men who might form independent convictions as to Jewish literature and life," he suggested, or it could easily become a narrow "Theological School of a petty sect in Judaism." Magnes also wrote to Louis Goldman, president of the UAHC, telling him that HUC had already become "a petty sectarian school," far from the ideals of I. M. Wise. Although the founder had not sympathized with Zionism, "as President of the College, he fully understood that a Zionist had at least as much place on the faculty as did an anti-Zionist." If the HUC did develop into a bastion of Reform anti-Zionism, as Magnes darkly hinted it might, he nonetheless felt that "from a certain point of view," that of Kohler and those in his camp, such a development unfortunately seemed "both justifiable and logical."[46] While Magnes felt no need to reconcile his Zionist fervor with his Reform background and could easily assert the primacy of the former, Heller could not sunder his allegiance to the institutions that had shaped his Americanization and his original loyalties as a Jewish professional.

But Zionists, including the Reform leadership (a minority), were not always mutually supportive. One of the most paradoxical illustrations of the fratricidal factionalism occurred in Heller's bid for the presidency of the CCAR.[47] In spite of his controversial views, his colleagues in the Conference that Heller had helped found responded to his loyalty and hard work by electing him vice president in 1907, to succeed president-elect David Philipson when his term expired. In his autobiography, written forty years later, Philipson recalled that the CCAR leadership that year confronted a situation in which irony abounded. Although both rabbis deserved to head the conference, the two were "diametrically opposed" on the issue of Zionism. Moses J. Gries, Philipson's "devoted" confidant, aware of the dilemma, worried that Philipson would find Heller's candidacy "objectionable," since "harmony between the two leading officers of the conference" was mandatory if the CCAR were to function effectively. Philipson noted that Gries granted him carte blanche in the decision making and told Philipson that his wishes "would guide the [nominating] committee." Philipson unequivocally stated that, due to his "services and seniority," Heller deserved the honor of the office. He assured the nominating committee that the two could "get along," and if Heller's name were submitted, Philipson would not contest the decision. He remembered that during the two years they served together, no "wrangling in the Executive Committee" disturbed the Conference. The forty-year interlude in Philipson's memory served to smooth over some of the "wrangling" between the two men. In the spring of 1909, in reaction to his vice president's criticism of Philipson's tract on "The Jew in America," he had sent Heller a scathing letter. While Heller had evidently wanted to approve the tract before it was distributed, Philipson denied that Heller had the right to censor the text. "I should not have permitted myself to be persuaded to write it [the tract]," Philipson complained, if he had anticipated needing Heller's approval. Philipson accused Heller of using the incident as an opportunity "again to pick at what you consider a flaw in my conduct of Conference affairs."[48]

While Philipson and Heller could resolve their differences in leading the Conference for the most part, Heller found himself unexpectedly opposed by Stephen S. Wise, his Reform Zionist cohort. In a strange turn of events during the fall of 1909, Wise actively campaigned to block Heller's assumption of the CCAR presidency. Already elected honorary vice president of the FAZ, Heller undoubtedly anticipated some opposition from the anti-Zionist coalition in the CCAR, which argued that Heller's open espousal of Zionism and active participation in the FAZ undermined the protocol of ascent within the Conference. To complicate matters, the FAZ planned to schedule a Zionist mass meeting in New York when the CCAR was holding its election meeting there. The proposed theme of the FAZ meeting, "Are Reform Judaism and Zionism Compatible?," would highlight the conflict between the CCAR's majority and Heller.[49]

Although he had anticipated an uphill battle, Heller was unprepared for Wise's letter-writing campaign promoting the candidacy of the arch–Radical Reformer and anti-Zionist Emil Hirsch. Wise refused to support Heller, obviously not on the grounds of the incompatibility of Zionism and Reform, but because Wise, a Radical Reformer as well as a Zionist, considered Heller too much a "counter-Reformer." Wise accused Heller of being too sympathetic to represent the Reform movement and the CCAR. In stressing the rational and the prophetic aspects of Judaism, Classical Reform had discarded rituals and ceremonies. By the mid-1890s, a small movement within Reform, including Heller, believed that rationalism had gone too far and called for reinstating some religious ritual—just as Temple Sinai had done in constructing its Sukkah. Solomon Schechter labeled this minority faction a "counter-Reformation." Judah Magnes, one of its prominent proponents, wanted to restore "to Jewish consciousness something of beauty and strength." At this early point in his long career, Stephen Wise felt that Judaism needed to be revitalized, not by returning to ritual, but by reemphasizing social justice, and his Free Synagogue had the reputation of being a "Torahless, Sabbathless synagogue." Heller defended those branded with the "terrifying bogey" of "Counter-Reformation" as battlers who, among other things, "dared" disapprove of the "Sunday-Sabbath" and condemned "the shifting or occasional abolition of our historical festivals." He believed that no "true friend of Reform" or Judaism could "witness without protest the excesses, the compromises with sheer convenience . . . of which the extremists in our ranks have been guilty.[50]

Furious with Wise, Heller felt betrayed by the "feeler" Wise had sent to test the winds for a Hirsch presidency. Heller considered himself "neither narrow enough nor sufficiently blinded by conceit" to see that some of his colleagues would feel that Hirsch would make a better president, but Wise's tactics particularly perturbed him. "What arouses my indignation . . . and partly robs me of the esteem in which I hold you," he told Wise, "is the secret and underhanded manner in which your movement is engineered." If Heller were initiating some action against Wise, he would have done it "in the open," with Wise "among the first" to have received any "circular." Wise, in turn, was infuriated with Heller's letter. Wise considered it "of such a character as to justify" his refusal to respond, but while denying that he had attempted to "undermine" Heller's candidacy, he justified his action at some length. As a Reform Zionist who saw no conflict between the aims of the two movements, Wise took an extraordinary stand against Heller. He and a "number of men" felt that "at this time, the Presidency . . . should not be lodged in a man who has . . . chosen to place himself in the forefront of the counter-reformation movement," a movement that Wise saw "fundamentally opposed to the principles of the Jewish Reformation." He assured Heller that the position against his candidacy had nothing whatsoever to do with the friendship and personal relations between Heller and those with whom Wise consulted. They simply felt that Hirsch, always in the vanguard of American Reform Judaism, "was entitled to the titular [recognition]," since "his is the real leadership of the American Jewish ministry." Wise had written Henry Berkowitz, a close professional associate of Heller in the CCAR, hoping that Berkowitz could demonstrate to Heller that no animosity existed behind the scheme to derail his candidacy. Amazingly, Wise had anticipated that Heller would not only sympathize with the pro-Hirsch faction but would also "step aside *for one year*" and "be magnanimous enough" to nominate Hirsch for the presidency![51]

Heller's angry response, of course, had dashed these hopes, and Hirsch himself opposed his own nomination. Wise indicated that some of those opposed to departing from precedent to support Hirsch might nonetheless do so to support someone other than Heller, someone "friendly to the Cincinnati cabal." Although striving for balance in the body of the letter, Wise concluded with an attack on Heller that revealed the transparency of at least some of his motives in supporting Hirsch. In comparison with Heller, Wise was much more the maverick Reformer, freer by nature and by economic circumstance to diverge from the norm. Wise reminded him that, in the *American Israelite* four years earlier, Heller had criticized Wise's promotion of freedom in the pulpit. In a much-publicized dispute between Louis Marshall and Wise concerning Wise's candidacy for the pulpit at Emanu-El in 1905, Wise had demanded a pulpit free from control of the board of trustees, a condition, Marshall assured him, that would never be met. Heller undoubtedly did not object to Wise's idea that the rabbi should represent his own inner beliefs above those of his congregation's, but he opposed Wise's audacity in the self-promotional *An Open Letter . . . on the Freedom of the Jewish Pulpit,* which was published the following year. Wise claimed that he had forgiven Heller and others who misunderstood the "importance of the fight I made for the entire Jewish ministry in America," but in the context of Heller's candidacy for CCAR president, the embers of Wise's resentment still glowed.[52] Although the Hirsch candidacy was now dead, the anti-Zionist, anti-Heller faction remained a problem that Heller needed to resolve immediately.

Unfortunately, Heller could not attend the election meeting and therefore could not lobby on his own behalf. Isidore Newman, the leading turn-of-the-century philanthropist in New Orleans, was at death's door, and the family expected Heller to remain at his side. Joe Stolz could not understand how one congregant's impending death could deter Heller from traveling to New York. Heller tried to explain that regional differences accounted for Stolz's inability to comprehend the delicacy of Heller's situation. The need to stay in favor with a leading Jewish family was not the principal motive behind Heller's refusal to abandon Newman. "You do me wrong to view my act from the millionaire angle," Heller complained, "you ought to know my defiant soul better than that." What Stolz failed to appreciate was the way in which, during a time of need, "Southerners cling to their minister." Heller had not been especially close to the Newman family, but his effectiveness as a southern rabbi might easily have suffered had he ignored his customary obligations to a prominent family's needs. He tried to justify his decision to remain with the dying man and his family by explaining, "I have yet to find one man or woman in this community" who suggested "that it would have been either wiser or nobler . . . to go to N.Y." That New York might further his "personal ambition" mattered relatively little when weighed against Newman's death. Newman had been not only the most important Jewish philanthropist in New Orleans but the "biggest giver in the South (among Jews)," supporting Jewish efforts in other parts of the United States, like the Jewish Hospital in Denver, in addition to his efforts on behalf of the New Orleans community. Heller's leaving at this time was truly "inconceivable," and if those in attendance did not understand, it was their loss. "If the Conference punishes that sort of a stand, so much the worse for the Conference," he concluded. Heller would have to depend on Stolz and Henry Cohen, his closest friends, to build support at the Conference without him.[53] Loyalty to his community, to those depending on his personal commitment to their needs, superseded his desire for prestige and national recognition.

As in the Emanu-El situation several years earlier, Heller chose to remain true to his inner convictions. And once again, the issue of Zionism threatened to become a stumbling block. In the fall of 1909, it was the potential conflict between Heller's presidency and his leadership role in the FAZ that perturbed Heller's supporters. Stolz worried that, among those favoring Heller, an issue would be made not about his pro-Zionist views but about the propriety of allowing an officer of the FAZ to assume the presidency of the CCAR. These supporters claimed, Stolz wrote, that "in the eyes of the public the two principles: Reform and Zionism will be identified and that therefore you should forego holding any office or be[ing] active in the work of the Federation while you are Pres of the Conference." Stolz considered this compromise "perfectly reasonable." Like Stephen S. Wise, Stolz also expressed his concerns about Heller's articles in the *American Israelite* that were sympathetic to and respectful of traditional Jews and traditional Judaism. Stolz feared that Heller's words might be misconstrued to mean that he favored the "reactionary party" and thus that he might use his influence "against Reform," even though Stolz realized that what Heller was fighting was only "a certain brand of Reform." Heller appreciated his friend's concern but refused to follow Stolz's advice. "As to my reactionary tendencies," he retorted, "they reside in the imagination of the radicals in whose sides I may have been a thorn at times," the same men who wanted to "read me out of the ranks of Reform . . . because I am making war upon their unhistorical vagaries." He further justified his stance by recalling I. M. Wise's philosophical positions. If the CCAR were against Heller because of his critique of the assimilationist extremes to which Reform had moved, it should never have elected Wise the first president of the Conference, since he "was a good deal less radical than I am."[54]

Others in attendance at the Conference also kept Heller up to date on the political climate in New York, informing him that Stephen Wise's efforts against Heller had yielded "*very poor* success." Henry Cohen sent affectionate and humorous notes to Heller from the convention. "Don't worry," Cohen consoled his friend. "We would rather have you with your Zionism & counter-Ref. than Hirsch with his—damned if I know what & he doesn't know himself." Cohen also tried to make light of the situation. In a note to Heller the night before the election, he included a little verse parody of "The Charge of the Light Brigade": "Rabbis in front of me / Rabbis at back of me / Rabbis at side of me / Would vote for Heller / There's not to make reply / There's not to reason why / There's but to say Oh! My! / He's just the Feller!" Fortunately, the FAZ understood that Heller's success might depend on the Zionist organization's keeping a low profile during the CCAR conference, and the FAZ meeting was postponed. The Federation secretary at the time was Reform rabbi Joseph Jasin, who reassured Heller that he had deferred the meeting as a precaution, although he felt certain that Heller would be elected regardless. To Jasin, "it seemed best that every possible pretext should be removed."[55]

Finally, Heller's solid work and committed involvement in the CCAR overcame opposition from every quarter. He was elected president. After the election, he told Philadelphia friends that when someone had advised him that his victory depended on his "pledging neutrality for my administration, toward Zionism and radicalism," he had refused. He had claimed that he would rather "forego the office" than "forfeit my liberty."[56] Heller's decision to remain by Newman's deathbed certainly helped him maintain his outspokenness in New Orleans as well; the quarrel with the *Times-Democrat* over the Christmas Doll and Toy Fund occurred the following month. Had he been less loyal to his local obligations, he would have encountered a more hostile response. He had waged other battles earlier with the *Jewish Ledger,* and the Crescent City's Jewish press ignored his election.[57]

Heller balanced his heady intellectual life with his more prosaic duties as a congregational rabbi. While he was emerging from his cocoon of deliberation and was testing his new wings as a publicist for Zionism on the American scene, he actively increased his influence over his congregation and community. In 1912, Tulane University in New Orleans appointed him professor of Hebrew and Hebrew Literature. He began his tenure with three lectures to the faculty and students. His topics, "The Strength and Charm of the Hebrew Language," "The Extent and Variety of Hebrew Literature," and the "The Essayist-Philosopher of the Hebrew Renaissance," neatly showcased his erudition, his pride in Jewish heritage, and his enthusiasm for the rebirth of Hebrew as a living language— a consequence of Zionism. His status as a member of the university faculty undoubtedly pleased his congregants, whether or not they agreed with his Zionism.[58]

In spite of the often conflicting expectations of his southern, Zionist, and Reform Jewish constituencies, Heller worked to maintain his intellectual and ideological independence. His need for stability and order pulled him in one direction, while his desire to break loose pushed him in another; his passionate support for issues close to his heart, therefore, was pockmarked by tension and ambivalence. In a telling passage to Stolz, he defended the restraint he had exercised as a Zionist. He claimed that he had never crammed his "convictions down unwilling throats . . . never discussed Zionism when a guest in some pulpit or even in my own except at the time when I opposed it." From Heller's perspective, his Zionism never had threatened his relationship with the *American Israelite.* The latter claim was an exaggeration, but he meant to flaunt his fair-mindedness before his non-Zionist friend. Heller's two terms as CCAR president while he served as FAZ honorary vice president provided a model for future American Jewish leaders seeking recognition for mainstream leadership while espousing unpopular causes.[59]

To keep his equilibrium, Heller constantly needed to check the tautness of the tightrope he walked. Even then, agitation from both Zionist and Reform colleagues tended to counter his best efforts to assert mutuality of interests and to achieve harmony among all sectors of the American Jewish community. While Heller refused to remain neutral in regard to his Zionism, prominent Zionists, like Louis Lipsky, the editor of the *Maccabaean*, belittled the Reform movement to which Heller owed his first allegiance. Lipsky felt no need to make an exception for Reform Zionists when the majority of the American Reform leaders had worked to eliminate Zionism "from every Jewish thing it has been interested in." In Lipsky's view, Zionist Reform rabbis, "by their ineffective presence and adherence," passively supported the CCAR and the artifacts of the Conference. He considered attacks on Reform Judaism to be a siege against "the enemy en bloc," and he believed that Reform rabbis should "dissociate themselves" from anti-Zionist organizations. As a borer from within, Heller, along with other less strident non-Reform Zionists, took the opposite view. In reprimanding Lipsky, FAZ president Harry Friedenwald explained that while Zionists might appropriately condemn "anti-Zionistic principles," the Zionist cause could not be furthered by alienating Reform rabbis and making their "allegiance to our movement more difficult than it already is."[60]

Goaded by naysayers on either side of him, Heller redoubled his journalistic efforts to reach out to both Reform and Zionist audiences simultaneously. His assumption of the CCAR presidency initiated his most productive period—in the pulpit, in the press, and in the forefront of American Reform Judaism. As in the preelection controversy with Stephen S. Wise, however, alliances tended to be both situational and mercurial. While Jewish leaders might perceive a need for unity over an issue, such as the resistance to discriminatory immigration laws, the tactics employed by each group varied widely and sometimes directly contradicted the efforts of another coalition.

In dealing with anti-immigrationists, the positions turned on the question of Jewish identity. In January 1909, at a UAHC meeting, Zionists and anti-Zionists struggled over a resolution requesting that the immigration authorities remove the word "Hebrew" from its list of possible immigrant nationalities.[61] The following January, Simon Wolf, a prominent Jewish attorney and spokesperson, actively fought the efforts of Senator Henry

Cabot Lodge and others by arguing that Jews constituted a people and not a race, even though the definition of "race" lacked the distinctiveness later ascribed to it.[62] Wolf's anti-Zionism was integrally linked to his feeling that those "racial" attributes ascribed to Jews resulted from "religious teaching and prescription, rules and regulations" rather than from any biological factors. He believed that the anti-immigrationists were manipulating a racial definition of Jewish identity as a weapon to restrict Jewish immigration, and he contended that, rather than denying Jewish "racial affinities," he was denying "the right of the government to discriminate." His underlying concern was that Zionists, in promoting national over religious identity for Jews, would inadvertently play directly into the hands of the immigration restrictionists.[63]

Heller also attacked individuals who opposed immigration, and he implicitly agreed with Wolf. The following year, in his presidential address to the CCAR, Heller spoke of religion as the "raison d'être of the Jew" and insisted that, in arguing for Jewish rights and citizenship here and abroad, Jews should be seen as "representatives of a religion." But while Wolf's central focus was access to rights in America and elsewhere, Heller's agenda went further. He wanted to ensure the survival of Jews as a distinct group. He returned to the theme of salvation he had enunciated a decade earlier and insisted that Zionism alone could save Jews from the twin threats of "racial dissolution" and "loss of individuality."[64]

Heller basically concurred with Horace Kallen's views, expressed in "The Ethics of Zionism," which appeared in the *Maccabaean* four years earlier: "If it is the Jew's right to survive, and Zionism asserts it is, it is his right by the vigor of his achievement and the effectiveness of his ideals." Kallen also discussed the physical attributes of the Jewish race that have survived, seeing both spiritual and physical aspects of a noteworthy "gift of resistance . . . , the physiological counterpart of the spiritual fervor we have found to characterize the Jewish race." For him, the anti-Semite was one who perceived the race struggle as the basic fact of social life and allowed "prejudice rather than wisdom to guide him in its prosecution." Interestingly, Kallen selected the South as the one American environment in which Jewish identity seemed most endangered. He focused in particular on "chameleon Jews," who "turn the color of their particular environments" but "remain the same chameleon under these many skins." Heller's concern, like Kallen's, remained "spiritual self-assertion."[65]

In his opening message as CCAR president at the twenty-first annual conference at Charlevoix, Michigan, the following June, Heller summarized the themes of his leadership and the central principles on which he acted in all realms of his professional life. He began by defending Reform Judaism in the context of the Enlightenment-engendered "current of liberation" against those who saw the movement merely as a "gospel of convenience." He directly confronted the issue of Zionism, stressing, as always, the reconciliation of Reform and Zionism. Tolerating antireligious Zionists no more than anti-Zionist Reform Jews, Heller emphasized the need for Jews to work together to combat "religious indifference" and the need to look past the conflict between Reform Judaism's "mission" and Zionism's nationalism.[66] In his passion for rapprochement, however, he failed to specify any way of attaining mutuality, even though his CCAR presidency personified the reconciliation of the two tenets he held dear— the necessity for Reform's revisionist approach to Jewish tradition in a modern world and the immutability of Zionism's claims for the continuity of Jewish identity. Max Raisin, a Reform rabbinical colleague, and an ardent Zionist, had published a similar, although far more terse, statement of the compatibility of the two movements in an article, "Reform Rabbis and Zionism," in the March 1910 issue of the *Maccabaean*. He concluded bluntly, "One thing, Reform surely is not: It is not a Mosaic ordinance from Sinai." Like Heller, Raisin placed his Jewish identity above his identity as a Reform Jew. Raisin was then serving as rabbi of a congregation in Meridian, Mississippi, although he spent most of his later career in New York.[67]

Reelected as CCAR president in 1911, Heller continued to use his weekly column in the *American Israelite* to voice his concerns over issues other than Zionism, while he used the *Maccabaean*'s pages to bridge the chasm that most Zionists and most Reform Jews perceived between the two movements. His writing was more direct and coherent in his *Maccabaean* essays, where he had the freedom to explore the identity crisis that he saw at the heart of the modern Jewish experience. Although Heller continued to write for the *American Israelite*, he still argued with Leo Wise about Zionism. Wise said, for example, that although he did not want to "dictate" to Heller by saying "Thou shalt," Wise felt that he could say " 'thou shalt not' . . . The columns of the 'Israelite' are not the place for propaganda of Zionism or adverse criticism of the leaders of our cause [Reform Judaism]."[68]

In "Zionism and the Mission," Heller moved to the position that dominated his mature career. He argued that Zionism signified the "mission of Judaism." This overarching ideal fueled his activism and gave him energy to pursue a "translation of the monotheistic idea into social righteousness." Henry Hurwitz, editor of the *Menorah Journal*, responded to this article by telling Heller, "I use your Zionist articles . . . (would only there were more of them!) to stir and persuade the doubting ones among my friends." Heller also rejected the views of many of his contemporary Reform colleagues, who viewed America as the Jewish ideal or who posited "a blending of Americanism and Judaism." He believed that the Reform movement needed Zionism as an antidote to the excessive idolatry of occidentalism. Zionism could remind American Jews that they were wrong in trying to make "Judaism small and Americanism great." Only Zionism could "free American Judaism from this incubus."[69]

By now Heller had successfully integrated the prophetic ideal into his sense of self. He sounded like a true Progressive in his belief that the tools of enlightened humanity could be used to solve the problems plaguing society. If the central tenet of progressivism was a belief in the ultimate perfectibility of humankind, then the creation of a Jewish state was the means of achieving that goal. Like Theodore Roosevelt, Heller employed images of masculinity almost obsessively when he addressed the problem of group or self-assertiveness. And for Heller, "manliness" and "manhood" also corresponded to arrival at the center of his own soul. Being a Zionist meant securing "the courage of one's inborn Jewish manhood to revitalize the body of Jewish nationality for the reinvigoration and the self-fulfillment of the Jewish spirit."[70] Although the creation of a Zionist state appeared to be a "distant vision" in 1911, the World War I era moved the target into the foreground and gave Heller the opportunity to demonstrate his "manly courage" in active pursuit of this dream.

CHAPTER VIII

❧❧❧

Mandate for "Moral Courage: American Ideals in the Light of Judaism"

Max Heller's belief that rational solutions could be found for any social problem colored every proposal he initiated or supported. He was very much a man of his time, a Progressive in spirit and in deed. Unlike those Reform rabbis who looked to Protestant theologians such as Walter Rauschenbusch and Washington Gladden for leadership in the area of social reform, Heller found ample inspiration in Judaism for the pursuit of social justice.[1] The same passion for social justice that underscored his commitment to the tenets of reform animated his Zionism and unified all his endeavors into a seamless whole. Jewish nationalism fueled his soul and created a field of energy that allowed him to move from one sphere of work to another with integrity and inner direction. Although Heller's "Judaicization" often led him to pursue social criticism beyond the limits imposed by southern white and middle-class norms, and to do so mainly on behalf of Zionism and justice for African Americans, he continued to position himself at the forefront of elite civic reform leadership on most issues. The pace and scope of his activism rapidly accelerated in the years leading up to the Great War.

Certain recurrent themes ran through Heller's Progressive ventures. Health was one of them. He worried and often commented on his own rather delicate health. His chronic severe hay fever was exacerbated by the heat and humidity of New Orleans. Tuberculosis had afflicted both his mother and his oldest sister. Cecile, his older daughter, suffered from severe diabetes, while Isaac, his younger son, walked with a limp after a bout of polio. Heller visited J. H. Kellogg's famous Battle Creek Sanitarium with Isaac and preached the blessings of healthful eating to those back home. Hoping that Heller might interest several of the "millionaires" in his congregation to contribute to Kellogg's enterprise, the health promoter remarked that Jews had done more for the "sanitary welfare of the world" than any other people, that civilized nations for 2,000 years had benefited from the "sanitary laws of Moses." Heller probably did not respond to the plea, since he was soliciting funds for Touro Infirmary at the time. He also worked hard to raise money for the National Jewish Hospital for Consumptives in Denver and later served on the board of directors.[2]

Given Heller's obsessive concerns with his own health and the public health issues that perpetually plagued New Orleans, it was natural for him to crusade to eliminate the city's sanitation problems. The aftermath of the 1897 yellow fever epidemic found the city's residents particularly aroused. Two years later, Heller and other ministers used their pulpits to promote a sewerage and drainage ordinance. In a letter to the editor of the *Times-Democrat*, Heller defended the ministry's action, arguing that the appeal had sought to arouse the "civic conscience" rather than to allow "the pocket" to decide. Civic action earned kudos from the Jewish community. The local YMHA paper, the *Owl*, commented on Heller's "public spirited earnestness" in waging the war for better sewerage and quoted Heller's lament, that "we shall always be mentioned in the same breath with Havana, until we shall have remedied this deficiency in which we may soon stand utterly alone, even among the fifth-rate cities of the United States." When the American Public Health Association met in New Orleans in 1902, Heller could boast to those assembled that the city that served as the "gateway of a continent" had triumphed over "adverse circumstances" of its "maligned climate" to reduce the death rate through better sanitation. And when the city did take a more forthright look at yellow fever in 1905, Heller appreciated the new reign of "absolute truthfulness." He remembered that in the 1897 epidemic, New Orleans citizens did not take sufficient precautions because the business community had consciously downplayed the extent of the devastation.[3]

Closely aligned with Heller's concern for improved health care was his desire to sanitize the city's physical and moral environment. He moved from advocating a modern sewerage facility to working for larger environmental issues. At one point, for example, his interest in minimizing the city's waste problems and improving the physical environment led him to meet and then correspond with a Chicago paper mill executive in hopes of interesting the firm in using recycled New Orleans newspapers, but the project evidently proved too ambitious. Heller then advocated mandatory drivers' licenses, believing that "unfailing identification" implied "personal responsibility" that would guard the public against "the reckless automobilist."[4]

Heller's preoccupation with moral issues began but did not end with criticism of congregants for emphasizing materialism over spirituality and idealism in the conduct of their daily affairs. In 1909, his concern with the question of local prostitution prompted him to send Frank D. Chretien, a judge of the Orleans Parish Criminal District Court, a book that sought to blame the "moral turpitude" of Europe on the presence there of legalized prostitution. Chretien replied that since laws in the parish neither legalized nor prohibited prostitution, the institution was tolerated. The judge believed that only if laws licensing "houses of plea-sure" were applied "rigidly, honestly & forcibly" would they "lessen the evil." That the police, on the other hand, might be more likely to apply them arbitrarily and "with favoritism" would only exacerbate the situ-ation. Chretien suggested that churches could more effectively combat "dissipation & debauchery" through the education and elevation of "the moral character of the community."[5]

When the American Purity Congress (APC) met in New Orleans in 1910, with Heller and Catholic archbishop James H. Blenk as two of the featured local speakers, the city's character became a major topic of con-tention. At the time, New Orleans and San Francisco were both bidding to host the upcoming Panama Exposition. The APC censured the two cit-ies, declaring them morally unfit, since each maintained a "segregated [red light] district." Although both cities were otherwise natural com-petitors for the prestigious exposition, the APC passed a resolution rec-ommending that the first to wipe out its red light district be given pref-erence as the host city. In its original form the resolution stated that the APC would petition the U.S. Congress to grant the Exposition to neither city unless their "cesspools of iniquity" were wiped out. Heller substi-tuted a statement that did not mention a petition to Congress. While the committee had a right to pass resolutions, he believed that congressmen would have trouble determining which city was purer. Heller rephrased the resolution to state simply that "in their present moral conditions, both San Francisco and New Orleans are wholly unfit to entertain the Panama Exposition." The APC adopted the resolution, which had been seconded by a local minister, with Heller's wording. The local press lauded his ef-forts, claiming that he had rescued New Orleans in proposing a compro-mise that rejected the role of Congress but "still left New Orleans in the San Francisco class, which was bad enough."[6]

The question of Jewish prostitution proved more difficult for Heller to confront. In 1909, *McClure's Magazine* had done an exposé on New York's Lower East Side brothels, and articles in the national Jewish press ex-pressed concern over the significant number of Jewish prostitutes, espe-cially in New York. Heller became squeamish, however, when Judge Henry Dannenbaum, a Zionist friend in Texas, made public statements mentioning the problem of Jewish white slavery. Heller felt that Dannen-baum's charges, "uncorroborated by any official statistics," were "only too liable to 'put a sword into the hands of our enemies.' " Dannenbaum responded pointedly, "Have you ever walked along the brilliantly lighted streets of New York or Chicago at midnight and observed what race is manifestly in the majority among the street solicitors, have you ever can-vassed the restricted district of your own city to see what race is rela-tively the largest represented as well as the most active in pursuing busi-ness . . . ? There is more to be said on the subject, but it is not pleasant to think about." Heller did not reply.[7]

In his formal remarks at the APC convention, the rabbi interjected a favorite theme, a "plea for moral courage." As societal changes made un-healthy temptations more easily accessible, Heller recognized that self-discipline and moderation became increasingly valuable assets in com-bating self-indulgence. He used this argument repeatedly in advocating temperance instead of prohibition. Although the latter was generally a favorite hobbyhorse of southern Protestant Progressives, the rabbi called prohibition a "species of intolerance and oppression, an insult to moral manhood." In an article in the *Texas Jewish Herald,* Heller admitted that a rabbi had to show "moral courage" in his discussion of the liquor ques-tion. Any hint of advocacy of prohibition "would be certain to incur the personal enmity of friends whose business interests are identified with the opposite side"; by inveighing against prohibition, on the other hand, he might seem to be "the lackey who trims his preaching to suit the pock-ets of his members." Although this stand broke with southern Progres-sives, who strongly favored the measure, it matched that of other Ameri-can Jews.[8]

Alcoholism was foreign to most Jewish families, Heller suggested, not because of religious prohibitions but because Judaism promoted temper-ance in its "positive training of moderation" and its emphasis on a "God-fearing life" to control "the lower appetites." Heller blamed puritanical fanaticism for the flourishing of the saloon in American society, and he considered it the responsibility of the "Jewish pulpit" to "warn against the futile attempt of legislating men into temperance." Not only did he regard legal measures as paternalistic infringements on personal free-dom, but he believed that such restrictions would lower "the standards of moral manhood," that only "inward, individual restraints of the moral will" could overcome excess. Fanaticism, he maintained, tinged those who lobbied for prohibition. Although he predicted that this "moral wave" would "rise into a flood of hypocrisy" where vice would "flourish the more grossly under pious cloaks," he believed that the American public would not long tolerate this "frenzy of faith" and would awaken from the bout of "intoxications to resume the path of sobriety and self-control." Heller never mentioned his own drinking habits, but wine plays a prominent role in Jewish ceremonies.[9]

While he promoted moral restraint in dealing with alcoholic beverages, Heller advocated an aggressive campaign to control gambling. He never explained why he believed that one vice could be checked by self-discipline while the other required governmental regulation. Just as he had fought the Louisiana Lottery in the 1890s, a quarter of a century later he condemned racetrack gambling as the "most stupendous gambling machine put forth in the South" since the defeat of the Lottery. In 1916, he scathingly attacked the state government by pointing out the duplicity in its antigambling raids. Some weeks earlier, a state militia had been mobilized to raid several small "gambling resorts" on the west bank of the Mississippi across from New Orleans, while the racetrack, "fathered by business men of standing," thrived, wreaking more devastation in the homes and careers of New Orleanians in one hour than the small establishments would have created in a year. He begged his congregants to spearhead an effort to "sweep this unclean gambling den out of our sight" and to place the good name of the city "above the unclean dollar, with the invisible tears of women and children clinging to it."[10]

Even when not out crusading on moral issues with other ministers, Heller kept his garden of alliances with non-Jewish clergy well watered. In a "good neighbor" move, he furthered interfaith cooperation by offering the facilities of Temple Sinai to the First Presbyterian Church while the church was being repaired. First Presbyterian accepted and expressed its gratitude to Heller and his "noble people." Heller later spoke to a group at the church, as he proudly told his sons, "probably the first time in this city that a rabbi was asked to teach a Protestant Bible Class." He did not confine interfaith cooperation to the middle-class white community, however. In the evening of the day that he taught the Bible class, he planned to give a lecture on Booker T. Washington at a local African American church. In 1902, he also joined several other prominent clerics and citizens, including Bishop David Sessums of the Episcopal Archdiocese and Professor James H. Dillard of Tulane University, in conducting an unofficial and independent inquiry into the grievances of striking local carmen. According to Bishop Sessums, the committee members did not offer themselves as mediators but banded together in the interest of the "convenience, safety and welfare of the community" and hoped that the information gleaned from the strikers "might be used to ease the situation."[11]

Heller's progressivism both preceded and mirrored a larger social justice movement within Reform Judaism. For many years he had preached and editorialized against an excessive materialism that put a premium on competition with a flagrant disregard for those who were not equal to the race. In the era of the Spanish-American War, he cautioned against imperialist bombast that nominally promised "civilizing protection" while "relieving" the "backward races" of "unworked wealth in the shape of forests, mines and other productive resources." Although his humanitarian concern was genuine, Heller, like other Progressives, often viewed the plight of his "weaker brothers" through a lens tinted by noblesse oblige. He believed that no nation could remain "morally sound" that did not "remember its duty toward the weak." In 1904, his Yom Kippur sermon, "Doing and Loving," included a section on workplace relationships. He asked the members of his congregation to put themselves in the place of those with whom they dealt. He hoped to prod his wealthy congregants to question the ethics of their day-to-day behavior, whether or not they appreciated his judgment. First he addressed businessmen directly, wondering whether they were protecting their customers with the same "jealous care" that they used to safeguard themselves. Then he shifted to manufacturers and inquired whether they treated those who worked for them as men or as "the kind of machine which is replaced without cost." He questioned whether other employers took advantage of their employees or deadened their ambition "by cutting off all hope of advancement." And he did not forget the domestic workers, mostly black, employed by many householders in the congregation. He asked the "mistress" of the household whether she dealt justly with the woman looking after her family. Alternatively, Heller asked, "is all your life one frantic dance about the devouring, never-sated idol of your selfishness?"[12]

The first national religious institutional response to progressivism occurred in 1908, when the Federal Council of the Churches of Christ in America adopted a platform that called for humanitarian measures in the workplace, including abolition of child labor, protection of workers from dangerous machinery and occupational hazards, and regulation of the conditions under which women worked. Another two years intervened before the CCAR, in 1910, responded to similar concerns while Heller served as president of the Conference. That year, the CCAR created the Committee on Synagogue and Labor to deal with the plight of the Jewish workingman. Although no issues were resolved immediately, and the rabbinical conference was torn between those who wanted to limit the discussion of social problems and those who wanted to commit themselves to overriding principles, social justice had moved from the rhetoric of the 1885 Pittsburgh Platform to heated debate on the floor of the conference itself.[13]

From early in his career, Heller had involved himself in organizations that sought to prevent child labor and cruelty to children, and in 1909, when the CCAR recognized the significance of the problem of child labor, he dedicated a column in the *American Israelite* to the issue. In Louisiana, he noted, Jews had been "well to the fore" among those "ardent humanitarians" who supported the women's movement and promoted child labor legislation. Heller's support of such legislation, however, went beyond his concern for children's physical, intellectual, and emotional development. He understood that eliminating child labor would raise adult wages and that a better educated, better paid citizenry would have "beneficent social consequences."[14]

While Heller often voiced his concern for the workers and chided employers to treat their employees fairly, only rarely in his campaigns for social betterment did he concentrate on labor issues. In the spring of 1911, for example, he worked to get a Mardi Gras holiday for a local union of retail clerks. Two years later, he served on the CCAR's Commission on Social Justice. The Commission investigated several areas—including child labor, housing reform, the regularization of industry (meaning the even distribution of work throughout the year to minimize unemployment in seasonal industries) and the right of labor organization—but it was not yet ready to suggest a practical program. Heller dissented, refused to sign the report, and turned in a minority report of his own. He branded the Commission's report inadequate because it was filled with statements that "skim the surface" and neither inform nor illuminate. He wanted a "practical survey" to replace what he considered "a sermon." And he suggested that the Conference more directly attack the social problems identified, first by issuing "a clear indictment of existing wrongs," then by agreeing upon "guiding principles" to deal with the "separate evils," and finally by using these principles to undergird a thorough analysis of the situation. These steps would lead logically to a practical solution. In 1916, the following year, Heller told Isaac, his son, then at Harvard Law School, that the young man should consider himself fortunate to be circulating among the great legal minds of the country, including William Howard Taft and Louis D. Brandeis. Rabbi Heller was especially impressed with Brandeis, whom he regarded as "*the* supreme Jew of this country." Heller deemed Brandeis's "work on behalf of the laboring classes . . . *the* summit of legal service."[15]

A muckraking article in the March 1913 issue of *McClure's* provoked Heller's sole investigative campaign into the relationship between capitalists and producers, a campaign that only concerned labor tangentially. In Heller's estimation, journalist Burton Hendricks had begun his series of articles to prove his contention that "in the next hundred years the Semitic influence [in business] is likely to be almost preponderating in the United States." Heller was outraged, worried that loose statements and statistical exaggerations would fuel the already strong nativist and anti-immigrant sentiment in the nation. He circulated the article and a personal letter to key figures he knew in various enterprises throughout the country, seeking objective confirmation of his views. Jewish preponderance, he felt, had surely been overstated. Interestingly, Jews who responded to Heller's circular politely took him to task. Much to his surprise, although none necessarily agreed with Hendricks's manipulation of statistical evidence, they found his interpretations and generalizations generally accurate. Writing from Savannah, M. B. Suskind told Heller not to waste his time trying to disprove Hendricks, because as far as "legitimate drama, vaudeville and moving picture business" were concerned, Suskind found that "Jewish influences largely control," although he saw nothing in that statement "to be sensitive or tender over." A New York realtor told Heller that he believed 80 percent of the buildings erected in the greater New York area had been built by Jewish builders or by corporations controlled by Jews. Jews' interest was primarily in real estate speculation—in acquiring and selling property "as fast as they possibly can" and frequently returning it "to Gentiles."[16]

Anti-Semitism was sufficiently real during the Progressive era to make Heller examine each incident critically, then vigorously fight the spread of racist discrimination and hatred. But definitions of "race," so loosely employed in the first decades of the twentieth century, could be used simultaneously by Zionists to promote Jewish nationalism and unity and by Jew baiters to stereotype all Jews as a degenerate "unmixed" race with universally pernicious and easily identifiable characteristics. Count Arthur de Gobineau, the French racial theorist, in his influential *Essay on the Inequality of Races,* sought to explain all history on a racial basis. Although he saw the whites as superior, he believed that white, yellow, and black—the three major racial divisions—had to be mixed to achieve "a truly great civilization" and that only "race hybrids" could be "civilized at all." Heller was obviously trying to indicate that Jews were "hybrid" in the best sense. He had to avoid the extremes of the "mixed" argument, however, because if it were carried too far, one would encounter the negative epithet "mongrel race," which was also hurled at Jews. Heller doubted whether another "race or nation" had historically been subjected to such an accumulation of sweeping generalizations. He refuted them one by one. While some non-Jews thought that all Jews were wealthy like the Rothschilds, he observed, others conjured up images of the medieval "wandering Jew," the penniless peddler who traveled from village to village. Even though Jews were often said to be born businessmen, the majority of Jews in the United States in 1908, according to Heller, were laborers, and a minority was beginning to enter the professions, especially journalism, theater, and music.[17] Some Jews promoted and profited from capitalism; others denounced the bourgeoisie and staunchly supported socialism. After arguing that a diversity of occupations and ideologies existed among Jews, Heller switched his discussion to physical characteristics, asserting that here too no single Jewish "type" prevailed. In fact, he considered Jews to be the "most mixed of all races," and students of "racial physiognomy" might find among Jews "every facial type—Egyptian . . . , Italian, German, Anglo-Saxon, Slavic . . . , Tartar—even negroid in rare instances." All bore the "imprint of their native country far more than any mutual resemblance as members of the same race," a strong verification of the "plastic adaptiveness" of the people.[18]

Heller sent a copy of this essay, "Promiscuous Generalizing about the Jew," to his friend Henry Cohen, in Galveston. Cohen agreed wholeheartedly with Heller's observations and, in his letter, included a brief sociological overview of Jewish occupations in his city. Cohen found that the majority of Galveston's Jewish males were dockworkers, although among other occupations he mentioned a couple of pawnbrokers, a banker, a theater owner, three cotton brokers, and a steamship agent. "In fact," Cohen concluded, "we are nearly, if not exactly like other people—not all black: not all white, but grey." Under most circumstances, Cohen tended to underplay the issue of anti-Semitism, probably because he found relatively little of it operating in Galveston, where Jews served as presidents of many secular and business-related institutions. He saw no social ostracism even in social clubs and organizations and, in fact, denied that any existed "throughout the whole South."[19]

Philo-Semitism, in fact, thrived in the Bible Belt. In 1907, while Heller and his family vacationed in Bay St. Louis, on the Mississippi Gulf coast, a local reporter wrote about his conversations with "the learned Doctor." Having gleaned much from his visits, the reporter discussed Jewish diversity in historical perspective, then admonished those who sought to revile "God's chosen race" through negative stereotypes of sharp business practices allegedly predominant among Jews. "But the Jew is tricky! Is he?" the journalist asked, then went on to demolish the negative Jewish archetype. "Were you ever taken in by a Methodist preacher on a real estate deal or a horse trade? Did you ever get in close quarters with a

Presbyterian elder in a speculation," or "buy mining stock from an Episcopalian broker," or "find lard in the butter sold by a New England
Puritan?" Heller's admirer concluded by praising universal brotherhood
and denouncing anti-Semitism as "un-Christian, inhuman, un-American."[20]

As Heller worked to counteract negative stereotypes about Jews, his
own stereotypes about women changed. His perception of the role of
women expanded significantly from his narrow belief in the 1890s that
women needed to concentrate on making their homes more reflective of
Jewish values. Although he still regarded the home, and the traditional
Jewish woman's place in it, as central, by 1903, he advocated more liberal
goals for the "gentler sex." In a sermon titled, "Woman in the World and
at Home," Heller praised the United States for offering great opportunities for women. Then, citing the presence of queens, judges, prophetesses,
and heroines in the Bible, he claimed that Jewish tradition gave women
"a right to enter upon every higher career." He couched his remarks in
the sexist phraseology of the time, however, when he added that women
always existed who were "gifted with masculine courage, masculine
logic, masculine force and determination." But he did not entirely short-
circuit his argument. "Shall we leave strong minds undeveloped?" he
asked. Invoking the progressive spirit of the period, he used language
similar to that employed when he addressed African American audiences: "Shall we trample upon brave hearts by denying them their right-
ful heritage in the grand upward struggle?"[21]

Heller early recognized the rising current that would sweep in women's
suffrage when he noted that "once we have placed the finely tempered
steel of education into women's hands we have put it beyond our power
to keep them out of the arena of public debate in which the oppressed
will obtain a hearing." In 1903, Heller sent a copy of his recent sermon
"Woman in the World and at Home" to the editor of the *Woman's Journal*,
who responded that since Heller's views reflected those of the editors
in advocating equal suffrage, he took "the liberty of republishing the discourse" in the journal's columns. He thanked the rabbi for his "valuable
contribution to the literature of the Suffrage Movement." The following year, Kate M. Gordon, a New Orleans resident who served as corre-
sponding secretary for the National American Woman Suffrage Association, asked Heller whether Temple Sinai could host a lecture featuring
Charlotte Perkins Gilman, a "distinguished poet, preacher and philosopher" who would be visiting the city. Gordon mentioned that Gilman's
lecture would not emphasize suffrage as much as "social uplift," since
her creed was "human work as an expression of human energy." Noted

11. *The Heller children, from left to right: Ruth, Cecile, Isaac, and James, circa 1914. Courtesy of Edward M. Heller and Theo M. Heller.*

speakers who brought the "best elements" of the New Orleans interdenominational community to Temple Sinai for such prestigious events would undoubtedly have pleased both the Sinai board and its general membership by placing the temple in the forefront of New Orleans's Progressive community. Herman Weil, president of the Temple Sinai board in 1916, sent Heller a note with the names of eleven prominent members, including himself, who had made contributions totaling $1,400 toward the rabbi's summer vacation. His spiritual leadership pleased them enormously. They expressed the hope that the time spent with his family would prove "restful and enjoyable."[22]

Finally, Heller advocated equality in the workplace when he resolved that men would have to make room for women "in the serious occupations of life." While he had always reflected normative Jewish values in praising the home as woman's special domain, Heller had come from a family of working women. In "Woman in the World and at Home," he could have been addressing his remarks to Ruth, his younger daughter, who in the following decade became a social worker, moved to New York City, and worked resourcefully there with Lillian Wald at the Henry Street settlement house. For someone like Heller, who had so much empathy for Jewish tradition and had touted the home as a sacred space for women, the most radical stand he took concerned the role of women in Reform Judaism. In 1922, he served on a committee, chaired by Henry Cohen, that formulated a statement expressing the CCAR's sentiment on the subject of ordination of women rabbis. The committee recognized that the question could not have arisen without the "evolution" of the woman's role in contemporary American life and concluded by declaring that "woman cannot justly be denied the privilege of ordination."[23]

As women fought for full citizenship rights, American Jews often felt compelled to justify their right to citizenship in an overwhelmingly Christian environment. The large influx of Jewish immigrants at the turn of the century triggered claims that the United States was a "Christian nation." As early as 1896, when the *Times-Democrat* editorialized in favor of inserting a statement into the Constitution of the United States recognizing Christianity, Heller took the offensive. In language reminiscent of Tocqueville's warning about the tyranny of the majority, Heller reminded the editor that "the power of majorities to impose their wishes upon minorities should not extend, in a free government, to the authoritative imposition of opinions and beliefs." He praised secular separation of church and state as one of the characteristics that made him proud to be an American, and he claimed that the proposed amendment would benefit no one and would only alienate those patriotic Jewish citizens who otherwise felt devoted to their country's well-being. He prayed that "merciful Providence" would "shield us from fanatics who would drag religion into politics."[24]

But as the number of Eastern and southern Europeans at the turn of the century increased, transforming the ethnic demography of the United States, nativist efforts to establish the essentially Anglo-Saxon and Christian character of the nation gained political momentum. One of the central battlegrounds targeted for pressing the Christian agenda was the public school. In 1906, the *Times-Democrat* informed the citizens of New Orleans that the Protestant Ministers' Association backed Bible reading in the schools and reminded the public of the terms of John McDonogh's generous bequest to the city's schools. McDonogh, a local antebellum philanthropist, had stipulated in his will that, in the "Free Schools" that he endowed, the "poor . . . of both sexes and all classes and castes of color" would be admitted, "free of expense . . . , provided . . . that the Holy Bible . . . shall be . . . forever made use of . . . as one (and the principal one) of the reading or class books.' "[25]

McDonogh's instructions for religious education had been scrupulously ignored, and now, more than sixty years after his death, Catholic and Jewish ministers protested strongly. Heller believed that where secular and religious teaching was concerned, there were only two possibilities: either complete separation or complete religious "interpenetration." Furthermore, if the latter course was taken, the public school, instead of functioning as "the melting pot of nations, races and faiths" that produced the "most varied types . . . with the stamp of broad and enlightened Americanism," would be broken "into sectarian fragments." While the needs of the Jewish child could not be served by teaching "equal reverence for the Old and New Testament," neither should the Christian child be forced to discriminate between the two. Finally, no matter how intelligent and skilled the faculty, none could be expected to approach religion with "absolute impartiality" or to teach the Bible "without any admixture of sectarian bias." As Christmas approached the following year, Heller wrote that although he realized that, for the majority of Americans, the holiday had lost most of its religious significance and had become "a mere social jollification," he genuinely wished that the "common man" found Christmas more meaningful and that the "lesson of peace and good will" went deeper. On the other hand, he also preferred to see "the Christmas exercise" confined to the religious school, "where it properly belongs." In closing, he acknowledged that it appeared as if some people were waging "an aggressive fight . . . on behalf of sectarian instruction" in public schools. He warned that if it continued, such militance might call for "determined resistance" by those who championed public education "as a meeting-ground of sects and classes." Heller struck a conciliatory note in his final sentence, however: "fortunately," no confrontation of that kind seemed "impending in our own genial Southland." The same article also quoted Leucht's remark that "to sing about Santa Claus, to dance around a Christmas tree, and to make and receive little Christmas presents is all right." But Leucht did not want school celebrations to go beyond this point.[26]

Perhaps sensitive to the Protestant belief that Jewish opposition to Bible reading was antireligious, Heller later slightly modified his position. In 1924, when the issue of Bible reading in public schools once again gained prominence, Heller still firmly spoke against any form of prayer in school. Now, however, he felt that the CCAR should participate in seeking conferences to select "fit parts of the Bible" for public school reading. Perhaps the religious backlash of the 1920s helped to change Heller's opinion, or perhaps he was pragmatically realizing that some Bible reading was bound to occur and that the rabbis should try to cooperate in choosing readings they deemed "constructive." Jewish interests were not served by appearing inherently antireligious.[27]

When the CCAR met in Philadelphia in the summer of 1909, the rabbis responded to the report of a committee that had been appointed to analyze the "interference of sectarianism with the principle of separateness between Church and State." Did those assembled consider the United States a Christian nation? In examining issues like Sunday laws and prayer and Bible reading in public schools, the rabbis recognized the tensions inherent in the "potent influence" exercised by the Christian majority. Heller made it a point to report to the *Daily Picayune* on his return to New Orleans, "The Jew feels that to call ours a Christian nation is to represent him as a perpetual alien to its civilization." He also warned against the danger of enthroning Christianity "in an authoritative relationship to the State," thereby threatening the principle of separation "fundamental to our civic welfare and to our essential democracy."[28]

While Heller reiterated the ideas that he had expressed earlier concerning Bible reading in the public schools, the issue remained open to debate. In 1914, while clergy were still battling over the specific language of the McDonogh will and Protestant ministers were protesting against the neglect of Bible reading in fulfillment of the demands of the document, an editorial in a local Jewish publication provided additional insight into the situation. The columnist acknowledged Heller as a battler against Bible reading, then analyzed the current dilemma, finding that "the same retaliatory denominationalism" and anti-Catholicism that prompted McDonogh remained solidly behind those pushing to uphold the "letter of the legacy." But the community had chosen to apply a looser interpretation. It had honored McDonogh's memory "by attributing to him the intent to bestow the broadest benefit" in education of the public rather than in promotion of Protestantism. Moreover, the writer conceded, if total compliance with the will had been followed, then many white children would have been denied proper training "in order to apply a large share to schools for negroes." Racism, not surprisingly, overrode religious niceties. He noted that none of the ministers had "appealed for such a redistribution" and concluded that they might best leave the matter "unagitated and undisturbed."[29]

With or without the peculiar New Orleans variant, the debate over religion in the public schools continued to be on the table at the CCAR conferences. In 1915, the rabbis considered various options that would permit students to get some religious or ethical training, on or off the campuses of public schools. Rabbi Samuel Schulman, who led the discussion, closed his remarks by reiterating the need for a "zealous watchfulness" of Jewish rights. But he also reminded those gathered that, as Americans upholding the "great ethical and spiritual traditions" of the nation, they needed to pursue a new policy. To promote the "moral and spiritual education" of the nation's citizenry might mean cooperating with "various movements" rather than merely criticizing their efforts. Heller protested vehemently, and reaffirmed his conviction that Zionism provided the only answer to the modern Jewish dilemma. He felt that church-state separation was constantly violated—in the cases of Sabbath observance, chaplaincies, and national religious holidays—and that religion increasingly suffused education, with the majority stamping "its individuality upon the customs, traditions and habits of the people." Only by identifying with the Zionist cause could an otherwise assimilating American Jewry hope to preserve its distinctive identity in the face of such a powerful onslaught. America, for all the opportunities offered its Jewish citizens, was still dominated by a Christian majority. Heller insisted that American Jews needed Palestine, a national historic homeland, to rekindle Hebraic culture and foster pride in Jewish identity. Schulman countered by arguing that Heller represented Zionist "despair." Speaking on behalf of an American Jewry that would not "subscribe to his [Heller's] ideas," Schulman suggested that a more positive goal for Jewish survival was the "eventual triumph" of the principle of separation of church and state in all countries.[30]

Issues of Jewish identity consistently colored any discussion of majority-minority status, whether or not anti-Semitism was directly involved. In addressing the problem of Jewish-gentile intermarriage, for example, Heller positioned himself as a strong opponent of what he considered a growing problem in a liberal society. He argued that his objection to intermarriage stemmed not from any "arrogant" belief in Jewish superiority but from his conviction that intermarriage had to be avoided "in the interest of the preservation of . . . [Jewish] religion and . . . race, using the latter term untechnically." In a country so dominantly Christian, he saw Judaism and Jewish culture assaulted continually by the "surrounding Christian atmosphere" that threatened both "the solidarity of Judaism and . . . the Jewish individuality." He believed that liberals who tolerated intermarriage tended to "undervalue the importance of religious conviction in shaping character." Heller practiced what he preached. When Cecile, his older daughter, fell in love with a non-Jewish man, the rabbi threatened to disown her if she married outside the faith. She ultimately found a Jewish husband.[31] Heller, like Theodore Roosevelt, worried about "racial suicide" and believed that intermarriage and assimilation ultimately resulted in a homogenization that would destroy the unique "racial types" that nurtured and strengthened American civilization.[32] Several years later, Heller likened Jewish social stratification to a pyramid, with the "diminishing top . . . continually breaking off through baptism and intermarriage." Ironically, to Heller, this "apostasy and union" of the upper classes was "tantamount to a revindication of Jewish capital," since he thought that a majority of that capital acquired by Jews became "dejudaized again" through intermarriage among the elites.[33]

Intermarriage was a fact of life in New Orleans, and although Rabbi Heller disapproved of Cecile when she contemplated marrying outside the faith, he had to be more liberal with his congregants. While he claimed that he would never officiate at a marriage not "sanctioned by both civil and Jewish law," once an intermarried couple became members of the congregation, he accepted them fully. In 1915, the rabbis of the three Reform congregations in New Orleans asked the boards of the Reform cemeteries to adopt a rule that permitted non-Jewish spouses to be buried alongside their mates. The previous year Heller also introduced the topic at the CCAR convention, with the proviso that no non-Jewish ceremonies be performed in connection with the funeral, that no non-Jewish symbols be carved upon the tombstone, and that there be "no violation of Jewish religious principles and sentiments."[34]

With large numbers of Eastern European Jews arriving yearly, it was not only (or simply) the "diminishing top" but the rapidly increasing base of the Jewish social pyramid that was becoming problematic for American Jewry. In 1907 at the peak of Jewish immigration, wealthy Jewish laymen, principally Jacob Schiff and Cyrus Sulzberger, believed that diverting incoming Jews to the port of Galveston might help diminish their concentration in New York. Schiff and Sulzberger thought that dispersal would also help derail nativism and anti-immigration efforts. Henry Cohen, with the monetary backing of I. H. Kempner, Galveston's most prominent Jewish citizen, was the key to the success of the Galveston Movement. Cohen predicted that, since the Jewish community favored the project and his "heart and soul" was in the work, it would succeed. He told Heller that Galveston's Jewish community (the "Yehudim" of the city)[35] was delighted that Galveston had been selected as the port of entry, although newly arriving Jews were not to remain in the city but would be transported to other Texas, southwestern, western, and midwestern communities where few Jews lived and the newcomers' labor would be welcome. "From the pier to the railroad station," Cohen confessed, was all that most would see of Galveston. The *New Orleans Item* supported the move and suggested that the South lagged behind other parts of the nation in industrial growth because the businessmen and industrial captains of the region had not promoted immigration. Since political and religious persecution seemed to be driving the Jews out of Eastern Europe and Germany, and Jewish philanthropists were diverting the immigrants to Texas, the editorialist hoped that some would immigrate directly through New Orleans as well, because the city could use an industrious element. "No people," he admitted, added more to the "wealth of the city."[36]

In a 1911 editorial in the *American Israelite*, Heller agreed with the principle of systematic distribution of immigrants. He even felt that the "colored problem" of the South could be resolved if "copious streams" of white immigrants entered the workforce. But New Orleans never became an additional port of entry, and not even the Galveston scheme worked out as Schiff had intended. Unlike their German coreligionists a half century earlier who spread themselves over the North American continent, most of the Eastern Europeans wanted to cluster in New York and other major cities of the Northeast and Midwest where a strong Jewish institutional support system and kinship networks could nurture and sustain them. By 1914, only 10,000 immigrants (approximately 1.2 percent) had chosen to enter the United States through the Texas Gulf port, and the movement was abandoned.[37]

Pro-immigration editorials seldom appeared in the general press, however, because nativist and racist sentiment outweighed other arguments. The efforts to stem the antirestrictionist tide made by American Jewish leaders like Simon Wolf proved insufficient when measured against the alleged threat to American social stability caused by the influx of so many newcomers who were thought to be racially inferior. While Theodore Roosevelt worried about diluting the Anglo-Saxon racial stock that he felt had given America its frontier-conquering strength, stronger appeals to overt racism and anti-Semitism made the former president's statements pale by comparison. Houston Stewart Chamberlain, an Englishman and the son-in-law of the German composer and arch-racist Richard Wagner, became so enamored of German metaphysics and music that he abandoned his British citizenship and declared himself a citizen of Germany. In the 1890s, be began to develop racial theories that, like those of his father-in-law, even sought to make Jesus into a Teuton, stating that "whoever makes the assertion that Christ was a Jew is either ignorant or insincere" or else simply wants "to curry favour with the Jews." In 1899, Chamberlain's most famous work, *Foundations of the Nineteenth Century*, was published in Germany and was widely distributed in many editions. In 1911, the English translation became available in the United States. While Roosevelt felt that a "queer vein of the erratic" marked a great deal of the work, he also found much that Chamberlain wrote to be "perfectly true . . . [and] emphatically worth considering." Coinciden-tally, that same year, the World's Congress of Races met in London, and the *American Hebrew* published several articles dealing with the "Jewish Problem." In "The Jewish Race and Its Problem," British author Israel Zangwill responded to a paper presented at the Congress by Ignaz Zoll-schan. Zangwill claimed that the "Jewish problem . . . springs exclusively from Christian or heathen injustice and intolerance, from the oppression of minorities, from the universal law of dislike for the unlike." Several months later, in response to Chamberlain, Zollschan contributed an ar-ticle of his own to the *American Hebrew*. He believed that the Jewish people were in the midst of a struggle between the poles of assimilation and nationalism. Those at the latter extreme were people desiring "the continued existence of the race . . . against the dissolving influences . . . [of] assimilation."[38]

An incident much closer to home cast an ominous shadow across the otherwise relatively sunny lot of southern Jewry. On Confederate Memo-rial Day in April 1913, Mary Phagan, a thirteen-year-old employee of the National Pencil Company in Atlanta, Georgia, was found murdered in the factory's basement. Suspicions fell almost immediately on Leo Frank, the young factory superintendent, who was the last person who admitted to having seen her alive. Although southern born, Frank had grown up and been educated in the North. As both a Yankee and a Jew, Frank ap-peared to be the quintessential outsider, culturally and economically, in the raw young metropolis filled with exploited working-class whites who had recently moved in from the country to seek work in Atlanta's bur-geoning mills and factories. Heller's first editorial in the *American Israel-ite* in 1913, "The Answer to Prejudice," seemed to presage the event. Hel-ler had considered the question "What shall we do . . . in answer to prejudice?" and responded that removing it seemed impossible while races and faiths remained "unbrotherly." Unfortunately, the Jew was a perennial target. As the "most unique of peoples," the Jew could not eas-ily escape the penalty of being eternally a stranger, "so long as, to the crude mind, to be strange means to arouse estrangement."[39]

Local journalists, including ex-Populist Thomas E. Watson, exploited the incident through sensationalist reporting that sought to establish Frank's guilt on the basis of prejudice unsupported by fact. One of Wat-son's columns included the following: "The next Leo Frank case in Geor-gia will never reach the Courthouse. THE NEXT JEW WHO DOES WHAT FRANK DID, IS GOING TO GET EXACTLY THE SAME THING THAT WE GIVE TO NEGRO RAPISTS."[40] The testimony of Jim Conley, the pencil factory's black janitor with a past record of petty

crimes, was most damaging because it implicated Frank as a sexual de-
viant. Solicitor General Hugh M. Dorsey, in charge of the state's case,
needed a conviction to promote his own career, and the conviction of a
Yankee Jew seemed to represent a more distinctive accomplishment than
the prosecution of an obscure black suspect like Conley. The media
aroused public sentiment against Frank. In addition, Frank's rather unattractive appearance and personality, and the defense attorneys' blun-
ders in handling the case, all damaged his cause. The jury did not take
long to convict him of murder and sentenced him to execution. A long
round of appeals followed, and the case, like the Dreyfus Affair, almost
immediately became a cause célèbre.[41]

Shortly after the trial, in the fall of 1913, Heller wrote a column in the
American Israelite that was sympathetic to Frank's defense, and Frank responded with a personal note of thanks. Frank hoped that articles on his
behalf would arouse the American public and "wear away the unreason-
able & unfair wall of prejudice & public animosity . . . so viciously . . .
reared against me." Frank felt that he "might as well have been tried by
the mob on the street," since the "spirit of the mob" had infected the
courtroom, and he hoped for a new trial. If justice were served, he believed he would surely be vindicated, and he thanked Heller for "words"
that tended to "mitigate the difficulty of our problem."[42]

No retrial was granted despite publicity like Heller's and the prodigious efforts coordinated by Louis Marshall and other leaders of the
American Jewish Committee (established in 1906) that spoke on behalf
of the national Jewish community "to prevent infringement of the civil
and religious rights of Jews." An enormous number of letters and peti-
tions to the governor of Georgia and to the Prison Commission pleaded
that Frank's sentence should be commuted to life imprisonment. Finally
in the spring of 1915, knowingly risking his political career, Governor
John M. Slaton inspected all evidence and detected a flaw in Conley's testimony. Despite letters that threatened his life and that of his wife, he
decided in favor of commutation. The governor declared that he could
not "stand the companionship of an accusing conscience." He intended
to grant Frank a full pardon as soon as the public could be persuaded to
view the event objectively. But mobs reacted by denouncing him as "King
of the Jews" and burning him in effigy, while others armed and marched
on his home north of Atlanta where state militiamen stopped them.[43]

In late June, Heller considered "Jewish aspects" of the Frank case in an
article for the *New Orleans American*. Heller compared the case to that
against Dreyfus in France and the more recent, though less familiar, trial
of Mendel Beilis in Russia. In the fall of 1913, not long after the Atlanta

jury found Frank guilty, a jury of Russian peasants had found Beilis innocent of the charges of ritual murder. Heller noted parallels of "unwarranted presumptions" of anti-Semitism in all three cases where Jews were looked upon as "peculiarly liable to inhuman and unnatural practices," the sort to be expected of a "species of fiends." But in what may have been a calculated effort to downplay the strength of southern prejudice, Heller denied that anti-Semitism was primary in the Frank case. Instead, he indicted "two conspicuously weak spots" in the American justice system. The first he called "the despotism of legal technicality"; the second was what he believed to be the "untrustworthiness of the jury system." That a "reasonable doubt . . . patently conceded" could not lead to a new trial because of legal technicalities seemed "shameful," while having a jury composed of men who yielded to the pressure of public excitement was a travesty. In discussing the Beilis case two years earlier, Heller had praised the Russians for the "moral virility" of the jurors. Now he asked who among the twelve jurors would have risked "ostracism, or even lynching" to save the life of a stranger. Only Slaton's courage "vindicated" American manhood. But Slaton's courage could not save Frank. In the aftermath of the Beilis case, Heller had wondered, rhetorically, whether Russia's Jews were clear of the scandal and the "dastardly" legend of ritual murder that had clung to them for centuries. But he realized that Jews could not shake themselves free of libel so easily; they still needed to defend themselves "against accusations which dispute our possession of the first elements of humanity." The Frank affair proved that America was not as exceptional as some Jews wanted to believe, even if anti-Semitism were secondary to the case. In July 1915, about two months after Slaton had commuted Frank's sentence, a mob dubbing itself the Knights of Mary Phagan stormed the prison, abducted Frank, and lynched him.[44] The Ku Klux Klan was revived shortly afterward.

In 1914, the *Jewish Immigration Bulletin* cited a column of Heller's that had been published in the *American Israelite* in which he discussed the supposed connection between the growth of U.S. anti-Semitism and the influx of Russian Jews that had begun in 1881 when Eastern European immigration began rising dramatically. Heller denied that a cause-and-effect relationship existed between the great numbers of recent arrivals with their "Russian costume and Ghetto habits" and the rise of anti-Jewish sentiment. Convinced that the anti-Semitic temper would have risen even if Russian Jews had never entered the United States en masse, he did not hold the less assimilated masses responsible. Heller pointed out that in the South and West, where Russian immigrants did not form a significant percentage of the Jews, anti-Semitism generally followed "the proportion of Jewish prosperity and success." Contrary to Henry Cohen's claims that no anti-Semitism existed in Galveston, Heller felt that prejudice against the Jew was "hardly less rife" in the urban South than in those eastern cities where Russian Jews formed the majority.[45]

While Heller's continued defense of Russian Jews earned him disapprobation among the assimilated, he basked in the affection of those he championed. At a CCAR meeting in 1908, when Reform rabbis had despaired of attracting the Russian Orthodox to their ranks, Heller felt that the Reform rabbinate lacked perspective. Russian Jews, he believed, preferred developing their own benevolent institutions, when possible, rather than enlisting "under the organizations of German philanthropy." Nor did they need to accept Reform Judaism "in bulk" to become well-adjusted American citizens. Heller understood that the Russian Jew simply had to find his own way, and the "old fogies" of Reform Judaism, rabidly anti-Zionist and still tied to the "hide-bound . . . intellectualism" of the "doctrines of 1848," seemed irrelevant to the new immigrants. A Judaism that "cared more to astonish the Gentile than to inspire the Jew" meant nothing to the Russian, who could not see Reform even as religion, "much less Judaism." Armed with his all-around solution to every problem of Jewish unity, Heller optimistically felt that the younger generation of Russian Jews would be attracted to a Reform Judaism "sufficiently seasoned by Zionism."[46]

In 1914, Rabbi Heller and his wife, Ida, celebrated their twenty-fifth anniversary. While Temple Sinai and many congregants showered the couple with "innumerable tokens of cordial feeling," the gesture that impressed Heller most was the gift from Congregation Beth Israel, the major Orthodox synagogue in New Orleans. Tellingly, Heller thought enough of the incident to describe it in the *Jubilee Souvenir* booklet that he wrote in 1922, on the occasion of Temple Sinai's fiftieth anniversary. Beth Israel presented the Hellers with a silver basket filled with white roses, and Heller believed that the gift was probably the first time, "at least in this country, that an orthodox congregation gave official recognition to the family festival of a Reform rabbi." Inclusion of the event in the published history of his congregation confirms the event's significance for Heller. The letter of thanks to Beth Israel allowed Heller to reveal a great deal about the strength of his personal feelings. He told Louis Pailet, the secretary of the congregation, that few things in Heller's life had given him more happiness than did "this cordial recognition of our friendship." Heller explained that although his "attachment to orthodoxy" and to his "orthodox coreligionists needed no stimulus," he was encouraged to feel that his "affection" had "not been without response." He recalled being brought up in an Orthodox home and told Pailet that he believed "orthodoxy was my mother which taught me Judaism." Heller also expressed regret that more "well-meaning" Reform rabbis had not been reared in "truly Jewish" homes. He concluded by praying that "Providence" would grant him "the boon of seeing Orthodoxy and Reform work hand in hand for the advancement of Judaism." He fully realized that only as the two denominations respected each other could they hope to rear their children in their ancient faith.[47]

Heller's desire for rapprochement between Orthodoxy and Reform brought him few kudos from within his own movement. In March 1912, Leo Wise wrote that although he disliked being "a bearer of unpleasant tidings," he needed to warn Heller that he did "not stand well with the college authorities" at HUC. Several days later Heller received a letter from J. Walter Freiberg, president of the board of the UAHC. Evidently Heller had let the UAHC know how disappointed he had been at not hearing from that organization on the twenty-fifth anniversary of his tenure at Temple Sinai. Freiberg apologized for his negligence, claiming that he heard about the celebration only after it occurred. Heller's major bone to pick with Freiberg concerned being discriminated against as "the only man of the first two classes [at HUC] . . . not given a Doctor's Degree by the College authorities." Freiberg claimed that Heller had evidently not complied with the requirement of filing a thesis or standing an examination or had otherwise not applied for the degree "in the ordinary manner." He also contended that all of Heller's charges could be subsumed under the rubric of his resentment and belief that, as a Zionist, he had been treated like an "outlaw who . . . must be disciplined." Like other members of the "Zionistic cult," whom Freiberg declared to be "super-sensitive" to criticism, he found that they all only "imagined a great deal of the opposition" to their movement and to themselves.[48]

But the maverick southern Zionist was not so easily kept in line. Just two months later, an infuriated Leo Wise wrote Heller that the *American Israelite* had received an "official communication" from the publicity chairman of a forthcoming Zionist convention. The announcement named Heller as one of the "distinguished visitors" who would be attending. Wise reminded Heller that the paper's position had been "uncompromisingly anti-Zionistic" and that the *Israelite* could not afford "to have our chief editorial contributor, who is generally looked upon throughout the country as our editor, take a prominent part in a National Zionist convention." Wise argued that Heller's participation there would "stultify the ISRAELITE" and "help nullify the work of my father's lifetime, which was to make as many good Americans out of Jews as could possibly be made out of Christians."[49]

Heller's reply contained his most complete summation of the American Zionist movement and of his involvement. "That I should consent to have my movements defined and my freedom of utterance (outside of your columns) hampered is something entirely new in our relationship," Heller retorted. No one who knew him or knew of him could have been unaware of his reputation as "an ardent and convinced Zionist." Wise surely knew that Heller had been writing Zionist articles for the *Maccabaean* and had argued on the floor of CCAR and UAHC conventions on behalf of Jewish nationalism, Heller reminded the publisher. "Your sainted father," Heller wrote with reference to I. M. Wise, was not afraid of other opinions, having asked one of the HUC professors to write a paper on Zionism for a CCAR conference. The senior Wise simply did not want the *Israelite*'s pages used for Zionist propaganda. If Leo Wise wanted Heller to continue writing for the *American Israelite*, then Wise should be aware that the "gentle Southern Zionist" had never taken his "cue from other people," and he had no intention of beginning to do so. Although Heller's Zionism had often threatened to splinter the relationship he had with the *Israelite*, philosophical differences did not cause the break. Just as friction over the straitened finances of the *Jewish Ledger* had brought Heller's writing for the local Jewish paper to an end, so too, Wise's concerns about the *Israelite*'s worsening economic prospects offered Heller an opportunity to quit his post.[50]

According to an editorial in the *American Hebrew,* when the CCAR met in April 1912, the majority of those assembled in Baltimore reaffirmed that religious principle alone bound Jews together. The rabbis rejected the idea that Jewish unity could be based on "the claims of race or nation." But Heller was never one who worried about majorities. In early July, when he stood in the pulpit of B'nai Jeshurun Temple in Cleveland to give the Sabbath eve sermon at the services that opened the fifteenth annual Zionist convention, he described Zionists as an idealistic minority. He took his sermon from a verse in Micah: "And the remnant of Jacob shall be among many nations like the dew from God, as a shower upon a meadow." In a world where racial and religious prejudice kept growing, Zionists were those who fervently believed that Israel would "yet be to the world as a divine dew and a refreshing rain."[51]

Heller's sermon made a fine impression in Zionist circles. The following September, Horace Kallen, professor of psychology and philosophy at the University of Wisconsin, urged Heller to come to Madison to lecture on Zionism. Kallen told Heller that "particularly the Zionists of the

Middle West" were "in need of a fresh voice and a revived message" and that Kallen could think of no one better to deliver it to them. Heller took another three years to get to a middle western college campus, but it turned out to be the University of Michigan instead of the University of Wisconsin, and Zionism was not the subject of his address.[52]

In mid-January 1915, Leo Franklin, supervising rabbi of the Jewish Student Congregation at the University of Michigan in Ann Arbor, invited Heller to deliver the sermon for the Jewish Union Service at the Hill Auditorium on campus. Franklin, an anti-Zionist, selected Heller for his speaking ability and acclaimed leadership in American Reform Judaism rather than for his propagandizing on behalf of Zionism. Heller was clearly excited about the invitation, especially when he found that he was to deliver his sermon in a large, interdenominational setting. The hall seated 5,000, he told his sons, and the opportunity would be "glorious . . . for saying something strong" if he had the "pluck and fortitude to do it." Later that month he learned that he was the first rabbi "to conduct this unique service." As he contemplated the "great responsibility" involved in delivering a meaningful sermon in Ann Arbor, he hoped to have the "vigor to face it adequately." Heller's summoning of his own "vigor" probably inspired the title he chose for the address, "Moral Courage: The Test of American Manhood." At the top of Heller's own printed copy of "Moral Courage," he wrote "American Ideals in the Light of Judaism," an apt title for this period of his life. He strongly identified with the exceptional American social environment that encouraged such a service and told the students that in older countries where religious lines were "sharply drawn," removing sectarian barriers "would seem inconceivable." Heller credited the freedom of the occasion to the principle of separation of church and state. He attributed the initiation of the service on the Ann Arbor campus to the remarkable reform character of the state of Michigan. Here he found the "greatest and most successful of our state universities," the "pioneer in proving that an eminent seat of learning can be established and maintained by the administrative agencies of a progressive and enlightened state."[53]

Heller spoke as a representative of "the mother faith of the civilized world." His entire sermon was a paean to American progressivism. With Europe already at war and German militarism threatening to destroy the secular environment that had nurtured Heller, he saw no reason to exalt "physical bravery." He called instead for an "inwardness of courage." He believed that the university had a key role to play in the development of moral courage, mainly in imparting "the manly vigor of intellectual independence," which alone could inspire "intellectual audacity." Democracies needed citizens able to exercise "on behalf of all, the manhood of unbiased . . . , self-reliant . . . , fearless judgment." Heller discussed some of the problems threatening civilization, principally the inequitable distribution of wealth, and he looked to students as the "rising generation" whose "moral manliness . . . will bring us nearer to equipoise." The future of the country demanded "public-spirited men" willing to "refuse alluring employment" to help the "downtrodden consumer," the underpaid laborer, the "hoodwinked voter." Only those unafraid to speak out could "organize the people to vigorous self-defense against aggressive franchises and overgrown privileges."[54]

In closing, he recalled his own first steps as a reformer in the struggle against the Louisiana Lottery. He told his interfaith audience that when friends had tried to warn him about "the risks involved in challenging so powerful a corporation," his heart was "sore and troubled." A Christian hymn seemed to lift his spirits and help him regain his courage:

Dare to be a Daniel,
Dare to stand alone,
Dare to have a purpose strong,
Dare to make it known.

For his final words, Heller turned to Hillel, a Jewish rabbi, whose concise statement "In a place where there are no men, strive to be a man" set forth the essence of the hymn. Hillel's timeless aphorism also embodied Heller's sermon and underscored the strivings of his own particular blend of American Judaism and progressivism.

As Leo Franklin told Joe Stolz, "Heller rose to the heights. I did not imagine with all my regard for him, that he could preach such a sermon in such a way." Franklin encountered "not a single superfluous word" in the delivery that he praised as tinged with the "obvious sincerity which is characteristically his [Heller's]." Franklin told Heller that the favorable impression he made on those who heard him in Ann Arbor would "not soon pass away." As usual when he was pleased with what he had written, Heller sent a copy of the sermon to those he felt would be interested. George Cornelson, Jr., replied that "Moral Courage" was an "inspiration . . . even in cold print" and told Heller to expect to bring some of his "thought and spirit" to Cornelson's "own flock" at the First Presbyterian Church in New Orleans.[55]

CHAPTER IX

❧❧

"The Zenith of My Career"

As the Balkan powder keg exploded and its flames ignited the rest of the European continent, Max Heller's professional energies peaked, sparked by enough "trouble to keep one's edges clean." World War I inspired both the Wilsonian vision of a world made safe for democracy and the Balfour Declaration, which promised the fulfillment of the Zionist dream. Together, these wartime impulses allowed Heller's idealism to soar to new heights. Although sometimes exhausted by his physical limitations, he nevertheless fiercely battled for his Progressive and Zionist principles. Heller well understood that the war years constituted a key era in his life. In fact, he admitted to his sons in 1916, "I am probably at the zenith of my career."[1]

Characteristically, Heller responded to the outbreak of the European conflict by becoming enthusiastically engaged in the promotion of peace. In October 1914 the *New Orleans Item* published his "Prayer for Peace," the first indication that he had enlisted in the ranks of the peace movement. He offered his prayer on behalf of the "misguided brothers . . . divided by bitter animosities" in hopes that God might speedily terminate "their efforts at mutual destruction." Heller hoped that, out of the anguish, some "incalculable good" might arise and that "hatred and prejudice . . . between races, nations and faiths" might vanish. In the earthly paradise he envisioned, the stronger would generously help the weaker in an effort to establish the "reign of genuine brotherhood."[2]

In June of the following year, the major headline of the *New Orleans American* carried news of the sinking of the *Lusitania*, and on the same page, a large photograph of Heller appeared with the caption "Jewish Leader of New Orleans Who, with His People, Stand for Peace." The long accompanying article quoted Heller extensively. "No nation ever existed for which the word peace had greater attraction than it always had for the Jew." In the years that preceded America's entrance into the Great War, Heller's activity in the American Peace Society yielded him leadership in the organization. He was twice elected as president of the local chapter. A Wilsonian in spirit, even before he openly campaigned for the president's reelection in 1916, Heller also worked with the Louisiana Society for International Concord. The promotional circular sent over his signature and that of three other leaders bore the imprint of his style. In advocating international law, the authors argued that they were not "commending a policy of peace in preference to justice" nor "peace at any price." While denouncing the spirit of militarism that might lead to "martial castes," the organization encouraged "military preparedness" for self-defense. Their sole purpose was to rouse public awareness, to insist that neutrality had not "lost all value."[3]

Before vigorously working for Woodrow Wilson's reelection, Heller had never taken an active role in a presidential campaign. Isaac, while a law student at Harvard, was also campaigning in the Boston area for Wilson. Calling Wilson "the greatest progressive President this or any other country has ever had," the father listed some arguments for his son to use in trying to persuade prospective voters. As the election approached, Heller worried about the prospects of the "schoolmaster turned practical reformer." He wrote to his sons that he wished he "were sure of W. W.'s election," adding that it would be "a real relief which would make me deeply thankful both for the sake of the country and of humanity in general." In an elated letter to Stephen Wise written shortly after the president's reelection, Heller pronounced the "Wilson triumph . . . a vindication of a great man of progressive policies" and of the "justice and good sense of the American people." The good news made the rabbi "feel like newborn."[4]

In the spring of 1916, Heller also campaigned enthusiastically for the Progressive Louisiana gubernatorial candidate, John M. Parker. Unlike other contemporary southern governors, Parker distinguished himself as an arch-enemy of the Ku Klux Klan and a fighter against bigotry. Attending a large campaign meeting for Parker, Heller bragged to his sons that he had seated himself "conspicuously" on the platform, "to emphasize my friendship for him." In the service of progressivism, Heller overcame some past grudges, even praising a speech of Charles Rosen's "which seemed to me very excellent." The hall where the Progressives met was jammed with a "splendid class of people." Parker's bid was successful, and the following November, Heller sang Parker's praises again because the governor had actively campaigned for Wilson's reelection. Telling a local friend, chairman of a banquet to be given in Parker's honor, that he would be "most eager" to be included on the guest list, Heller added that he wanted to pay tribute to Parker at the affair. When Parker saw Heller's letter, the governor called it "the finest compliment paid me" and asked Heller's permission to publish it. Heller gladly consented and confided to Stephen S. Wise that Parker was a man "after your and my heart, with moral courage and staunch backbone, a sincere friend of the Jews and a real lover of progress."[5]

But work on behalf of war sufferers abroad demanded much more of Heller's energies than did politics. In the fall of 1914, even as he solicited funds to help the civilians displaced by war, he worried that Jewish agencies like the B'nai B'rith and the American Jewish Committee might duplicate efforts and waste precious money raised. Heller told Isaac that although "*schnorring* [begging] for the Jewish war-sufferers" proved to be "a nasty and difficult job," the older Heller derived a great deal of satisfaction from using the skills he had developed in "fighting hard for justice." Now he considered himself "in prime time for attacking tight purses and flinty hearts."[6]

Encouraged by the FAZ to make an appeal to the Reform rabbinate on behalf of Zionism, Heller had sent out a circular to most of his Reform colleagues, encouraging them to rethink their attitudes toward Palestine in the light of the war. He admitted that he was writing as a "radical Zionist" but asked his colleagues, "Are not many of us, despite their opposition to political Zionism, disposed to favor the setting aside of Palestine as a neutral zone of Jewish shelter? It is a queer coincidence," Heller noted, "that orthodox Jews and Julius Rosenwald should understand that monthly contributions are called for, not skimpy donations." He told them that, as rabbis, their positive influence could go far in remedying "prevailing indifference toward Palestine."[7]

Good Progressive and amateur sociologist that he was, Heller decided to poll the Reform rabbinate and included a list of four questions that he wanted answered briefly and returned. This circular and questionnaire marked his first systematic efforts to create a dialogue on Zionism within the rank and file of the CCAR membership. The effort to relieve suffering among Jews abroad had opened a door for Heller's larger mission of reconciliation between the two movements that might otherwise have remained locked. Heller was very much aware of his role. In January 1915, he told his sons that he now realized that the circular constituted "a highly important step, together with my appeal for funds, in the rapprochement between Zionism and Reform Judaism." The effort enabled him "to prove that at least $\frac{1}{3}$ of the CCAR membership" sympathized with Zionism "(41 replies, so far out of 209)." By February, fifty-five had notified him that they would help raise funds to support the colonies in Palestine.[8]

By early February 1915, Louis Brandeis, recently converted to Zionism and already its leading American spokesperson, had sent Heller a telegram, urging him to collect funds for Palestine, where suffering was particularly intense. Heller expressed his frustration to his sons, "Find myself utterly unable to do more than to send of my own. From the people I cannot collect again." Less than two weeks later Cyrus Sulzberger, secretary of the American Jewish Relief Committee (AJRC), told Heller that, thus far, no funds "commensurate with the well-known generosity of the South" had been raised in Louisiana. Sulzberger felt compelled by the "crisis in the affairs of our coreligionists abroad" to call upon Heller to take the chairmanship for the AJRC for the state. Heller may have wished to refuse but could not do so. He worked hard to raise whatever additional funds he could.[9]

Heller's additional responsibilities placed new items on an already crowded agenda. After resigning from his position as weekly columnist for the *American Israelite* in the fall of 1914, he had begun publishing more regularly in the *Maccabaean*. In January 1915, Louis Lipsky, the journal's editor, wrote that he was "heartily glad" that Heller had turned all his "literary abilities to Zionist service" and affirmed his interest in Heller's monthly contributions to the *Maccabaean*. But even as Heller responded to Lipsky's call, he found himself deeply enmeshed in a policy crisis at HUC that involved James, his son, who had enrolled there as a rabbinical student.[10]

The previous December, when James and three other students who formed the board of the college's Literary Society learned that Horace Kallen would be coming to Cincinnati, they invited him to speak on a subject of his choice at the Literary Society meeting the evening before his address to the Menorah Society. Kallen accepted and told the student board that his topic would be "The Meaning of Hebraism." Two days before Kallen's scheduled arrival, the president of the Literary Society telegraphed him that the HUC authorities "commanded" the board to rescind the invitation because of some of the positions Kallen had taken publicly. Kallen was deeply disturbed by the affair not so much for the criticism of his Zionism or atheism as because he worried about the apparent lack of academic freedom at an institution responsible for training American rabbis. He told Stephen S. Wise that restrictions on academic freedom would only weaken the *morale* of the rabbinate and would undermine "the freedom of Judaism." Furious, Wise demanded of Heller, "Is nothing to be said or done about this? Are you satisfied with that spirit at the college and are you going to sit silent under it?" Personally, professionally, and philosophically, Heller could hardly avoid being swept into the vortex of the dilemma.[11] More fireworks lay ahead. The members of the Literary Society's board apologized to Kallen, stating that the invitation had been canceled "over our heads" and that they were writing "at the risk of appearing disloyal" to the college. They made the mistake of sharing the letter with Kohler, who, in turn, initiated disciplinary actions against them for insubordination. Wise and Heller protested to the HUC Board of Governors, and the board president issued an all-expenses-paid invitation to both of them to attend a special executive conference in Cincinnati at which they could express their grievances. Before leaving to meet the board, Heller circulated a letter to its members outlining the situation. Heller contended that HUC's current rage of censorship discredited I. M. Wise's spirit of "broad toleration." Heller cleverly argued that Kohler's policy only resulted in "rendering Zionism the more alluring to youths of independent spirit" while fostering "habits of servility and toadyism in those who are disposed to cater to superior power." He entreated the board members, as "spiritual heirs of Dr. Wise" to "exercise their influence on behalf of a reasonable measure of academic liberty" when they met in Cincinnati in mid-February.[12]

Even before the mid-February meeting, Heller anticipated success. He persuaded the HUC board members to pass a resolution stating that the topic of political Zionism was not too dangerous for discussion, provided that the lecturer were "competent" and free of "insulting hostility to the institution [HUC] or its officials" and could "speak in a spirit consonant with genuine religiousness." Moreover, a student could advocate Zionism from the chapel's pulpit if the "temper and manner of his Zionist support" were "sincerely religious." Heller felt gratified by the "open-minded earnestness" that the board had displayed in considering the proposals he had presented.[13]

Involvement with the demands of congregation and community and commitment to Zionism and with the problems at HUC did not detract from his concern as a parent for his younger son, Isaac. Although a deeply spiritual man, once he became a rabbi, Heller rarely talked about God, preferring such terms as "divine Providence" when he infrequently approached the subject in a sermon. Thirty years of serving in the rabbinate heightened his sense of spiritual maturation. While Isaac was attending Harvard Law School, Max received a letter not unlike the postcard he had mailed from Prague to his own father nearly forty years earlier. Isaac had entertained the idea of becoming a rabbi, but he wrote to say that he had definitely decided not to do so.[14]

Unlike Simon, his father, Max was able to identify with the feelings Isaac expressed. Telling Isaac that his letter "touched me deeply," Max recalled his own rebellion. "A father tries his best to guide his boys right; when he himself was crowded [?] away by such circumstances from the dream of his childhood he cannot, especially as a believer in self-guidance, force a vocation on his boy," Max replied. "Because a boy goes through the feverish measles of scepticism [sic] and agnosticism therefore he thinks the ministry is not for him, or else his brother is already studying, or his father has a stormy road to travel. But all the time that boy does not know the deep fountains of his yearning at the bottom of his nature . . . , the hunger for the . . . eternal values of the soul-life, the unspeakable satisfaction of pouring out one's being in the communication of one's innermost to souls that long for their food. Religion which is my blockhead's joke to-day, has been the intoxicating wine and the nourishing meat of all the deepest and most luminary souls in history." But Max did not push the rabbinate. Instead, he reassured Isaac that, as an attorney, he could "do a great deal of good in Judaism . . . , broadening and deepening your moral life, owing to the contact you may have had with these strange sides of human nature." To show Isaac that he accepted his decision, Max warmly told him that he was sending him a tallis (prayer shawl). "It belonged to your great-grandfather on my father's side," Max wrote, and then he shared instructions about the proper way to wear it. Prayer shawls were not used in Reform worship, but Heller was now anxious to initiate his son into more traditional Jewish forms, even if Isaac had chosen to pursue a career different from that of his father and older brother. He trusted that Isaac would also carry on the fight for Zionism.[15]

At the CCAR conference at Charlevoix, Michigan, in 1915, Heller practically single-handedly championed the Zionist point of view. While Stephen S. Wise was beginning to feel overwhelmed by the obstinate leadership within the CCAR and did not attend the conference, he relayed to Heller that younger Zionist rabbis present had spoken of his superb fight "against the powers of darkness." Heller and Wise differed radically in their approach to the CCAR. When frustrated by intransigence, Wise was ready to pull out of the organization, but Heller's loyalties to his HUC education and to the memory of I. M. Wise made him persist in attempts at reconciliation. Perhaps the unpleasant isolation at the conference inspired Heller's powerful attack, waged in October 1915, in the *Jewish Comment*. Calling his pulpit enemies "Philistines," Heller excoriated them for the "colorless liberalism" that seldom ventured beyond safe platitudes rooted in middle-class comfort. He deplored such rabbis' effusive discourses on social maladjustments, with their tendency to represent social justice "as the core of Judaism," and simultaneous criticism of Brandeis's leadership in the American Zionist movement. Brandeis, the model of social justice, had no formal Jewish training, but, Heller wondered, "Must a man know Hebrew grammar in order to be entitled to an opinion on Jewish psychology?" Wise again communicated his frustrations. He agreed with Heller that the future battles in Judaism would be waged not between the Orthodox and the Reform "but over a real and fundamental Jewishness expressed racially or, if you please, nationally, and with milk-and-water emasculate Judaism which is the sad survival of the German-Jewish Reformation." Moving far from the position he had taken in opposition to Heller's bid for CCAR president some years earlier, Wise now claimed to feel closer to Orthodox Jews not ashamed of their Judaism than to "our reform colleagues many of whom have fundamentally ceased to be Jews, who prate about the religion of the Jew when religion is furthest from their own souls."[16]

Just as Heller had opened 1915 by giving a memorable address at the University of Michigan, so he closed the year with another major sermon on Jewish identity delivered in mid-December at Temple Israel in St. Louis, at the Jewish Chautauqua Service. In "The Jewish Consciousness," he traced the historic evolution of Jewish consciousness, dwelling particularly on the dilemmas posed by emancipation. He saw the Jew unhappily caught "between the Scylla of truculent self-assertion and the Charybdis of shame-faced self-obliteration." In his confusion, the modern Jew lacked the appropriate language for self-definition, unsure whether to call the bonds between him and his brethren racial, religious, or national. Heller eloquently pleaded for a synthesis, for a Jewish manhood yearning to be its "unhampered self." He believed that all humanity needed "the soil-rootings of nationality" in order to flourish, a condition clearly impossible in the "assimilative environments" of the West. In a similar vein, earlier that month, Heller had published an unsigned article, "Uprooted," in which he argued that while a "man without a country" was a pathetic creature, even sadder was the man "whose heart has cut itself loose from all rootage in its natural soil." Even as Heller realized that nationalism run amok had plunged Europe in the throes of war, he embraced nationalism as an "indispensable" ingredient in the evolution of consciousness, "a prime factor in the cultural diversification and, thereby, the progressive unfoldment, of the human race."[17]

Heller's continued allegiance to Zionism only renewed and deepened his commitment to the larger themes of brotherhood. Strengthened by his own insights and his determination to spread the gospel of his own convictions, in December Heller also returned to preach at the Central Congregational Church in New Orleans, in the same pulpit from which he had first addressed an African American audience several years earlier. This time he gave a memorial sermon, "Booker T. Washington, a Modern Prophet." Heller compared Washington to Moses; both men had found their mission in building the foundations for their people. Washington deserved praise, Heller argued, because he had taught and uplifted his race without renouncing his dignity, his self-worth, and his race pride. Like a Jew concerned with fulfilling God's laws, Washington had spent his entire life in "one consistent preachment of duties, rather than a demand for rights." Heller prophesied that the time would come when the South would "count it among her glories" that one "dark-skinned man, in the space of one generation," had fought his way "out of the night of slavery into the full daylight of wide esteem and incalculable service."[18]

But Heller well understood the limits of the gains that Washington had made. Just a few months after the sermon, Heller wrote his sons that he and Ida had gone to see *The Birth of a Nation*, D. W. Griffith's neoconfederate racist epic. Heller was appalled. He found it "replete with prejudice of the worst kind and historic misrepresentations." Although he considered sending a letter to the *Times-Picayune*, "warning parents against sending their children to see it and denouncing this way of stirring up feeling against the negro," or preaching a sermon against both the film and the book on which it was based, he eventually did nothing. Temporarily exhausted from his exertions or unwilling to face a fresh barrage of criticism, he admitted that he was "not in the mood . . . to take up another fight." He added that, unfortunately, no one else seemed ready to "trouble himself about it."[19]

In 1916, however, Heller did take up another fight. Even though he was not a central protagonist in the battle to establish an American Jewish Congress, his presence made a difference in the conference skirmishes where he debated the mainstream leaders of the CCAR and in the editorial bouts where his pen became his weapon of choice. The war in Europe coincided with and helped change the structure of the American Jewish community. The increase in the needs of Jews abroad placed additional pressure on communal resources already stretched to meet the demands of the large numbers of immigrants who had arrived steadily before war broke out in Europe.

When the thoroughly assimilated Louis D. Brandeis mediated a garment workers' strike in 1910, he encountered Russian immigrant Jews for the first time and as a pragmatic idealist found himself deeply moved by the workers' intellectual acumen and Jewish pride. The journey from sympathy to activism proved short, as it had for Heller a decade earlier. Tutored by his friend Horace Kallen, Brandeis converted to Zionism.

When he took over the leadership of the Zionist Provisional Executive Committee, which sought to alleviate the emergencies of Jews overseas, he used his immense energies to transform American Zionism into a movement that could more efficiently meet the needs abroad. "Men! Money! Discipline!" he demanded. In addition to the prestige and organizational abilities that Brandeis brought to American Zionism, he offered his own synthesis of Kallen's cultural pluralism, which proved to be the perfect formula for recruiting. He smoothly blended American patriotism with Zionism, a fusion that harmonized the tensions inherent in the specter of "dual loyalties" feared by assimilated German-American Jews. "To be good Americans," he announced, "we must be better Jews, and to be better Jews, we must become Zionists."[20]

The movement mushroomed under his leadership, and the ideals of his skillfully engineered progressivism seeped not only into Zionism but also into a movement to organize democratically for Jewish defense, to establish an American Jewish Congress that truly represented the American Jewish community. Brandeis became the titular head of the pro-Congress group. Before the fight for and establishment of an American Jewish Congress, the exclusive and oligarchic American Jewish Committee (AJC) had represented the Jewish community with prestigious patriarchal leaders like Jacob Schiff and Louis Marshall. At the opposite end of the spectrum, the working-class Zionist organizations spearheaded the Congress movement, which by 1916 was being actively debated at the CCAR convention. Heller asked the organization to support the Congress movement, "endorsed by the masses of our people," instead of the AJC, which had resisted the idea of a democratically elected organization. Although democratization in the American Jewish community reflected larger trends in American political culture like the Seventeenth Amendment that provided for the direct election of senators, Heller's close friend, Joseph Stolz, disagreed with his support of an American Jewish Congress, fearing that the Congress would destroy the AJC.[21]

Although Stolz and Henry Cohen had been Heller's closest friends in the rabbinate, neither sympathized with his Zionism, and now Stolz argued against the Congress movement. When, in the fall of 1916, Isaac dejectedly wrote that the young woman he loved no longer returned his affections, his father responded by revealing his own disappointment in friends. Isaac worried that his limp from his bout with polio had made him unattractive. Heller reassured him that some day he would meet an "aspiring, noble-hearted woman, the sympathetic echo of your innermost yearnings." Although Rabbi Heller had often boasted that he had "the two most admirable friends of any one in the rabbinate, your Uncles

Joe and Henry" and many others, he rhetorically asked Isaac, "Do you imagine I have one perfect friend, one solitary friend whom I could trust to the very end?" He added defensively, "Don't you know how often my friends have failed to stand by me, not because they didn't love me, but because they lacked the moral courage?" The father's own moral courage did not diminish the loneliness he experienced because he advocated unpopular positions.[22]

As the United States moved away from its policy of isolation, Heller continued to support Wilson. Heller told his congregants that the country could remain neutral no longer, since modern civilization had already "entangled us into alliances without number which bind up our commerce, our intellectual progress, our sympathies, our daily life with the welfare and the peace of Europe." When the United States entered the war in the spring of 1917, Heller professed boundless optimism and was fully invested in Wilson's democratic mission. In his sermon "Boons from the World War," Heller asked his congregants, "Is there not such a thing as a democracy of nations as well as of individuals?" The metaphors he had been using for the past decade when addressing the needs of African Americans and Eastern European Jews he found serviceable once more. He foresaw a day when even the "least gifted and most backward nations" would be able to live and develop freely, having been given "its right of unhampered unfoldment" in living "according to the inner law of its own individuality," rather than subsumed under the "selfish interests of some powerful elder-brother nation." Heller believed that from the current travails there might "emerge as victor the dove of peace bringing the olive-leaf of perfect reconciliation, of universal disarmament" and "free fellowship."[23]

That same spring, Heller accepted an invitation to give the commencement address at Tuskegee Institute. With the international situation very much on his mind, he found striking parallels between the international struggle for minority rights and the fight against racial barriers confronting African Americans at home. He told the graduates that he had always been "deeply touched by the problem of the Negro." His sympathies were aroused on behalf of the downtrodden race, "partly because, as a Jew, the perplexity of national problems and race problems comes home to me as it would not to other men." Heller confessed that he had been too often "depressed" by the "bigoted prejudice" that had hindered the efforts of "even otherwise well-meaning people" in attacking the "delicate problems of race." He cleverly merged the Wilsonian concern in the international arena for smaller nations and the national rights of minorities with the racial situation in America. Now his paternalistic devotion to African

Americans, expressed in "The Elder Brother" title of his sermon, had broader overtones than a simple echo of Atticus Haygood. Heller took for his biblical passage Genesis 25:23, "One people shall be mightier than the other, but the elder shall serve the younger." He moved from questioning how the stronger might protect the weaker individual or race to wondering how the small nations and "backward races" might be protected "against the aggressions and exploitations, against the violences and rapacities of their brother-nations and races." While he did not offer any innovative solutions to the aggressive segregation of the day, Heller did admit that, especially in the South, there could be no prosperity "while our colored brother is languishing." The South could foster no "enduring culture" while shutting out the black citizen "from the best which our generation has to offer." The only real solution was to "take our colored brother with us on our march of progress" or else "lag with him in the rear, as we shall, then, deserve to lag." He also compared the difficult road ahead for the aspiring, educated black student with the plight of the Jewish people, some of whom had "climbed to the heights of culture," while the other half had "only left Russian bondage" two months earlier.[24]

The next month in the *Jewish Ledger*, Heller once again advocated an American Jewish Congress. He believed that the projected meeting of a Congress presented a significant departure from the historic methods of self-defense Jews had used for centuries to fight bigotry. Typically, prominent Jews had pleaded "against injustice as individuals." Although later external circumstances departed radically from those of medieval Poland, essential features of the initial pattern of self-defense endured. Structurally, the most intriguing feature was the emergence of the *shtadlan*, the "intercessor" who presented himself to the gentile community as the representative of the Jews, as one acting in their behalf. Inevitably, the shtadlanim were also *maskilim*, or enlightened Jews. The enlightened, assimilated, secular Jewish leader acted at the expense of the traditional *kehilla* authority—the rabbi—but the self-appointed leadership function of the shtadlanim did not go unchallenged by working-class Jews. The latter refused to identify with either the assimilationist means or the bourgeois ends of the community elites. Now, for the first time, in America, "under the shadow of the greatest of democracies, under a President who seems to be the world's outstanding champion of democracy," Heller saw Jews who were ready to model themselves in the image of the country of their allegiance. They were choosing a democratic method of organization to unite in offering assistance to those abroad. "To impress upon the nations the rights of our brothers to freedom and self-unfoldment we must stand together," he counseled. In June, when elections for delegates were held throughout the United States, Heller was selected from New Orleans. But the meeting of the Congress was postponed for a year and a half. With the country now at war, American Jews decided to put their energies into the war effort and put aside their own agenda until after peace had been reestablished.[25]

The "zenith" of Heller's career as a journalist began at the end of 1916, when he told Stephen Wise that he was looking for a forum that would allow him to try his hand at "joining Zionism with Liberal Judaism." A new format in the *Maccabaean* provided the perfect venue for Heller's forceful essays. Beginning in the spring of 1917, Heller produced a frequent column in a section entitled "With Malice Toward None." The timing proved to be particularly fortuitous, because 1917 was a turning point both for progressivism and Zionism, and Heller had positioned himself to comment on both to a national audience.[26]

"Dollarland Spirituality" was the first column to appear in which Heller blasted those who preached "blessing and prosperity" as salvation. "What a fine gospel from unctuous pulpit-lackey to beatific millionaire!" he sneered, as if "our millions" could "bring back the faded Jewish life" or prosperity could "cure our snobbish attitude towards Jewish history." He deemed anti-Zionism a certain brand of "commercialized soul life" fit only for the philistines who still championed the obsolete notion of a Jewish mission in dispersion. "The Mission in Dispersion" followed. Here he used suggestive natural images of weakening, like the "subsidence of Jewish consciousness" or spiritual "barrenness" that occurred when Jews were planted in soil too rich in diversions, a condition "notoriously unsuited to the blossoming forth of religious genius."[27]

Just before the CCAR met in Buffalo the following July, Heller published in the *Maccabaean* a column, "Nationalism and Religion," that went beyond Brandeis's formula equating being a good American with being a better Jew, or a Zionist. Heller succeeded in his resolution of the central tensions in liberal Judaism by claiming that Jewish nationalism and religious Judaism were completely interdependent. Responding to the Zionists who discounted religiosity as well as to Reform Jews who discounted nationalism, Heller achieved his own synthesis. He maintained that Jewish nationalism needed the "consecration of Judaism" just as Judaism, "in the long run," needed nationalism to "maintain life."[28]

But the majority of the rabbis present in Buffalo, including Joe Stolz, reaffirmed the Jewish mission idea, declaring that "that essence of Israel as a priest-people" lay in its "religious consciousness . . . , not in any political or racial national consciousness." Heller submitted his own minority report, arguing that the tenets of Reform Judaism did not "insist on the dispersion of the Jews as an indispensable condition for the welfare and progress of Judaism." Attempting to secure a "publicly and legally safe-guarded home for Jews in Palestine," he declared, violated none of the principles of the Reform movement. He and Stolz parted ways again when the subject of the American Jewish Congress was debated, and this time Heller's other dear friend, Henry Cohen, also opposed the Congress. Heller tried to point out that because the American Jewish Congress already had a slate of delegates, the new body stood "before the world" in representing American Jewry, and the CCAR needed to be counted among its participants and supporters. Like the majority of his colleagues, Cohen disagreed, feeling that because a Zionist majority had been elected as delegates to the Congress, that body did not truly represent "American Israel." Three other southern rabbis present, Edward Calisch of Richmond, Morris Newfield of Birmingham, and David Marx of Atlanta, sided with Cohen. Heller's New Orleans colleague Rabbi Emil Leipziger, Leucht's successor at Touro Synagogue, editorialized on the CCAR conference in the *Jewish Spectator*. He mentioned that the majority had achieved "a significant diplomatic victory." Even though a resolution opposing Zionism would have caused the "secession of a number of valuable men from the Conference," one favoring Zionism would have been "unthinkable in the rabbinical body." As with his positions on Zionism and race, the Congress movement found Heller isolated again both in the CCAR and in his region.[29]

Despite defeat at Buffalo, Heller remained optimistic, discerning in the movement "a strong, influential and growing minority . . . openly espousing Zionism," while the majority had refused to condemn Zionism completely. Only a small group of "rabid irreconcilables" remained, and their numbers, he believed, were "dwindling." Heller believed that the younger men, those with "triumphant enthusiasm," might yet revitalize American Reform Judaism. Stephen Wise agreed, telling Heller, "As you rightly put it, the best thing about the debate on Zionism was the fact that we now see that the younger men are with us,—and that is everything."[30]

In "Our Spiritual Golus [diaspora]," however, Heller expressed the darker side of his feelings and fears about America, even as he proudly championed the president, the war effort, and Jewish patriotism. This essay in the *Maccabaean* conveyed the depths of discomfort in the Americanized immigrant's soul. Convinced that the Jew could not be "welcomed, as Jew, into the innermost life of American culture" and therefore faced outsider or pariah status in the United States, Heller discussed social anti-Semitism as "the silent unarticulated, but invincible power of a sense of uncongeniality" increasingly prevalent in America, from board-rooms and hotels to fraternities and schools that sought to exclude Jews from their midst. Although Heller was a liberal intellectually, his life experiences in the South and his observation of recent Western European Jewish history had forced him to qualify his trust in liberalism. "We ought to be abundantly aware," he cautioned, how much more "administrative policy, public feeling, social atmosphere matter" above the "mere formal letter of the law." He cited countries like Austria, in which "even the socialist and radical have not been above entering into bargains at the expense of the Jew." In his adopted country, Heller was wary because Americanization tended to equal "de-Judaization," a process that set up an "insoluble antagonism" for the Jewish citizen. Zionism, with its "restoration to our historic soil," provided the only cure for "spiritual homelessness."[31]

In the fall of 1917, the British issuance of the Balfour Declaration, recognizing Jewish rights to a homeland in Palestine, cast such light onto the Zionist world that Heller's diaspora depression lifted. He busily set to work to rally support among American Jews and gentiles alike. Earlier that spring, when the Russian Revolution seemed to offer relief for all the oppressed minorities there, including the Jews, David Philipson had predicted that it would lead to "Zionism's End." When the Balfour Declaration and the Bolshevik Revolution occurred almost simultaneously, Heller and the Zionists were vindicated. "In these days of the Russian chaos," he crowed, "as little as the Jewish problem is susceptible of a lightning solution, just so little is the Zionist movement in danger of a sudden and complete collapse." As Russia retreated from liberation and reverted to "pogrom conditions," Heller hailed Great Britain, "the greatest empire in the world," declaring itself "in full accord with the aims and aspirations of the Zionist movement." To Jacob de Haas, Heller cabled, "England, politically the ripest of commonwealths, boldly hews the path towards this triumph of international justice. America is certain to follow." While Heller believed that the world had been moving in the direction England now spearheaded, he understood that "the last to be convinced" would be "the snobs and autocrats in our ranks," although they, too, would ultimately "fall into line."[32]

David Philipson, one of the principal unnamed "autocrats," wrote an editorial for the *American Israelite* in which he proudly defended his allegiance to America, and he claimed that the Balfour Declaration in no way changed the terms of debate on Judaism's mission. "Are the Jews an international religious people unique and distinct in their status," he queried, "or are they merely a small nation in the political sense like other small nations of the earth?" For Philipson, the ideologue, no doubt existed as to the answer. He pledged his allegiance to the United States, considering Palestine "dear only as a memory," having been the "home of my very remote ancestry." Besides, he considered Judaism "much larger than Zionism," an essential element in his argument that Jews formed a religious and not a national group.[33]

Heller's close friend, Henry Cohen, was also among those who fell in line with the anti-Zionist activists after the Balfour Declaration, and the correspondence between the two leading southern rabbis never quite recovered its prior warmth and rapport. In late December, challenging his Galveston colleague, Heller wondered if the "historic changes" of the past few weeks had softened Cohen's attitude toward Zionism. Heller wanted to know the outer limits of Cohen's anti-Zionism, how far Cohen aligned himself with "rabid, purblind, selfish Anti-Zionists in fearing a nationalist experiment as prejudicial to the safety and comfort of Western Judaism." Henrietta Szold, a passionate Zionist and the founder of Hadassah, planned a trip to Galveston. If Cohen were to "chime in with that chorus" of anti-Zionists, Heller feared, it would seem "your holy duty to proscribe or, at least, cold-shoulder Henrietta." Heller assured Cohen that he was not trying to "beg a favor," but respecting and loving both Szold and Cohen, he would feel "greatly pained" if a conflict ensued. "What's the use, Max?" Cohen had responded to a similar request. "We've threshed the matter out thoroughly, for lo! these many moons & that's the result. Why you should call it intolerance I don't know!" Cohen tried to patch over their differences. "Seemingly your experiences are different," he told Heller, "but I know mine. You are a Zionist & your people know it. I am not & my people know it."[34]

The Moravian-born historian Gotthard Deutsch, Heller's close friend at HUC, was an anti-Zionist intellectually but emotionally kept his distance from those like Kohler and Philipson. Deutsch enjoyed playing the devil's advocate. Complimenting Heller on one of his journalistic pieces on anti-Zionism, Deutsch could not resist asking if Heller actually believed that a Jewish commonwealth in Palestine would help retain the "Judah P. Benjamins . . . , the Joseph Pulitzers . . . , and even the Mary Antins and their descendants within the fold of Judaism." Deutsch believed that the assimilationists would always find an "easier way of slipping out of Judaism," just as, with the intense anti-German sentiment of wartime America, prominent Americans of German descent were now proclaiming that their ancestry was "a matter of strictly historic interest."[35]

A real maverick, Deutsch intensely admired German culture and had never become an American citizen. In April 1917, he was completely disheartened, upset with the injustice of what he considered an unjust war. Factional problems between Zionists and anti-Zionists seemed beside the point. Deutsch still had family in Germany. James Heller and Deutsch's sons were all in the army. To Deutsch, the "great need of the moment" was to make the American nation "appreciate the monstrosity of a patriotism that demands of my boys to consider it the highest virtue to kill the only son of a widow who happens to be their father's only sister." Deutsch's sympathies during the war were becoming problematic. He sarcastically commented to Heller, "You go on preaching the making of the world safe for democracy, when 100 innocent niggers are cruelly done to death in broad daylight." Deutsch's vulnerability wounded him. While Heller preached democracy, the Board of Governors warned Deutsch to abandon his activity with the "council for peace and democracy," an organization evidently critical of the war. Deutsch closed with the line, "Give me humanity or Cherokkeee canibalism [sic]."[36]

In a city with so large a German population, when wartime anti-German feeling crested, Deutsch came under suspicion for his German affections and his German citizenship. He was accused of disloyalty. Many in Cincinnati's German Jewish community, fearful lest Deutsch's idiosyncrasies cast aspersions on their own patriotism, tried to pressure the HUC Board of Governors to dismiss him. Deutsch's loyal out-of-town friends on the board of HUC alumni, including Stolz and Heller, came to his aid, and the college retained him. In a statement submitted to the board by the Alumni Association, the organization decided that Deutsch should make a "public declaration of loyalty" to clear the college of suspicion. After Deutsch was exonerated, Heller congratulated him but warned him that he needed to be "watchfully discreet," "to abstain" from giving the "slenderest provocation."[37]

Following Deutsch's death in 1921, Heller wrote a biographical sketch of him for the *Hebrew Union College Monthly* in which he tried to explain Deutsch's wartime problems. Heller maintained that Deutsch's "heart clung to the German people" and that "his affections . . . ruled his judgment." But, Heller continued, Deutsch had also been stung by the "general discredit under which everything associated with Germany had fallen in the exaggerated wave of chauvinistic bigotry which had come with the war." Heller himself had sent a letter to the editor of the *Times-Picayune* to protest when the local school board threatened to remove German from the public high school curriculum. Heller argued that teaching the German language perpetuated "that glorious German spirit" that far antedated and would long survive "the menacing spectre of Prussian Kultur."[38]

Heller's overwhelming concern, after the issuance of the Balfour Declaration, however, lay in publicizing the renewed possibility that Zion would be restored, a subject he entertained both in the pulpit and in the local press as well as in the Jewish press. Unlike Deutsch, Heller was now caught up in the vision of a Jewish Palestine, the most "glowing romance of the world war." But while the younger men in the CCAR well may have sympathized with Zionism and, like many American Jews formerly indecisive over the issue, were more likely to embrace the movement since the appearance of the Balfour Declaration, the anti-Zionists were motivated to organize as never before. In the spring of 1918, Heller's venom reached a literary peak in a letter to the editor of the *American Israelite* in which he compared the anti-Zionist to the Bolshevik, arguing that the two exhibited "many points of congeniality and resemblance." He called the Anti-Zionist the "Bolshevik of Jewishness." Both Bolsheviks and anti-Zionists were prisoners of their own dogma; both would discover, "too late, that by their blindness, they have struck their adored cause of actualized social justice a stunning blow from which it will take a long time to recover." The anti-Zionist belatedly might awaken to learn that he had "injured the prestige of his own faith and race by stubbornly seeking to retard" what was already "beyond his power to prevent."[39]

The following June, Heller was jockeying behind the scenes to shape the CCAR summer convention in Chicago, even though he had decided not to attend. He stayed away, he sarcastically remarked, because the unpleasant decisions at the Buffalo convention had "satisfied" him "for some time to come." Although he refused to resign from the CCAR and was "keeping Wise and [Martin] Meyer from doing so," he complained to Stolz that he felt "worn out with the pettiness, weakness and folly of the rank and file" and "nauseated by the spirit of leaders like Philipson and Schulman." The "blinkered" positions spouted by Heller's antagonists on issues from Zionism to "social maladjustments" and "industrial evils" dampened both his "pride of vocation and glow of idealism." A "divorce" may have been out of the question, but he needed a period of "separation" from the Conference. The leadership's response to the Balfour Declaration particularly displeased him, and in referring to the subject, Heller revealed his peevishness even to Stolz. "If the rest of you cannot recognize an epoch when it has come," he wrote, "I want to be absent when you record yourselves" standing in the way of historical development. Although he still felt the tug of old loyalties and apologized for the bitterness in his heart, he concluded that it was best to stay away even while he continued to work for the CCAR in other areas.[40]

Heller's premonitions were sound. He was far from being paranoid on the growing intransigency of the anti-Zionists, even if he remained un-aware of the extent of their underground activities. In late April 1918, a group of rabbis and laymen, including Schulman and Herman Enelow, met in New York at the request of Ephraim Frisch, a young anti-Zionist rabbi there. Frisch wanted to initiate a League of American Jews, an official anti-Zionist organization similar to the League of British Jews. In July, as Heller was lobbying for a more positive statement from the CCAR on the subject of the Balfour Declaration, Frisch, Philipson, and other anti-Zionists were busily planning a counterattack. Philipson noted that since the CCAR had reaffirmed its position at Buffalo, the Conference had to deal with Zionism again at the 1918 convention only because the Balfour Declaration had been issued, bringing "Zionistic propaganda into the field of practical world politics." The CCAR very much favored facilitating the immigration of Jews to Palestine when "economic neces-sity or political and religious persecution" made Palestine the obvious haven, he argued, but the Conference refused to subscribe to the phrase in the Declaration stating that Palestine was to be designated as "a na-tional home-land for the Jewish people." The CCAR opposed the idea of Palestine as "THE homeland of the Jews" and maintained that the Jewish people had a right to be at home wherever they chose to live.[41]

Heller waged his attack on the outcome of the CCAR convention in an essay, "Zionism and Our Reform Rabbinate," in an unusually long *Mac-cabaean* column that presented a concise historical overview of the en-counter between America's Zionists and anti-Zionists during the preced-ing two decades. Now that more of the seminary's students were of Eastern European parentage, Heller believed that perhaps a majority were sympathetic toward the movement, but he sadly noted that, when faced with the hostility of their congregants, many of these young men would "abandon their Zionist ideals" in order to maintain their pulpits. As if predicting that more favorable conditions might exist in the fu-ture, he mentioned that Zionist rabbis now headed five of the largest con-gregations in the country—New York, Philadelphia, Cleveland, San Fran-cisco, and New Orleans—and that the most influential rabbi in the movement [unnamed, but undoubtedly Stephen S. Wise] was also a Zi-onist. Again equating anti-Zionism with philistinism, Heller concluded, "Whenever, if ever, the multitudes of the prosperous will adopt Zionism into fashion, they will be followed, reluctantly by their spiritual lead-ers."[42]

Anti-Zionists wasted no time in pushing their agenda past a limited audience of Reform Jews—rabbinical and lay. Just a few days after the Chicago meeting, Henry Cohen sent a letter to Robert Lansing, Wilson's secretary of state. No friend of the Jews, Lansing was a logical and well-chosen target of anti-Zionist propaganda. In December 1917, he had already cautioned Wilson to "avoid endorsing the British position." Cohen's letter got to the point very quickly. He told Lansing that "an overwhelming majority of native born Americans and numbers of Jews who have made the United States the country of their adoption" appreciated Balfour's good intentions, but felt the Declaration to be an "act of mistaken kindness." He argued that Reform Jews, having "outgrown the conception of Jewish nationality," were much "too deeply attached" to the United States to seek another political affiliation. Truly, these anti-Zionists reacted "with repugnance and alarm" to the very idea of a newly established Jewish state. Obviously, Cohen wished to pressure the State Department, and ultimately the president, to withhold support for the British Declaration.[43]

Now when he advocated the Zionist position, Heller used Wilsonian-Brandeisian terminology, seeing the new Jerusalem "in the shape of a realized pattern of social justice." The Jews would establish in their regained homeland a "perfectly ethical social order," which would lead to "higher spirituality." In another article, he spoke of the harmony that would exist in the homeland, where "every class-interest and party-complexion" would be assuaged.[44]

The dream of Jewish harmony in the promised land vividly contrasted with the intraethnic fighting that the idea of a revived Palestine provoked. In August 1918, both the Reform Zionists and the anti-Zionists were aggressively promoting their viewpoints. Heller, Stephen Wise, and Martin Meyer circulated a counterstatement (endorsed by several other Zionists within the CCAR) to the recent CCAR resolution. When Cohen received his, he scribbled a response at the bottom, castigating Zionists for propagandizing to members of Congress. Evidently he interpreted his "private" letter to Lansing in a different light. At the end of August, Frisch, Philipson, and Cohen, among others, were ready to put forward their League of American Jews and proposed that a conference be held in New York at the end of October. While the anti-Zionist organizers exchanged letters containing a variety of agendas for the meeting and their future campaign against the Declaration, on the last day of August, President Wilson's Jewish New Year's greeting to Stephen S. Wise undermined all of their plans. Wilson warmly endorsed the progress American Zionists had made since the Balfour Declaration and generally looked forward to the British government's fulfillment of its promise to facilitate the establishment in Palestine of a national homeland for the Jewish people.[45]

Zionist leaders capitalized on the statement by sending copies to rabbis throughout the country, suggesting that they read it aloud to their congregants during high holiday services. In light of Wilson's pro-Zionist sentiment, anti-Zionists like Kaufman Kohler decided that the time was not propitious for launching a new anti-Zionist organization. He worried that such an action would not only expose the "weakness and smallness of numbers" in the anti-Zionist camp but might even seem un-American. "I consider it detrimental to our cause to start an opposition during war time," he told his cohort David Philipson, since the League could be "looked upon as unpatriotic." Kohler decided not to allow his name to be used in the call for the anti-Zionist conference. "I trust . . . that you yourself have by this time come to the same conclusion," he added. Louis Marshall's letter was even stronger. "I not only am unwilling to permit the use of my name" in calling for a League conference, "but I sincerely hope that you and your associates may abandon the project," Marshall began. He warned that only negative consequences would result from the effort, creating "a bitter feeling among the Jews of this country and of misapprehensions which can only bode evil."[46]

Frisch, however, followed his own counsel and, after Wilson's letter to Wise had been published, telegraphed the president himself. Embarrassed by Frisch's ill-timed, impetuous, and bold reaction, Zionists and anti-Zionists alike castigated him. In his statements to the press, the unseasoned young rabbi had, perhaps inadvertently, revealed the plans for the League of American Jews. Henry Berkowitz, an influential Philadelphia rabbi originally sympathetic to the League, now reversed himself. "Circumstances have placed us in a position in which we are robbed . . . of doing anything that would prove effectual," he told Philipson. Berkowitz regretted that Frisch had destroyed any possibilities "to make known our position in a dignified and effective way to the President and the country." But the die-hards like Philipson, Cohen, Frisch, and some committed laymen did not give up so easily.[47]

Frisch's action motivated Heller to vent his anger in a scalding letter to the editor of the *American Israelite*, which remained one of the most ideologically anti-Zionist publications in the country. He acknowledged that Zionists had been portrayed as "impractical dreamers . . . irreligious or even anti-religious in tendency." But now that the national association of Orthodox Rabbis had endorsed Zionism, the argument that the movement was anti-religious could be seen as fallacious. While Heller acknowledged that the president's letter was not an official sanction, he nevertheless believed that Wilson, in "speaking on behalf of 'all Americans' " and in alluding to Palestine's "promise of spiritual rebirth," favored the cause. Heller's conclusion was particularly strong. "If Zionism succeeds, the glory will certainly be that of the Jew and Judaism," he predicted. But should the movement fail, "the discredit can not be escaped by Jew and Judaism," especially if the failure resulted, "not from outward impediments," but from "inner divisions and factious antagonisms." Elsewhere Heller called antinationalism a "prejudice" that Jews still needed to outgrow. He continued to blame an assimilated, comfortable American Jewish community who refused "to measure a world-wide question otherwise than with the yardstick of domestic interests."[48]

Although now badly crippled, the anti-Zionists continued to work more discreetly. After armistice was declared in November 1918, the core of League-supporting anti-Zionists now hoped to limit the Zionist influence on the peace process. When the American Jewish Congress finally convened in Philadelphia the following month, and Judge Julian Mack, Brandeis's disciple and president of the Zionist Organization of America, was elected to chair the delegation going to Paris,[49] anti-Zionists felt duty bound to redouble their organizational efforts.

President Wilson's reassurance to Stephen S. Wise that he would stand by his promise to help secure a "Jewish commonwealth," only spurred the anti-Zionists to find a leader to deliver their message to the president. In March 1919, the same month that Wilson personally met with the American Jewish Congress delegation, California Congressman Julius Kahn presented the president with an anti-Zionist manifesto that had been signed by nearly 300 prominent American Jews, including rabbis from nearly every major Reform congregation in the South except Temple Sinai.[50] These leaders identified completely with the Classical Reform mission of dispersion, an attitude reinforced by the anxieties aroused by wartime antihyphenated campaigners like Theodore Roosevelt, who stridently insisted that America was for Americans. David Philipson quoted the California congressman whose concluding remarks praised the recent elimination of "hyphenism" in the United States. "Thank God for it! . . . And what is Zionism endeavoring to do? Create a new form of hyphenism? . . . We want no such thing. For me the United States is my Zion and San Francisco is my Jerusalem." But these sentiments proved to be practically the anti-Zionists' last hurrah of the World War I era.[51]

In response to the renewed anti-Zionist thrust, Heller continued to promote the message of the essential reciprocity between Reform and Zionism as he patiently and passionately explained that the two movements needed each other. In his neatly balanced argument, he ably described the inner reconciliation that allowed him to fight actively for the two movements that, at the moment, appeared to be poised in opposition.

Significantly, he now perceived both as processes that, in time, were bound to "fructify and interpenetrate one another." While Zionism needed the "liberal temper . . . to save for Judaism its vigor and freshness of ever renewed readaptation to historic environments," Reform Judaism required "the inspiring wing-beat of the Zionist hope" with its "hot, red blood of Jewish loyalty and . . . brotherhood, its thirst for the sincerity and the fulfillment of being ourselves." Now when he waged his war of words, Heller called those who still opposed a Jewish homeland not anti-Zionists but anti-Semites. Paraphrasing Brandeis's famous call for men, money, and discipline, he implored American Jews to "observe discipline ourselves." Then he presented his own plea. "Let us fall into line," he urged, "uphold our leaders and build the one permanent refuge for our downtrodden brothers." Rabbi Leon Harris, a non-Zionist from St. Louis and a friend of Heller's, provided a positive long-term perspective on the Zionist question within the Reform movement. He agreed that to oppose the rehabilitation of Palestine was not anti-Zionistic but anti-Semitic, and he believed that there was "room in Jewry . . . for those who are sympathetic with Zionistic aspirations, without actually sharing them."[52]

At the two major CCAR events of 1919, the celebration in Cincinnati in April in honor of the centenary of I. M. Wise and the annual summer convention to which Heller was now ready to return, the New Orleans rabbi underscored his major arguments with new variations on his well-worn theme of rapprochement. Although anti-Zionism remained the official position of the Reform movement, Heller detected in the turn of events since the Balfour Declaration the beginning of the sea change he had anticipated in the Reform rabbinate. In spite of much waving of the "bloody Anti-Zionist shirt" at the Wise celebration, he discerned the "Zionist skeleton at the Reform feast" apparent in the momentous topics assiduously avoided in the CCAR president's address. Missing was all reference to Palestine, Wilson's communiqués to Wise, the meeting of the American Jewish Congress and the Zionist presence at the peace conference—clearly the most noteworthy recent events in American Jewish life. Heller could see that the "best men" in Reform Judaism had become "painfully aware" that the movement had lost its vitality. Any rabbi sensitive to his own Jewishness would be troubled to see that the officially sanctioned Jewishness among CCAR leaders consisted merely of "trite quotations and cant phrases" uttered by men whose minds were as "inelastic as their hearts" were cold. The topic of Zionism, however, served as fair game for constant dissection and denouncement in other venues at the centenary. In an intriguing metaphor, Heller noted that although Jewish nationalism had played the role of "St. Sylvester to a shower of passing arrows," he still believed that "conversion to Zionism" had to precede the "revitalization, in America, of Reform Judaism."[53]

In his critique of the president's paper at the CCAR summer convention, Heller parted ways with the dominant Brandeisian Zionism that had won over so many American Jews. The souring of the Progressivist vision in the ashes of World War I, coupled with the xenophobia and racial hysteria that ran rampant throughout the country in 1919, served as elements to diminish, once again, his belief in American exceptionalism. He echoed sentiments that he had expressed earlier that year when he noted that those Jews who worried about Zionism and dual loyalty and who readily denounced "Ghetto ways" were actually those most clearly bearing the "deepest Ghetto marks." They were undoubtedly the Jews who were unsure of their acceptance in American society, and their anxiety expressed itself as "Ghetto Americanism" with its frantic appeals to Zionists not to "substitute Jerusalem for Washington." While Heller exalted America as "the ideal of perfection . . . above all other national loyalties," he considered excessive patriotism to be in bad taste, indicative of insecure Jews' desperate need to feel equal to other Americans. The ills of assimilation had lessened his expectations that Judaism could thrive on American soil. "We have lost our Sabbath and our Jewish feeling towards the Sabbath," he complained. Having known the Sabbath as a "child of the ghetto" in Prague, Heller understood the great value of that loss, and he for the first time openly said that he wished to live in Palestine, where he could celebrate the Sabbath as the essence of a Jewish way of life. Although he acknowledged that, in his "advanced years," he had "nothing to offer Palestine at this time," his sentiment was not as a result "any less sincere."[54]

If Heller had been younger or stronger that year, he would have been able to participate in a couple of events that he would have found stimulating. Stephen Wise invited him to join Justice Brandeis on a fact-finding mission to Palestine, an experience that could later be used in pro-Zionist fund-raising. Heller declined because he did not think he had the physical stamina to "repay that wonderful experience by an adequate propaganda tour"; his energies would have to be devoted to the efforts of his own congregation in building a new temple. He told Wise that he planned to ask his congregation for a winter vacation in recognition of his thirty-five years in Sinai's pulpit, and he hoped to make the pilgrimage to Palestine at that time. He also declined another propaganda tour, this time under the auspices of the National Association for the Advancement of Colored People (NAACP). Among the several rabbis who had written to James Weldon Johnson, executive director of the NAACP, offering to speak on race relations on behalf of the organization, Heller was the only Southerner. Now he felt that his poor health precluded his participation in promoting "the cause of an Association . . . very dear to me." He hoped that the following year he would be sufficiently rested to do so.[55]

Unfortunately, while Heller was never able to speak on behalf of the NAACP, he did muster the vigor, psychological as well as physical, to face the CCAR convention the following summer. Between the two meetings, the British mandate for Palestine had been confirmed at the San Remo Conference. Heller undoubtedly realized that the CCAR leadership might still not bow before the reality of this momentous decision. He was right. The committee on the president's message found that it could not "rejoice" when the mandate for Palestine was heralded as the "Redemption of Israel." The Reform movement remained "convinced" that the mission of the Jew was to trumpet ethical monotheism throughout the world, rejecting any assertion of Jewish nationality as "long ago outgrown." Israel's Redemption would be realized only "when the Jew will have the right to live in any part of the world" with "all racial and religious prejudice and persecution ended."[56]

Heller, along with Horace J. Wolf, a younger Zionist rabbi, dissented. The CCAR, they argued, must realize that "conditions annihilate theories." The treaty of San Remo had "stamped the sanction of the civilized world upon the program of political Zionism," and the CCAR should go along with the majority of Jews throughout the world in lifting "our hearts in fervent gratitude to the mysterious Providence . . . guiding the Jewish people . . . into the Promised Land." Although the majority report received the lion's share of the vote, Heller felt that a strongly "spiritual aspect" was already surfacing at the convention. The majority had trounced the Zionists' report, but Heller believed that "in Judaism, minorities have a trick of changing to majorities." He and Stephen Wise had already recognized that Zionism held an attraction for younger rabbis. Now Heller felt that more rabbis could flock to the "standards of Zionism, despite . . . pressure . . . exercised in the opposite direction."[57]

Anti-Semitism, moreover, was once again on the rise, even in the United States, in the resurgence of the Ku Klux Klan and in the pages of Henry Ford's *Dearborn Independent*. Heller felt that Jews could not continue to deceive themselves that no danger existed here. In "Dangers of the Hour," Heller mentioned the reappearance of "deep-rooted antagonisms" that would "take generations to overcome." He also identified signs of a brighter future to come. First, the "guiding principle of minority rights" had been recognized in the postwar peace negotiations, and

Jews had succeeded in sending representative delegations to the peace conference at Paris. Most important, even though Jewish persecution was on the rise, the prospect of a national homeland "endorsed by the great powers of civilization" offered some hope of rescue. Heller prophetically perceived that the next few decades would prove to be "a critical period in Jewish history" that would "largely determine the nature and scope of our contribution to the reborn world." A Jewish world divided between assimilationists and nationalists could not respond adequately to the dual tasks of rebuilding a Jewish homeland and rehabilitating "our impoverished brothers" in Europe "where they would never be able to live at peace." During the early 1920s, in addition to occasional articles and essays in the local press and in Jewish publications where he had earlier published, Heller served as a special correspondent to the *B'nai B'rith News.* In article after article, he analyzed the rise of anti-Semitism abroad and at home. In January 1925, Heller's article "The Quandary of the Apostate Jew" appeared in the *B'nai B'rith Magazine.* Now the rabbi's analysis gained a new sense of urgency, eerie in its insights of the changing nature of anti-Semitism. "The anti-Semite becomes impatient with science," he warned. "Refractory archaeologists have disappointed him by failing to discover any mysterious Arian meaning in the history of his cherished Swastika; another science must come to the rescue; anti-Semitic microscopes promise to detect Jewish blood, nay, even the half-blood the quarter-blood."[58] Although Heller could not imagine the dimensions of the dangers he envisioned, he truly believed that moral courage and the spiritual vision of a reunited Jewish people would ultimately triumph.

CHAPTER X

The Legacy of a Righteous Life

In the spring of 1924, the *Times-Picayune* published a daily series of interviews with New Orleans residents entitled "What I Would Do If I Had Only One Year to Live." In Heller's interview, which was featured, the sixty-four-year-old rabbi declared that, first, he would prepare himself mentally so that he might "meet the situation bravely and calmly" and complete whatever "duties" remained unfinished. From systematically arranging his affairs to framing directions for a modest funeral, Heller was concerned to handle all unpalatable tasks so that the work he began could continue "under the most favorable auspices." He hoped that those who would "make the wisest use of them" would inherit whatever possessions he had acquired. By so organizing his days, he hoped to spare his family unnecessary pain and help them face the "impending separation with courage and dignity."[1] Heller's last decade more than fulfilled these modest aims as he productively concluded his career by attempting to shape the legacy he would leave his family, his congregation, his community, and American Judaism.

From the time Heller arrived in New Orleans, he maintained a strong interest in the education of the congregation's children. In 1887 he had insisted that the religious school classes have dedicated classrooms; by 1915, he had made sure that none but trained teachers or college graduates would teach the classes. The next year, Heller suggested that the confirmation class furnish one of the large classrooms as its gift to the temple. He hoped that other confirmation classes would follow this example, making the kind of improvements that would be "transferrable [*sic*] to a new temple whenever our congregation should feel itself in a position to undertake that greatly-needed forward step."[2]

As young adults, Heller's children Isaac and Cecile participated actively in the religious school. During the World War I years, Isaac served as principal of the religious school, while Rabbi Heller's love of the He-

12. *Ida and Max Heller in a rowboat, circa 1925. Courtesy of Edward M. Heller and Theo M. Heller.*

brew language and enthusiasm for the Balfour Declaration motivated him to create a simulated "Trip to Palestine" for the Hebrew students. Ships sailing to Palestine represented the various Hebrew classes, and Cecile Heller drew on her artistic talents to prepare the map for the "voyage." As Heller grew older, his hair and beard became completely white, and his manner, so fierce in debates with his CCAR colleagues and others, turned gentle and solicitous with fellow Zionists and the students of Temple Sinai's religious school. Those whom Rabbi Heller confirmed remember him as the man "who looked like God." Before illness incapacitated Heller, he and Ida each year invited the entire confirmation class to their home for the Passover seder. Walter A. Lurie, a member of the last confirmation class that Heller taught, recalled Heller as a great teacher. "When he was too ill to meet us, he would have us come to his house, often conducting class from his bed," Lurie wrote. Heller had been too ill to attend the confirmation service, so the students went to his home afterward to be blessed, "and not until then did we feel the full solemnity of the occasion; through all the beautiful services, we had missed the presence of the one who was most closely connected in our hearts, with matters religious and spiritual."[3]

Young Walter Lurie may have found the rabbi inspiring, but Heller consistently had trouble getting adults to attend services. The majority of his congregants simply did not take religious observances seriously, and the temple was no longer near the geographic center of the New Orleans Jewish community. In February 1917, Heller criticized board members for their lack of attendance at Shabbat services; none of them had appeared on a recent Friday night, and now Heller chastised them: "Either the congregation has a service, choir, cantor and minister which repel the people, or else its officers are, to put it mildly, lacking in enthusiasm and faithfulness." And these were his words for people in leadership positions![4]

Heller's own children adored him, and they considered his personal strength and integrity truly awesome, even in times of personal tragedy. James and Ruth were the first of his children to marry, and in 1920, the spring when Heller rejoiced in the signing of the San Remo treaty, Cecile, his oldest child, followed suit. Cecile's physical development, like that of her brother Isaac, had been inhibited by health problems. She had diabetes, and her family devoted much energy to seeing that she got the best care possible. Not six months after her wedding to the Chicagoan Edward Lasker, an author of books on chess who competed internationally, Cecile was hospitalized for tonsillitis, and she had to undergo surgery. Although she had apparently begun to recuperate, she died suddenly just a few days later from complications related to her diabetes. The family was in shock. It is unclear whether Heller reached Chicago before her death, but her mother and James, as well as her new husband, were at her side. The family returned home to New Orleans on the Panama Limited, and Heller conducted a private funeral at the Union Passenger Terminal immediately upon the train's arrival in the city. Only a deep well of faith could have sustained the grieving father sufficiently to allow him to fulfill his duties as a rabbi despite the immense loss.[5]

The year 1920 also marked Heller's sixtieth birthday. For the first time, Temple Sinai began to look for an associate rabbi. Worn out from battles over Zionism and the emotional ordeal of Cecile's death, Heller was undoubtedly ready for some assistance, although the temple found no suitable permanent candidate. Coincidentally, James was also moving into an associate position. Leaving behind his own pulpit in Little Rock, Arkansas, James was elected to assist Louis Grossman, Heller's old classmate at HUC, at the Plum Street Temple in Cincinnati. Plum Street Temple was the "mother" temple of the American Reform movement, having been Isaac M. Wise's congregation during his tenure in Cincinnati. Heller's older son was now positioned to carry on his father's work and assumed Grossman's pulpit when he retired. James ultimately be-

13. *Max Heller with the 1922 Temple Sinai confirmation class.*
Courtesy of Edward M. Heller and Theo M. Heller.

came I. M. Wise's biographer, CCAR president, and a major Zionist leader in his own right.[6]

Isaac, for a time attracted to the rabbinate, was the only Heller child to return to New Orleans, where he married and raised a family. An able attorney, Isaac, like his father, took a great interest in public education and from 1929 to 1941 served as a "dissident member" of the Orleans Parish School Board, where he tirelessly championed better facilities and opportunities for black students. Both sons carried on their father's example and proved their mettle in the late 1930s in helping Jewish refugees from Nazi Germany enter the United States. Isaac Heller's legal expertise sliced through the bureaucratic bulwarks so effectively that representatives from the Catholic archdiocese approached him to help rescue German Catholics. Mildred, Heller's wife, served as president of the local Council of Jewish Women during that harrowing crisis. She recalled spending many hours at the Union Passenger Terminal seeing to the needs of transient refugees. Isaac also joined James in stumping for Zionism at national meetings.[7]

In 1922, Temple Sinai reached two milestones. March marked Heller's thirty-fifth year as Sinai's spiritual leader, and in November the congregation celebrated its fiftieth anniversary. The local paper noted that, historically, Heller was one of only four rabbis in the United States who had occupied the same pulpit continuously for such a length of time. In his anniversary address, he contrasted the congregation that had welcomed him in 1887 with the one now seated before him. The late nineteenth-century New Orleans Jewish community, like the city itself, was not only smaller but also more compact, and the earlier congregants lived much closer to the temple. As residential neighborhoods developed along St. Charles Avenue and spread further uptown, Reform Jews in New Orleans took part in the demographic shift.

Heller felt that something vital had been lost in the changes. He detected a "new snobbishness" strongly suggesting that his congregants had drifted apart socially as well as geographically. As their lives and relationships became more atomized, the congregants had also floated free of "honored old anchorages, and religion had been one of those stabilizing rudders." The other Reform congregations, Gates of Prayer and Touro Synagogue, were much more accessible to the increasingly uptown Jewish community. The lay leaders of Temple Sinai, as well as Heller, had been looking into a new location for some years. By moving further uptown, Heller hoped that the temple would once again be convenient, and therefore more vital, to its congregants. At the fiftieth anniversary celebration, when the congregation showed Heller its appreciation for his service by presenting him with a purse "said to contain $3500," Heller returned the gift, announcing that it would be the first subscription in the building fund for a new temple.[8]

For over a decade, the rabbi had consulted with other rabbis about erecting a new facility. He knew exactly the kind of structure that he wanted his congregation to build. When one rabbi sent Heller a picture of the new temple in his community, Heller remarked that he was "delighted" to see that the style selected was not that of a "meaningless, snobbish, non-religious, library-museum-concert hall" so popular among congregations seeking assimilative anonymity. Instead, he found that the temple erected stood "manfully for Jewish identity, for the imposingly and impressively religious" and the "frankly historical rather than the non-descript." The building that local Jewish architect Emile Weil designed and completed for Temple Sinai six years later at the corner of Calhoun and St. Charles Avenue in the fashionable university section of uptown New Orleans matched Heller's ideal (illustration 14). No one could mistake the massive domed edifice for a secular building. The rabbi saw his aesthetic choices becoming bricks and mortar. Today the sanctuary

14. *New Temple Sinai. Courtesy of the Historic New Orleans Collection.*

still comfortably and majestically seats the congregation more than a half century later in a location that has remained central for a majority of the congregants.[9]

For the congregation's "jubilee" celebration in November 1922, Heller's tribute bore the distinct mark of his careful scholarship and astute observations. At the anniversary banquet at the Harmony Club, each guest received a small bound volume entitled *Jubilee Souvenir of Temple Sinai, 1872–1922,* which Heller had lovingly "compiled." One hundred and fifty pages in length, complete with photographs, footnotes, and index, the publication contained much more than its title modestly suggested. Not only did the *Jubilee Souvenir* painstakingly portray the saga of the congregation, it chronicled the entire century of New Orleans Jewish history. Heller expanded the parameters of the volume because he felt that the congregational history could be understood only "out of its origins and antecedents." No one before him had "taken the trouble of putting together the main events in the early career of New Orleans Jewry where they might be conveniently accessible to the casual searcher."[10]

Since Heller meticulously documented his sources, his volume has remained the starting point for any serious scholarly inquiry into the origins and evolution of the entire New Orleans Jewish community. In the pages of the *Jubilee Souvenir*, Heller also discussed the ecumenicism that existed between the New Orleans Jewish and non-Jewish communities, and he credited the periodic epidemics that plagued the city with having inadvertently stimulated both "religious toleration and interdenominational courtesy." The threats to public health required a community of laymen and clerics alike who necessarily worked together to ensure better public health protection for all. Interestingly, Heller included portraits of Reverend Theodore Clapp and Dr. Benjamin Palmer, the city's most dynamic Protestant leaders of the nineteenth century.[11]

Heller also integrated Temple Sinai into its larger set of origins and antecedents. He evaluated the half century of American Jewish history that followed the congregation's birth and retraced the roots of the American Reform movement from David Einhorn to Isaac M. Wise. While he noted that the Reform movement had progressed "towards a bolder radicalism" and "more effective organization," he also identified the "revival of vital religious observances" for which he had worked during most of his career. This revival coupled with the creation of new ceremonies that promised to deepen "modern religious life" meant that Reform Judaism was beginning to show "a more mature reverence for the authority of history and tradition," a condition that had to exist before rapprochement and American Jewish unity could prevail.[12]

Again Heller alluded to periodic public health crises. He drew an analogy between yellow fever, which had reinforced the ecumenical spirit in New Orleans, and anti-Semitism, which had catalyzed Reform Judaism. Like a debilitating disease, anti-Semitism retarded "all movements in the direction of discarding inheritances and wiping out what is Jewishly characteristic." As in choosing a distinctive architectural style for a synagogue, a Jew could assert his integrity only by standing up proudly for his entire history and culture, including its unique Orientalisms. Not surprisingly, Heller's closing paragraphs extolled Zionism—although few of his congregants shared his broad perspective—as the prescriptive for Jewish identity, for kindling and bracing "Jewish consciousness" against the disintegrating processes of emancipation and assimilation. Although another four decades passed before the majority of Temple Sinai members followed Heller's example, earlier than anyone else in a major southern pulpit, he had planted the roots of Zionism in the fertile soil of Reform Judaism and had claimed that heritage for his congregation.[13]

Since his twenty-fifth year in the Reform rabbinate, Heller had been accusing those in leadership positions at HUC of punishing him for his

Zionism by refusing to grant him a doctoral degree. In 1925, Heller became critically ill while visiting in New York and was confined to Mount Sinai Hospital. Several colleagues in the Reform rabbinate who were aware of Heller's fragile condition wrote to express their wishes for his return to health. Some probably believed that he would not recover and sought a reconciliation while he was still alive. They included Samuel Schulman of New York's Temple Emanu-El, who acknowledged that the two men had disagreed in many ways but told Heller that "one of the joys of life" was to "differ with those whose talents and character one profoundly respects." Schulman admired Heller's "mentality," his "zeal on behalf of Judaism," his literary style, and his "challenging and at the same time, entertaining wit and sarcasm," which made the southern rabbi "always a refreshing influence in American Judaism." Julian Morgenstern, president of HUC, went even further and, writing to Heller on his sickbed, proposed to confer upon him the degree of doctor of Hebrew law. An honorary title at one time might have meant something to Heller's ego and career, but the degree now was useless, an insult inasmuch as he had achieved great stature without such a title. Illness had done nothing to diminish Heller's "entertaining wit and sarcasm." He dictated a letter to Ida from his bed, telling Morgenstern that he was "restrained" from accepting "any such degree" from the college. Having protested to the Board of Governors on several occasions against the "unfair and mischievous, un-Jewish and un-American" methods used by HUC in conferring doctoral degrees, Heller now refused to reverse himself. In declining the title of doctor of Hebrew law, Heller claimed that he knew enough of the Jewish Law "(which is the one alluded to) to be clearly and unalterably aware that my acquaintance with it is far from sufficient to enable me, with honesty and dignity, to accept and wear such a title." He preferred "not to be perpetually reminded" how far he was from "having mastered" the law. He claimed that he owed it to the memory of his "illustrious great-grandfather, Reb Nachum Kassowitz . . . , one of the 'jurists' " of the Prague Jewish community, "not to be a party to such . . . ill-proportioned pretensions." In deference to his own self esteem and "in justice to the wider issues involved," the refusal would be "given due publicity in the Jewish press."[14]

Recovering from his illness, Heller remained in the pulpit long enough to celebrate his fortieth anniversary at Temple Sinai, and then he resigned. In his farewell sermon, "Forty Years of Effort and Companionship," he told his congregants that when he entered the rabbinate, he knew better than to expect a "visible or tangible reward." In the first address to the congregation in 1887, he had stressed the value of spiritual over material rewards. Now, at the end of his career, Heller realized more than ever that "invisible things are greater than steel or bronze." Significantly, Heller's closing sermon also reemphasized the theme of reconciliation. He spoke of the union he had strived constantly to realize between the Orthodox and the Reform communities and between Jew and non-Jew. Monte M. Lemann, one of the most prominent Sinai members, responded that, through the years, Heller had only continued to increase the "strong hold on his people." But Lemann also noted Heller's role as a dissident. Although Heller's "reasoning" had not always agreed with that of some of his congregants, the rabbi had "ever held their hearts close to his own."[15]

Stephen S. Wise wrote to the congregation that he considered Heller "a mighty utterer of truth and righteousness in the pulpit." While "utterly loyal to the liberal movement," Heller had "avoided the terrible mistake of viewing the liberal movement as a schism or divisiveness within Israel." Instead Heller had "done much to heal the breach between Reform and Orthodox Jews in our country." Community leaders honored Heller's retirement with a farewell reception at the Athenaeum the following evening. Among those who spoke were Rev. Robert S. Coupland, rector of Trinity Church, and Dr. A. R. Dinwiddie, president of Tulane University.[16]

At last Heller could fulfill two of his most closely cherished dreams. He made a pilgrimage to Palestine that included a stop in Basel, Switzerland, to attend the World Zionist Congress (WZC). In the 1890s, Heller had penned accounts of his European travels for the *Jewish Ledger*. In the early 1920s, he traveled to postwar Europe and described his impressions in the pages of the *B'nai B'rith News*. Now he shared his experiences in the Middle East with readers of the *New Orleans States*. Each Sunday, from October 1927 to January 1928, the paper ran a column of his sketches of life in the Holy Land. As he told an audience after his return, "I went to Palestine, not as an expert nor as a scholar, but as one primarily interested in human happiness, justice and progress." Filled "with the love of my own people in my heart," Heller went to see for himself the land that was to be both a refuge for Jews fleeing oppression and the future center for developing Jewish culture.[17]

As the ship sailed from Alexandria to Jaffa, Heller passionately described his emotions upon seeing Palestine for the first time from the deck. When, at daybreak, "through clouds and a faint mist," the sun at last revealed the hills of Judea, Heller wrote, "My heart seemed to leap into my mouth." Alone at such an early hour, he burst into tears, "mostly of joy, not unmingled with mourning." This was the land of "Jewish love

15. *Max Heller in Egypt, 1927. Courtesy of Edward M. Heller.*

and Jewish pride," on which he was about to set foot at long last. He anticipated both Palestine's "beauty and its desolation" as he mentally reviewed the Jewish people's triumphs and struggles on this hallowed soil. While others remained asleep in their cabins, Heller walked for the next half hour, trying to contain his "bittersweet excitement."[18]

Historic sites and hardy twentieth-century Zionist pioneers rekindled Heller's faith as a Progressive. Through Heller's eyes, the Jewish homeland became the Brandeisian ideal of perfect democracy, with no differences in rank or station. He expressed a deep contentment. His soul felt satisfied and refreshed as he had so often dreamed it might be. The visit

16. *Max Heller in Palestine, 1927. Courtesy of the American Jewish Archives, Hebrew Union College–Jewish Institute of Religion, Cincinnati.*

convinced him that it was impossible to appreciate Zionism fully without traveling to Palestine.[19]

After serving as a delegate to the World Zionist Congress, Heller also believed that one could not understand the rebirth of a Jewish homeland without witnessing the biennial conference of its leaders. The diversity of the contemporary Jewish experience that excited him at the American Jewish Congress gathering in Philadelphia now impressed him in Basel. Although the American Jewish Congress more fully represented all classes and ranks in that experience, Heller claimed that the WZC was the first Jewish conference in twenty centuries to gather Jews from "the four corners of the globe." Jewish dispersal meant a Babel-like confusion. Since no common language existed, one address "was couched in . . . six languages: German, French and English, Hebrew, Yiddish and Russian." The need for translations required more patience from the audience than most of its members were willing to give. Just as being in the recently reestablished Jewish homeland made Heller more acutely aware of the strong pulse of the Jewish past and its continuity with the Jewish future, so did his presence at the WZC reassure him that world Jewish leaders like Chaim Weizmann could help translate the messianic future into a viable present. Heller's inner tensions could, at long last, rest.[20]

17. *Max Heller at retirement, 1927. Courtesy of the American Jewish Archives, Hebrew Union College–Jewish Institute of Religion, Cincinnati.*

Heller died in New Orleans on 30 March 1929, just two months after his sixty-ninth birthday, the day the one hundred and tenth birthday of I. M. Wise was observed. He had lived to see the new Temple Sinai dedicated and to preach the baccalaureate sermon at the Jewish Institute of Religion, the Reform seminary that Stephen S. Wise had founded in New York several years earlier as an alternative to HUC. Wise wanted Heller to review his "rich and serviceable years" in the rabbinate, and Heller chose as his commencement topic "Modernized Judaism and the Modern Rabbi." Heller insisted that, above all, a rabbi needed to radiate an "unashamed Jewishness," to be "a son of his people." In one of his rare references to God, Heller spoke of the core of Jewish identity. "To be a Jew," he stated, meant caring "for the inward" while yearning "intensely for harmony with the Unseen, as the kernel of one's faith in the Unity." By striving to embody these "ultimate and victorious instincts of the Jewish soul, the prophetic flashes of Jewish genius . . . , we, most truly and completely, fulfill ourselves." After the address, Wise told Heller that his "message to the men was one of rare beauty," that he had "touched their hearts." Heller died a fulfilled Jew.[21]

Headlines and a photograph on the front page of the local papers told the city of his death. Fifteen hundred people reportedly attended his funeral at Temple Sinai, overflowing from the sanctuary into the doorways and even onto the sidewalks. Rabbi Louis Binstock, Heller's successor, conducted the services. He asked those gathered to remember their former rabbi metaphorically as "a sunglass that gathered the bright beams of light of understanding and intelligence and focused them to a point where they rendered the most good." Heller's pallbearers included two men from fields in which Heller had been active beyond his rabbinical duties. General Allison Owen, head of the Community Chest campaign was one; Ephraim Lisitzky, the renowned Hebrew poet and superintendent of New Orleans Communal Hebrew School, was the other. An editorial in a local paper noted that "on a foundation of Czech and German culture and philosophy," Heller had erected "with Jewish industry a structure of American citizenship as notably high and fine as that achieved by several other public men with that background." The journalist recognized that Heller's works beyond his ministry were as noteworthy as those directed toward the Jewish community. Another local editorial mentioned that, although Heller was "of foreign birth, he was an American to the core, and New Orleans never had a citizen more devoted to her upbuilding."[22]

Heller's death also captured national interest. The *New York Times* carried a photograph as well as a double-column article that quoted both

Stephen S. Wise and Louis Marshall. Wise noted that Heller's traditional European background was coupled with "the modernist's spirit of
searching and resolute inquiry . . . [He was] one of the few teachers in
our time to discern and to do battle against the menace of sectarianism
in Jewish reform." He called Heller "a complete and uncompromising
Jew" who devoted his life "to his people and his adopted country." Marshall recognized Heller's "cultivated intelligence," which allowed him to
wield a "facile pen" in disseminating ideas "illumined by scholarly
thought, good taste and sound sense." Heller's "deep and sincere interest" in everything pertaining to the "advancement of the Jewish people"
also impressed the prominent lay leader. In fact, Marshall was the first to
mention that even those who differed with Heller "never failed to respect
him for his intellectual honesty and his sterling and genuine manhood."[23]

At the memorial service held at Temple Sinai in early May, Julian Morgenstern, looking back over the quarter century of their acquaintance,
realized that he and Heller had almost always "stood on opposite sides."
He remembered no "vital question or action in which we were in agreement" but felt that the differences of opinion had never "affected our mutual friendship and our confidence in each other's sincerity of conviction
and purpose." The HUC president emphasized that while Heller understood Reform Judaism as a product of "stern irresistible, historic necessity," he had refused to "make a fetish" out of the movement or to make
of it "an end in itself." Instead, Heller saw Reform "in its true, historical
significance, as merely another stage in this endless process of evolution," and insisted on building "wisely in our own day for those tomor-
rows still to come." Morgenstern believed that Heller, "sooner than did
most of us," saw Reform not as an isolated, self-sufficient entity but as
one facet in the "world-unity of Israel." He predicted that the ideas and
principles that Heller had championed would become increasingly influential. Morgenstern mentioned the doctoral degree that Heller had refused to accept four years earlier and expressed regret that the institution had been able to pay Heller appropriate homage only after his death.
Others delivering eulogies represented the range of the rabbi's friendships. They included S. Walter Stern, president of Temple Sinai, Reverend
William McFaddin of the Prytania Street Presbyterian Church, and
Joseph Stolz and Henry Cohen, Heller's oldest friends in the rabbinate.[24]

Heller would have found several tributes particularly pleasing. One
journalist in the Jewish press claimed that no other Reform rabbi was as
respected by his Orthodox and Reform colleagues. Heller had the special
gift of an acute intelligence and an arresting personality that allowed

him to campaign brilliantly for the sometimes unpopular causes that he advocated, but he also had the humility that endeared him to the Jewish masses that he loved. As Heller's close friend Ephraim Lisitzky wrote in his eulogy in the *Jewish Ledger*, Heller had undergone painful self-scrutiny. Heller's spiritual journey had forced him to uproot the "liberal Judaism grafted with assimilation" that had been implanted at Cincinnati and to effect "a new grafting." His achievement lay in his successful cultivation of "liberal Judaism, liberated from assimilation with Zionism," which he had replanted "in the bleeding soil of his soul," where "it took root, blossomed and yielded both flowers and fruit." Another eulogy noted that "American Jewish life derived from him far more than it conferred upon him," because Heller had "adorned it with the dignity and grace he so well personified." But Heller, as a longtime fighter against injustice, would have been most pleased by the words of his Reform colleague Maurice H. Harris: "We loved him for the enemies he made."[25]

Heller's career in New Orleans attests both to the courage he manifested in speaking out and to the survival skills he acquired in testing the limits of racial thought and Jewish nationalist aspirations at the turn of the century. Although many of his Jewish contemporaries disagreed and sought to distance themselves from him, he inspired followers. Even before the 1960s, Temple Sinai served as the spiritual center of Jewish civil rights leadership in New Orleans, from Binstock's successor, Rabbi Julian Feibelman, Heller's son Isaac, and Edgar B. and Edith Rosenwald Stern to more contemporary activists.[26] While American Reform Judaism was still hostile to Zionism at the time of Heller's death, by the 1930s, nationally, the tide had begun to turn in support of the position that Heller had been among the first to espouse. His remarkable sense of righteousness informs his legacy. His cardinal principles impelled him to speak out, to act, and above all, to "stand unswayed."

APPENDIX

❧

THE PITTSBURGH PLATFORM, 1885

In view of the wide divergence of opinion, of conflicting ideas in Judaism to-day, we, as representatives of Reform Judaism in America, in continuation of the work begun at Philadelphia, in 1869,[1] unite upon the following principles:

First. We recognize in every religion an attempt to grasp the Infinite, and in every mode, source or book of revelation, held sacred in any religious system, the consciousness of the indwelling of God in man. We hold that Judaism presents the highest conception of the God-idea as taught in our Holy Scriptures and developed and spiritualized by the Jewish teachers, in accordance with the moral and philosophical progress of their respective ages. We maintain that Judaism preserved and defended, midst continual struggles and trials and under enforced isolation, this God-idea as the central religious truth for the human race.

Second. We recognize in the Bible the record of the consecration of the Jewish people to its mission as priest of the one God, and value it as the most potent instrument of religious and moral instruction. We hold that the modern discoveries of scientific researches in the domains of nature and history are not antagonistic to the doctrines of Judaism, the Bible reflecting the primitive ideas of its own age, and at times clothing its conception of Divine Providence and justice dealing with man in miraculous narratives.

Third. We recognize in the Mosaic legislation a system of training the Jewish people for its mission during its national life in Palestine, and to-day we accept as binding only the moral laws, and maintain only such ceremonies as elevate and sanctify our lives, but reject all such as are not adapted to the views and habits of modern civilization.

Fourth. We hold that all such Mosaic and rabbinical laws as regulate diet, priestly purity and dress originated in ages and under the influence of ideas altogether foreign to our present mental and spiritual state. They fail to impress the modern Jew with a spirit of priestly holiness: their observance in our days is apt rather to obstruct than to further modern spiritual elevation.

Fifth. We recognize in the modern era of universal culture of heart and intellect the approaching of the realization of Israel's great Messianic hope for the establishment of the kingdom of truth, justice and peace among all men. We consider ourselves no longer a nation, but a religious community, and therefore, expect

The text of the Platform appeared in Meyer's *Response to Modernity*, 387–388.

neither a return to Palestine, nor a sacrificial worship under the sons of Aaron, nor the restoration of any of the laws concerning the Jewish state.

Sixth. We recognize in Judaism a progressive religion, ever striving to be in accord with the postulates of reason. We are convinced of the utmost necessity of preserving the historical identity with our great past. Christianity and Islam being daughter religions of Judaism, we appreciate their providential mission to aid in the spreading of monotheistic and moral truth. We acknowledge that the spirit of broad humanity of our age is our ally in the fulfillment of our mission, and therefore, we extend the hand of fellowship to all who cooperate with us in the establishment of the reign of truth and righteousness among men.

Seventh. We reassert the doctrine of Judaism that the soul of man is immortal, grounding this belief on the divine nature of the human spirit, which forever finds bliss in righteousness and misery in wickedness. We reject, as ideas not rooted in Judaism, the beliefs both in bodily resurrection and in Gehanna and Eden (Hell and Paradise) as abodes for everlasting punishment and reward.

Eighth. In full accordance with the spirit of Mosaic legislation, which strives to regulate the relation between the rich and poor, we deem it our duty to participate in the great task of modern times, to solve, on the basis of justice and righteousness, the problems presented by the contrasts and evils of the present organization of society.

Table 1. Membership of Temple Sinai, 1886

Membership	Address	Occupation/firm
Herman Aaron	h: 367 Carondolet	Cotton
Henry Abraham[a]	h: 194 Jackson Avenue b: 119 Gravier	Henry Abraham and Sons, Cotton Factors/ Commission Merchants
Edward Adler[a]	h: 150 Delord b: 119 S. Peters	Edward Adler and Sons, Hides and Wool
Selim Barnett	h: 444 Camp Street b: 40 Camp	Katz and Barnett, Whls. Fancy Goods
Bertrand Beer[a]	h: 1007 St. Charles Avenue b: 76 Baronne	H. & B. Beer, Cotton Buyers
Julius Beer	h: 346 Magazine b: 51 Poydras	Wise & Beer Commission Merchants
Theodore Berkson	h: 209 Third b: 12 & 14 S. Peters	Berkson Brothers, Whls. Grocers
Simon Bloch	h: 204 Esplanade b: 42 Union	Cotton, Sugar, Rice Factor, Dealer
Henry Block	h: 502 St. Charles Avenue b: 12 S. Peters	Liquors

Membership	Address	Occupation/firm
Albert Bloom[a]	h: St. Charles, corner Felicity b: 56 Magazine	Bloom & Son, Sugar & Molasses
Isaac Bloom	h: 246 St. Mary b: 56 Magazine	Bloom & Son, Sugar & Molasses
Elie Blum	h: Second, between Chippewa & Annunciation b: 18 S. Peters	J. W. Demarest Company, Fruit Whls.
G. Brown[a]		
E. Brunner	(no record)	
Edgar M. Cahn		Ass't. Supt., Post Office
Leon Cahn[a]	h: 722 Magazine b: 15 Magazine	Keiffer Bros., Whls. Boots & Shoes, Travel Agent
Joseph Cohn	h: 161 Robin b: 26 Magazine	Whls. Clothing
Simon Cohn[a]	h: 422 Magazine b: 70 & 72 Common	Cohn & Feibelman, Whls. Clothing
David Danziger[a]	h: 196 Jackson b: 131 Canal	Retail Dry Goods
Theo Dennery	h: 393 Magazine b: 80 Customhouse	Manufactures' Agent
Abraham Dinkelspiel	h: 286 Philip	
Joseph Dinkelspiel	h: 267 Sixth b: 36 Carondolet	New York Life Ins., Gen. Agent
Max Dinkelspiel[a]	h: 286 Philip b: 81 St. Charles Avenue	Braughn, Buck, & Dinkelspiel, Attorney
Ben Dreyfus	h: 150 Race	Agent
Leon Dreyfus	h: 257 St. Mary b: 18 Chartres	Koch & Dreyfus, Whls. Jewelers
Bernard Feibelman	h: 404 St. Charles Avenue b: 70 & 72 Common Street	Cohn & Feibelman, Whls. Clothing
Edward Feibelman	h: 234 Baronne b: 21 & 23 S. Peters	E. Feibelman & Sons, Grocers
August Feiber	h: 240 Baronne b: 76 Baronne	H. & B. Beer, Commission Merchants
Emanuel Forchemier	h: 338 Magazine b: 24 St. Charles Avenue	A. Rosenfield Co., Whls. & Gents Furnishing Goods
Emanuel Frank	h: 229 Baronne b: 57 Magazine	

Membership	Address	Occupation/firm
Michael Frank	h: 169 Prytania b: 100 Common	
Laz. (Leon?) Godchaux	h: 182 Esplanade b: 81 & 83 Canal	Whls. Clothing
P. L. Godchaux[a]	h: 182 Esplanade b: 81 & 83 Canal	L. Godchaux & Co., Bookkeeper
Prosper Godchot	h: 163 Third b: 89 Canal	Girot & Godchot, Whls. Clothing
Edward Goetz	h: 402 S. Rampart b: 51 to 59 Customhouse	F. Hollander & E. Goetz, Whls. Liquors

Ferdinand
Goldsmith[a]
	h: 338 St. Charles Avenue
	b: btw. St. Thomas
	  & Chippewa,
	  Richard & Market
		Smith & Goldsmith,
		Commercial Cotton Press

Morris Goldsmith	h: 322 St. Andrew
	b: btw. St. Thomas
	  & Chippewa,
	  Richard & Market
		Clerk, Smith &
		Goldsmith, Commercial
		Cotton Press

Adolph Goldstein	h: 193 Poydras b: 189 to 193 Poydras	Louis Goldstein & Sons, Fancy Goods
Julius Goldstein	h: 193 Poydras b: 193 Poydras	Louis Goldstein & Sons, Fancy Goods
Henry Grabenheimer	h: 310 Terpsichore b: 73 Poydras	Commission Merchant
Jacob Grossman	h: 244 Thalia b: 11 & 13 S. Peters	Herrmann & Grossman, Whls. Grocers
Cornelius Gumbel	h: 348 Josephine b: 36 Perdido	Gumbel Bros. Mayer, Cotton Factors/Commission Merchants
Simon Gumbel[a]	h: 264 Prytania b: 192 Gravier	S. Gumbel & Co., Cotton & Sugar/Commission Merchants
Henry Gutmann	h: 223 Terpsichore b: NE corner, Baronne & Gravier	Collector, Jewish Widows' and Orphans' Home
Morris Gutmann	h: 356 St. Charles Avenue	Laborer
Isidore Haas	h: 450 Baronne b: 96 Common	Mayer & Haas, Whls. Clothing
Abraham Haber	h: 227 Baronne	

Membership	Address	Occupation/firm
Lewis Hart	h: 197 Terpsichore b: 199 Gravier	Clerk, Lehmann & Stern, Cotton Factors
Isidore Hernsheim[a]	h: 659 St. Charles Avenue b: 25 & 27 Tchoupitoulas	S. Hernsheim & Bros., Cigar & Cigarette Mfgs.
Sam Heymann	b: 455 Dryades	Clerk, M. Lehman, Dry Goods
Jonas Hiller[a]	h: 444 Camp Street b: 34 Perdido	Hyman, Lichtenstein, & Co., Cotton Factors/ Commission Merchants
Cerf Hirsch	h: 452 Magazine	
Frederick Hollander	h: 400 S. Rampart b: 51 & 59 Customhouse	F. Hollander & E. Goetz, Whls. Liquors
Abraham Isaac[a]	h: 724 Magazine b: 199 Gravier	Salesman, H. Abraham & Sons, Cotton Factors/ Commission Merchants
Sam Isaac(s)	h: 724 Magazine b: 199 Gravier	Correspondent, H. Abraham & Sons, Cotton Factors/Commission Merchants
Lizar Joseph	h: 298 St. Mary b: 43 & 45 Magazine	Wackerbarth & Joseph, Tobacco Mfgs.
Gabe Kahn[a]	h: 161 Annunciation b: Market & St. Thomas	Cotton Pickery
Solomon Kahn	b: 367 Chartres	Solomon Kahn, Retail Dry Goods
Sigmund Katz	h: 709 Magazine b: 36 to 40 Camp	Katz & Barnett, Whls. Notions & Fancy Goods
Isidore Keiffer[a]	h: 424 Magazine b: 15 Magazine	Salesman, Keiffer Bros., Whls. Boots & Shoes
Julius Keiffer[a]	h: 401 Carondolet b: 15 Magazine	Keiffer Bros., Whls. Boots & Shoes
Leopold Keiffer[a]	h: 869 St. Charles Avenue b: 15 Magazine	Salesman, Keiffer Bros., Whls. Boots & Shoes
Sigmund Keiffer[a]	h: 869 St. Charles Avenue b: 15 Magazine	Keiffer Bros., Whls. Boots & Shoes
H. Kern	h: St. Charles Avenue, cor. b: Camp, SW cor. Poydras & 110 Baronne	Henry Kern, Retail Dry Goods

Membership	Address	Occupation/firm
E. I. Kursheedt	h: 434 St. Charles Avenue b: 114, 118, 120 Camp Street	Kursheedt & Bienvenu, Hardware, Monuments, Tombstones, Iron Mantels
Elias Landauer[a]	h: 94 Constance b: 17 Camp	Gerber, Meyer, & Co., Hats, Whls. & Retail
Emile J. Lang	147 Dumaine	Jeweler
Calme Lazard	h: 285 Esplanade b: 29 to 33 Canal	C. Lazard & Co., Whls. Clothing
H. L. Lazarus	h: 440 Magazine	Judge, Civil District Court
Simon Lehmann	h: 248 Felicity b: 9 St. Ferdinand	Box Mfgs.
Wm. H. Lengsfield	h: 126 Terpsichore b: 192 Gravier	S. Gumbel & Co., Cotton & Sugar
Ben Leopold	h: 177 Eighth b: 52 Canal	Clerk, Konig, Dwyer, & Co., Whls. Fancy Goods
Isaac Levi	h: 198 Baronne b: 9 Baronne	Jeweler
Isidore Levi	h: 371 Camp b: 36 to 40 Camp	Travel Agent, Katz & Barnett, Whls.
J. C. Levi	131 Chartres	Clerk, Bonds
Felix U. Levy	h: 509 Magazine b: 82 Canal	Levy, Loeb, Scheurer, & Co., Whls. Dry Goods
Frank L. Levy		Clerk, The Bradstreet Co., Mercantile Agency
Isaac Levy[b]		
Isaac K. Levy		I. K. Levy & Sons, Whls. Fancy Goods
M. Levy[b]		
Marx Levy[b]		
Sam Levy[b]		
Charles Lob[a]	h: 718 Magazine b: 21 Chartres	Charles Lob's Sons, Whls. Cloths, Cassimeres & Vestings
Felix Loeb[a]	h: 593 St. Charles Avenue b: 21 & 23 Decatur	Felix Loeb & Bros., Whls. Wines & Liquors
Leopold Loeb[a]	h: 162 Felicity b: 82 Canal Street	Levy, Loeb, Scheurer, & Co., Whls. Dry Goods
Ike Loewengardt	h: 29 Prytania b: 103 & 105 Canal Street	M. Scooler & Loewengardt, Jewelers

Membership	Address	Occupation/firm
Joseph Magner	h: (boards) 15 Royal b: 192 Gravier	Correspondent, S. Gumbel & Co., Cotton & Sugar
Moses Mann	h: 308 St. Charles b: 56 S. Peters	Clerk, B. Meyer & Co., Commission Merchants
Adolph Marks[a]	98 Gravier	Mfgs. Agent
Ferd Marks[a]	h: 473 Carondolet b: 58 Carondolet	Cotton Broker
Morris Marks	h: 464 St. Charles Avenue b: 30 Carondolet	Marks & Bruenn, Lawyers
Henry Marx	h: 313 Chippewa b: Cotton Exchange Bldg.	Sec., N. O. Seed Co.
Abe Mayer[a]	h: 169 Prytania b: 100 Common	Crockery
Daniel A. Mayer	h: 416 Carondolet b: 18 St. Charles Avenue	Mayer & Seeskind, Gents' Furnishing Goods
Moses Mayer	h: 8 Old Magazine b: 97 & 99 Common	Mayer & Weill, Whls. Cigars & Tobacco
Sigmund Mendelsohn	h: 386 St. Charles Avenue b: 59 Customhouse	Mfgs. Agent
Jac Meyers	(no record)	
Sam Meyers	h: 277 Magazine b: 53 Poydras	Commission Merchant
Bernard Moses	h: 157 Hospital b: same	Moses & Massicot, Photographers
Meyer L. Navra	h: 190 Canal b: 167 Canal	China, Crockery, Glassware
Herman Neugass	h: 206 Esplanade b: 20 Carondolet	Stock Broker
Charles Newman[a]	h: 41 Prytania b: 218 Gravier	H. & C. Newman, Cotton Factors/Commission Merchants
Henry Newman	h: 294 St. Charles Avenue b: 218 Gravier	H. & C. Newman, Cotton Factors/Commission Merchants
Isidore Newman[a]	h: 48 Prytania b: 26 Carondolet	Stock Broker
Ephraim Offner[a]	h: 366 St. Charles Avenue b: 174 Canal	Crockery

Membership	Address	Occupation/firm
Sam Picard	h: 368 Magazine b: Julia NW cor. Peters	Boss Drayman
Henry Roos	h: 1536 St. Charles Avenue b: 64 Common	Commission Merchant
Julius Rose	h: Villere between Clouet & Louisa	Laborer
Abe Rosenfield[a]	h: Baton Rouge b: 24 St. Charles Avenue	A. Rosenfield Co., Gents' Whls. & Furnishing Goods
Joseph (M. or U.) Rosenthal	b: 25 Canal Street	Rosenthal Bros., Clothing
Mathias Salomon	h: 301 St. Charles Avenue b: 112 Magazine Street	Diefenthal & Salomon, Butchers
Isaac Scherck	h: 235 Chestnut b: 214 Gravier	Adler, Goldman & Co., Commission Merchants, Cotton Factors
Louis Scherck[a]	h: 439 Magazine b: 69 Gravier	Clerk, R. H. Chaffe, Whls. Grocers
Louis Scherer	h: 568 Rampart	Laborer
Max or Morris Schwabacher[a]	b: 91 & 93 Poydras	J. & M. Schwabacher, Commission Merchants
Louis Schwartz[a]	h: 158 Clio b: 98 to 102 Magazine	Louis Schwartz Machinery Depot
Moses Schwartz	h: 450 Magazine b: 39 Magazine	Machinery
Maurice Scooler	h: 23 Prytania b: 103 & 105 Canal	M. Scooler & Ike Loewengardt, Jewelers
Joseph (Judah) Seidenbach[a]	h: 392 Magazine b: 66 & 68 Canal	Cashier, A. Lehmann & Co., Whls. Dry Goods
Sigmund A. Seeskind	h: 166 Orange b: 158 Common	Stockbroker
Max Seligman	h: 402 Camp	Jewelers
Alex Shlenker	h: 340 Magazine	
Charles Simon[a]	h: 684 Magazine b: 16 to 20 Magazine	Simon & Kohn, Whls. Hats & Trunks
Joseph Simon	h: 725 Magazine b: 16 to 20 Magazine	Simon & Kohn, Whls. Hats & Trunks
Sam L. Simon	b: 16 to 20 Magazine	Salesman, Simon & Kohn, Whls. Hats & Trunks

Membership	Address	Occupation/firm
Henry Stern	h: 438 Magazine b: 35 Chartres	H. Stern & Co. Auctioneers, Whls. Boots & Shoes
Maurice Stern[a]	h: 446 Camp b: 199 Gravier	Lehmann, Stern, Co., Cotton Factors
Sol Stern	h: 387 Magazine b: 78 Decatur	Solomon Stern, Produce & Fertilizer
Charles Stich[a]	h: 306 St. Charles Avenue b: 75 Poydras	Moritz Stich & Son, Produce & Provisions, Commission Merchant
Emil Weil	(no record)	
Max Weil[a]	h: 261 St. Mary b: 98 to 102 Magazine	Louis Schwartz, Machinery Depot
David T. Weill[a]	h: 334 Carondolet b: 97 & 99 Common	Mayer & Weill, Whls. Cigars & Tobacco
Julius Weis[a]	h: 213 Jackson b: 30 & 32 Perdido	Julius Weis & Co., Cotton Factors
Sam E. Worms	h: 97 Prytania b: 76 & 78 Canal	S. Dalsheimer & Co., Fancy Goods, Notions

[a] Indicates membership in the Harmony Club, 1899, as indicated in Louis W. Marcott, comp., *Membership Roster of New Orleans Clubs, 1899* (New Orleans: D. J. Searcy-Wm. Pfaff, Printers, 1899), Louisiana Collection, Tulane Library.

[b] Names like this will be listed as members only. Since duplicate entries exist in the City Directory, without additional information, there is no way of identifying which of the same name were members of the temple.

Source: Membership meeting roll, 28 November 1886, Temple Sinai Minutes; There is no extant membership list from this period, so the names here reflect only those present at the meeting. All members were men. Information on addresses and occupations taken from the New Orleans City Directories of 1886 and 1887. The information in the City Directory varies from person to person, so that some entries are more complete profiles than others, depending upon what the individual was willing to pay for or what he wanted published.

LETTER REGARDING CHARGES AGAINST LEUCHT'S DIRECTORSHIP

copy   New Orleans, April 21st, 1898

To the Committee investigating the office of Vice President of Touro Infirmary—
Gentlemen.

In accordance with your request of the 19th I herewith present an outline of my charges against the administration: The material at my command is so large that I have concluded for the present at any rate, to confine myself to 2 principal charges, which Providence favoring I expect to establish to your satisfaction:

First. That the dispensor of our charity has by harsh, pitiless, rude and summary methods made his name a terror to the deserving poor, until many of them prefer any extremity to the treatment which they would experience on soliciting his aid.

Second. That he has lowered the standing of the minister and of his charitable office by conduct which is certain to reflect on both.

I shall establish charge No 1

A—by witnesses which will testify to it in general as being a fact.

B—by the following specific charges, applying to the now quoted particular cases.

Specified Charges

Name	Approximate Time	Charge
A. Lichtbad	1896	Refusal to listen
Openhain Family	1895	Harsh treatment
B. Ruchwaldy	1897	Harshness & persecution
I. Stern	1896	Aggravated discourtesy
Mrs. Lucha	1897	Refusal to listen, rudeness
——Isaacs	1896	Gross and utterly unjustified rudeness
Abr. Rosenkrant	1897	Refusal to listen
Isaac Moirovitz	1898	Cruel disrespect
Nachman Rathoosky	1898	Refusal of all access
——Goldsmith	1897(?)	Refusal to listen
Isidor Deitsche	1897	Refusal to listen
A Weiner	1898	Systematic harshness, resulting most seriously
Mrs. A Rosenbloom	1895	Harshness arising to violence
Mrs. I. Gordon	3 months ago	Heartless taunting
H. Dasorov	6 months ago	Refusal to keep promise
——Grossman	4 years ago (?)	Rough refusal of needed aid
Robert Auspach	1893	Repulse of a repenting convert
——Judinski	1895(?)	Threw him down stairs

I shall be glad to add to these cases others on which as yet I have not gathered satisfactory information.

I shall of course adhere strictly to the requirement of furnishing an outline of these further charges before submitting them to the form of testimony.

Under principal charge No 2 I claim that inquiries which were made at the offices of all transportation companies and of the Charity Organization Society for the purpose of casting a doubt on my veracity as well as the request which I was in turn compelled to urge at the same quarters, that these tended to cast a serious reflection upon two ministers, the Infirmary, and indirectly upon the jewish [*sic*] community.

Trusting that this information may prove to correspond with your desires, I am, gentlemen,

Very truly yours,
(signed)   Max Heller

NOTES

Abbreviations

AJA   American Jewish Archives
AJRC   American Jewish Relief Committee
CCAR   Central Conference of American Rabbis
HCP   Henry Cohen Papers
HUC   Hebrew Union College
HUC-JIR Hebrew Union College–Jewish Institute of Religion
HUCP   Hebrew Union College Papers
JIRP   Jewish Institute of Religion Papers
MHP   Max Heller Papers
SCHTL   Special Collections, Howard Tilton Library
SSWP   Stephen S. Wise Papers

Chapter 1

1. Temple Sinai Records, 13 February 1887, vol. 4, Temple Sinai Papers; Edgar Cahn, New Orleans, to Max Heller, 10, 14 February 1887, Box 1, Folder 15, MHP; *Daily Picayune*, 14 February 1887.

2. I use the word "assimilation" throughout to mean "a process of seeking integration into a larger society and increasingly taking one's ideas and customs from it" (Rubin, *Assimilation and Its Discontents*, xiv).

3. Mildred Heller, Max Heller's daughter-in-law, interview with the author, 1 February 1989; Dumas Malone, ed., *Dictionary of American Biography*, vol. 8 (New York: Charles Scribner's Sons, 1932), s.v. "Maximilian Heller"; Steiner, " 'The Girls in Chicago,' " *American Jewish Archives* 26 (April 1974): 8; Joseph Stolz, "Dr. Max Heller—Rabbi and Teacher," memorial address, 3 May 1929, New Orleans, reprinted in the *Reform Advocate*, 18 May 1929, Box 6, Folder 16, MHP, mentioned that the distinguished rabbis among Max's forebears included, on his father's side, Lipmann Heller, and on his mother's, Solomon Judah Loeb Rapoport.

4. Tales of the golem date back 400 years to medieval Prague, when the great Rabbi Loeb, known as the Maharal, created a precursor to Frankenstein to defend the Jewish ghetto when it was being viciously attacked during a Passover blood libel plot. See Serwer, "The Mechanical Man of Prague," 39–54; Buck, in "The Paradoxes of Prague," 122–133, 154–161, reminded me of the myth and its relationship to Prague.

5. For background on Czech Jewry, see works by Gary B. Cohen, Hillel Kieval, and Guido Kisch cited in the bibliography.

6. Kieval, "Caution's Progress," 71; Kieval, *The Making of Czech Jewry*, 5–6.

7. Heller, *Isaac M. Wise*, 19–20, 27; Katz, *Out of the Ghetto*, 57–79; in "Jews Between Czechs and Germans," 31–33, Ruth Kestenberg-Gladstein notes that until 1848, only the "upper stratum of the Jewish population" desired assimilation. Most Jews still lived in ghettos and maintained their traditional way of life, untouched by urbanization and industrialization.

8. Pulzer, *The Rise of Political Anti-Semitism in Germany and Austria*, 5, links the fate of Jews to that of liberalism. Since Jews actively participated in creating and then benefiting from liberal institutions, the enemies of liberalism could readily attack them. Jewish interests nicely accommodated the assertiveness of the bourgeoisie. Orton, *The Prague Slav Con-*

gress of 1848, 1–29; Thomson, *Czechoslovakia in European History,* 119–135; Sachar, *Modern Jewish History,* 111–113; Kisch, *In Search of Freedom,* 26–57, provides a thorough discussion of the "On to America" movement.

9. Sachar, *Modern Jewish History,* 102; Cohen, *The Politics of Ethnic Survival,* 21; Kohn, "Before 1918 in the Historic Lands," 15–16; Kieval, *The Making of Czech Jewry,* 5–6; Kerstenberg-Gladstein, "Jews Between Czechs and Germans," 24–25; Steiner, " 'The Girls,' " 8.

10. Gary B. Cohen, *The Politics of Ethnic Survival,* 45–46; Kieval, *The Making of Czech Jewry,* 6–7, 12; Kerstenberg-Gladstein, "Jews Between Czechs and Germans," 26–28; Cohen, "Jews in German Society: Prague, 1860–1914," *Central European History* (1977): 37, notes that the "Bohemian public equated the test of language with one of nationality."

11. Cohen, *The Politics of Ethnic Survival,* 22–23.

12. Mildred Heller interview; *Dictionary of American Biography,* 8:511–512; Steiner, " 'The Girls,' " 8; Adler, *American Jewish Yearbook, 1903–1904,* p. 62. The correspondence in German between Simon (already in Chicago) and Max Heller (Prague) dating from the late 1870s in MHP (Folder 7, 8) indicates that this was the language of choice for the Hellers.

13. Cohen, *The Politics of Ethnic Survival,* 66–85; "Jews in German Society," 39, 48–49; Kieval, *The Making of Czech Jewry,* 15–16, 21; Kieval, "Education and National Conflict," 55. *American Jewish Yearbook, 1903–1904,* p. 62.

14. Max Heller, New Orleans, to Henry Hurwitz, New York, 4 September 1918, Box 18, Folder 9, Henry Hurwitz Menorah Society Papers, AJA.

15. Bauer, *A History of the Holocaust,* 38.

16. Meyer, *Response to Modernity,* 153–155, 192–193; Carl E. Schorske, *Fin-de-Siècle Vienna,* 149.

17. Zweig, *The World of Yesterday,* 22; Clare, *Last Waltz in Vienna,* 63–74; Max Heller, "The Chanukah of My Boyhood," clipping from unidentified source, 19 December 1919, Box 14, Folder 5, MHP; Cohen, "Jews in German Society," 45–46.

18. Glanz, "The German-Jewish Mass Emigration," 66, pointed out that since German Jewish emigrants came from urban settings in Europe, they deliberately looked for urban areas in their new home in hopes of making a smooth economic transition; Clare, *Last Waltz in Vienna,* 69; Zweig, *The World of Yesterday,* 14–15; Heller, *Isaac M. Wise,* 43; Mildred Heller interview; *Dictionary of American Biography,* 8:511–512; Steiner, " 'The Girls,' " 8.

19. Box 7, Folder 8, MHP, contains the correspondence, in old German script, between Max and his family as well as his Neustadter Gymnasium report cards and a "Certificate of Poverty," 8 November 1878, granted by the Prague Magistrate. Max had to obtain the certificate when he applied for a student stipend, "attesting that he earns monthly 16 florin by giving private lessons—of which he has to pay 12 fl. 50 for cost and lodging, that he has no other income, no property, and no support." The Prague papers cited here were translated for this study by Hilda Weltman, Cincinnati, 1989. Anna Heller, Chicago, to Max Heller, Prague, 12 August 1877; Simon Heller, Chicago, to Max Heller, Prague, 25 September 1877.

20. Bodnar, *The Transplanted,* 57, explained that since "families and friends were in close contact even when separated . . . , immigrants seldom left their homelands without knowing exactly where they wanted to go and how to get there"; Steiner, " 'The Girls,' " 8–9.

21. Steiner, " 'The Girls,' " 8–9. A Talmud Torah was a communally run Hebrew school that held classes in the afternoon after public schools were dismissed.

22. Abraham Cahan poignantly described such role reversal in his depiction of mother and daughter Dora and Lucy Margolis in *The Rise of David Levinsky.*

23. Steiner, " 'The Girls,' " 10.

24. Simon Heller, Chicago, to Max Heller, Prague, 11 March 1878, Box 7, Folder 8, MHP, translated for this book by Hilda Weltman.

25. Steiner, " 'The Girls,' " 9–10. According to the *Dictionary of American Biography,* 8:512, Max sailed for America because he had heard that his tubercular mother had only a short

time to live. Simon Heller, Chicago, to Max Heller, Prague, 25 September 1877, 11 March 1878, 20 May 1879, Box 7, Folder 8, MHP, translated for this study by Hilda Weltman; Joseph Stolz, "Maximilian Heller," memorial address, *CCAR Yearbook* 39 (1929): 222; Simon Heller, Chicago, to Max Heller, Prague, 17 October 1878, Box 7, Folder 8, MHP, translated for this book by Hilda Weltman.

26. Simon Heller, Chicago, to Max Heller, Prague, 17 October 1878, Box 7, Folder 8, MHP, translated for this book by Hilda Weltman.

27. Simon Heller, Chicago, to Max Heller, Prague, 27 June 1879, Box 7, Folder 8, MHP, translated for this book by Hilda Weltman.

28. Simon Heller, Chicago, to Max Heller, Prague, 27 June 1879, Box 7, Folder 8, MHP, translated for this book by Hilda Weltman.

29. Simon Heller, Chicago, to Max Heller, Prague, 20 May 1879, Box 7, Folder 8, MHP, translated for this book by Hilda Weltman.

Chapter 2

1. Mostov, "A 'Jerusalem' on the Ohio," 9; Meyer, "The Hebrew Union College," 7, claims that by the Civil War Cincinnati had already attracted about 10,000 Jews; Stephan Thernstrom, ed., *Harvard Encyclopedia of American Ethnic Groups* (Cambridge, Mass.: Harvard University Press, 1980), s.v. "Jews."

2. Jick, *Synagogue*, 69–70; Bauman, "A Functional Approach," 13–16; Karp developed the idea of various survival strategies in America in "Ideology and Identity," 310–334; Martin, "Americanization," 39–40, cited David Philipson and Louis Grossman, eds., *Selected Writings of Isaac Mayer Wise*, 14, for Wise's reading of Cooper.

3. Henry Howe was the late nineteenth-century Ohio historian cited by Jonathan D. Sarna, " 'A Sort of Paradise for the Hebrews,' " 131, 136–137. My thanks to Jonathan for calling my attention to his chapter; Max Heller, letter to the *American Hebrew*, 1 June 1900, cited in "Hebrew Union College–Jewish Institute of Religion," 151–153; "America's Leading Jew," *Times-Picayune* (New Orleans), 27 March 1900. According to Nadel, "Jewish Race and German Soul," 10, originally, *Die Deborah* was published "with special regard for the ladies," and women constituted Wise's main readers.

4. Meyer, "The Hebrew Union College," 7–8; Meyer, "A Centennial History," 10, pointed out that until the founding of Hebrew Union College, all Reform rabbis in America were dependent on German training in order to be ordained; Max Heller, "Shall Our Theological Schools Unite?" *American Hebrew* (September 1900): 19–22; Max Heller, "Shall the Hebrew Union College Be Moved?" *American Israelite* (Cincinnati), 17 May 1900; Fox, "On the Road to Unity," 149.

5. Meyer, "The Hebrew Union College," 8; Meyer, "A Centennial History," 26–27, notes that the largest budgetary item the first few years were the funds expended for the "indigent" student; Jick, *Synagogue*, 80–81; Wiebe, in *The Search for Order*, discusses the tendency of institutions to imitate the centralization and professionalization current in industrializing America; *Encyclopedia Judaica*, vol. 16, s.v., "Isaac Mayer Wise"; Meyer, "A Centennial History," 13.

6. Meyer, "The Hebrew Union College," 9–10, 16; Isaac Mayer Wise, Cincinnati, to Max Heller, Chicago, 22, 23 September 1879, Isaac Mayer Wise Correspondence, translated for this book by René Lehmann, New Orleans, February 1990. Lehmann points out that the salutation Wise used in addressing Max, "Geehrter Herr Heller," was "somewhat condescending," although "there is no English equivalent for this nuance." Evidently, the elder was letting the young man know that his status as a student would imply deference; René Lehmann, New Orleans, to Bobbie Malone, New Orleans, 8 February 1990, letter in the writer's possession.

7. "America's Leading Jew," *Times-Picayune* (New Orleans), 27 March 1900, quoted Max Heller's description of Wise after the latter's death; Simon Heller, Chicago, to Max Heller, Cincinnati, 25 November 1879, Box 7, Folder 8, MHP, translated for this book by Hilda Weltman; Jacob Rader Marcus, interview with Bobbie Malone, Cincinnati, July 1989. Marcus, the son of a poor Russian immigrant, came to HUC in 1910 and remained to teach after his ordination. To a large extent, his experience as a student paralleled that of young men three decades earlier. The anecdote about the businessman and other details about the college years appears in Meyer, "The Hebrew Union College," 18-19.

8. Isaac M. Wise, "Opening the Eighth Annual Scholastic Year, 1882-1883," quoted in full in "Hebrew Union College-Jewish Institute of Religion—A Centennial Documentary," 127; Meyer, "A Centennial History," 11; *Dictionary of American Biography*, 8:512; Steiner, " 'The Girls,' " 11; Feingold, *Zion in America*, 72, 99, 142; Korn, "German-Jewish Intellectual Influences," 108.

9. Meyer, in "German-Jewish Identity," 247-259, discusses the complex relationship of Wise's Bohemian roots to his evolving sense of a unique American Judaism.

10. Karp, "Ideology and Identity," 315.

11. *Encyclopedia Judaica*, vol. 16, s.v. "*Wissenschaft des Judentums*"; Liebman, "The Training of American Rabbis," 6-7.

12. Meyer, "A Centennial History," 8-10; Liebman, "The Training of American Rabbis," 9.

13. "America's Leading Jew"; Heller, "Shall the Hebrew Union College Be Moved?"; Michael Meyer, "A Centennial History," 123-124.

14. Nadel, "Jewish Race and German Soul," 10. As Michael Meyer points out in "A Centennial History," 15, Wise felt no commitment to maintaining the German language in either hymnal or prayerbook in the United States: English was to be the language of American Reform Judaism.

15. *Proceedings of the UAHC*, vol. 2, 1880-1885, AJA; Actually, the invitation to join the Phi Beta Kappa Society at the University of Cincinnati is undated, but the fraternity honors undergraduates, Box 4, Folder 16, MHP.

16. Max Heller, Cincinnati, to "Parents," Chicago, 19 June 1882, Box 7, Folder 8, MHP, translated for this book by Hilda Weltman.

17. "University of Cincinnati Graduation Programme, 1882," University of Cincinnati Archives, Belgen Library; Box 15, Folder 1, MHP.

18. Board Minutes, University of Cincinnati, September 1883-December 1891, University of Cincinnati Archives; Heller, "Shall the Hebrew Union College Be Moved?"; Heller, letter to the *American Hebrew*, 25 May 1900, in "Hebrew Union College-Jewish Institute of Religion—A Centennial Documentary," 151.

19. Max Heller, "Shall the Hebrew Union College Be Moved?" Heller, letter to the *American Israelite*, 24 May 1900, in "Hebrew Union College-Jewish Institute of Religion—A Centennial Documentary," 151; Bloom, "The Rabbi as Symbolic Exemplar," 201-202, indicates that the nexus of the problem of seminary training lay in providing the seminarian with a traditional rabbinic model to be emulated, that of a "life-time student and pious scholar," a model inappropriate to the needs of the pulpit. From his late twentieth-century perspective, he believed that the "relative newness of the pulpit rabbinate means that there is little in the way of a time-tested model of the pulpit rabbi." Heller had been one of the first to express such concerns.

20. *Dictionary of American Biography*, 8:512, refers to the "permanent impairment" of Heller's health but does not clarify the nature of such impairment. Family correspondence dealt extensively with matters of health, and perhaps Max's frustrated desire to become a physician underlay his obsession with his family's problems and his own physical ailments.

21. Seltzer, *Jewish People, Jewish Thought*, 393-408; May, *Protestant Churches and Industrial America*, 47-50, 142-147 (reprint edition); Feingold, *Zion in America*, 97.

22. Heller, "Maimonides and the Philosopher of Evolution"; Plaut, "Reform Judaism," 5.

23. Meyer, "The Hebrew Union College," 23; *Times-Picayune,* 12 November 1922, clipping in Box 4, Temple Sinai Papers.

Chapter 3

1. The quotation of UAHC president Moritz Loth appeared in Fox, "On the Road to Unity," 181. Loth mentioned nine rabbis who had graduated, but the actual number was eight, four in 1883 and another four in Max's class.

2. Simon Heller, Chicago, to Max Heller, Prague, 25 September 1877, Box 7, Folder 8, MHP, translated for this book by Hilda Weltman; Glanz, "The German-Jewish Mass Emigration," 52, notes that this " 'pulling-after' of brothers, sisters, and other relatives is indeed the most significant feature of the German Jewish immigration to America." Family movement, on the other hand, characterized East European immigration.

3. *Encyclopedia Judaica,* vol. 6, s.v. "Bernhard Felsenthal"; *American Jewish Year Book, 1903–1904,* 53; Meyer, "German-Jewish Identity," 261, 267, quotes Felsenthal's *Judisches Schulwesen in Amerika;* Karp, *Haven and Home,* 84–86; Meyer, *Response to Modernity,* 263, cites Felsenthal's comments on Wise from the *Occident* (Chicago), 20 July 1883.

4. Samuel Stein, Chicago, to Max Heller, Cincinnati, 22 May 1884, Box 8, Folder 4, MHP; Ludlow, "Bernhard Felsenthal," 205.

5. Isaac M. Wise, Cincinnati, to Max Heller, Chicago, 3 August 1884, Box 6, Folder 6, MHP; Wise addressed the letter, "My dear Friend Heller." This collegiality is very different from the formal tone in the first letter he sent; see chapter 2, note 6.

6. Max Heller, Chicago, to Joseph Stolz, location unknown, 18 August 1884, Box 8, Folder 6, MHP.

7. Ludlow, "Bernhard Felsenthal," 205, felt that the two men "served amicably together." A letter from Joseph Stolz, Little Rock, Arkansas, to Max Heller, New Orleans, 25 April 1887, Box 8, Folder 6, MHP, refuted this interpretation. When Felsenthal retired, and Stolz applied for the position of rabbi at Zion Congregation, Stolz thanked Max for his using influence to see that Stolz was considered as a candidate. Stolz added, "I anticipate opposition from Felsenthal, because he is so prejudiced against you & the College."

8. See the appendix for a complete copy of the eight planks of the platform.

9. In its issue of 8 January 1886, the *American Israelite* correspondent reported on the Southern Rabbinical Conference that met in the city. The southern rabbis felt that the principles of the Pittsburgh conference were "in harmony with the spirit of progressive Judaism," but they, "individually and collectively, reserve the right to dissent from any practical deductions that have or may be drawn from them." They affirmed, in addition, that "the observance of the Sabbath of the Decalogue and the practice of the Abrahamic rite [circumcision] are just as binding today upon Israel as they ever were."

10. Karp, "Ideology and Identity," observed that late nineteenth-century Reform Jews were "closer in spirit and practice to liberal Christianity than to traditional Jews," 317; Sarna, "New Light," 361–363; Leon Jick, "The Reform Synagogue," in *The American Synagogue, A Sanctuary Transformed,* ed. Jack Wertheimer (New York: Cambridge University Press, 1987), 91; Feldman, *Dual Destinies,* 133–137.

11. Meyer's *Response to Modernity* contains the Pittsburgh Platform in the appendix; May, *Protestant Churches and Industrial America,* 170–181 (reprint edition); *Harvard Encyclopedia of American Ethnic Groups,* 578; Karp, *Haven and Home,* 78; Sarna, "New Light," 362.

12. "An Intimate Portrait of the Union of American Hebrew Congregations—A Centennial Documentary," *American Jewish Archives* (April 1973): 18–20, includes a reminiscence by one of those graduating and a copy of the menu that destroyed Wise's fragile coalition; Michael A. Meyer, "A Centennial History," 41–42, warns against exaggerating the negative re-

percussions of the banquet and credits the arrival of Orthodox Eastern European Jews in America with the ascendancy of the Conservative movement.

13. Meyer, *Response to Modernity*, 265–267; Sarna, "New Light," 368; Polish, "The Changing and Constant in the Reform Rabbinate," 177, mentions that "contrary to the widespread general impression . . . , the Reform movement's formative principles were not monolithic and instead presented a dialectic between a clearly dominant majority and an articulate minority or, at times between balanced ideological adversaries."

14. *Dictionary of American Biography*, 8:512; Stolz, "Maximilian Heller," 221.

15. Felsenthal did resign in 1887 when Max's friend Joseph Stolz, with Heller's warm endorsement, followed him to Zion Congregation and remained there as rabbi for his entire career; Joseph Stolz, Chicago, to Max Heller, New Orleans, 25 April 1887, 13 October 1887, Box 8, Folder 6, MHP.

16. *Encyclopedia Judaica*, vol. 6, s.v. "Bernhard Felsenthal"; J. Greenwood, Secretary of Zion Congregation, Chicago, to Max Heller, 22 May 1886. He assured Heller that the board of directors would try to "define the duties of both Rabbis and thereby avoid any clashing of ill feeling that may arise. *We all understand your positions thoroughly.*" Microfilm of Max Heller's correspondence, MHP; *American Israelite*, 29 January 1886; 30 April 1886.

17. E. Raphael, Houston, to Max Heller, Chicago, 2 August 1886, Box 4, Folder 24, MHP. Correspondence from Henry Fox of Beth Israel, Houston, and Heller, dating from 1884, indicates that Heller was actively in touch with the congregation long before he accepted a position there, Box 2, Folder 8, MHP.

18. E. Raphael, Houston, to Max Heller, Chicago, 16 August 1886, Box 4, Folder 24, MHP; I. M. Wise, Cincinnati, to Max Heller, Chicago, 5 September 1886, Box 6, Folder 6, MHP.

19. Silverstein, *Alternatives to Assimilation*, 82–83, 94–95, suggests that by the 1880s prominent Reform congregations were hiring young rabbis and were instituting innovative programs to attract new members. He sees Wise as the "critical link between many rabbinic candidacies and temple employment." Silverstein, 96, also mentions that the young rabbis often vied for the same jobs. Joseph Krauskopf, another HUC graduate, accepted the position at Philadelphia after turning down Temple Sinai's offer. M. Wise, Cincinnati, to Max Heller, Houston, 13 December 1886, Box 6, Folder 6 MHP; I. M. Wise, Cincinnati, to Max Heller, Houston, 7 January 1886, I. M. Wise Correspondence. The letter dated 7 January 1886 must actually be from 1887. It is likely that Wise dated the letter improperly (the letter was written early in the new year). The events mentioned in the letter make sense only in the context of January 1887.

20. I. M. Wise, Cincinnati, to Max Heller, Chicago, 5 September 1886, microfilm, MHP.

21. I. M. Wise, Cincinnati, to Max Heller, Houston, 13 December 1886, 7 January 1886, Box 6, Folder 6, I. M. Wise Correspondence; Max Heller, undated letter of resignation to Temple Beth Israel (scratch copy), microfilm, MHP.

22. Edgar Cahn, New Orleans, to Max Heller, Houston, 10 February 1887, Box 1, Folder 15, MHP.

23. Edgar Cahn, New Orleans, to Max Heller, Houston, 10 February 1887, Box 1, Folder 15, MHP; Shpall, *The Jews in Louisiana*, 40; Sussman, "Isaac Leeser," 1–19.

24. As Roy Lubove points out in the introductory chapter of *The Professional Altruist*, during the 1880s, American charitable institutions, in creating efficient and rational policies for distribution of funds, began looking to models in the corporate sector. Leucht was therefore quite up to date in his methods.

25. Shpall, *The Jews in Louisiana*, 40; I. L. Leucht, New Orleans, to Max Heller, Houston, 23 December 1886, Box 3, Folder 25, MHP.

26. Edgar Cahn, New Orleans, to Max Heller, Houston, 14 February 1887, Box 1, Folder 15, MHP.

27. Max Heller, undated letter of resignation to Temple Beth Israel (scratch copy), Box 1, Folder 4, MHP.

28. Edgar Cahn, New Orleans, to Max Heller, Houston, 25 February 1887, Box 1, Folder

15, MHP. There is a slight discrepancy between the official minutes of Temple Sinai, which show the vote as 91–9, and Cahn's mention of the results as 92–8.

29. Max Heller, "A Tale of Thirty-Five Years," 3 March 1922, Temple Sinai Papers.

Chapter 4

1. Raphael, "Intra-Jewish Conflict in the United States," 7, points out that even within the German Jewish community in America, hostilities existed that began in Germany "with the growing distinction between the more culturally emancipated elements and the more 'unenlightened' Jews in Prussia's Polish provinces" where westernization was accomplished more slowly; Korn, *The Early Jews of New Orleans*; Ashkenazi, *The Business of Jews*, 6–8, points out that most of the German Jews of the area came from Bavaria and Alsace Lorraine. My own primary research for "New Orleans Uptown Immigrants," 239–265, indicates that differences in social and economic status further divided the newly arriving immigrants of that generation from their counterparts who had arrived earlier from the same areas of Germany.

2. Korn, *The Early Jews of New Orleans*, 228, writes that early "large-scale acceptance" of Jews in New Orleans "meant that there was no negative pressure . . . to create a congregation or to develop an intensive religious life."

3. In New Orleans, "above" and "below" Canal Street are common geographic references, since the twisting Mississippi River that gives the "crescent city" its nickname renders the typical compass points particularly ineffective. Canal Street was and remains the main business thoroughfare in New Orleans. "Above" Canal Street, or upriver toward Baton Rouge, is "uptown," while "below" Canal Street, or downriver toward the mouth of the Mississippi, is "downtown."

4. Bennetts, "Black and White Workers," 10; Shugg, *Origins of Class Struggle*, 283 (reprint edition), refers to the American sector as the old Faubourg Ste. Marie of the First District; Jackson, *New Orleans in the Gilded Age*, 17.

5. Stern, "Origins of Reform Judaism"; Ashkenazi devotes chapters 1 and 4 to the European roots of Jews in Louisiana and to the relevance of this socioeconomic legacy to the businesses in which they thrived after coming to the state. The five synagogues were listed in the 1886 city directory; Heller's correspondence with Sigmund Hecht, Montgomery, Alabama, 1886–1887, Box 3, Folder 5, and especially with Henry Berkowitz, Mobile, Alabama, during the winter of 1886–1887, discussed the vacancy at Temple Sinai and the politics of hiring Gutheim's successor, Box 1, Folder 7, MHP; Letter fragment, only page 1 extant (the letter therefore appears unsigned) on F. Marks letterhead, New Orleans, to Max Heller, Houston, 25 February 1887, Box 4, Folder 1, MHP.

6. Clark, "The German Liberals," 139, mentions that in 1842, Joseph Cohn, a German Jewish immigrant, had established the *Deutscher Courier*, the city's leading German newspaper; Raimund Berchtold's "The Decline of German Ethnicity in New Orleans, 1880–1930" (master's thesis, University of New Orleans, 1984), is devoted to the subject of cultural assimilation; Cohen, *The Politics of Ethnic Survival*, 22–23; Cohen, "Jews in German Society," 32; Kieval, *The Making of Czech Jewry*, 10.

7. Ashkenazi, *The Business of Jews*, chaps. 1 and 4; Temple Sinai membership list, 28 November 1886, taken from Temple Sinai minutes, Temple Sinai Collection, then traced through the New Orleans city directories, 1886–1887, to provide an economic and demographic overview. See list in appendix. The Harmony Club's membership undoubtedly claimed more Sinai members in 1899 who were not included in the 1886 list; Marcott, *Membership Roster*. In *Alternatives to Assimilation*, 15–18, Alan Silverstein compares the economic profiles of the lay founders of the nation's four "cathedral congregations," one of which is Temple Sinai. The occupations of the founders and those of the congregants a decade and a half later were very much alike. They were also similar to the profiles of two of the other

congregations studied by Silverstein, Kehillah K'doshah B'nai Yeshurun in Cincinnati and Temple Emanu-El in San Francisco.

8. Marcus, *To Count a People*, 81; Andriot, *Population Abstract of the United States*, 1:321; Korn, *Early Jews*, 74–90; "The Golden Jubilee: Isidore Newman Manual Training School Dedicated," *Jewish Ledger* (New Orleans), 13 January 1905; "Isidore Newman Dead; Man Widely Mourned," *New Orleans Picayune*, 1 December 1909; "Isidore Newman," *Jewish Ledger*, 3 December 1909.

9. Malone, "1888's Social Confrontation," features the 1 December 1888 *Mascot* cartoon from the William R. Hogan Jazz Archives, Tulane University; Mayo, *The Ambivalent Image*, 19, cites Abram Isaacs, who in the 1890s wrote that American writers treated Jews with either "superlative praise or superlative condemnation." Higham, *Strangers in the Land*, 26–27, observes that the European Shylock image that attached to the Jew during the Civil War acquired a "significant new dimension" during the Gilded Age as "an indictment of Jewish manners for vulgarity and ostentation." In an era when few who achieved wealth were willing to criticize the basis for their rise in status, the Jew provided a ready target as "a symbol of the parvenu spirit"; Joseph Cohen, "The Jews of New Orleans and the Mardi Gras"; *Membership Roster of New Orleans Clubs, 1899*.

10. Stern, "The Role of the Rabbi in the South," 23–24, notes that as Jewish Southerners built their congregations, they were intensely aware of "Mah yomru hagoyim?" or "What will the Gentiles say?" This concern remained significant in the region until after the establishment of the state of Israel; *American Israelite*, 10 September 1886; Max Heller, "Why So Much Money?" Bulletin of the Isaac M. Wise Memorial Fund (New Orleans, 1901), Louisiana Collection, Tulane University.

11. Dethloff and Jones, "Race Relations in Louisiana," mention that black voters were still able to "exert an important influence as an independent factor" in elections and that, until 1890, more blacks than whites were registered in the state; Jackson, "Crime and the Conscience of a City," notes that crime and violence had been on the rise since the days of Reconstruction and that during the last twenty years of the nineteenth century, "a general atmosphere of lawlessness plagued New Orleans" beyond the scandal in politics.

12. Bennetts's introductory chapter in "Black and White Workers," 1–35, analyzes the status of New Orleans as the twentieth century approached. He mentions that while New Orleans was still the largest city in the South in 1900, the growth was due to "the advantage gained prior to the Civil War," 8. See also Goldfield, *Cotton Fields and Skyscrapers*, 126–127; Brownell and Goldfield, *The City in Southern History*, chaps. 3 and 4.

13. Arnesen, "Waterfront Workers," 160; Ettinger, "John Fitzpatrick," 345–346. Black voting during the Gilded Age was not unified, and since neither faction dominated local politics, both the machine politicians and the business reform elites needed and actively solicited black support only to reject it as soon as the election had taken place. Since the two sets of white Democrats held similar racist attitudes, fraud and violence during elections were commonplace.

14. Everard, "Bourbon City," 241, stresses the complexity of the city's ethnic class base; Haas, "John Fitzpatrick," 9–11; Jackson, *New Orleans in the Gilded Age*, 6, 55, 60; Wall, *Louisiana*, 227; Nussbaum, "Progressive Politics," 11–12, argues that the evolving ethnic composition of New Orleans, with its successive waves of immigrants, uniquely colored the political structure of the city; Schott, "John M. Parker," 11; Bennetts, "Black and White Workers," 1–35; Ettinger, "John Fitzpatrick," 341–347, notes that political chaos was fueled by "economic instability, racial strife and social tension," which made it virtually impossible "for any faction to govern effectively."

15. The 1887 New Orleans city directory listed the officers and directors of local insurance companies and banks. Six Temple Sinai members sat on bank boards, and eight served on the boards of insurance companies.

16. Everard, "Bourbon City," 242–243, mentions that New Orleans "had a long history of wishing to avoid any adverse publicity to its health problem"; Shugg, *Origins of Class*

Struggle, 281–282; Hair, *Bourbonism,* 112, blames the state's failure to attract outside business-men on its inability "to improve its political and social climate."

17. Jackson, *Gilded Age,* 60–63, 82–96; Haas, *Political Leadership,* 16–17; interviews with Ruth Dreyfous, 1988–1995; Ruth Dreyfous with Bobbie Malone, "Felix Jonathan Dreyfous: A Life of Integrity and Service Remembered with Love," New Orleans, 1995 (photocopy), 20–24, in possession of Ruth Dreyfous.

18. Max Heller, New Orleans, to Oscar J. Cohen, Mobile, 29 January 1889, scratch copy, Box 1, Folder 19, MHP.

19. Temple Sinai minutes, 1887–1890, Temple Sinai Papers; Joseph Stolz, Little Rock, Arkansas, to Max Heller, New Orleans, 25 April 1887, Box 8, Folder 6, MHP; Ernestine Heller, Chicago, to Max Heller, New Orleans, 13 December 1890, Box 6, Folder 17, MHP; Jack Bloom, "The Rabbi as Symbolic Exemplar," 30.

20. *Encyclopedia Judaica,* vol. 7, s.v. "James Koppel Gutheim"; *Jewish Ledger,* 22 May 1896.

21. Minutes, 29 November 1889, Conference of the Rabbis of Southern Congregations, Papers of the Conference of Southern Congregations, AJA; Max Samfield, Memphis, to Max Heller, New Orleans, 9 February 1888, Box 5, Folder 3, MHP; Raphael, *Profiles in American Judaism,* 38, 49. *CCAR Yearbook* (1890–91): 21–22, 32.

22. Ida's father's name was Joseph H. Marks III; see the Marks (New Orleans) family tree as depicted in Stern, *Americans of Jewish Descent;* interview with Mildred Heller, January 1989.

23. Anna Heller Stein, Chicago, to Max Heller, New Orleans, 3 November 1888, Box 8, Folder 2, MHP; Bloom, "The Rabbi as Symbolic Exemplar," 195.

24. Rischin, "Germans Versus Russians," 131; Raphael, "Intra-Jewish Conflict," contrasts the attitudes of groups of Jewish immigrants that arrived earlier and later.

25. Lubove, *Professional Altruist,* 6–8. "Best men" is used here as Sproat defines it in *"The Best Men,"* 7: "the men of breeding and intelligence, of taste and substance." Sproat notes that "no other group of men had better intellectual and moral equipment to deal with the problems of the Gilded Age"; Myron Berman, *The Attitude of American Jewry,* 42–43, 49–68; Bennetts, "Black and White Workers," 9–10, Steven Hertzberg, *Strangers Within the Gate City,* 77–78.

26. Shugg, *Origins of Class Struggle,* 297, comments that Louisiana's benevolent institutions had more inmates than did those of other southern states; Heller, *Jubilee Souvenir,* 8.

27. I. L. Leucht, New Orleans, to Max Heller, New Orleans, 26 June 1888, Box 3, Folder 25, MHP; Urofsky, *American Zionism,* 59, writes that the "human flood" of East Europeans threatened the "German Jewish aristocracy," who saw "those people" as "barbaric vestiges of the Middle Ages." According to the *Hebrew Standard,* the "thoroughly acclimated American Jew" is "closer to the Christian sentiment around him than to the Judaism of these miserable darkened Hebrews."

28. In Hebrew, there is no word for charity. *Tzedakah* translates as social justice, of which charitable acts are a part. According to "The Three Pillars," a well-known Hasidic saying that deals with the concept of justice, "three pillars support the world: teaching, service, and good deeds, and, as the world approaches its end, the first two will shrink, and only good deeds will grow. And then what is written will become truth: 'Zion shall be redeemed with justice' " (Buber, *Ten Rungs,* 115 [reprint edition]).

29. Max Samfield, Memphis, to Max Heller, New Orleans, 15 January 1887, 22 February 1888, 9 February 1888, 24 December 1889, microfilm, MHP; I. M. Wise, Cincinnati, to Max Heller, New Orleans, 27 December 1888; Funeral Service for Rabbi Heller, *Morning Tribune,* 1 April 1929; "A Rabbi's Wedding," unidentified clipping, in the possession of Edward Heller family.

30. *American Israelite,* 10 January 1890; circular from Max Heller, New Orleans, to David Danziger, New Orleans, 31 March 1890; Isaac M. Wise Correspondence, AJA; David Danziger, New Orleans, to Max Heller, New Orleans, 4 April 1890, Box 1, Folder 22, MHP.

31. Board minutes, 5 June 1887, 24 November 1889; Temple Sinai Collection; Louis Gross-

man, Detroit, to Max Heller, New Orleans, 2 January 1888, congratulating Heller on his engagement, Box 2, Folder 23, MHP; *Dictionary of American Biography,* 8:512; Mildred Heller interview; New Orleans city directories, 1887–1890; interview with Ruth Dreyfous, August 1989, New Orleans, Louisiana. Ruth Dreyfous, a ninety-three-year-old native of New Orleans, was born on Jackson Avenue, where her parents built their home about the time the Hellers moved there. Several other prominent Jewish and non-Jewish families lived on the street, which formed one of the boundaries of the Garden District, still the most prestigious neighborhood in Uptown New Orleans.

32. *American Israelite,* 5 December 1889.

33. *Times-Democrat* (New Orleans), 28 October 1889, 17 November 1889; *American Israelite,* 21 November 1889.

34. *Times-Democrat,* 2, 3, 4, 8, 22, 24 January 1890; *American Israelite,* 9, 30 January 1890; Shugg, *Origins of Class Struggle,* 43, notes that as early as 1860, "trade in a few villages was monopolized by Jewish storekeepers who stood their guard, ready to undersell bold interlopers and peddlers."

35. *Jewish Chronicle,* 17, 31 January 1890, Louisiana Collection, Tulane University; Scrapbook, 1889–98, Box 15, Folders 7 and 8, MHP. Holmes has provided the most extensive analysis of whitecapping in several articles, "Whitecapping in Mississippi," 134–148; "Moonshiners and Whitecaps," 31–49; "Whitecapping," 244–261.

36. Jackson, "Crime and the Conscience of a City," 239–243; Jackson, *Gilded Age,* 244–253; Nelli, *The Business of Crime,* 36–37, notes that Sicilians in New Orleans with criminal records in the homeland did participate in "legal and semi-legal" activities in the city. If they were not former mafiosi, as Sicilians they were familiar with "the traditions and characteristics" of the Mafia.

37. Cinel, "Sicilians in New Orleans," 1, indicates that prejudice against the local Italian community was a preexisting condition in New Orleans, since, among other factors, "unlike any other American state with large Italian immigration, Louisiana openly stated that Italians were desirable only as a replacement of black labor."

38. Accounts of the lynching vary both in details and in interpretation. Schott, "John M. Parker," 33–36; Jackson, "Crime and the Conscience of a City," 239–243; Jackson, *Gilded Age,* 244–253; Cinel, "Sicilians in New Orleans," 27–31, notes that the "Hennessy affair was the confrontation between a modern society based on an objective system of law, and a traditional society where power struggles were solved from within by the sheer use of private force"; *American Israelite,* 24 March 1891; *Times-Democrat,* 15 March 1891; "Seligman" is sometimes spelled "Seligmann," depending on the source. Seligmann was a Temple Sinai member; Ernestine Heller, Chicago, to Max Heller, New Orleans, 16 March 1891, Box 6, Folder 17, MHP.

39. Politically, New Orleans was divided into seven districts, and each, according to Bennetts, "Black and White Workers," 6–7, "came to have cultural and social significance as well, as each had its own peculiar characteristics"; in the well-documented appendix of *Political Leadership in a Southern City,* 121–155, Haas provides biographical information on the members of the New Orleans reformers (in the Citizens League of 1896) and Regular Democrats, many of whom founded the Choctaw Club. Meyer, as a professional politician, was a member of the latter group.

40. *American Israelite,* 9 September 1889, mentioned that Jonas had been the collector of the port of New Orleans until Cleveland's defeat the previous year; *American Israelite,* 23, 30 October 1890, 13 November 1890; *Daily States,* 4 October 1890, 2 November 1890.

41. *Times-Democrat,* 19 October 1890, 15 March 1891.

42. Heller, *Jubilee Souvenir,* 72; Ernestine Heller, Chicago, to Max Heller, New Orleans, 3 December 1890, Box 6, Folder 17, MHP; Schott, "John M. Parker," 44; Jackson, *Gilded Age,* 249.

43. Jackson, *Gilded Age,* 116, 121.

44. Jackson, *Gilded Age,* 129–130; Alwes, "Louisiana State Lottery," 964, 1034; Wickliffe,

"The Louisiana Lottery," 571; Thomas Cary Johnson, *The Life and Letters of Benjamin Morgan Palmer* (Richmond, Virginia: Presbyterian Committee of Publication, 1906), 553–554, 636–637; *Dictionary of American Biography*, 8:512; Nussbaum, 8; Guerin, "James Campbell Moise," 88; interviews with Ruth Dreyfous, 1988–1995.

45. Wall, *Louisiana*, 223, 115–116, 121–126.

46. Alwes, "Louisiana State Lottery," 1040–1041; *Daily States*, 25 May, 9 June 1890; Jackson, *Gilded Age*, 129.

47. Unidentified article containing Heller's Shreveport speech included in Henry Mortimer Favrot's "Scrap Book of Louisiana Lottery Collected by H. M. Favrot, #3," Favrot Collection, Special Collections, Tulane University Library; Ruth Heller Steiner, "Glimpses Through the Mist," 11, February 1965, revised January 1982 (photocopy), AJA.

48. Karp, *Haven and Home*, 93; Glazer, *American Judaism*, 48; Feingold, *Zion in America*, 102–103; Korn, "German-Jewish Intellectual Influences," 110.

49. Smith, "Religion and Ethnicity," 1161; Heller, "Why So Much Money?"

50. Wickliffe, "Louisiana Lottery," 571; *Mascot* (New Orleans), 15 April 1890, microfilm in Jazz Archives, Tulane University Library. Very few issues exist, none of them containing the articles that Henry Favrot collected, but the *New Delta* was the only paper in New Orleans not owned or controlled by the Lottery and was therefore the likely source for the item on Max Heller's address, Scrap Book #3, Favrot Collection; John H. Stone, Clinton, Louisiana, to Max Heller, New Orleans, 9 April 1890; Max Heller, New Orleans, to C. H. Parker, New Orleans, 23 May 1890, Box 5, Folder 2, MHP.

51. Alwes, "Louisiana State Lottery," 1060, 1064; Edgar Cahn, New Orleans, to Max Heller, New Orleans, 11 August 1891, Box 1, Folder 15, MHP; Ida Heller, Chicago, to Max Heller, New Orleans, 9 August 1891, Box 7, Folder 1, MHP.

52. *Shreveport Times*, 14 August 1891; *New Orleans Item*, 30 August 1891, 1–3 September 1891; T. F. Bell, Shreveport, to Max Heller, New Orleans, 14 August 1891, Box 1, Folder 4, MHP; Bell thanked Heller for delivering a "handsome, cogent, and convincing address."

53. *American Israelite*, 27 August, 10 September 1891; A. Lewenthal, Brookhaven, Mississippi, to Max Heller, 5 September 1891, Box 3, Folder 22, MHP; A. Krauss, Brookhaven, Mississippi, to Max Heller, New Orleans, 20 November 1891, MHP.

54. Ida Heller, Chicago, to Max Heller, New Orleans, 10 September 1891, Box 7, Folder 1, MHP; Henry Cohen, Galveston, to Max Heller, New Orleans, 6 May 1890, Box 1, Folder 18, MHP.

Chapter 5

1. *American Israelite*, 1888–1890, 31 October, 7 November 1889, 10 December 1890; sermon notes, 12 January 1890, Box 9, Folder 1, MHP.

2. Arnesen, "Waterfront Workers," 157; Ettinger, "John Fitzpatrick," 341–346.

3. Steiner, "Glimpses Through the Mist," 9.

4. David Marx was a New Orleans native; Mervis, "The Social Justice Movement," 174–175; Bauman and Shankman, "The Rabbi as Ethnic Broker," 53–55; Cowett, "Rabbi Morris Newfield," 52–74.

5. *Jewish Ledger*, 23 October 1896.

6. Feldman, "The Social Gospel," 310, links the humanitarian principles of the social gospel movement with "the heart of Judaism," quoting Morris Adler's statement, "Judaism is a God-centered faith whose chief concern is man." Max Heller, "Commencement Address at HUC," 14 June 1895, in *American Israelite*, 18 June 1895.

7. Zunz, "American History," 66, indicates that social historians, "in our hurry to enshrine workers as heroes and to condemn robber barons as villains," have often overlooked "the powerful influence of the middle-classes" in shaping immigrant assimilation at the turn of the century and, in the Progressive period, "Conservatism"; see *Jewish Ledger*, 17 July

1896. In the introduction to *Ethnic Leadership in America*, 3, John Higham distinguishes between "accommodation and protest as alternative strategies" for ethnic leaders to employ when dealing with the larger society. Heller's discussion of the conflicting roles of prophet and priest addressed similar issues. *Jewish Ledger*, 20 August 1897.

8. Raphael, "Intra-Jewish Conflict," 56, quoted I. M. Wise; *Jewish Chronicle* (Mobile, Alabama), 3 November 1899; *Daily Picayune*, 3 December 1896.

9. Augustus A. Levey to Hermann Makower, secretary for German Central Committee for Russian Refugees, 21 July 1882, cited in Urofsky, *American Zionism*, 60; Rischin, *The Promised City*, 19-75 (reprint edition); *Jewish Chronicle*, 17 January 1890; Mandel, "Attitude of the American Jewish Community," 28. Attitudes among the New Orleans Jewish establishment paralleled those discussed in Robert Rockaway's study "Ethnic Conflict in an Urban Environment," 133-150.

10. *Daily States* quoted in the *American Israelite*, 9 October 1890, 12 November 1891.

11. The organizations represented at the initial meeting included Temple Sinai, Touro Synagogue, Touro Infirmary, the Jewish Home for Widows and Orphans, Tefilah Congregation, Ahavath Sholom Congregation, Home Lodge and Grand Lodge, and B'nai B'rith.

12. *Times-Democrat*, 17 March 1891, 9 November 1891; *American Israelite*, 9 April 1891.

13. Temple Sinai minutes, 1 November 1891; *American Israelite*, 12, 19, 26 November, 31 December 1891, 21, 28 January, 4, 18, 25 February 1892; Raphael, "Intra-Jewish Conflict," 45.

14. By 1890, Ernestine offered to type Heller's sermons. Ernestine Heller, Chicago, to Max Heller, New Orleans, 7 November 1890, Box 6, Folder 17, MHP; Steiner, " 'The Girls in Chicago,' " 11-12; Max Heller, New Orleans, to Ernestine and Louise Heller, Chicago, 24 November 1891, Box 6, Folder 17, MHP; G. Bamberger, Chicago, to Max Heller, New Orleans, 1 December 1899, TL, Box 1, Folder 4, MHP.

15. Max Heller, New Orleans, to Julius Weis, New Orleans, 26 February 1897, Box 6, Folder 2, MHP.

16. *American Israelite*, 14 January 1892; Edgar Cahn, New Orleans, to Max Heller, Bad St. Moritz, Switzerland, 18 July 1892, Box 1, Folder 15, MHP; Max Heller, Bad St. Moritz, to Ida Heller, Chicago, July-August 1892, Box 7, Folder 1, MHP; Heller, *Jubilee Souvenir*, 90.

17. Steiner, "Glimpses Through the Mist," 10-11.

18. Max Heller, New Orleans, to Ernestine and Louise Heller, Chicago, 14 January 1893, Box 6, Folder 17, MHP; *Biennial Report*, 4, 37; Alcée Fortier, New Orleans, to Max Heller, New Orleans, 3 September 1893, 2 September 1896, 10 September 1898, Box 2, Folder 8, MHP; Everard, "Bourbon City," 972.

19. *Jewish Ledger*, 26 April 1895, 12 July 1895; Alcée Fortier, Biloxi, Mississippi, to Max Heller, New Orleans, 3 September 1893, Box 2, Folder 8, MHP; Jackson, *Gilded Age*, 116-118.

20. *Jewish Enquirer*, 2 March 1894, Louisiana Collection, Tulane University, one copy—possibly the only issue; A. J. Hollander (advertiser), New Orleans, to Max Heller, 12 March 1894, Box 3, Folder 1, MHP, in which Hollander explains that he must give up publishing the *Enquirer* because he cannot afford the financial risk; *Jewish Ledger*, 1 January 1896-30 December 1897.

21. *Jewish Ledger*, 17 April 1896, 15 May 1896; Cremin, *The Transformation of the School*, 85, stresses the observation that "humanitarians of every stripe saw education at the heart of their effort toward social alleviation."

22. Greene, *American Immigrant Leaders*, 15, addresses his study to leaders of " 'internal' elite who function as the group's representative and advocate," a definition that Heller could have applied to himself; Bauman, "Centripetal and Centrifugal Forces," 98. Jonathan Sarna notes that with the rise of rabbis as " 'representative Jews' . . . , laymen now welcomed rabbinic participation in public affairs; indeed, they took pride in showing their rabbis off."

23. *Jewish Ledger*, 26 March 1897.

24. *Jewish Ledger*, 16 April 1897.

25. Grantham, *Southern Progressivism*, 22-23; Feldman, "The Social Gospel and the Jews," 312, notes that in the 1890s for the first time in many years Jews and Christians could talk

about religion, a topic that "for centuries had been held to be sacred and mutually exclusive"; Heller, *Jubilee Souvenir,* 33; Temple Sinai Minutes, 1 November 1891, 22 February 1895; *American Israelite,* 7 December 1893, 12 April 1894, 27 November 1896; *Times-Democrat,* 9 April 1894. Two studies, that of Mark Cowett, "Rabbi Morris Newfield," and Bauman and Shankman, "The Rabbi as Ethnic Broker," depict rabbinic careers in Birmingham and Atlanta, respectively, that in many ways paralleled that of Heller, especially during this early and more socially conservative part of his work.

26. *Times-Democrat,* 27 November 1896; Karp, "Ideology and Identity," 317, argues that classic Reform Jews were closer in spirit and practice to liberal Christianity than to traditional Jews; Meyer, *Response to Modernity,* 289–290; Heller, *Jubilee Souvenir,* 103–104.

27. Ten adult Jewish men constituted a traditional *minyan,* the minimum necessary to gather for prayers according to Jewish tradition; Silverstein, *Alternatives to Assimilation,* 50–52.

28. According to Temple Sinai Minutes, 25 November 1895, the board approved Heller's plans to preach on the circuit; *Jewish Ledger,* 6 December 1895, 3 January 1896; *Southwestern Presbyterian,* 10 December 1896, clipping in scrapbook, Box 15, Folder 3, MHP.

29. Max Heller, "Pioneer Types in Louisiana and Mississippi," undated typescript, Box 11, Folder 5, MHP.

30. Max Heller, New Orleans, to Temple Sinai president and Board of directors, New Orleans, 13 December 1893, Box 5, Folder 20, MHP; *Summit Sentinel,* quoted in the *Jewish Ledger,* 10 January 1896. According to the *Jewish Ledger,* 15 May 1896, Heller left for Heidelberg "where he intends to take medical advice, as he has not been in good health for some time"; Ben Forchheimer, Summit, Mississippi, to Max Heller, New Orleans, 6 March 1896, Box 2, Folder 8, MHP. The editorials discussing circuit preaching did not mention Heller by name but instead referred to an "urban Israelite" who had been active in circuit preaching, and Heller was the only one involved in the movement; *Jewish Ledger,* 22, 29 July 1898.

31. Silverstein, *Alternatives to Assimilation,* 156; Raphael, *Profiles in American Judaism,* 34–35, explains that Sunday services were but one facet of the larger "Radical" Reform trend. Several factors provoked the movement, including Darwinian theory, and the "intellectual climate" created by scientific discoveries and theories, scientific analysis of the Bible and the new study of comparative religions, and "profound shifts in moral and religious attitude, particularly those resulting from the impact of positivistic naturalism and the thoroughgoing challenge to supernaturalism." The same forces produced radical changes in Christianity as well as in Reform Judaism. In "The Undertow," appearing in the *Jewish Ledger,* 3 January 1897, Heller described his own view of the changes, which supports Raphael's analysis: "Beneath the varied doings and sayings of individual men, beneath the purposes and undertakings of communities . . . , there are silent underground streams of public opinion with which must change the convictions, the wishes and hopes of men. . . . it is the logic of cause and effect . . . , as Herbert Spencer would call it, which explains, most rationally . . . these frequently puzzling drifts."

32. Max Heller, "Conference Sermon," *American Israelite,* 6 July 1891; *American Israelite,* 3 December 1891.

33. Meyer, *Response to Modernity,* 289–291; *Jewish Ledger,* 3 January 1896, 22 January, 25 May 1897; Max Heller, "Occidentalism, A Friday Evening Talk," *American Hebrew,* undated scrapbook clipping, Box 14, Folder 1, MHP. According to the *Jewish Ledger,* 15 November 1895, the *St. Louis Jewish Voice* lauded Heller's article, "Occidentalism," while an editorial in the *American Jewess* (Chicago), October 1897, attacked his suggestion that ceremonialism could "interrupt the fierce strife for personal advancement"; *Jewish Ledger,* 22 January, 7 July, 3 September 1897.

34. The Bat Mitzvah ceremony, where women were also called to the Torah, is a mid-twentieth-century creation; Simon Heller, Chicago, to Max Heller, Prague, 22 April 1875, MHP, translated for this book by Rose Karpel; Scott, *The Southern Lady,* preface; Fredrickson, *Black Image,* 279–281.

35. *Jewish Ledger,* 20, 27 November, 11 December 1896, 8 January, 26 February 1897.

36. *Jewish Ledger,* 1, 15, 22 January, 1897; Max Heller, New Orleans to "Folks," Chicago, 4 February 1897, Box 7, Folder 3, MHP.

37. Max Heller, Bad St. Moritz, to Ida Heller, Chicago, 1 August 1892, Box 7, Folder 1, MHP.

38. Max Heller, New Orleans, to Ernestine and Louise Heller, Chicago, 14 January 1893; Max Heller, Bad St. Moritz, to Ida Heller, Chicago, 17 July 1896.

39. Max Heller, Bad St. Moritz, to Ida Heller, Chicago, 22 July 1896, Box 7, Folder 1, MHP.

40. Ernestine also held her own with her brother and was willing to confront him in angry rebuttal. Ernestine Heller, Chicago, to Max Heller, New Orleans, 4 October 1897, TL, Box 6, Folder 17, MHP; Ida Heller, Chicago, to Max Heller, New Orleans, 4, 15 October 1897, Box 6, Folder 17, MHP; Scott, *The Southern Lady,* x; Calder, *The Victorian Home,* 121–152, suggests that, because of the restrictions placed upon the home and family, the domestic ideal could easily become the "domestic prison." Although she described conditions in England, society's expectations of women among the elite were similar on both sides of the Atlantic; *American Israelite,* 31 May 1900; Max Heller, *Jubilee Souvenir,* 96.

41. John Ruskin cited in Calder, *The Victorian Home,* 10; Max Heller, New Orleans, to "Folks," Chicago, 1, 25 March 1895, Box 7, Folder 1, MHP; Hernsheim, in addition to serving as vice president of S. Hernsheim and Company, a cigar manufacturing firm, was president of the National Automatic Fire Alarm Company; Edward F. Haas, *Political Leadership,* 48.

42. Max Heller, New Orleans, to "Folks," Chicago, 28 December 1896, Box 7, Folder 1, MHP.

43. Clipping from the *Mechanic Dealer and Lumberman,* 1 January 1896, Box 15, Folder 2, MHP, includes a detailed description of the materials used in construction and the photograph; *Jewish Ledger,* 20 September 1895; city directory, 1896.

44. *American Israelite,* 14 November 1895; 30 April 1896; Max Heller, "The Root of All Evil," *Jewish Ledger,* 24 April 1896; Haas, *Political Leadership,* 41, 52.

45. Schott, "John M. Parker," 70–71; Jackson, *New Orleans in the Gilded Age,* 315. According to Schott, "John M. Parker," 73, "the irony of 1896 in Louisiana history is that alluvial planters, manipulating thousands of Negro votes, helped win the fight for the Democracy, and then turned around and eliminated the Negro as a factor in the future politics of the state." Schott interprets the move toward disfranchisement as a response to the threat of fusion of class over racial interests.

46. Everard, "Bourbon City," 249–250; Dethloff and Jones, "Race Relations," 310–311, Schott, "John M. Parker," 72; *Jewish Ledger,* 5 April 1895; 1, 8 May 1896.

47. *Jewish Ledger,* 5, 8, 24 April, 1 May 1896; *Daily Picayune,* 8 April 1896.

48. *Jewish Ledger,* 16 October 1896.

49. *Jewish Ledger,* 16, 23 October 1896.

Chapter 6

1. As Dyer, *Theodore Roosevelt,* 21, writes, "To explain history, society, and individual and group character in racial terms appeared both logical and scientific in the light of the best scholarly opinion of the day." Heller's use of the word "race" is consistent with Dyer's explanation.

2. Max Heller, "A National Problem," *American Israelite,* 17 March 1904.

3. In his introduction to *The Crucible of Race,* Joel Williamson defines three distinct "mentalities" in the mind of the white South—liberals, conservatives, and radicals. Liberalism was strongest during the 1880s when its adherents believed that the South had not yet given the African American a fair chance to "absorb white culture." Although few in number, liberals were "articulate, highly energetic, and conspicuous," 5–6.

4. Raphael quotes Wise in "Intra-Jewish Conflict," 87–88, and noted, 29–30, that while German Jews had carried their English dictionaries with them as they crossed the Atlantic, the Russian Jews had brought their prayer books.

5. Max Heller, "Bernhard Felsenthal," eulogy, *American Israelite*, 23 January 1908; Felsenthal, *Bernhard Felsenthal*, 64.

6. Max Heller, New Orleans, to Moses Gries, Cleveland, 30 September 1895, Box 1, Folder 14, MHP; Max Heller, "The Future of the Jew in America," reprinted in the *Jewish Ledger*, 23 May 1897; Silverstein, *Alternatives to Assimilation*, 158–159, points out that by the end of the first decade of the twentieth century, other Reform rabbis had begun to understand the impact that Russian Jews would have on American Judaism. He cites Rabbi Martin Meyer of San Francisco's Temple Emanu-El, who wrote in 1911, "Frankly, the future of the Jew in America will be in the hands of the Russian-descended contingent . . . because of the preponderance of the numbers."

7. *Jewish Ledger*, 5 February, 19 February, 5 March 1897; *Daily Picayune*, 13 February 1897.

8. "Report of the First Vice-President," *Annual Report*, Touro Infirmary and Hebrew Benevolent Association, 1889–1902, Touro Infirmary Archives, New Orleans, Louisiana; *Jewish Daily News*, 25 August 1901, Box 15, Folder 2, MHP.

9. *Mascot*, 14, 21 March 1896; I. L. Leucht, New Orleans, to Max Heller, New Orleans, 20 May 1895, two undated letters, Box 3, Folder 25, MHP; Sam Blum, New Orleans, to Max Heller, New Orleans, 3, 10 June 1895, MHP, *Jewish Ledger*, 14 February 1896.

10. *Jewish Ledger*, 2 July 1897. At the end of 1897, Heller and Steeg, the publisher of the *Ledger*, had a dispute over Heller's salary, and Heller resigned. Complaining of dire financial straits, Steeg had asked Heller to consider writing for the paper gratis until Steeg recovered, but Heller declined, stating that no one else on the staff was expected to work without compensation. A. Steeg, New Orleans, to Max Heller, New Orleans, 17 December 1897, 26 December 1897, Box 5, Folder 2, MHP.

11. According to Howe and Greenberg, *A Treasury of Yiddish Stories*, 629 (reprint edition), a *maggid* (or *magid*) is a traveling preacher.

12. Julius Weis (?), undated, Box 5, Folder 2, MHP; W. Willner, Meridian, Mississippi, to Max Heller, New Orleans, 2 February 1898, Box 6, Folder 2, MHP; "Report of the First Vice-President," *Annual Report*, Touro Infirmary and Hebrew Benevolent Association, 1895, Touro Infirmary Archives, New Orleans, Louisiana.

13. Julius Weis (?), undated, Box 5, Folder 2, MHP.

14. Undated typescript, MHP (see appendix for copy).

15. Julius Weis (?), undated, Box 5, Folder 2, MHP; Max Heller, New Orleans, to "Folks," Chicago, 12 May 1898, Box 7, Folder 3; Gus Lemle, New Orleans, to Max Heller, New Orleans, 11, 13, 18, 29, 30 April 1898, Box 3, Folder 22, MHP.

16. *Jewish Spectator*, 20 May 1898; *Jewish Chronicle*, 1 July 1898, clippings, Box 15, Folder 3, MHP; *Jewish Ledger*, 6, 13, 20 May, 8, 22 July, 5, 26 August 1898; *American Israelite*, 16 June 1898.

17. *Chicago Israelite*, 9 July 1898, clipping, Box 15, Folder 3, MHP.

18. Simon Weis, New Orleans, to Max Heller, New Orleans, 13 June 1898, Box 6, Folder 2, MHP; Maurice Stern, New Orleans, to Max Heller, New Orleans, 13 June 1898, Box 5, Folder 2, MHP.

19. Urofsky, *American Zionism*, discusses the conflicts in his chapter, "Zionism Comes to America," 90–116; Schorske, *Fin-de-Siècle Vienna*, 146–180. In "Germans Versus Russians: An Update," *American Jewish History* 73 (December 1983): 142–156, Selma Berrol argues that the intense intraethnic fighting between Russian and German Jews in this country perpetuated tendencies even more explicit in the German cities where they originated. On both sides of the Atlantic, assimilated German Jews blamed their less acculturated Russian brethren for the rising tide of anti-Semitism, which, ironically, paralleled the rise to prominence of German Jewish businessmen and professionals.

20. Urofsky, *American Zionism*, 96, calls Heller "the most outspoken of the Zionists."

21. *Jewish Ledger,* 26 March, 16 April 1897 as discussed in chapter 5.

22. Cable, *The Silent South,* 53.

23. *Jewish Ledger,* 1 May 1896. In *The Strange Career of Jim Crow,* 18–21, Woodward emphasizes the fact that, before the Civil War, "racial discrimination in political and civil rights was the rule in the free states and any relaxation the exception." After the Civil War, the North could not provide a very inspiring precedent for enacting racial equality.

24. Max Heller, "The Root of All Evil," *Jewish Ledger,* 21 April 1896.

25. Urquhart, "The American Reaction to the Dreyfus Affair," 3; "The World's Verdict; Rabbi Heller Discusses the Dreyfus Trial and Decision," *Daily Picayune,* 10 September 1899.

26. Schorske, *Fin-de-Siècle Vienna,* 146–158.

27. Karp, "Ideology and Identity," 319.

28. *Jewish Ledger,* 30 July 1897.

29. See Hair, *Bourbonism;* Kousser, *The Shaping of Southern Politics,* 152–165.

30. *Biographical and Historical Memoirs of Louisiana,* 1:520; *The Convention of '98,* 12–16; Kruttschnitt obituary, *Daily Picayune,* 17 April 1906; E. B. Kruttschnitt, New Orleans, to Max Heller, New Orleans, 21, 24 February 1898, Box 3, Folder 14, MHP; *Times-Democrat,* 4–28 February 1898; Heller's opening prayer was on 28 February, mentioned in the paper 1 March 1898.

31. Fredrickson, *Black Image,* 228–282; Gossett, *Race,* 144–175; 253–286, 84–122 (reprint edition); Heller, "Modern Intolerance," *Times-Democrat,* 19 February 1898; Newby, *Jim Crow's Defense,* 7–13.

32. Max Heller, "Modern Intolerance"; Cable, "The Freedman's Case in Equity," 7.

33. "The Psychology of Race Prejudice," 42–43; Harlan, "The Secret Life of Booker T. Washington," 393–394; Williamson, *Crucible of Race,* 111–139.

34. Booker T. Washington, "Taking Advantage of Our Disadvantages," *A.M.E. Church Review,* April 1894, in *The Booker T. Washington Papers,* 3:408–411.

35. Du Bois, "Strivings of the Negro People," 194; Max Heller, "The Curse of Consciousness," *American Israelite,* 6 February 1902.

36. August Meier, "The Paradox of W. E. B. Du Bois," in *Negro Thought in America,* 182–183, 190–206 (reprint edition); Elliott M. Rudwick, *W. E. B. Du Bois: Propagandist of the Negro Protest* (New York: Atheneum, 1968), 36–37.

37. Gossett, *Race,* 144–175, 253–286 (reprint edition); Mosse, *Confronting the Nation,* introduction; Fredrickson, *Black Image,* 228–282.

38. Woodward, *The Strange Career of Jim Crow,* 31–65; Wynes, *Forgotten Voices;* Sosna, *Southern Liberals and the Race Issue;* Degler, *The Other South;* Bailey, *Liberalism in the New South,* 17–50; Mann, *Atticus Haygood;* Turner, *George Washington Cable,* 223; Fredrickson, *Black Image,* 204–220; in "Race and Mastery," 190, Bauman argues that the presence of dissent was no aberration but an indication that there existed "a multitude of minds of the South."

39. Newby, *Jim Crow's Defense,* 7–13.

40. Max Heller, New Orleans, to Board of Directors of Temple Siani, New Orleans, 16 November 1899, Box 5, Folder 20, MHP.

41. Hair, *Carnival of Fury,* 95–97. Interestingly, the only white person who had anything good to say about Robert Charles, the black man whose desperate murder of New Orleans policemen instigated the riot, was Hyman Levy. Although Hair does not mention it, Levy, a Dryades Street merchant from whom Charles bought clothes, was most likely a Jew.

42. Zola, "Maximilian Heller," 375–397.

43. "Speaks on Atonement; Rabbi Heller Talks at Temple Sinai," newspaper clipping, hand dated "T. D. Sept. 25," Box 14, Folder 2, MHP. Although Heller did not write the year on the clipping, the language and the incidents cited indicate that the sermon dated from the turn of the century; Open Letter Club postcards, George Washington Cable Collection, Box 125, SCHTL; Turner, 263–273 (quotation, 264); Williamson, *Crucible of Race,* 104–107; Morton Sosna mentions that although Haygood, unlike Cable, refrained from attacking

segregation, "he did argue that the debate over social equality was irrelevant" and maintained that black suffrage was just; *Southern Liberals and the Race Issue*, 7.

44. A *shlemiel*, or "Shlemihl" in Heller's phonetical spelling, is a Yiddish word for a "clumsy bungler" or fool. See Kogos, *A Dictionary of Yiddish Slang and Idioms*, 66; "For a Community of Interest," *Jewish Daily News*, 25 August 1901, clipping in Box 15, Folder 2, MHP.

45. Francis G. Caffey, Montgomery, to Max Heller, New Orleans, 31 March 1900, MHP.

46. Fredrickson, *Black Image*, 283–285, identifies the white moderate search for "interracial harmony and accommodation" as "accommodationist racism," a reaction against the "brutality" of the Darwinian racial extremists, and he sees these moderate Progressives as the natural heirs of the 1880s "paternalists" like Atticus Haygood.

47. In this passage and the following one, Heller is referring to social separation in terms of interpersonal relations, that is, interracial marriage only. Elsewhere, he opposed intermarriage between Jews and gentiles. His advocacy of "racial" separation was consistent, although such separation was voluntary only in the instance of Jewish-gentile intermarriage.

48. Murphy quoted by Bailey, *Edgar Gardner Murphy*, 59–61; Max Heller, "A National Problem," *American Israelite*, 17 March 1904.

49. Murphy, *The Present South*, 160–161; Heller, "A National Problem."

50. Louis Marshall, New York, to Max Heller, New Orleans, 28 February 1905, Box 4, Folder 5, MHP. Whether Marshall was responding to Heller's fears about, or acceptance of, segregation, at this point, remains unclear.

51. Bailey, *Edgar Gardner Murphy*, 39; "Temple Sinai Holds a Touching Service," *Daily Picayune*, 20 September 1901.

52. Edward Barnes, New Orleans, to Max Heller, New Orleans, 21 September 1901, Box 1, Folder 4, MHP.

53. *Times-Democrat*, 9, 12 November 1904.

54. "The Negro Scholar and Gentleman," *Times-Democrat*, 17, 21 November 1904; "The Point of View," two newspaper clippings, unidentified (*Times-Democrat?*), Box 15, Folder 5, MHP. In "The Heart of the Race Problem," Ewing, an Episcopal priest serving a congregation in a hamlet in southwestern Louisiana, wrote that, for the white Southerner, the race problem lay not in the observation of the black man's inferiority but rather in the problem of "how to keep him what he is in relation to the white man."

55. Harlan, "Booker T. Washington's Discovery of the Jews," 154. Harlan also mentions that Tuskegee's major white supporters in Alabama were Jews and that, as early as 1905, a rabbi had delivered the commencement address, 155–156.

56. "The Golden Jubilee: Isidore Newman Manual Training School Dedicated," *Jewish Ledger*, 13 January 1905.

57. "An Impudent Nigger," *Jewish Ledger*, 22 September 1905; on Thomas Dixon, see Fredrickson, *Black Image*, 280.

58. "How to Meet Prejudice; An Interesting Sermon by Rabbi Max Heller," *Times-Democrat*, 16 February 1907; "Impressive Ceremonies Mark Eve of Atonement," *Times-Democrat*, 5 October 1908; Frances Joseph-Gaudet, New Orleans, to Max Heller, New Orleans, 11 October 1908, Box 2, Folder 16, MHP.

59. Max Heller, Manitoa Springs, Colorado, to Joseph Stolz, Chicago, 18 July 1905, Box 8, Folder 7, MHP; William Benjamin Smith, *The Color Line: A Brief in Behalf of the Unborn* (New York: McClure, Phillips, 1905), x–xi; Max Heller, New Orleans, to R. K. Bruff, 6 November 1925, Max Heller, New Orleans, to William Benjamin Smith, New Orleans, 10 November 1915, University Archives, SCHTL.

60. Max Heller, "Abraham Lincoln," *American Israelite*, 11 February 1909.

61. Max Heller, "Atonement Eve Address," *American Israelite*, 16 September 1909.

62. "Dr. Heller on 'Christmas Confusions'; The Doll and Toy Distribution," *Times-Democrat*, 30 December 1909.

63. "A Criticism of the Doll and Toy Fund," *Times-Democrat*, 30 December 1909.

64. "Dr. Heller's Position," *Times-Democrat*, 31 December 1909.

65. W. E. Myers, *The Israelites of Louisiana* (New Orleans: W. E. Myers, [1905?]), 83; interview with Bill Rosen, New Orleans, April 1990; Malone, "Reform and Dissent," chaps. 2–Epilogue; "Dr. Heller's Views," *Times-Democrat*, 1 January 1910.

66. "Rabbi Heller's Letter," *Times-Democrat*, 1 January 1910; "Another Letter from Rabbi Heller," *Times-Democrat*, 5 January 1910. *Jewish Ledger*, 7 January 1910.

67. A. R. Perkins, Chicago, to Max Heller, New Orleans, 4, 5, 9 January 1910, Box 4, Folder 17, MHP; J. W. Hawthorn, Alexandria, to Max Heller, New Orleans, 8 January 1910, Box 3, Folder 1, MHP; Valcour Chapman, New Orleans, to Max Heller, 5 January 1910, Box 1, Folder 14, MHP.

68. "Unfair Treatment of Negro," *Times-Democrat*, 2 January 1910; "The Times-Democrat and the Negro Race," *Times-Democrat*, 9 January 1910, newspaper clippings, Box 14, Folder 4, MHP.

69. Heller, "A Departure in Jewish Philanthropy," *American Israelite*, 12 January 1911.

70. Central Congregational Church's guest speakers during 1910–1911 included W. E. B. Du Bois and Professor James H. Dillard, president of the Jeanes Fund and director of the Slater Fund, Central Congregational Church notes, Historical Events Notebook, Central Congregational Church Papers; *Times-Democrat*, 13 February 1911; *Daily Picayune*, 13 February 1911, clippings from scrapbooks, MHP.

71. *Times-Democrat*, 13 February 1911; *Daily Picayune*, 13 February 1911, clippings from scrapbooks, MHP; *Jewish Ledger*, 17 February 1911.

72. *Times-Democrat*, 13 February 1911, *Daily Picayune*, 13 February 1911, clippings from scrapbooks, Box 15, Folder 5, MHP.

73. *Times-Democrat*, 13 February 1911; Meier, "The Paradox of W. E. B. Du Bois," 182–183; W. E. B. Du Bois, "Racial Prejudice," *Crisis* 1 (April 1911): 6; Heller, "Manliness Versus Prejudice," 859–862.

74. Heller, "Manliness Versus Prejudice," 862; Max Heller, "Difficult Friendships," *American Israelite*, 11 May 1911.

Chapter 7

1. Heller, "Our Salvation"; Bernhard Felsenthal, Chicago, to Max Heller, New Orleans, 31 March 1902, Box 2, Folder 9, MHP.

2. David Philipson, Cincinnati, to Max Heller, New Orleans, 28 March 1902, Box 4, Folder 18, MHP; Jacob S. Raisin, Port Gibson, Mississippi, to Max Heller, New Orleans, 12 March 1902, Box 4, Folder 22, MHP; Zola, "Maximilian Heller," 380–381. In "Converts to Zionism in the American Reform Movement," 2–4, Jonathan Sarna notes that during the last thirty years of the nineteenth century, the majority of those attending key conferences of the Reform Jewish movement (the Philadelphia Rabbinical Conference in 1869, the 1885 Pittsburgh conference, the 1897 meeting of the CCAR, and the 1898 UAHC meeting) passed resolutions against Zionism.

3. Heller, "Bernhard Felsenthal."

4. Heller, "Zionism and the Mission," *Maccabaean*, January 1911, pp. 20–21; for an in-depth look at the conflicts between Reform and Zionism at the turn of the century, see Cohen, "The Reaction of Reform Judaism," 361–394, and Sternstein's "Reform and Zionism," 11–31; Greenstein, *Turning Point*, 73.

5. Higham, *Strangers in the Land*, 198–199; Toll, "Ethnicity and Freedom," 160: Kallen, "Democracy Versus the Melting-Pot, Part Two," 220.

6. "Rabbi Heller Discusses Zionism," *Daily Picayune*, 18 November 1899; "Zionism," *Southwestern Presbyterian*, 30 November 1899; Zola, "Maximilian Heller," 379–380.

7. Stephen S. Wise, New York, to Max Heller, New Orleans, 4 December 1899, Box 6, Folder 8, MHP.

8. Zola, "Maximilian Heller," 380, feels that Wise's death was pivotal in giving Heller the intellectual and emotional freedom to convert to Zionism, but he may have seen more in the coincidence than did Heller; Gotthard Deutsch, Hyde Park, Ohio, to Max Heller, New Orleans, 25 November 1898, Box 2, Folder 1, MHP; Max Heller, New Orleans, to "Folks," Chicago, 3 December 1898, Box 7, Folder 3, MHP; Max Heller, New Orleans, to Gotthard Deutsch, Cincinnati, 20 December 1898, Box 2, Folder 9, MHP.

9. Hair, *Carnival of Fury.*

10. "An Utopian Dream or a Practical Solution?" *Times-Democrat,* 12 December 1901.

11. Heller, "Our Salvation."

12. Israel Zangwill, "The Jewish Race and Its Problem," quoted in the *American Hebrew,* 18 August 1911; Kallen, "Jewish Life Is National and Secular," 527.

13. Heller, "Our Salvation."

14. Zola, "Maximilian Heller," 375, believes that Heller's dedication to the reconciliation of Reform Judaism and Zionism was his main achievement as a Reform Jewish leader, his singular accomplishment as "pioneer on the path toward establishing Zionism as an integral component within the philosophy of Reform Judaism." Michael A. Meyer successfully refutes the belief that anti-Zionism was ever hegemonic in the Reform Jewish movement in his seminal article "American Reform Judaism and Zionism."

15. Arthur Hertzberg, ed., *The Zionist Idea: A Historical Analysis and Reader* (New York: Atheneum, 1972), 495. Gottheil's son, Richard, was one of the foremost early Zionists in America, founder of the Federation of American Zionists, the first national American Zionist organization; see Diner, *A Time for Building,* 223.

16. Gustav Gottheil, New York, to Max Heller, New Orleans, 6 April 1902, Box 2, Folder 21, MHP.

17. Jacob de Haas, New York, to Max Heller, New Orleans, 10 September 1902, Box 3, Folder 2, MHP.

18. Jacob de Haas, "Mr. de Haas's Tour," *Maccabaean,* January 1908, p. 27.

19. Leo Wise, Cincinnati, to Max Heller, New Orleans, 9 January 1903, Box 6, Folder 7, MHP; "Reform and Zionism," unnamed and undated column that referred to the *Jewish Comment,* Box 14, Folder 4, MHP.

20. Max Heller, New Orleans, to Isaac Heller, Cambridge, Massachusetts, 20 November 1914, Box 17, Folder 10, MHP.

21. Meyer Stern, New York, to Max Heller, New Orleans, 5 April 1889, Box 5, Folder 2, MHP; Max Heller, New Orleans, to Marcus Kohler, New York, 27 November 1894, Box 3, Folder 14, MHP; Tobias Schanfarber, Mobile, to Max Heller, New Orleans, 11 and 16 January 1899, Box 5, Folder 4, MHP; Max Heller, New Orleans, to Philip Cowen, New York, 12 January 1900, Box 1, Folder 20, MHP.

22. Joseph Stolz, Chicago, to Max Heller, New Orleans, 19 March 1903, Box 8, Folder 6, MHP.

23. *Hebrew Standard,* 10 and 17 April 1903; *Times-Democrat,* hand dated and illegible; *New York Times,* 13 April 1903; *Jewish Exponent,* 17 April 1903; *American Hebrew,* 17 April 1903.

24. Philip Cowen, New York, to Max Heller, New Orleans, 2 April 1903, Box 1, Folder 20, MHP; Max Heller, New Orleans, to Philip Cowen, New York, 4 April 1903, Box 1, Folder 20, MHP; Joseph Stolz, Chicago, to Max Heller, New Orleans, 27 April 1903, Box 8, Folder 6, MHP; Richard Gottheil, New York, to Max Heller, New Orleans, 21 April 1903, Box 2, Folder 21, MHP.

25. Louis Marshall, New York, to Max Heller, New Orleans, 15 June 1903, Box 4, Folder 5, MHP; the two men developed a lasting relationship and maintained a correspondence over the years. Heller told Stolz that meeting his New York host, the cotton broker Emanuel Lehman, Solomon Schechter, and Louis Marshall "will always seem to me a more than ample compensation for the trouble of going to New York, even for my probable defeat"; Max Heller, New Orleans, to Joseph Stolz, Chicago, 11 September 1903, Box 8, Folder 6, MHP.

26. Max Heller, New York, to Ida Heller, New Orleans, 3 May 1903, Box 7, Folder 3, MHP.

27. "Our Place Today," *American Hebrew,* 8 May 1903; *Jewish Exponent,* 8 and 29 May 1903, in an unidentified article, hand dated by Heller, 8 May 1903, the journalist speculated about Heller's chances of being elected to Emanu-El, mentioning that the *American Hebrew,* "whose influence in the best Jewish circles in the Metropolis is positive," strongly favored him, Box 15, Folder 4, MHP; *American Hebrew,* 1 May 1903; Henry Cohen, Galveston, to Max Heller, New Orleans, 9 May 1904, Box 1, Folder 18, MHP.

28. Max Heller, New Orleans, to Joseph Stolz, Chicago, 19 June 1903, Box 8, Folder 6, MHP; Joseph Stolz, Chicago, to Max Heller, New Orleans, 11 February 1904; Max Heller, New Orleans, to Joseph Stolz, Chicago, 15 February 1904, Box 8, Folder 6, MHP. In his *Memories of an American Jew,* 396–397, Philip Cowen mentioned that Heller (and Galveston's Henry Cohen) were two rabbis whom he wanted to see in New York pulpits, although both "held their positions for life." Cowen referred to a beautiful letter that Heller had written to Marshall in which he eliminated himself from consideration for Emanu-El because he felt that his talents and needs were not those that Emanu-El sought in a rabbi; Louis Marshall, New York, to Philip Cowen, New York, 16 February 1904, Box 4, Folder 5, MHP.

29. *Jewish American,* 2 January 1903; Beverly Warner was the minister leaving New Orleans, *Times-Democrat,* 8 January 1905.

30. Max Heller, "The Rationale of Modern Judaism," *Maccabaean,* July 1903, pp. 32–34.

31. *Times-Democrat,* 27 January 1905.

32. "By Way of Contrast," *Maccabaean,* March 1903, pp. 173–174; Max Heller, "Aristocracies and the Jew," *American Israelite,* 27 April 1911.

33. Heller, "The Rationale of Modern Judaism," *Maccabaean,* July 1903, pp. 32–34; Toll, "Ethnicity and Freedom," 160; Kallen, "Jewish Life Is National and Secular," 527; "The Longing for Orthodoxy," *American Israelite,* 23 October 1902; Max Heller, "Object-Lesson in Judaism," *Jewish Comment,* 29 June 1900; *Maccabaean,* March 1903, p. 176.

34. The term "Russian Jews" generically encompasses all new arrivals from various parts of Eastern Europe. Many had seen their European homes incorporated into the Russian empire; Rosalie Cohen and Mike Brener, interviews by author, 1989, 1993, tape recordings; I. M. Levy, Joseph Goldman, Elias Brener, Elias Pailet, New Orleans, to Max Heller, New Orleans, 27 May 1901, Box 3, Folder 22, MHP; *American Israelite,* 6 June 1901, A. Rabonowitz (?), New Orleans, to Max Heller, New Orleans, 19 August 1903, Box 4, Folder 21, MHP; *Times-Democrat,* 5 January 1903, 14 December 1903; J. D. Dresner, New Orleans, to Max Heller, New Orleans, 20 March 1906, 21 June 1907, Box 1, Folder 22, MHP; *Daily Picayune,* 2 April 1906.

35. Max Heller, "Object-Lesson in Judaism," *Jewish Comment,* 29 June 1900; "For a Community of Interest," *Jewish Daily News,* 25 August 1901.

36. *CCAR Yearbook* 14 (1904): 64–65.

37. *Jewish Daily News,* 20 March 1910.

38. *CCAR Yearbook* 18 (1908): 179–210 (quotations, 205, 210, 215).

39. In the chapter "Zionism Comes to America," in *American Zionism,* 81–115, Melvin Urofsky provides a complete overview of the structural and organizational problems facing American Zionists before World War I.

40. Ohavei Zion program, New Orleans, 18 December 1903, Box 15, Folder 4, MHP; "Eloquent Address of Dr. Heller," unidentified clipping, 21 December 1903, Box 15, Folder 4, MHP; Max Heller, "About to Throw Away a Rare Opportunity," *Jewish Comment,* 19 December 1904, Box 15, Folder 2, MHP; Zola, "Maximilian Heller," 382; as Urofsky explains (*American Zionism,* 27), Herzl did not mean for Uganda to replace Palestine. Instead, he considered it a "temporary refuge until Palestine could be secured." But he had to read the lines "If I forget thee, O Jerusalem" from Psalm 137 to reaffirm his devotion to Palestine in his final speech before the Congress. Exhausted from his efforts, he died at forty-four the following summer.

41. Max Heller, "Moral Zionism Absurd," *Menorah* (June 1904): 331–332; August Heidenheim, New Orleans, to Max Heller, New Orleans, 16 March 1904, Box 3, Folder 1, MHP.

42. "The Minister and the Business Man," 7 November 1902, "The Elements of Business Morality," 4 November 1902, *Temple Sinai Pulpit* (1902).

43. "Significance of Feast," *Times-Democrat*, 11 April 1906; Judah Magnes, FAZ secretary, told Heller, "I think I understand the situation in New Orleans, and your loneliness there from a Zionist point of view," Judah Magnes, New York, to Max Heller, New Orleans, 27 November 1906, Box 4, Folder 2, MHP; *Times-Democrat*, 10 December 1906; Yom Kippur Sermon, *Daily Picayune*, 19 September 1904; *CCAR Yearbook* 17 (July 1907): 137–138; *CCAR Yearbook* 18 (July 1908): 93–94.

44. Max Heller, *Jubilee Souvenir*, 92; Silverstein, *Alternatives to Assimilation*, 157: Joseph Stolz, Chicago, to Max Heller, New Orleans, 23 December 1909, Box 8, Folder 7, MHP.

45. Judah Magnes, New York, to Max Heller, New Orleans, 28 October 1907, Box 4, Folder 2, MHP; Max Margolis, Cincinnati, to Max Heller, New Orleans, 26 April 1907, Box 4, Folder 5, MHP; Charles S. Levy, Peoria, Illinois, to Max Heller, New Orleans, 14 May 1907, Box 3, Folder 22, MHP; Cohen, "The Reaction of Reform Judaism," 373–381; Polish, *Renew Our Days*, 97, briefly discusses the plight of Caspar Levias, a fourth HUC Zionist who, also in 1907, was dismissed from his professorship at HUC. Zionism, ostensibly, was the reason for his dismissal, as it had been for the other three who left that year. In *Hebrew Union College–Jewish Institute of Religion at 100 Years*, Samuel E. Karff notes that Solomon Schechter, president of New York's Jewish Theological Seminary, HUC's new rival institute, declared himself a Zionist in 1906 and speculated that his announcement might have compelled the leadership at HUC to reaffirm the college motto "America is our Zion." The attitude expressed by the slogan jeopardized the careers of the Zionist professors there.

46. Leo Wise, Cincinnati, to Max Heller, New Orleans, 23 January, 14 March, 26 April 1907, Box 6, Folder 7, MHP; Judah Magnes, New York, to Max Heller, New Orleans, 19 April 1907, Box 4, Folder 2, MHP; Judah Magnes, New York, to Louis Goldman, Cincinnati, 15 May 1907, Box 26, Folder 4, UAHC Collection, AJA; Sarna, "Converts to Zionism," 4, agrees with Meyer, "A Centennial History," 44–46, 62–69, that, although disagreements in the Reform movement over Zionism were fundamental, no schism occurred.

47. Zola, "Maximilian Heller," 383–385, discusses the election, mentioning that the CCAR elected Heller president in 1910. The election took place at the end of 1909, and his term of office began in 1910.

48. Philipson, *My Life as an American Jew*, 193; David Philipson, Cincinnati, to Max Heller, New Orleans, 15 April 1909, Box 4, Folder 18, MHP.

49. A. S. (name indecipherable), Chairman FAZ Propaganda Committee, New York, to Max Heller, New Orleans, 23 September 1909, Box 2, Folder 8, MHP.

50. Shapiro, *A Reform Rabbi*, 209–210; Floyd Lehman Herman in "Some Aspects of the Life of Stephen S. Wise to 1925" (master's thesis, HUC-JIR, 1964).

51. Max Heller, New Orleans, to "Dear Colleague" (Stephen S. Wise), New York, 10 November 1909, unsigned, Box 6, Folder 8, MHP; Stephen S. Wise, New York, to Max Heller, New Orleans, 13 November 1909, Box 6, Folder 8, MHP.

52. Urofsky, *A Voice That Spoke for Justice*, 49–58.

53. Max Heller, New Orleans, to Joseph Stolz, Chicago, 5 November 1909, Box 8, Folder 7, MHP. Stolz was not the only person to whom Heller unburdened himself; realizing his predicament in not being able to attend the conference himself, he tried to rally support from other friendly colleagues; Max Heller, New Orleans, to Samuel Schulman, New York, 3 November 1909, Box 1, Folder 45, Samuel Schulman Papers, AJA; Max Heller, New Orleans, to Julian Morgenstern, Cincinnati, 4 November 1909, Box 5, Folder 5, CCAR Papers, AJA.

54. Joseph Stolz, New York, to Max Heller, New Orleans, 10 November 1909, Box 8, Folder 7, MHP; Max Heller, New Orleans, to Joseph Stolz, New York, 13 November 1909, Box 8, Folder 7, MHP.

55. Henry Cohen, New York, to Max Heller, New Orleans, Friday (otherwise undated),

Box 1, Folder 18, MHP; Henry Cohen, New York, to Max Heller, New Orleans, Tuesday night (otherwise undated), Box 1, Folder 18, MHP; Moise Bergman, New York, to Max Heller, New Orleans, 11 November, 12 November 1909, Box 1, Folder 6, Moise Bergman Correspondence, AJA; Joseph Jasin, New York, to Max Heller, New Orleans, 12 November 1909, Box 3, Folder 13, MHP.

56. Heller credited Judah Magnes with tactical aid in postponing the FAZ meeting. Heller realized that his absence from the conference redounded to his ultimate victory. He claimed that had he been there, he would never have allowed the FAZ to call off a meeting just to assure his success; Max Heller, New Orleans, to Mr. and Mrs. C. J. Teller, Philadelphia, 26 November 1909, Box 5, Folder 19, MHP; Joseph Silverman, New York, to Max Heller, New Orleans, 19 November 1909, Box 5, Folder 9, MHP.

57. On its editorial page, the *Jewish Ledger,* 5 November 1909, noted that the twentieth annual meeting of the CCAR was to be held in New York the coming week and briefly outlined its program but failed to mention that Max Heller was the vice president and expected to succeed to the presidency. No mention is made of the meeting nor the election results in the weeks that follow.

58. Max Heller, *Jubilee Souvenir,* 115.

59. Cited by Zola, "Maximilian Heller," 385.

60. Louis Lipsky, New York, to Harry Friedenwald, Baltimore, 7 January 1910, unsigned, Box 3, Folder 29, MHP; Harry Friedenwald, Baltimore, to Louis Lipsky, New York, signed "H.L.," Box 3, Folder 29, MHP; Meyer, "American Reform Judaism and Zionism," 50, notes that Lipsky "held out no hope that Reform Judaism might ever become Zionistic."

61. *Philadelphia Inquirer,* 21 January 1909, clipping in Box 15, Folder 5, MHP. The article featured photographs of some of the prominent spokespersons at the conference, including Heller.

62. Dyer, *Theodore Roosevelt,* 23, carefully tackles the murky definition of "race" in the early twentieth century and finds that terms like "race feeling" and "race consciousness" hint of "quasi-mystical qualities associated with racial identity . . . , a self-knowledge of race membership which approximates the concept of fellow feeling."

63. Simon Wolf, Washington, D.C., to Max Heller, New Orleans, 11 February 1910, Box 6, Folder 9, MHP; Panitz, *Simon Wolf,* 121–131.

64. "Message of Rabbi Max Heller, President of the Central Conference of American Rabbis, to the Twenty-second Annual Conference, at St. Paul, Minn., July 2, 1911," *CCAR Yearbook* 21 (1911): 133–134; Heller, "What Zionism Saves."

65. Kallen, "The Ethics of Zionism," 61–71.

66. "Message of Rabbi Max Heller, President of the Central Conference of American Rabbis, to the Twenty-first Annual Convention, at Charlevoix, Mich., June 28, 1910," *CCAR Yearbook* 20 (1910): 137–169.

67. Raisin, "Reform Rabbis and Zionism," 100–101; Max Raisin, New York, to Max Heller, New Orleans, 18 September 1905, and other correspondence between Raisin and Heller, 1905–1913, Box 4, Folder 23, MHP; Max Raisin, autobiographical typescript, Paterson, New Jersey, 1953, AJA; H. D. Uriel Smith, "Out of the Books of Rabbi Max Raisin's Life," term paper, HUC-JIR, AJA. In Gary Zola's synopsis of Raisin's memoirs, *Misefer Khayai: Zikronot Urishimot Otobiografayim (From the Book of My Life),* 13, term paper, Small Collections, AJA, he discusses Raisin's concern for Meridian's black citizens and his shock when members of his congregation opposed his speaking out "against this injustice."

68. Leo Wise, Cincinnati, to Max Heller, New Orleans, 30 January 1911, Box 6, Folder 7, MHP.

69. Zola, "Maximilian Heller," 386–387; Heller, "Zionism and the Mission," 20–21; Henry Hurwitz, Dorchester, Massachusetts, to Max Heller, New Orleans, 1 February 1911, Box 3, Folder 8, MHP; "Anti-Zionist Supposition," article in *Modern View,* 1911, Box 14, Folder 4, MHP.

70. Dyer, *Theodore Roosevelt,* acknowledges Roosevelt's obsession with masculine images

and terms. For example, 48–49, Roosevelt glowingly described the superiority of white Americans who derived from their Teutonic forebears their boldness and intelligence, their ability to show "their best in an emergency"; Heller, "Zionism as the Leaven," 95–96; Sarna, "Converts to Zionism," 16, also cites "Zionism as the Leaven."

Chapter 8

1. Urofsky, *A Voice That Spoke for Justice,* 40, writes that the sermons Wise wrote as a young rabbi "derived in large part" from the works of Josiah Strong, Lyman Abbott, Gladden, and Rauschenbusch. In both his earlier article, "Rabbi Morris Newfield," and his biography, *Birmingham's Rabbi,* 12, 77–78, Mark Cowett argues that Newfield, Heller's younger southern colleague, paid a great deal of attention to Social Gospelers. For broad discussions of the subject, see Feldman, "The Social Gospel and the Jews," and *Dual Destinies,* 132–138; Mervis, "The Social Justice Movement," 171–227.

2. In Heller's correspondence with family and friends, his health and that of his family were always topics that he mentioned in some detail, MHP; J. H. Kellogg, Battle Creek, Michigan, to Max Heller, New Orleans, 19 October and 26 November 1908, Box 3, Folder 14, MHP; (signature illegible), Treasurer, Touro Infirmary, New Orleans, to Max Heller, New Orleans, 7 November 1908, Box 5, Folder 12, MHP; S. Pisko, Denver, Colorado, to Max Heller, New Orleans, 31 January 1916, Box 4, Folder 17, MHP.

3. "The Ministry and the Sewerage Election," *Times-Democrat,* 12 January 1899 (Heller letter dated 10 January 1899); *Owl,* 1899, Box 15, Folder 1, MHP; "Health Association," *Times-Democrat,* 19 December 1902; unidentified clipping, 1905, Box 15, Folder 5, MHP.

4. Henry C. Flonacher, Chicago, to Max Heller, New Orleans, 14 December 1905, Box 2, Folder 18, MHP; "Public Needs Protection," open letter from Max Heller, New Orleans, to Harold W. Newman, Commissioner of Public Safety, 25 May 1914, *Times-Picayune,* 26 May 1914.

5. Frank D. Chretien, New Orleans, to Max Heller, New Orleans, 23 June 1909, Box 1, Folder 14, MHP.

6. "Purity Talks End in Peace," *Daily Picayune,* 28 October 1910; "Flays Purity Congress," *Times-Democrat,* 31 October 1910.

7. Max Heller, "In Re Dannenbaum," typed manuscript, undated, Box 1, Folder 24, MHP; Henry J. Dannenbaum, Houston, to Max Heller, New Orleans, 17 March 1912, Box 1, Folder 24, MHP; in an undated issue of the New Orleans *Blue Book,* a directory listing the names of prostitutes and establishments in the city's red light district, several Jewish names were listed—including Dora Cohen, Alvera Frumenthal, Sadie Freidburg, and Lena Silberman—but the majority were not Jewish; Henry Levi Collection, Vault, 15–5, Box 5, SCHTL; Dick Allen, archivist at the William R. Hogan Jazz Archives, Howard Tilton Library, Tulane University, New Orleans, showed me another edition of the *Blue Book* from the 1890s in which Jewish prostitutes, like African Americans, advertised separately. Allen thought their reason for doing so was that the separateness made them seem more exotic; conversation with Dick Allen, summer 1991; Sachar, "The Shame of Our Daughters," 164–168; Sorin, *A Time for Building,* 84–85.

8. "Rabbi Heller Talks on Issue of Prohibition," *Times-Democrat,* 19 April 1908; "Ministers and Lawmakers," Max Heller, letter to the editor, dated 7 June 1908, *Times-Democrat,* undated clipping, Box 14, Folder 4, MHP; Max Heller, "Prohibition in the Light of Judaism," *Texas Jewish Herald,* 11 February 1915.

9. "Rabbi Heller Talks on Issue of Prohibition," *Times-Democrat,* 19 April 1908; "Ministers and Lawmakers," Max Heller, letter to the editor, 7 June 1908, *Times-Democrat,* undated clipping, Box 14, Folder 4, MHP; Dewey Grantham, *Southern Progressivism,* xix, xxi, 160–177; *American Israelite, Jewish Ledger,* 1908–1918.

10. "Rabbi Max Heller Denounces Race Track Gambling," *American,* 26 February 1916.

11. George H. Cornelson, New Orleans, to Max Heller, New Orleans, 4 October 1915, Box 1, Folder 14, MHP; Max Heller, New Orleans, to "Boys," Cincinnati and Boston, 12 December 1915, Box 17, Folder 10, MHP; "Civic Leaders Gather, But Say Their Conference Was Merely to Learn the Strikers' Views," unidentified clipping, 1902, Box 14, Folder 4, MHP.

12. Max Heller, "Diverging Tendencies," *American Israelite*, 15 March 1906; other examples of his sermons and editorials dealing with materialism include "Rich and Poor," *Daily Picayune*, 31 January 1902; "Extravagance," *Times-Democrat*, 4 January 1908; "Pocket Patriotism," *Times-Democrat*, 28 November 1908; "Jews Observe Yom Kippur," *Daily Picayune*, 19 September 1904.

13. Mervis, "The Social Justice Movement," 175–177.

14. "Rev. Max Heller, Rabbi Temple Sinai, Expresses His Opinion as to the Fresh Air Outing for Poor Children," column from a publication of the Louisiana Society for the Prevention of Cruelty to Children, 1896, Box 15, Folder 1, MHP; Dr. J. C. Orcutt, Louisiana Society for the Prevention of Cruelty to Children, New Orleans, to Max Heller, New Orleans, 7 November 1898, Box 1, Folder 14, MHP; Heller, "Child Labor," *American Israelite*, 8 April 1909.

15. F. Gerstner, Recording Secretary, Retail Clerks International Protective Association, Local No. 706, New Orleans, to Max Heller, New Orleans, 17 March 1911, Box 2, Folder 16, MHP; "Report of the Commission on Social Justice," *CCAR Yearbook* 25 (1915), 96–103; Max Heller, New Orleans, to Isaac Heller, Boston, 12 November 1914, Box 17, Folder 8, MHP. In the same letter Heller mentioned how glad he was that Brandeis had become a Zionist. "I know of no man (even Schiff or Rosenwald)," he wrote, "whom I would rather have seen in our ranks."

16. Circular, Max Heller, New Orleans, to "Friend," 26 February 1913, Box 1, Folder 1, MHP; S. Harby Plough responded to the circular that, from his point of view, the cigar business was "unquestionably controlled by Jews"; Harby, New York, to Max Heller, New Orleans, 7 March 1913, Box 4, Folder 17, MHP; Jacob J. Abt, president of the Wholesale Clothiers Association of Chicago, told Heller that when Hendricks wrote, "The Jew is the greatest shoe-string capitalist in the world," in the clothing business, the statement was "in some measure, true"; Abt, Chicago, to Max Heller, New Orleans, 8 March 1913, Box 1, Folder 1, MHP; M. B. Suskind, Savannah, to Max Heller, New Orleans, 8 March 1913, Box 5, Folder 2, MHP; Benjamin Mordecai, New York, to Max Heller, New Orleans, 10 March 1913, Box 4, Folder 1, MHP.

17. Horace Kallen's claim that the Jewish workforce clustered in the "garment-making industries, tobacco manufacture, and in the 'learned professions' " supports Heller's argument, "Democracy Versus the Melting-Pot, Part I," *Nation*, 18 February 1915, p. 194.

18. Max Heller, "Promiscuous Generalizing about the Jew," *Jewish Voice*, 2 April 1909, reprinted from the *Item* (handwritten notation; no dates given); Gossett, *Race*, 343–344.

19. Henry Cohen, Galveston, to Max Heller, New Orleans, 30 December 1908, Box 1, Folder 18, MHP; "The New Jewry of the South: Interview with Rabbi Henry Cohen of Galveston," *American Hebrew*, 13 September 1912.

20. "Dr. Max Heller and the Hebrews," *Sea Coast Echo*, 31 August 1907.

21. "Woman in Talmud," *Times-Democrat*, 2 April 1901; "Woman's Work," *Times-Democrat*, 6 February 1903; "Woman in the World and at Home," *Temple Sinai Pulpit*, 10 April 1903.

22. Henry B. Blackwell, Boston, to Max Heller, New Orleans, 26 April 1903, Box 1, Folder 4, MHP; the article appeared in the journal, 2 May 1903; Kate M. Gordon, New Orleans, to Max Heller, New Orleans, 17 November 1904, Box 2, Folder 16, MHP; Herman Weil, New Orleans, to Max Heller, New Orleans, 5 June 1916, Box 5, Folder 20, MHP.

23. *CCAR Yearbook* 32 (1922), 50–51.

24. Max Heller, "To Amend the Constitution," letter to the Editor, *Times-Democrat*, 13 November 1896; Cohen, *Jews in Christian America*, deals with the legal challenges implicit in the "Christian America" agenda; Feldman, *Dual Destinies*, 150.

25. DeVore and Logsdon, *Crescent City Schools*, 33–35; "Strenuous Opposition to Bible in the School," *Times-Democrat*, 4 April 1906.

26. "Rabbis and Christmas," *Times-Democrat,* 7 December 1907.

27. *CCAR Yearbook* 34 (1924): 84; Naomi Cohen discusses the issue extensively in *Jews in Christian America.*

28. "The Jewish Congress; Rabbi Heller Returns from Philadelphia Convention," *Daily Picayune,* 27 June 1909.

29. "The Bible in the Schools," *Athenaeum,* 15 February 1914.

30. "Round Table on Bible Reading in Public Schools," *CCAR Yearbook* 25 (1915): 423–429.

31. Cecile told her father that she had tried to talk her boyfriend into converting, but he felt that it would be hypocritical to begin the marriage with a lie, since he was agnostic but culturally Catholic; Cecile Heller, Philadelphia, to Max Heller, New Orleans, 6 April 1918, Box 8, Folder 1, MHP; James, already a rabbi himself, sided with his sister. He wanted his father to give Cecile his blessing, and love, even if he refused to attend the wedding ceremony; James Heller, Philadelphia, to Max Heller, New Orleans, 8 April 1918, Box 7, Folder 5, James Heller Papers, AJA. The issue was apparently resolved when Cecile agreed to wait until after World War I to marry. In early 1920, she married Edward Lasker, a Jewish chess champion from Chicago, but within the year, she died tragically from diabetic complications following minor surgery; "Funeral of Rabbi Heller's Daughter," unidentified newspaper clipping, 13 November 1920, Box 15, Folder 6, MHP.

32. Heller may have borrowed Roosevelt's words and adapted his ideas to fit Jewish identity issues, but Roosevelt's deep-seated concern about the possibility of race suicide was of an entirely different order. He perceived that the "fertility of old-stock Americans" was declining even as people of inferior racial stock (including Jews) surged into the country in greater numbers, and he became morbidly concerned for the country's future. Although Roosevelt found "militant political anti-Semitism . . . reprehensible," many of his comments suggested that he was not beyond employing anti-Semitic stereotypes "of the more common variety"; Dyer, *Theodore Roosevelt,* 143–167, 124.

33. "Rabbi Heller Answers 'Liberal,' Letters from the People," *Times-Democrat,* 23 November 1908; "The Jew's Fabled Wealth," *Literary Digest,* 13 September 1913.

34. Max Heller, New Orleans, to the president and board members of Temple Sinai, New Orleans, 24 November 1915, Box 5, Folder 20, MHP; *CCAR Yearbook* 24 (1914): 155.

35. *Yehudim,* both Hebrew and Yiddish for "Jews," was a term that Eastern Europeans used in referring to the German-Jewish American community.

36. Henry Cohen, Galveston, to Max Heller, New Orleans, 25 January 1907, Box 1, Folder 18, MHP; "Jewish Immigration," *New Orleans Item* cited in the *Hebrew Standard,* undated clipping, Box 15, Folder 5, MHP.

37. Max Heller, "Anti-Alienism," *American Israelite,* 19 January 1911; Sorin, *A Time for Building,* 65–67.

38. Dyer, *Theodore Roosevelt,* 45–68; Gossett, *Race,* 347–353, calls Chamberlain "the most grandiloquent prophet of German racism" and mentions that American racists gained from their German mentor "a method for countering the arguments of anthropologists which belittled the importance of racist theory"; Charles S. Myers, "Is There a Jewish Race?" *American Hebrew,* 5 August 1911; Israel Zangwill, "The Jewish Race and Its Problem," *American Hebrew,* 18 August 1911. In an editorial, "The Universal Races Congress," *American Hebrew,* 15 September 1911, the journalist noted that the problems "aroused by the differences of pigmentation in men's skins" attracted "the attention of the thoughtful"; Ignaz Zollschan, "The Jewish Race Problem," *American Hebrew,* 9 February 1912.

39. Dinnerstein, *The Leo Frank Case,* is the most comprehensive account of the Leo Frank case; Hertzberg, *Strangers Within the Gate City,* 202–215, provides a brief summary of the events and analyzes its effects on the Atlanta Jewish community; Lindemann, *The Jew Accused,* 194–272, introduces a provocative revision by considering the case in a comparative framework and emphasizes the class dimensions of the case.

40. Woodward, *Tom Watson,* 443.

41. Woodward, *Tom Watson,* 431–450.

42. Max Heller, "The Answer to Prejudice," *American Israelite,* 2 January 1913; Leo Frank, The Tower, Atlanta, to Max Heller, New Orleans, 24 November 1913, Box 2, Folder 8, MHP.

43. Sorin, *A Time for Building,* 211–223; Eugene Levy, "Is the Jew a 'White Man?': Press Reaction to the Leo Frank Case, 1913–1915," *Phylon* 35 (1974): 212–222, mentions that after Frank was lynched, one northern Jewish paper declared that blacks "were 'the only defender of [Georgia's] good name,' in that a black man was the only one to come forward to supply his wagon to carry away Frank's body, thus preventing its mutilation and burning," 219; Lindemann, *The Jew Accused,* 270; Hertzberg, *Strangers Within the Gate City,* 210.

44. Max Heller, "Jewish Aspects of Frank Case," *American,* 24 June 1915; Max Heller, "Some Lessons of Ritual Murder Trial in Russia," *Times-Picayune,* 15 November 1913; Hertzberg, *Strangers Within the Gate City,* 210–211.

45. "A Misleading Explanation of Prejudice," *Jewish Immigration Bulletin,* March 1914, Box 14, Folder 5, MHP; interview with Rabbi Henry Cohen of Galveston," *American Hebrew,* 13 September 1912.

46. "Reform Rabbis on the Future of Reform Judaism," *American Hebrew,* 27 November 1908, p. 91.

47. Heller, *Jubilee Souvenir,* 115–116; Max Heller, New Orleans, to Louis Pailet, New Orleans, 2 April 1914, Box 4, Folder 17, MHP.

48. J. Walter Freiberg, Cincinnati, to Max Heller, New Orleans, 18 March 1912, Box 2, Folder 11, MHP; Zola, "Maximilian Heller," 388–389.

49. Leo Wise, Cincinnati, to Max Heller, New Orleans, 10 May 1912, Box 6, Folder 7, MHP.

50. Leo Wise, Cincinnati, to Max Heller, New Orleans, 17 September 1914, Box 6, Folder 7, MHP; Leo Wise, Cincinnati, to Max Heller, New Orleans, 29 September 1914, Box 6, Folder 7, MHP; Max Heller, New Orleans, to Isaac Heller, Boston, 2 October 1914, Box 17, Folder 8, MHP.

51. *American Hebrew,* 19 April 1912; "American Zionists at Cleveland," *Jewish Exponent,* 5 July 1912; Louis Lipsky wrote Heller the following week, thanking him for his participation at the convention and telling him that the delegates had elected him honorary vice president, "leaving the naming of other vice-presidents to the executive committee, according to the rule," Louis Lipsky, New York, to Max Heller, New Orleans, 12 July 1912, Box 3, Folder 29, MHP.

52. Horace Kallen, Madison, Wisconsin, to Max Heller, New Orleans, 26 September 1912, Box 3, Folder 15, MHP.

53. Max Heller, New Orleans, to "Boys" (Isaac and James Heller), Boston and Cincinnati, 12 January 1915, Box 17, Folder 10, MHP; Max Heller, New Orleans, to "Boys" (Isaac and James), Boston and Cincinnati, 31 January 1915, Box 17, Folder 10, MHP; "Moral Courage," printed program, Box 14, Folder 2, MHP.

54. Heller, "Moral Courage."

55. Heller, "Moral Courage"; Leo Franklin, Detroit, to Joseph Stolz, Chicago, 22 February 1915, Box 2, Folder 10, MHP; George H. Cornelson, Jr., New Orleans, to Max Heller, New Orleans, 12 March 1915, Box 1, Folder 14, MHP; Simon Wolf paid Heller a fine compliment. To Wolf, the sermon had "the true manly ring," and he told Heller, "I wish there were more men like you who have not only the courage of their convictions, but also the intellectual force to give them emphasis"; Simon Wolf, Washington, D.C., to Max Heller, New Orleans, 11 March 1915, Box 6, Folder 9, MHP.

Chapter 9

1. Max Heller, New Orleans, to "Boys" (Isaac and James), Cincinnati and Boston, 3 February 1916, Box 17, Folder 11.

2. Max Heller, "Prayer for Peace," *Item,* 3 October 1914.

3. Max Heller, New Orleans, to "Boys" (Isaac and James), Cincinnati and Boston, 29 March 1916, Box 17, Folder 11, MHP; Arthur D. Call, Executive Director, American Peace Society, Washington, D.C., to Max Heller, New Orleans, 8 July 1915, Box 1, Folder 14, MHP; "Orleans Jews Are in Sympathy with Peace Movement," *American,* 3 June 1915, clipping, Box 14, Folder 5, MHP; untitled promotional circular on stationery from the Louisiana Society for International Concord, New Orleans, 20 January 1916, Box 6, Folder 15, MHP.

4. Max Heller, New Orleans, to "Boys" (Isaac and James), Cincinnati and Boston, 29 October 1916, Box 17, Folder 11, MHP; Max Heller, New Orleans, to "Boys" (Isaac and James), Cincinnati and Boston, 9 November 1916, Box 17, Folder 11, MHP; Max Heller, New Orleans, to Stephen S. Wise, New York, 14 November 1916, Box 45, Folder 16, SSWP.

5. Matthew James Schott, "John M. Parker of Louisiana and the Varieties of American Progressivism" (Ph.D. diss., Vanderbilt University, 1969), 409–465; Max Heller, New Orleans, to "Boys" (Isaac and James), Cincinnati and Boston, 5 April 1916, Box 17, Folder 11, MHP; Max Heller, New Orleans, to Harold A. Mosie, New Orleans, 15 November 1916, Box 4, Folder 1, MHP; Moise told Heller that Parker "requested that this letter be saved for him to hand down to his children and grand children [*sic*]," Harold A. Moise, New Orleans, to Max Heller, New Orleans, 17 November 1916, Box 4, Folder 1, MHP; Max Heller, New Orleans, to "Boys" (Isaac and James), Cincinnati and Boston, 18 November 1916, Box 17, Folder 1, MHP; Max Heller, New Orleans, to Stephen S. Wise, New York, 14 November 1916, Box 45, Folder 16, SSWP.

6. Adolf Kraus, president, B'nai B'rith, Chicago, to Max Heller, New Orleans, 27 November and 2 December 1914, Box 3, Folder 14, MHP.

7. Max Heller, New Orleans, to Isaac Heller, Boston, 20 November 1914, Box 17, Folder 8, MHP; Max Heller, New Orleans, to Samuel Rosinger, Beaumont, Texas, 8 October 1914, Box 4, Folder 21, MHP; Bernard A. Rosenblatt, honorary secretary, FAZ, New York, to Max Heller, New Orleans, 18 August 1914, Box 4, Folder 21, MHP; David Philipson, Cincinnati, to Max Heller, New Orleans, 3 September 1914, Box 1, Folder 7, David Philipson Papers, AJA.

8. Max Heller, New Orleans, to Stephen S. Wise, New York, 31 December 1914 (circular), SSWP, Box 111, Folder 8; Max Heller, New Orleans, to "Boys" (Isaac and James), Cincinnati and Boston, 1 January 1915, Box 17, Folder 10, MHP; Max Heller, New Orleans, to "Boys" (Isaac and James), Cincinnati and Boston, 11 January 1915, Box 17, Folder 10, MHP; Martin A. Meyer, San Francisco, to Max Heller, New Orleans, 29 March 1915, Box 4, Folder 10, MHP.

9. Brandeis, *Zionism and Patriotism;* Cyrus Sulzberger (?), AJRC, Philadelphia, to Max Heller, New Orleans, 14 January 1915, Box 1, Folder 1, MHP; Max Heller, New Orleans, to "Boys" (Isaac and James), Cincinnati and Boston, 2 February 1915, Box 17, Folder 10, MHP; AJRC, unsigned circular, Philadelphia (?), to Max Heller, New Orleans, 2 February 1915, New York, Box 1, Folder 1, MHP; Cyrus Sulzberger, Philadelphia, to Max Heller, New Orleans, 11 February 1915, Box 5, Folder 22, MHP; Cyrus Sulzberger, Philadelphia, to Max Heller, New Orleans, 24 May 1915, 25 February 1916, Box 1, Folder 1, MHP.

10. Louis Lipsky, New York, to Max Heller, New Orleans, 15 January 1915, Box 3, Folder 29, MHP.

11. Summaries of the Kallen-HUC affair can be found in Urofsky, *A Voice That Spoke for Justice,* 89–90; Zola, "Maximilian Heller," 391; Horace Kallen, letter to the editor, *Jewish Comment,* 25 December 1914. When James told his father what had happened, Heller replied, "Too bad about Kallen. . . . He is one of the most glorious human beings I have ever met, though very eccentric," Max Heller, New Orleans, to "Boys" (Isaac and James), Cincinnati and Boston, 27 December 1914, Box 17, Folder 10, MHP; Horace Kallen, Madison, Wisconsin, to Stephen S. Wise, New York, Box 3, Folder 15, SSWP; Stephen S. Wise, New York, to Max Heller, New Orleans, 28 December 1914, Box 6, Folder 8, MHP; editorial, *Jewish Comment,* 1 January 1915.

12. Sam S. Mayerberg, Simon Cohen, I. J. Sarasohn, James G. Heller, Cincinnati, to Horace Kallen, Madison, Wisconsin, Box 13, Folder 1, Horace Kallen Papers, AJA; Isaac Bloom, sec-

retary, HUC Board of Governors, Cincinnati, to Max Heller, New Orleans, 27 January 1915, Series D, Box 8, Folder 15, HUC Papers, AJA; Stephen S. Wise, New York, to Isaac Bloom, Cincinnati, to Stephen S. Wise, New York, undated, Box 3, Folder 17, SSWP; Max Heller, New Orleans, to "Boys" (Isaac and James), Cincinnati and Boston, 28 January 1915, Box 17, Folder 10, MHP; Max Heller, New Orleans, to Edward Heinsheimer, president, HUC Board of Governors, Cincinnati, 29 January 1915, Series D, Box 8, Folder 15, HUC Papers; unsigned (secretary of the HUC Board of Governors?), Cincinnati, to Max Heller, New Orleans, 1 February 1915, Series D, Box 8, Folder 1, HUC Papers; Max Heller, New Orleans, to Henry Cohen, Galveston, 1 February 1915, Series 3, Box M233, HCP; Max Heller, New Orleans, to Stephen S. Wise, New York, 3 February 1915, Box 3, Folder 17, SSWP; J. Leonard Levy, Pittsburgh, to Max Heller, New Orleans, 3 February 1915, Box 3, Folder 26, MHP; Max Heller, New Orleans, to Joseph Stolz, Chicago, 5 February 1915, Box 8, Folder 7, MHP.

13. Max Heller, Chicago, to Joe Stolz, Chicago, 18 February 1915, Box 8, Folder 7, MHP; Max Heller, New Orleans, to Isaac Blum, Cincinnati, 1 March 1914, Series D, Box 8, Folder 15, HUC Papers; Blum replied that Heller's "expressions of pleasure and satisfaction at the happy finale of our conference sound[ed] a note of pleasure in the hearts of all those who attended the meeting," Isaac Blum, Cincinnati, to Max Heller, New Orleans, Series D, Box 8, Folder 15, HUC Papers; Zola, "Maximilian Heller," 391–392.

14. Max Heller, New Orleans, to Isaac Heller, Boston, 16 October 1912 (?), Box 17, Folder 8, MHP.

15. Max Heller, New Orleans, to Isaac Heller, Boston, 16 October 1912 (?), Box 17, Folder 8, MHP. Isaac's sons, Theo and Edward Heller, both assert that their father had a personality and temperament far better suited for the rabbinate than that of his older brother, James; informal conversations, New Orleans, 1989–1994.

16. *CCAR Yearbook* 25 (1915): 497–499; Urofsky, *A Voice That Spoke for Justice*, 9–10; Max Heller, "The Philistines Are Upon Thee, Samson," *Jewish Comment*, 2 October 1915; Stephen S. Wise, New York, to Max Heller, New Orleans, 15 November 1915, Box 6, Folder 8, MHP.

17. Max Heller, "The Jewish Consciousness," *Temple Israel Pulpit*, 31 December 1915; "By a Prominent Rabbi" [Max Heller], "Uprooted," *American Jewish World*, 10 December 1915.

18. "I speak to the negroes to-night on Booker Washington," Heller mentioned to his sons, Max Heller, New Orleans, to "Boys" (Isaac and James), Cincinnati and Boston, 12 December 1915, Box 17, Folder 10, MHP; Historical Events Notebook, Central Congregational Church Records, Amistad Research Center, Tulane University, New Orleans, Louisiana; Max Heller, "Booker T. Washington," *Olio* 30 (January 1916): 2–6, Box 15, Folder 2, MHP.

19. Max Heller, New Orleans, to "Boys" (Isaac and James), Cincinnati and Boston, 3 April 1916, Box 17, Folder 1, MHP.

20. Urofsky, *American Zionism*, 127–129.

21. Sorin, *A Time for Building*, 211–223; Urofsky, *American Zionism*, 127–129. The Jews already settled in Palestine also impressed Brandeis, and he again drew a thoroughly American analogy to their struggle. He regarded them as "Jewish Puritans" and saw Zionism as the "Pilgrim inspiration and impulse over again"; Sachar, *A History of the Jews in America*, 252, 228–229. Brandeis also added a neat summation about the work of the "Jewish Pilgrim Fathers"; Brandeis, *Zionism and Patriotism*, 2; *CCAR Yearbook* 26 (1916): 88–89; Sachar, *A History of the Jews in America*, 262–264; Stephen S. Wise, New York, to Max Heller, Kennebunk Port (sic), Maine, 10 August 1916, Box 6, Folder 8, MHP; Joseph Stolz, Chicago, to Max Heller, New Orleans, 27 April 1916, Box 8, Folder 7, MHP.

22. Max Heller, New Orleans, to Isaac Heller, Boston, 16 October 1916, Box 17, Folder 8, MHP.

23. Max Heller, "Rabbi Indorses [sic] Peace Proposal of President," *Times-Picayune*, 27 January 1927; Max Heller, "War Will Result in Great Benefit, Says Rabbi Heller," *Times-Picayune*, 28 April 1917.

24. Heller, "The Elder Brother."

25. Max Heller, "The Need of a Jewish Congress," *Jewish Ledger*, 29 June 1917; Stephen S.

Wise, New York, to Max Heller, Kennebunkport, Maine, 15 July 1917, Box 6, Folder 8, MHP; Lederhendler, *The Road to Modern Jewish Politics*, 84–110, clearly and perceptively analyzes the emergence and role of the *shtadlanim;* Sachar, *The Course of Modern Jewish History*, 265–266.

26. Max Heller, New Orleans, to Stephen Wise, New York, 14 November 1916, Box 45, Folder 16, SSWP; Zola, "Maximilian Heller," 394.

27. Max Heller, "Dollarland Spirituality," *Maccabaean*, April 1917, pp. 198–199; Max Heller, "The Mission in Dispersion," *Maccabaean*, May 1917, pp. 224–225.

28. Max Heller, "Nationalism and Religion," *Maccabaean*, June-July 1917, pp. 247–248.

29. *CCAR Yearbook* 27 (1917): 132–145; *Jewish Spectator*, 20 July 1917.

30. Max Heller, "Zionism at the Buffalo Convention," 1917, *American Jewish Chronicle;* Stephen S. Wise, New York, to Max Heller, Kennebunkport, Maine, 15 July 1917, Box 6, Folder 8, MHP; Zola, "Maximilian Heller," 393.

31. Max Heller, "Our Spiritual Golus," *Maccabaean*, August 1917, pp. 314–315.

32. Henry Hurwitz, New York, to Max Heller, New Orleans, 5 April 1917, Box 3, Folder 8, MHP; Max Heller, New Orleans, to Editor of *New York Times*, New York, 9 April 1917, Box 6, Folder 15, MHP; Max Heller, "Nationalism in English Diplomacy," *Maccabaean*, December 1917, p. 415; Max Heller, Chicago, to Jacob de Haas, New York, undated, Box 3, Folder 2, MHP.

33. David Philipson, "The British Declaration," *American Israelite*, 29 November 1917; Douglas Kohn, "David Philipson: American Anti-Zionist," manuscript, HUC-JIR, 1986, AJA, presents an excellent discussion of Philipson's consistent ideology, forged when he was a student of I. M. Wise and maintained until his death sixty-six years later.

34. Max Heller, New Orleans, to Henry Cohen, Galveston, 31 December 1917, Box 3M, Folder 236, HCP; Henry Cohen, Galveston, to Max Heller, New Orleans, 27 January (year?), Box 1, Folder 18, MHP.

35. Gotthard Deutsch, Cincinnati, to Max Heller, New Orleans, 6 February 1918, Box 2, Folder 2, MHP.

36. Gotthard Deutsch, Cincinnati, to Max Heller, New Orleans, 14 April 1917, Box 2, Folder 2, MHP; Gotthard Deutsch, Cincinnati, to Max Heller, New Orleans, 30 July 1917, Box 2, Folder 2, MHP; Olitzky, Sussman, and Stern, *Reform Judaism in America*, s.v. "Gotthard Deutsch."

37. Olitzky et al., *Reform Judaism in America*, 38–39; circular to Executive Members of the HUC Board of Alumni Association, from Julian Morgenstern, President, Board of Alumni, Cincinnati, HUCP, Box G1, Folder 9, AJA; Max Heller, Kennebunkport, Maine, to Gotthard Deutsch, Cincinnati, 28 June 1918, Box 2, Folder 9, Gotthard Deutsch Papers, AJA.

38. Heller, "The Personality of Gotthard Deutsch," 149–152; *Times-Picayune*, 5 September 1917.

39. "Rebirth of Holy Land Glowing Romance of War; Rabbi Max Heller Speaks on Restoration of Palestine at Temple Sinai," unidentified newspaper clipping, 17 February 1918, Box 14, Folder 7, MHP; "Rabbi Heller Tells of Plan for the New Jerusalem," *New Orleans Item*, undated clipping, Box 14, Folder 5, MHP; Max Heller, "An Intellectual Affinity," *American Israelite*, 14 March 1918.

40. Max Heller, Kennebunkport, Maine, to Joseph Stolz, Chicago, 13 June 1918, Box 8, Folder 7, MHP.

41. Knee, *The Concept of Zionist Dissent*, 49–50; Untitled, 29 April (1918), Box 1, Folder 1, Ephraim Frisch Papers, AJA, contains a list of those present; unsigned circular, initialed "DP/PF," undated, Box 1, Folder 15, David Philipson Papers; David Philipson, "The Rabbinical Conference on the Balfour Declaration and Zionism," editorial, *American Israelite*, 11 July 1918.

42. Max Heller, "Zionism and Our Reform Rabbinate," *Maccabaean*, July 1918, pp. 180–181, 190–191.

43. Urofsky, *American Zionism*, 196, 206, 210, 216; Henry Cohen, Galveston, to Honorable

Robert Lansing, Washington, D.C., 15 July 1918, Box 3M, Folder 236, HCP; David Philipson, Cincinnati, to Henry Cohen, Galveston, 19 July 1918, Box 3M, Folder 236, HCP.

44. Max Heller, "A Realized Pattern of Social Justice," *Menorah Journal,* August 1918, p. 236; Max Heller, "A National Resurrection," *Times-Picayune,* 8 September 1918.

45. Edward N. Calisch, Richmond, Virginia, to David Philipson, Cincinnati, 3 August 1918, Box 1, Folder 2, David Philipson Papers; circular suggesting the formation of an organization "somewhat along the lines of the League of British Jews," signed David Philipson, Chairman, and Ephraim Frisch, Secretary, 8 August 1918, Box 3M, Folder 236, HCP; circular from Max Heller, Martin A. Meyer, Stephen S. Wise, New York, 8 August 1918, Box 3M, Folder 236, HCP; Ephraim Frisch, New York, to Leo Franklin, Detroit, 24 August 1918, Box 1, Folder 2, Leo Franklin Papers, AJA; Leo Franklin, Detroit, to Ephraim Frisch, New York, 26 August 1918, Box 1, Folder 2, Leo M. Franklin Papers; Ephraim Frisch, New York, to Henry Cohen, Galveston, 26 August 1918, Box 3M, Folder 236, HCP; A. H. Fromenson, New York, to Henry Cohen, Galveston, 5 September 1918, night lettergram, Box 3M, Folder 287, HCP.

46. Circular from Julian W. Mack and Jacob de Haas, New York, 5 September 1918, Box 3M, Folder 287, HCP; Kaufman Kohler, Cincinnati, to David Philipson, Cincinnati, 4 and 5 September 1918, Box 1, Folder 10, David Philipson Papers; Louis Marshall, New York, to David Philipson, Cincinnati, 5 September 1918, Box 1, Folder 13, David Philipson Papers.

47. Ephraim Frisch, New York, to President Woodrow Wilson, Washington, D.C., undated, Box 1, Folder 15, David Philipson Papers; Ephraim Frisch, New York, to David Philipson, Cincinnati, undated, Box 1, Folder 5, David Philipson Papers; Ephraim Frisch, New York, to Max Raisin, Brooklyn, undated, Box 11, Folder 16, CCAR Papers; Max Raisin, Brooklyn, to Ephraim Frisch, New York, 19 September 1918, Box 11, Folder 16, CCAR Papers; "Messages Favoring and Opposing Zionism Sent President Wilson by American Jews," *Independent,* 13 September 1918; David Philipson, Cincinnati, to Henry Cohen, Galveston, 11 September 1918, Box 3M, Folder 326, HCP; Henry Berkowitz, Philadelphia, to David Philipson, Cincinnati, 11 and 13 September 1918, Box 1, Folder 1, David Philipson Papers; Louis Wolsey, Cleveland, Ohio, to David Philipson, Cincinnati, 12 and 13 September 1918, Box 2, Folder 4, David Philipson Papers; Ephraim Frisch, New York, to David Philipson, Cincinnati, 20 September 1918, Box 1, Folder 5, David Philipson Papers; Kolsky, *Jews Against Zionism,* 34–35, 44, notes that, after the 1937 Columbus Platform of the CCAR (for which James Heller fought strongly) affirmed Palestine as a "center of Jewish culture and spiritual life" as well as a "haven for the oppressed." Those dissenting from the Columbus Platform founded the anti-Zionist American Council for Judaism, and the leaders included veterans of the League of American Jews.

48. Max Heller, "The Status of Zionism," *American Israelite,* 3 October 1918; Max Heller, "Outlived Viewpoints," *B'nai B'rith News,* September-October 1918.

49. Max Heller, "Impressions of the American Jewish Congress," *Chicago Israelite,* 26 December 1918.

50. Included among those signatories to the anti-Zionist manifesto were rabbis of the following southern pulpits: William Rosenau of Baltimore, Morris Newfield of Birmingham, William Greenburg of Dallas, Henry Cohen of Galveston, Harry Merfeld of Greenville, Mississippi, Henry Barnstein of Houston, Louis Witt of Little Rock, James Rauch of Louisville, William Fineshriber of Memphis, Isidore Lewinthal of Nashville, Emil Leipziger of Touro Synagogue, New Orleans, Moses Jacobson of Shreveport. Notably absent was also David Marx of Atlanta, even though he was an anti-Zionist, "Citizens of the U.S. of America: Signers of the Manifesto to the Peace Conference at Paris delivered to President Wilson by Congressman Julius Kahn, March 1919," small collections, documents file, AJA.

51. "The Hon. Julius Kahn Sounds a Warning Note," *American Israelite,* 6 February 1919, Sachar, *A History of Jews in America,* 264–267; Knee, *The Concept of Zionist Dissent,* 55; Higham, *Strangers in the Land,* 198; Kolsky, *Jews Against Zionism,* 31. A representative sampling of the rich vein of anti-Zionist materials of this brief period scattered in the collections of the AJA

includes the papers of Max Senior, David Philipson, Samuel Schulman, and Henry Berko-witz; secondary accounts of personalities and issues in the anti-Zionist camp include Micah D. Greenstein, "Classicity in the American Reform Rabbinate: A Study Based on the Unpublished and Published Papers, Sermons, and Works, of Moses J. Gries and William Rosenau, Two Presidents of the Central Conference of American Rabbis" (rabbinical thesis, HUC-JIR, 1991); Goldblatt, "The Impact of the Balfour Declaration in America," 455–515; Cohen, "The Reaction of Reform Judaism," 361–394.

52. "Synopsis of Rabbi Max Heller's Address at Carnegie Hall, Jan. 15," *Jewish Criterion*, 17 January 1919; Max Heller, "The Congress Question," *Jewish Ledger*, 7 March 1919; Leon Harris, St. Louis, to Max Heller, New Orleans, 21 February 1919, Box 3, Folder 4, MHP.

53. Max Heller, "A Zionist's Appraisement of the Isaac M. Wise Centenary," *Jewish Expo-nent*, 18 April 1919; Max Heller, "When Zionism and Reform Meet," *Maccabaean*, May 1919, pp. 112–114. After the centenary, Stephen Wise promised Heller that, should the CCAR pass a "really anti-Zionist resolution" at its summer convention, "I for one will have to withdraw, and I think my congregation would go with me," Stephen S. Wise, New York, to Max Heller, New Orleans, 16 April 1919, Box 6, Folder 8, MHP.

54. Max Heller, "Americanism and Zionism," *Maccabaean*, March 1919, p. 69; *CCAR Year-book* 29 (1919): 229, also cited by Michael A. Meyer in "American Reform Judaism and Zion-ism," 63–64.

55. Stephen S. Wise, New York, to Max Heller, New Orleans, 9 May 1919, Box 6, Folder 8, MHP; Max Heller, New Orleans, to Stephen S. Wise, New York, 15 May 1919, Box 45, Folder 16, SSWP; Max Heller, New Orleans, to James Weldon Johnson, Washington, D.C., 18 March 1919, NAACP Administration Files, C-172, Manuscript Division, Library of Congress, Washington, D.C. "List of Speakers for NAACP Meetings," NAACP Administration Files, C-172, Manuscript Division, Library of Congress; a footnote in Diner, *In the Almost Promised Land*, 159, alerted me to Heller's communications with the NAACP.

56. Knee, *The Concept of Zionist Dissent*, 58, notes that the CCAR accepted the San Remo decision because the majority of the members believed that the decision would serve as a "death blow to Zionism"; *CCAR Yearbook* 30 (1920): 138–143.

57. Max Heller, "San Remo and the Reform Rabbis," *Maccabaean*, August 1920, pp. 39–41; Michael A. Meyer, "American Reform Judaism and Zionism," 64; Max Heller, "The Roch-ester Convention from a Zionist Viewpoint," *Scribe*, 23 July 1920, also cited by Zola, "Maxi-milian Heller," 345.

58. Max Heller, "Dangers of the Hour," *Maccabaean*, September 1919, pp. 270–271; Louis Marshall, New York, to Henry Ford, Dearborn, Michigan, 3 June 1929, copy of telegram, Box 4, Folder 5, MHP; Dearborn Publishing Company, Dearborn, Michigan, to Louis Mar-shall, New York, 5 June 1920, copy of telegram, Box 4, Folder 5, MHP; Max Heller, "The Quandry of the Apostate Jew," *B'nai B'rith Magazine*, January 1925, pp. 138–139, 149; Heller, "The Anti-Semitic Twins," 165–166, 183.

Chapter 10

1. "What I Would Do If I Had Only One Year to Live: An Interview with Rabbi Max Heller," *Times-Picayune*, 24 May 1924.

2. Max Heller, New Orleans, to president and board of Temple Sinai, 24 May 1916, Box 5, Folder 20, MHP.

3. Some of the students who mentioned that Heller "looked like God" were Ruth Drey-fous, Moise Steeg, Hélène Godchaux, and Mary Anna Feibelman, interviews, 1990–1993; undated, Box 16, Folder 5, MHP; Heller, *Jubilee Souvenir*, 91–92.

4. Max Heller, New Orleans, to Temple Sinai board members, 28 February 1917, Box 5, Folder 20, MHP.

5. Cecile Heller Lasker, Chicago, to Max and Isaac Heller, New Orleans, 6 November

1920, Box 8, Folder 1, MHP; "Jew Is the Western Chess Champion Again," *Chicago Israelite*, 30 October 1920; "Funeral of Rabbi Heller's Daughter," *Times-Picayune*, 12 November 1920; interview with Mildred Heller.

6. S. Walter Stern, New Orleans, to Max Heller, New Orleans, 28 February and 25 March 1920, Box 5, Folder 15, MHP; Henry Englander, Cincinnati, to Max Heller, New Orleans, 23 February 1920, Box 2, Folder 7, MHP; Joseph L. Baron, Cincinnati, to Max Heller, New Orleans, 6, and 21 May 1920, Box 1, Folder 4, MHP; "Rev. Heller to Be Associate of Dr. Grossman," *Cincinnati Times-Star*, 14 October 1920; "Congregation Selects Rabbi James G. Heller," unidentified clipping, Box 15, Folder 6, MHP; "Plum Street Temple Congregation Elects Associate Rabbi," *American Israelite*, 28 October 1920; "Plum Street Temple—Installation of Rabbi Heller," *American Israelite*, 28 December 1920; *Isaac M. Wise* is James Heller's study of his father's mentor.

7. DeVore and Logsdon, *Crescent City Schools*, 171, 176, 182, 183, 197; interview with Mildred Heller; Edward Heller recalls that when he was a child, his father arranged for Booker T. Washington School to host entertainer Paul Robeson. Robeson refused to perform for a segregated group, and Isaac Heller somehow managed to ensure that an integrated audience would be present. Edward Heller was in the audience; phone interview with Edward Heller, son of Mildred and Isaac, 12 May 1994.

8. Max Heller, "A Tale of Thirty-Five Years," 3 March 1922, Box 4, Temple Sinai Papers; "Congregation Temple Sinai," 18 May 1911, Box 5, Folder 20, MHP; "Rabbi Gives Purse to Temple Fund," *Times-Picayune*, 5 March 1922; in the wake of Heller's unselfish action, an editorial in the *Hebrew Standard* declared, "All honor to him," 31 March 1922.

9. Max Heller, New Orleans, to Solomon Foster, Newark, 3 October 1913, Box 1, Folder 12, Solomon Foster Papers, AJA; the *New Orleans States* featured sketches of both the old and proposed temples, "Dream to Be Reality Soon," no date, Box 15, Folder 16, MHP; telephone conversation with Herbert Barton, Temple Sinai administrator, spring 1993.

10. Heller, *Jubilee Souvenir*, I.

11. Heller, *Jubilee Souvenir*, 15–16, 26–30, 32–38, 129.

12. Heller, *Jubilee Souvenir*, 121–125.

13. "Temple Sinai Anniversary: New Point in Noble Life," *Times-Picayune*, 12 November 1922; Heller, *Jubilee Souvenir*, 15–16, 27, 30–33, 120–125. In *The Synagogues of Kentucky*, Lee Shai Weissbach discusses synagogue architecture as an expression of Jewish identity; Rabbi Julian Feibelman, Sinai's well-loved rabbi from 1936 until his retirement to emeritus status in 1967, was active in the anti-Zionist American Council for Judaism, as were many Temple Sinai members, although he admitted that Israel's statehood and recognition by President Harry Truman "brought down the curtain on the last act." Feibelman resigned from the American Council, claiming that he "neither could nor would argue with history"; Feibelman, *The Making of a Rabbi*, 384–397 (quotation, 395).

14. Samuel Schulman, New York, to Max Heller, 14 October 1925, Box 5, Folder 6, MHP; Max Heller, New Orleans, to Members of the (HUC) Board of Governors, Cincinnati, October 1918, L (scratch copy), Box 5, Folder 20, MHP; Max Heller, New York, to Julian Morgenstern, Cincinnati, 16 October 1925, Series A, Box 12, Folder 4, HUC Papers.

15. "Dr. Max Heller Gives Farewell Sermon as Rabbi," *Times-Picayune*, 5 March 1927.

16. Stephen S. Wise, New York, to Temple Sinai (board members), New Orleans, 23 February 1927, Box 45, Folder 16, SSWP; "Dr. Heller Paid Farewell Honors," *Times-Picayune*, 6 March 1927.

17. " 'Workable' Religion Seen as World Need: Humanity Has Been 'Preached At' Long Enough, View of Rabbi Heller," *Birmingham News*, 2 April 1928. The day before, the three Birmingham temples, Emanu-El, K'nesseth Israel and Beth El, honored Heller on his return from Palestine; see Cowett, *Birmingham's Rabbi*, 163.

18. After his father's death, James Heller had the articles published as *My Month in Palestine*, 23.

19. Heller, *My Month in Palestine*, 228.

20. Heller, *My Month in Palestine*, 229–247.

21. "The Passing of a Great Jew," *B'nai B'rith Magazine*, May 1929, p. 253; Stephen S. Wise, New York, to Max Heller, New Orleans, 16 February 1928, Box 5, Folder 11, JIRP; "Excerpts of an address given by the Rev. Maximillian Heller, Rabbi Emeritus of Temple Sinai, New Orleans, La., on 'Modernized Judaism and the Modern Rabbi,' at the Third Annual Baccalaureate Service of the Jewish Institute of Religion," Box 5, Folder 11, JIRP; Stephen S. Wise, New York, to Max Heller, New York, 1 June 1928, Box 5, Folder 11, JIRP, AJA; Temple Sinai Dedication Program, 2–4 November 1928, Klaus Library, HUC-JIR, Cincinnati.

22. "City Mourns the Death of Dr. Max Heller," *New Orleans States*, 30 March 1929, "1500 Attend Services for Rabbi Heller," *Morning Tribune*, 1 April 1929; "Dr. M. M. Heller," unidentified clipping, Box 15, Folder 6, MHP; "Dr. Max Heller," editorial, *States*, 31 March, 1929; "Rabbi Heller's Rites to be Held this Afternoon," *Times-Picayune*, 1 March 1929.

23. "Dr. Heller Dies: A Zionist Pioneer Known Throughout World as Champion of Rebuilding of Palestine, Pillar of Liberal Judaism," *New York Times*, 1 April 1929.

24. Julian Morgenstern, Box 16, Folder 4, MHP; "Memorial Service for Dr. Max Heller," 3 May 1919, program, Box 16, Folder 4, MHP.

25. Emanuel Gamoran, "Dr. Max Heller—A Tribute," *American Israelite*, 12 April 1929; Ephraim Lisitzky, "Dr. Max Heller," *Jewish Ledger*, 12 April 1929; "A Severe Loss," *Jewish Tribune*, 5 April 1919; Maurice H. Harris is quoted in the *Jewish Daily Bulletin*, 2 April 1919.

26. Feibelman, *The Making of a Rabbi*, 436–438, describes the time in 1949 when Ralph Bunche, the distinguished African American and U.S. delegate to the United Nations, spoke at Temple Sinai. It was the first time a large integrated audience had gathered in the city. Feibelman offered the temple's facilities when Tulane University and the New Orleans Civic Auditorium declined to welcome Bunche. The activists of the 1960s included Helen Mervis, Margie Stich, Ruth Dreyfous and her sister-in-law, Mathilde Dreyfous, Jane Buchsbaum, and many others. In 1994, Max Heller's great-grandson, Mark Heller, served on the board of the temple, as chairman of the Federation's Community Relations Committee and was the Jewish Federation Men's Division campaign chair, 1994–1995.

Appendix

1. The Philadelphia Conference of 1869 was called by David Einhorn and Samuel Adler. According to Meyer, *Response to Modernity*, Einhorn and Adler invited only "their theologically educated colleagues, who favor decided religious progress," to "concur on basic principles that would set Reform clearly apart from Orthodoxy." The discussion was entirely in German. Wise attended, but when traditionalists attacked the radicals, he distanced himself from the Conference, probably because he realized that "while most congregations were in favor of progress, they abhorred radicalism" (Meyer, *Response to Modernity*, 255–258).

SELECTED
BIBLIOGRAPHY

Primary Sources

Archival Materials

American Jewish Archives, Hebrew Union College–Jewish Institute of Religion,
Cincinnati, Ohio
> Henry Berkowitz Papers
> Central Conference of American Rabbis Papers
> Gotthard Deutsch Papers
> Herman Enelow Papers
> Solomon Foster Papers
> Leo M. Franklin Papers
> Ephraim Frisch Papers
> Hebrew Union College Papers
> James Heller Papers
> Max Heller Papers
> Henry Hurwitz Menorah Society Papers
> Jewish Institute of Religion Papers
> Horace M. Kallen Papers
> Louis Marshall Papers
> David Philipson Papers
> Jacob Schiff Papers
> Samuel Schulman Papers
> Senior Family Papers
> Isaac Mayer Wise Correspondence
> Stephen S. Wise Papers
> Union of American Hebrew Congregations Papers

American Jewish Historical Society Archives, Brandeis University, Waltham,
Massachusetts
> Stephen S. Wise Papers

Amistad Research Center, Tulane University, New Orleans
> Central Congregational Church Papers, New Orleans
> Lucille L. Hutton Papers

The Center for American History, University of Texas at Austin
    Henry Cohen Papers

Howard-Tilton Library, Tulane University, New Orleans
    William R. Hogan Jazz Archives
    Louisiana Collection
    Special Collections
        George Washington Cable Papers
        Henry Mortimer Favrot Papers
        Henri Levi Papers
        National Council of Jewish Women Papers
        Temple Sinai Papers
        Touro Synagogue Papers

Klaus Library, Hebrew Union College–Jewish Institute of Religion, Cincinnati, Ohio

Library of Congress, Washington, D.C.
    National Association for the Advancement of Colored People Papers, Administration File

Louisiana Collection, New Orleans Public Library

Touro Infirmary Archives, New Orleans

University of Cincinnati Archives, Belgen Library, Cincinnati, Ohio
    University of Cincinnati Papers

Interviews

Brener, Mike. Interview with the author. 14 April 1993. New Orleans. Tape recording.
Cohen, Rosalie. Interviews with the author. 16 March 1989; 6, 17 June 1993. New Orleans. Tape recordings.
Dreyfous, Ruth. Interviews with the author. 12 November 1988, 13 February 1989, 20 June 1993. New Orleans. Tape recordings.
Feibelman, Mary Anna, and Alice Fellman. Interview with the author. 24 September 1988. New Orleans. Tape recording.
Godchaux, Hélène. Interview with the author. 16 March 1989. New Orleans. Tape recording.
Heller, Mildred. Interview with the author. 1 February 1989. New Orleans. Tape recording.
Marcus, Jacob Rader. Interviews with the author. 28 July 1989, 19 July 1990, 24 July 1993, 16 November 1993. Cincinnati. Tape recordings.
Steeg, Moise. Interview with the author. 22 March 1993. New Orleans. Tape recording.

Newspapers and Periodicals

American Hebrew, New York, New York, 1900–1920
American Israelite, Cincinnati, Ohio, 1885–1929
B'nai B'rith News, scattered issues
Daily Picayune, New Orleans, Louisiana, scattered issues
Item, New Orleans, scattered issues
Jewish Ledger, New Orleans, Louisiana, 1895–1929
Maccabaean, 1900–1929
Mascot, New Orleans, Louisiana, 1884–1891
Menorah Journal, 1900–1929
States, New Orleans, Louisiana, scattered issues
Times-Democrat, New Orleans, Louisiana, scattered issues

Secondary Sources

Adler, Cyrus, ed. *American Jewish Yearbook, 1903–1904.* Philadelphia: Jewish Publication Society of America, 1904.

Alwes, Berthod C. "The History of the Louisiana State Lottery Company." *Louisiana Historical Quarterly* 27 (October 1944): 964–1118.

Andriot, John L., ed. *Population Abstract of the United States,* vol. 1. McLean, Va.: Andriot and Associates, 1983.

"An Intimate Portrait of the Union of American Hebrew Congregations—A Centennial Documentary." *American Jewish Archives* 25 (April 1973): 18–20.

Arnesen, Eric. "Waterfront Workers of New Orleans: Race, Class, and Politics, 1863–1923." Ph.D. diss., Yale University, 1986.

Ashkenazi, Elliott. *The Business of Jews in Louisiana, 1840–1875.* Tuscaloosa: University of Alabama Press, 1988.

Bailey, Hugh C. *Edgar Gardner Murphy, Gentle Progressive.* Coral Gables, Fla.: University of Miami Press, 1968.

——. *Liberalism in the New South: Southern Social Reformers and the Progressive Movement.* Coral Gables, Fla.: University of Miami Press, 1969.

Bauer, Yehuda. *A History of the Holocaust.* New York: Franklin Watts, 1978.

Bauman, Mark K. "Centripetal and Centrifugal Forces Facing the People of Many Communities: Atlanta Jewry from the Frank Case to the Great Depression." *Atlanta Historical Journal* 23 (Fall 1979): 25–54.

——. "A Functional Approach to the Study of the American Rabbinate." Photocopy. Atlanta Metropolitan College, Atlanta, 1989.

——. "Race and Mastery: The Debate of 1903." In *From the Old South to the New: Essays on the Transitional South,* edited by Walter J. Fraser, Jr., and Winfred B. Moore, Jr. Westport, Conn.: Greenwood Press, 1981.

Bauman, Mark K., and Arnold Shankman. "The Rabbi as Ethnic Broker: The Case of David Marx." *Journal of American Ethnic History* 2 (Spring 1983): 51–68.

Bennetts, David Paul. "Black and White Workers: New Orleans, 1880–1900." Ph.D. diss., University of Illinois at Urbana-Champaign, 1972.

Berman, Myron. *The Attitude of American Jewry Towards East European Immigration, 1881–1914*. New York: Arno Press, 1980.

Biennial Report of the State Superintendent of Public Education to the General Assembly, 1892–1893. Baton Rouge: Advocate, 1894.

Biographical and Historical Memoirs of Louisiana, vol. 1. 1892. Reprint ed. Baton Rouge: Claitor's Publishing Division, 1975.

Bloom, Jack. "The Rabbi as Symbolic Exemplar." Ph.D. diss., Columbia University, 1972.

Bodnar, John. *The Transplanted: A History of Immigrants in Urban America*. Bloomington: University of Indiana Press, 1985.

Brandeis, Louis D. *Zionism and Patriotism*. New York: Federation of American Zionists, 1915.

Brownell, Blaine A., and David R. Goldfield, eds. *The City in Southern History*. Lexington: University Press of Kentucky, 1977.

Buber, Martin, ed. *Ten Rungs: Hasidic Sayings*. New York: Schocken Books, 1947.

Buck, Joan Juliet. "The Paradoxes of Prague." *Condé Nast Traveler*, June 1989, pp. 122–133, 154–161.

Cable, George Washington. *"The Silent South" Together with "The Freedman's Case in Equity" and "The Convict Lease System."* New York: Charles Scribner's Sons, 1885.

Cahan, Abraham. *The Rise of David Levinsky*. 1917. Reprint ed. New York: Harper and Row, 1960.

Calder, Jenni. *The Victorian Home*. London: B. T. Batsford, 1977.

Cinel, Dino. "Sicilians in the Deep South: The Ironic Outcome of Isolation." *Studi Etudes Emigrazione Migrations* 97 (March 1990): 55–86.

Clare, George. *Last Waltz in Vienna: The Destruction of a Family, 1842–1942*. London: Pan Books, 1980.

Clark, Robert T., Jr. "The German Liberals in New Orleans, 1840–1869." *Louisiana Historical Quarterly* 20 (1937): 137–151.

Cohen, Gary B. *The Politics of Ethnic Survival: Germans in Prague, 1861–1914*. Princeton, N.J.: Princeton University Press, 1981.

Cohen, Joseph. "The Jews of New Orleans and the Mardi Gras." Photocopy. Tulane University, New Orleans, 1982.

Cohen, Naomi. *Jews in Christian America: The Pursuit of Religious Equality*. New York: Oxford University Press, 1992.

———. "The Reaction of Reform Judaism in America to Political Zionism (1897–1922)." *Publications of the American Jewish Historical Society* 40 (June 1951): 361–394.

The Convention of '98. New Orleans: William E. Myers, Publisher, 1898.

Cowen, Philip. *Memories of an American Jew*. New York: Arno Press, 1975.

Cowett, Mark. *Birmingham's Rabbi: Morris Newfield and Alabama, 1895–1940*. Tuscaloosa: University of Alabama Press, 1986.

——. "Rabbi Morris Newfield and the Social Gospel: Theology and Societal Reform in the South." *American Jewish Archives* 34 (April 1982): 52–74.

Cremin, Lawrence A. *The Transformation of the School: Progressivism in American Education, 1876–1957.* 1961. Reprint ed. New York: Vintage Books, 1964.

Dethloff, Henry C., and Robert R. Jones. "Race Relations in Louisiana, 1877–1898." *Louisiana History* 9 (Fall 1968): 301–323.

DeVore, Donald E., and Joseph Logsdon. *Crescent City Schools: Public Education in New Orleans, 1841–1991.* Lafayette: University of Southwestern Louisiana, 1991.

Diner, Hasia R. *In the Almost Promised Land: American Jews and Blacks, 1915–1935.* Westport, Conn.: Greenwood Press, 1977.

——. *A Time for Building: The Third Migration, 1880–1920.* Baltimore: Johns Hopkins University Press, 1992.

Dinnerstein, Leonard. *The Leo Frank Case.* New York: Columbia University Press, 1968.

Du Bois, W. E. B. "Strivings of the Negro People." *Atlantic Monthly* 80 (August 1897): 194–198.

Dyer, Thomas G. *Theodore Roosevelt and the Idea of Race.* Baton Rouge: Louisiana State University Press, 1980.

Ettinger, Brian Gary. "John Fitzpatrick and the Limits of Working-Class Politics in New Orleans, 1892–1896." *Louisiana History* 26 (Fall 1985): 341–367.

Everard, Wayne M. "Bourbon City: New Orleans, 1878–1900." *Louisiana Studies* 11 (Fall 1972): 240–251.

Ewing, Quincy. "The Heart of the Race Problem." *Atlantic Monthly* 103 (March 1909): 389–397.

Feibelman, Julian B. *The Making of a Rabbi.* New York: Vantage Press, 1980.

Feingold, Henry L. *Zion in America: The Jewish Experience from Colonial Times to the Present.* New York: Twayne Books, 1974.

Feldman, Egal. *Dual Destinies: The Jewish Encounter with Protestant America.* Chicago: University of Illinois Press, 1990.

——. "The Social Gospel and the Jews." *American Jewish Historical Quarterly* 53 (March 1969): 308–329.

Felsenthal, Emma. *Bernhard Felsenthal, Teacher in Israel: Selections from his Writings with Biographical Sketch and Bibliography by his Daughter.* New York: Oxford University Press, 1924.

Fox, Steven A. "On the Road to Unity: The Union of American Hebrew Congregations and American Jewry, 1873–1903." *American Jewish Archives* 32 (November 1980): 145–193.

Fredrickson, George M. *The Black Image in the White Mind: The Debate on Afro-American Character and Destiny, 1817–1914.* New York: Harper and Row, 1971.

Glanz, Rudolf. "The German-Jewish Mass Emigration, 1820–1880." *American Jewish Archives* 22 (April 1970): 49–66.

Glazer, Nathan. *American Judaism.* Chicago: University of Chicago Press, 1957.

Goldblatt, Charles Israel. "The Impact of the Balfour Declaration in America." *American Jewish Historical Quarterly* 57 (June 1968): 455–515.

Goldfield, David R. *Cotton Fields and Skyscrapers*. Baltimore: Johns Hopkins University Press, 1982.

Gossett, Thomas. *Race: The History of an Idea in America*. Dallas: Southern Methodist University Press, 1963.

Grantham, Dewey. *Southern Progressivism: The Reconciliation of Progress and Tradition*. Knoxville: University of Tennessee Press, 1983.

Greene, Victor R. *American Immigrant Leaders, 1800–1910: Marginality and Identity*. Baltimore: Johns Hopkins University Press, 1987.

Greenstein, Howard R. *Turning Point: Zionism and Reform Judaism*. Chico, Calif.: Scholars Press, 1981.

Guerin, Kenneth R. "James Campbell Moise: Louisiana Lottery Opponent." *Louisiana Studies* 9 (Spring 1972): 84–98.

Haas, Edward F. "John Fitzpatrick and Political Continuity in New Orleans, 1896–1899." *Louisiana History* 22 (Winter 1981): 7–30.

———. *Political Leadership in a Southern City: New Orleans in the Progressive Era, 1896–1902*. Ruston, La.: McGinty Publications, 1988.

Hair, William Ivy. *Bourbonism and Agrarian Protest: Louisiana Politics, 1877–1900*. Baton Rouge: Louisiana State University Press, 1969.

———. *Carnival of Fury: Robert Charles and the New Orleans Race Riot of 1900*. Baton Rouge: Louisiana State University Press, 1976.

Harlan, Louis R. "Booker T. Washington's Discovery of the Jews." In *Booker T. Washington in Perspective: Essays of Louis R. Harlan*, edited by Raymond W. Smock. Jackson: University Press of Mississippi, 1988.

———. "The Secret Life of Booker T. Washington." *Journal of Southern History* 37 (August 1971): 393–416.

Haygood, Atticus. *Our Brother in Black: His Freedom and His Future*. New York: Phillips and Hunt, 1881.

"Hebrew Union College–Jewish Institute of Religion—A Centennial Documentary." *American Jewish Archives* 26 (November 1974): 151–153.

Heller, James G. *Isaac M. Wise: His Life, Work, and Thought*. New York: Union of American Hebrew Congregations, 1965.

Heller, Max. "Americanism and Zionism," *Maccabaean*, March 1919, p. 69.

———. "The Anti-Semitic Twins." *B'nai B'rith Magazine*, February 1925, pp. 165–166, 183.

———. "Atonement Eve Address." *American Israelite*, February 11, 1909.

———. "Bernhard Felsenthal." *Reform Advocate*, December 31, 1921.

———. "Booker T. Washington." *Olio* 30 (January 1916): 2–6.

———. "Dangers of the Hour." *Maccabaean*, September 1919, pp. 270–271.

———. "Dollarland Spirituality." *Maccabaean*, April 1917, pp. 198–199.

———. " 'The Elder Brother': A Commencement Sermon at Tuskegee Institute, May 20, 1917." *Southwestern Christian Advocate*, June 7, 1917.

———. *Jubilee Souvenir of Temple Sinai, 1872–1922*. New Orleans, 1922.

——. "Maimonides and the Philosopher of Evolution." Master's thesis, University of Cincinnati, 1884.

——. "Manliness Versus Prejudice." *American Missionary*, April 1911, pp. 859–862.

——. "The Mission in Dispersion." *Maccabaean*, May 1917, pp. 224–225.

——. *My Month in Palestine: Impressions of Travel.* New York: Bloch Publishing, 1929.

——. "Nationalism and Religion." *Maccabaean*, June-July 1917, pp. 247–248.

——. "Nationalism in English Diplomacy." *Maccabaean*, December 1917, p. 415.

——. "Our Salvation." New York: Press of Philip Cowen, 1902. (Reprinted from the *Menorah*, December 1901, January 1902.)

——. "Our Spiritual Golus." *Maccabaean*, August 1917, pp. 314–315.

——. "The Personality of Gotthard Deutsch." *Hebrew Union College Monthly*, March 1922, pp. 149–152.

——. "Pioneer Types in Louisiana and Mississippi." Undated typescript. Max Heller Papers.

——. "The Quandary of the Apostate Jew." *B'nai B'rith Magazine*, January 1925, pp. 138–139, 149.

——. "The Rationale of Modern Judaism." *Maccabaean*, July 1903, pp. 32–34.

——. "A Realized Pattern of Social Justice." *Menorah Journal*, August 1918, 236.

——. "San Remo and the Reform Rabbis," *Maccabaean*, August 1920, pp. 39–41.

——. "What Zionism Saves." *Maccabaean*, February 1910, pp. 47–48.

——. "When Zionism and Reform Meet." *Maccabaean*, May 1919, pp. 112–114.

——. "Zionism and the Mission." *Maccabaean*, January 1911, pp. 20–21.

——. "Zionism and Our Reform Rabbinate." *Maccabaean*, July 1918, pp. 180–181, 190–191.

——. "Zionism as the Leaven." *Maccabaean*, March-April 1911, pp. 95–96.

Hertzberg, Steven. *Strangers Within the Gate City: The Jews of Atlanta, 1845–1915.* Philadelphia: Jewish Publication Society of America, 1978.

Higham, John. *Ethnic Leadership in America.* Baltimore: Johns Hopkins University Press, 1978.

——. "Social Discrimination Against Jews in America, 1830–1930." *Publications of the American Jewish Historical Society* 47 (1957): 1–33.

——. *Strangers in the Land: Patterns of American Nativism, 1860–1925.* New Brunswick, N.J.: Rutgers University Press, 1955.

Holmes, William F. "Moonshiners and Whitecaps in Alabama, 1893." *Alabama Review* 34 (January 1981): 31–49.

——. "Whitecapping: Anti-Semitism in the Populist Era." *American Jewish Historical Quarterly* 58 (March 1974): 244–261.

——. "Whitecapping in Mississippi: Agrarian Violence in the Populist Era." *Mid-America* 15 (1973): 134–148.

Jackson, Joy. "Crime and the Conscience of a City." *Louisiana History* 9 (Summer 1968): 229–244.

——. *New Orleans in the Gilded Age: Politics and Urban Progress.* Baton Rouge: Louisiana State University Press, 1969.

Jick, Leon A. *The Americanization of the Synagogue, 1820–1870*. Hanover, N.H.: University Press of New England for Brandeis University Press, 1976.

Kallen, Horace M. "Democracy Versus the Melting-Pot, Part One." *Nation*, 18 February 1915, pp. 190–194.

———. "Democracy Versus the Melting-Pot, Part Two." *Nation*, 25 February 1915, pp. 217–220.

———. "The Ethics of Zionism." *Maccabaean*, August 1906, pp. 61–71.

———. "Jewish Life Is National and Secular." In *The Zionist Idea*, edited by Arthur Hertzberg. 1959. Reprint ed. New York: Atheneum, 1972.

Karff, Samuel E., ed. *Hebrew Union College–Jewish Institute of Religion at 100 Years*. Cincinnati: Hebrew Union College Press, 1976.

Karp, Abraham J. *Haven and Home: A History of the Jews in America*. New York: Schocken Books, 1985.

———. "Ideology and Identity in Jewish Group Survival in America." *American Jewish Historical Quarterly* 55 (June 1976): 310–334.

Katz, Jacob. *Out of the Ghetto: The Social Background of Jewish Emancipation, 1770–1870*. Cambridge, Mass.: Harvard University Press, 1973.

Kestenberg-Gladstein, Ruth. "The Jews Between Czechs and Germans in the Historic Lands, 1848–1918." In *The Jews of Czechoslovakia: Historical Studies and Surveys*. Philadelphia: Jewish Publication Society of America, 1968.

Kieval, Hillel. "Caution's Progress: The Modernization of Jewish Life in Prague, 1780–1830." In *Toward Modernity: The European Jewish Model*, edited by Jacob Katz. New Brunswick, N.J.: Transaction Books, 1987.

———. "Education and National Conflict in Bohemia: Germans, Czechs, and Jews." *Studies in Contemporary Jewry* 3 (1987): 49–71.

———. *The Making of Czech Jewry: National Conflict and Jewish Society in Bohemia, 1870–1918*. New York: Oxford University Press, 1988.

Kisch, Guido. *In Search of Freedom: A History of American Jews from Czechoslovakia*. London: Edward Goldston and Son, 1949.

Knee, Stuart E. *The Concept of Zionist Dissent in the American Mind, 1917–1941*. New York: Robert E. Speller and Sons, 1979.

Kogos, Fred. *A Dictionary of Yiddish Slang and Idioms*. New York: Paperback Library, 1967.

Kohn, Douglas. "David Philipson: American Anti-Zionist." American Jewish Archives, Hebrew Union College–Jewish Institute of Religion, Cincinnati, 1986.

Kohn, Hans. "Before 1918 in the Historic Lands." In *The Jews of Czechoslovakia: Historical Studies and Surveys*. New York: Jewish Publication Society of America and Society for the History of Czechoslovak Jews, 1968.

Kolsky, Thomas A. *Jews Against Zionism: The American Council for Judaism, 1942–1948*. Philadelphia: Temple University Press, 1990.

Korn, Bertram Wallace. *The Early Jews of New Orleans*. Waltham, Mass.: American Jewish Historical Society, 1969.

———. "German-Jewish Intellectual Influences on American Jewish Life, 1824–

1972." In *Tradition and Change in Jewish Experience*, edited by A. Leland Jamison. Syracuse, N.Y.: Syracuse University Press, 1978.

Kousser, J. Morgan. *The Shaping of Southern Politics: Suffrage Restriction and the Establishment of the One-Party South, 1880–1910*. New Haven: Yale University Press, 1974.

Lederhendler, Eli. *The Road to Modern Jewish Politics: Political Tradition and Political Reconstruction in the Jewish Community of Tsarist Russia*. New York: Oxford University Press, 1989.

Liebman, Charles. "The Training of American Rabbis." In *American Jewish Yearbook 69*, edited by Martha Jelenko. Philadelphia: Jewish Publication Society of America, 1968.

Lindemann, Albert S. *The Jew Accused: Three Anti-Semitic Affairs: Dreyfus, Beilis, Frank, 1894–1915*. New York: Cambridge University Press, 1991.

Lubove, Roy. *The Professional Altruist: The Emergence of Social Work as a Career, 1889–1930*. Cambridge, Mass.: Harvard University Press, 1965.

Ludlow, Victor Leifson. "Bernhard Felsenthal: Quest for Zion." Ph.D. diss., Brandeis University, 1984.

Malone, Barbara S. "Reform and Dissent: The Americanization of Max Heller, 1860–1898." Master's thesis, Tulane University, 1990.

Malone, Bobbie. "1888's Social Confrontation: The Upwardly Mobile Jew Versus the Club." *Community* (New Orleans), 18 August 1989, p. 6.

——. "New Orleans Uptown Immigrants—The Community of Congregation Gates of Prayer, 1850–1860." *Louisiana History* 32 (Summer 1991): 239–278.

Mandel, Irving Aarin. "Attitude of the American Jewish Community Toward East-European Immigration as Reflected in the Anglo-Jewish Press (1880–1890)." *American Jewish Archives* 1 (1948): 11–36.

Mann, Harold W. *Atticus Haygood: Methodist Bishop, Editor, and Educator*. Athens: University of Georgia Press, 1965.

Marcott, Louis W., comp. *Membership Roster of New Orleans Clubs, 1899*. New Orleans: D. J. Searcy–William Pfaff, Printers, 1899.

——. *To Count a People: American Jewish Population Data, 1585–1984*. New York: University Press of America, 1990.

Martin, Bernard. "The Americanization of Reform Judaism." *Journal of Reform Judaism* (Winter 1980): 33–58.

May, Henry F. *Protestant Churches and Industrial America*. 1949. Reprint ed. New York: Octagon Press, 1963.

Mayo, Louise A. *The Ambivalent Image: Nineteenth-Century America's Perception of the Jew*. Teaneck, N.J.: Fairleigh Dickinson University Press, 1988.

Meier, August. *Negro Thought in America, 1880–1915: Racial Ideologies in the Age of Booker T. Washington*. 1963. Reprint ed. Ann Arbor, Mich.: University of Michigan Press, 1966.

Mervis, Leonard J. "The Social Justice Movement and the American Reform Rabbi." *American Jewish Archives* 7 (June 1955): 171–227.

Meyer, Michael A. "American Reform Judaism and Zionism: Early Efforts and Ideological Rapprochement." *Studies in Zionism* 7 (Spring 1983): 49–64.

———. "A Centennial History." In *Hebrew Union College–Jewish Institute of Religion at 100 Years,* edited by Samuel E. Karff. Cincinnati: Hebrew Union College Press, 1975.

———. "The Hebrew Union College—Its First Years." *Cincinnati Historical Society Bulletin* 33 (Spring 1975): 7–23.

———. *Response to Modernity: A History of the Reform Movement in Judaism.* New York: Oxford University Press, 1988.

Mosse, George L. *Confronting the Nation: Jewish and Western Nationalism.* Hanover, N.H.: Brandeis University Press, 1993.

Mostov, Stephen. "A 'Jerusalem on the Ohio': The Social and Economic History of Cincinnati's Jewish Community, 1840–1875." Ph.D. diss., Brandeis University, 1981.

Murphy, Edgar Gardner. *The Present South.* New York: Macmillan, 1904.

Myers, W. E. *The Israelites of Louisiana.* New Orleans: W. E. Myers, [1905?].

Nadel, Stanley. "Jewish Race and German Soul in Nineteenth Century America." *American Jewish History* (Spring 1987): 6–26.

Nelli, Humbert S. *The Business of Crime: Italians and Syndicated Crime in the United States.* New York: Oxford University Press, 1976.

Newby, I. A. *Jim Crow's Defense, Anti-Negro Thought in America, 1900–1930.* Westport, Conn.: Greenwood Press, 1965.

———, ed. *The Development of Segregationist Thought.* Homewood, Ill.: Dorsey Press, 1968.

Nussbaum, Raymond O. "Progressive Politics in New Orleans, 1896–1900." Ph.D. diss., Tulane University, 1974.

Orton, Lawrence D. *The Prague Slav Congress of 1848.* Boulder, Colo.: East European Quarterly, 1978.

Panitz, Esther L. *Simon Wolf: Private Conscience and Public Image.* Rutherford, N.J.: Fairleigh Dickinson University Press, 1987.

Philipson, David. *My Life as an American Jew.* Cincinnati: Hebrew Union College Press, 1941.

Plaut, W. Gunther. "Reform Judaism: Past, Present and Future." *Journal of Reform Judaism* (Summer 1980): 1–11.

Polish, David. "The Changing and the Constant in the Reform Rabbinate." In *The American Rabbinate: A Century of Continuity and Change, 1883–1983,* edited by Jacob R. Marcus and Abraham J. Peck. Hoboken, N.J.: Ktav, 1985.

———. *Renew Our Days: The Zionist Issue in Reform Judaism, 1885–1948.* Jerusalem: Zionist Library, 1976.

Pulzer, Peter G. J. *The Rise of Anti-Semitism in Germany and Austria.* New York: John Wiley and Sons, 1964.

Race Problems in the South—Report of the Proceedings of the First Annual Conference Held Under the Auspices of the Southern Society for the Promotion of the Study of

Race Conditions and Problems in the South . . . at . . . Montgomery, Alabama, May 8, 9, 10, A.D. 1900. Richmond, Va.: B. F. Johnson, 1900.

Raisin, Max. "Reform Rabbis and Zionism." *Maccabaean,* March 1910, pp. 100–101.

Raphael, Marc Lee. "Intra-Jewish Conflict in the United States, 1869–1915." Ph.D. diss., University of California, Los Angeles, 1972.

———. *Profiles in American Judaism: The Reform, Conservative, Orthodox, and Reconstructionist Traditions in Historical Perspective.* San Francisco: Harper and Row, 1984.

Rischin, Moses. "Germans Versus Russians." In *The American Jewish Experience,* edited by Jonathan D. Sarna. New York: Holmes and Meier, 1966.

———. *The Promised City: New York's Jews, 1870–1914.* Cambridge, Mass.: Harvard University Press, 1962.

Rockaway, Robert. "Ethnic Conflict in an Urban Environment: The German and Russian Jew in Detroit, 1881–1914." *American Jewish Historical Quarterly* 60 (December 1970): 133–150.

Rubin, Barry. *Assimilation and Its Discontents.* New York: Random House, 1995.

Rudwick, Elliot. *W. E. B. Du Bois: A Study in Minority Group Leadership.* Philadelphia: University of Pennsylvania Press, 1960.

Sachar, Howard M. *The Course of Modern Jewish History.* Cleveland, Ohio: World Publishing, 1958.

———. *A History of the Jews in America.* New York: Alfred A. Knopf, 1992.

Sarna, Jonathan D. "Converts to Zionism in the American Reform Movement." 9 July 1990, revision. Photocopy.

———. Introduction to "The American Rabbinate: A Centennial View." *American Jewish Archives* 35 (November 1983): 98.

———. "New Light on the Pittsburgh Platform of 1885." Review of *The Changing World of Reform Judaism: The Pittsburgh Platform in Retrospect,* edited by Walter Jacob. *American Jewish History* (March 1987): 361–363.

———. " 'A Sort of Paradise for the Hebrews.' " In *Ethnic Diversity and Civic Identity: Patterns of Conflict and Cohesion in Cincinnati Since 1820,* edited by Henry Shapiro and Jonathan Sarna. Urbana: University of Illinois Press, 1992.

Schorske, Carl E. *Fin-de-Siècle Vienna: Politics and Culture.* New York: Vintage Books, 1981.

Schott, Matthew James. "John M. Parker of Louisiana and the Varieties of American Progressivism." Ph. D. diss., Vanderbilt University, 1969.

Scott, Anne Firor. *The Southern Lady: From Pedestal to Politics, 1830–1930.* Chicago: University of Chicago Press, 1970.

Seltzer, Robert M. *Jewish People, Jewish Thought.* New York: Macmillan, 1980.

Serwer, Blanche Luria, comp. and ed. "The Mechanical Man of Prague." In *Let's Steal the Moon: Jewish Tales, Ancient and Recent.* Boston: Little, Brown, 1970.

Shankman, Arnold. "Brothers Across the Sea: Afro-Americans on the Persecution of Russian Jews, 1881–1917." *Jewish Social Studies* 37 (Spring 1975): 114–121.

Shapiro, Robert D. *A Reform Rabbi in the Progressive Era: The Early Career of Stephen S. Wise.* New York: Garland Press, 1988.

Shpall, Leo. *The Jews in Louisiana.* New Orleans: Steeg Publishing, 1936.

Shugg, Roger W. *Origins of Class Struggle in Louisiana: A Social History of White Farmers and Laborers During Slavery and After, 1840–1875.* Baton Rouge: Louisiana State University Press, 1939.

Silverstein, Alan. *Alternatives to Assimilation: The Response of Reform Judaism to American Culture, 1840–1930.* Hanover, N.H.: University Press of New England for Brandeis University Press, 1994.

Smith, Timothy L. "Religion and Ethnicity in America." *American Historical Review* 4 (October 1978): 1155–1185.

Sorin, Gerald. *A Time for Building: The Third Migration, 1880–1920.* Baltimore: Johns Hopkins University Press, 1992.

Sosna, Morton. *Southern Liberals and the Race Issue: In Search of the Silent South.* New York: Columbia University Press, 1977.

Sproat, John G. *"The Best Men": Liberal Reformers in the Gilded Age.* New York: Oxford University Press, 1968.

Steiner, Ruth Heller. "Glimpses Through the Mist." February 1965, revised January 1982. Photocopy, American Jewish Archives.

———. " 'The Girls in Chicago.' " *American Jewish Archives* 26 (April 1974): 5–22.

Stern, Harriet. "Origins of Reform Judaism in New Orleans." Master's thesis, University of New Orleans, 1977.

Stern, Malcolm H., comp. *Americans of Jewish Descent: A Compendium of Genealogy.* Cincinnati: Hebrew Union College Press, 1960.

———. "The Role of the Rabbi in the South." In *Turn to the South: Essays on Southern Jewry,* edited by Nathan M. Kaganoff and Melvin I. Urofsky. Waltham, Mass.: American Jewish Historical Society, 1979.

Sternstein, Joseph. "Reform and Zionism, 1895–1904." *Herzl Yearbook* 5 (1963): 11–31.

Stolz, Joseph. "Maximilian Heller." *Central Conference of American Rabbis Yearbook* 39 (1929): 218–226.

Sussman, Lance. "Isaac Leeser and the Protestantization of American Judaism." *American Jewish Archives* 38 (April 1986): 1–9.

Thomas, William I. "The Psychology of Race Prejudice." In *The Development of Segregationist Thought,* edited by I. A. Newby. Homewood, Ill.: Dorsey Press, 1961.

Thomson, S. Harrison. *Czechoslovakia in European History.* Princeton, N.J.: Princeton University Press, 1944.

Toll, William. "Ethnicity and Freedom in the Philosophy of Horace M. Kallen." In *The Jews of North America,* edited by Moses Rischin. Detroit: Wayne State University Press, 1987.

Turner, Arlin. *George W. Cable: A Biography.* Baton Rouge: Louisiana State University Press, 1966.

Urofsky, Melvin I. *American Zionism from Herzl to the Holocaust.* Garden City, N.Y.: Doubleday, 1975.

———. *A Voice That Spoke for Justice: The Life and Times of Stephen S. Wise.* Albany: State University of New York Press, 1982.

Urquhart, Ronald Albert. "The American Reaction to the Dreyfus Affair: A Study of Anti-Semitism in the 1890s." Ph.D. diss., Columbia University, 1975.

Wall, Bennett, ed. *Louisiana: A History.* Arlington Heights, Ill.: Forum Press, 1984.

Washington, Booker T. *The Booker T. Washington Papers,* edited by Louis R. Harlan, vol. 3, 1889–1895. Urbana: University of Illinois Press, 1974.

Weissbach, Lee Shai. *The Synagogues of Kentucky.* Lexington: University of Kentucky Press, 1995.

Wickliffe, John C. "The Louisiana Lottery: A History of the Company." *Forum* 12 (January 1892): 569–576.

Wiebe, Robert H. *The Search for Order, 1877–1920.* New York: Hill and Wang, 1967.

Williamson, Joel. *The Crucible of Race: Black-White Relations in the American South since Emancipation.* New York: Oxford University Press, 1984.

Woodward, C. Vann. *The Strange Career of Jim Crow.* 3d rev. ed. New York: Oxford University Press, 1974.

———. *Tom Watson: Agrarian Rebel.* 1938. Reprint ed. New York: Oxford University Press, 1963.

Wynes, Charles E., ed. *Forgotten Voices: Dissenting Southerners in an Age of Conformity.* Baton Rouge: Louisiana State University Press, 1967.

Yearbook of the Central Conference of American Rabbis, 1890–1929. Cincinnati: Bloch Publishing, 1891–1930.

Zola, Gary. "Maximilian Heller: Reform Judaism's Pioneer Zionist." *American Jewish History* 4 (June 1984): 375–397.

Zunz, Oliver. "American History and the Changing Meaning of Assimilation." *Journal of American Ethnic History* 4 (Spring 1985): 53–81.

Zweig, Stefan. *The World of Yesterday.* New York: Viking Press, 1943.

INDEX

Abbott, Lyman, 27, 239 (n. 1)
Abt, Jacob J., 240 (n. 16)
Academica, 19
Adler, Morris, 227 (n. 6)
Adler, Samuel, 249 (n. 1)
African Americans, 84–108; and Frank case, 242 (n. 43); Heller declines to tour on behalf of NAACP, 186–87; Heller speaks at Central Congregational Church, 170–71; political influence, 224 (n. 11), 230 (n. 45); Temple Sinai and, 203, 249 (n. 26); Tuskegee Institute, 173–74, 233 (n. 55)
Ahavath Chesed (New York), 116–17
Ahavath Sholom Congregation (New Orleans), 228 (n. 11)
Alcoholism, 142–43
Alexander II, Czar, 59
American Committee for the Amelioration of the Conditions of Russian Immigrants, 61
American Council for Judaism, 246 (n. 47), 248 (n. 13)
American Hebrew, 119, 156, 161, 236 (n. 27)
American Israelite, 70; on Citizens' League, 80; and conflict between Leucht and Heller, 89–90; and Frank case, 157; on Heller, 28; Heller criticizes Stephen Wise in, 131–32; Heller resigns as columnist for, 167; on Heller's acceptance by congregation, 69; Heller writes on "Christmas confusions" in, 103–4; on Hennessy murder, 48–49; Isaac Mayer Wise and, 14, 30; and child labor, 145; and immigration, 155, 158; on New Orleans' Jewish community, 47, 61; on Southern Rabbinical Conference, 221 (n. 9); supports Heller's anti-Lottery activities, 54–55; and Zionism, 115, 128, 134, 137, 160–61, 180, 183–84
American Jewess, 229 (n. 33)
American Jewish Committee (AJC), 157, 166, 172

American Jewish Congress, 171–72, 174–75, 176, 184, 185, 199
American Jewish Relief Committee (AJRC), 167
American Missionary Association, 107
American Peace Society, 164–65
American Protective Association (APA), 68
American Public Health Association, 140
American Purity Congress (APC), 141, 142
"The Answer to Prejudice" (Max Heller), 156
Anti-Lottery League, 51–55, 57, 65, 78
Antin, Mary, 178
Anti-Semitism: and Dreyfus Affair, 92, 93–94; discussed in *Jubilee Souvenir*, 195; in Europe, 3; and Frank case, 158; and immigration, 121–22, 158–59; in New Orleans, 37–38; in New York, 121; in northern Louisiana, 47–48; and racism, 84–85, 93–94; Roosevelt and, 241 (n. 32); in Russia, 59; in United States, 82–83, 146–47, 176–77, 187–88; and Zionism, 121–22
Aristotle, 20
Ashkenazi, Elliott, 223 (nn. 1, 5, 7)
Atheism, 10–11
Atlantic Monthly, 95
Attucks, Crispus, 107

Balfour Declaration, 164, 177–78, 180–82, 185, 190
Bamberger, Gabriel, 62, 101
Barnstein, Henry, 246 (n. 50)
Beilis, Mendel, 157–58
Benjamin, Judah P., 49, 178
Bennetts, David Paul, 224 (n. 12)
Berkowitz, Henry, 131, 183, 246 (n. 47), 247 (n. 51)
Berrol, Selma, 231 (n. 19)
Binstock, Louis, 201, 203
Birth of a Nation, 171
Bismarck, Otto von, 113

Wise, Isaac Mayer, 25, 27, 41, 185; attends Philadelphia Conference of 1869, 249 (n. 1); death, 235 (n. 8); Felsenthal and, 24, 28; and HUC, 13–19; influences on, 239 (n. 1); in *Jubilee Souvenir*, 195; on Jewish patriarchy, 5; and Jewish immigrants, 59, 85; at Plum Street Temple, 191; and Reform Judaism, 113; relationship with Heller, 29–30, 46, 133, 169; and use of English, 220 (n. 14); and Zionism, 92, 111–12, 128, 161, 168

Wise, Leo, 115, 127–28, 137, 160–61

Wise, Stephen S., 133, 165, 166, 175, 184; and CCAR, 169–70; on Heller, 197; on Heller's death, 202; invites Heller to travel to Palestine, 186; and Jewish Institute of Religion, 201; and Kallen's attempts to speak at HUC, 167; *An Open Letter . . . on the Freedom of the Jewish Pulpit*, 131–32; opposes Heller for CCAR president, 129–32, 135; and Zionism, 111, 176, 180, 181, 182, 187, 247 (n. 53)

Wissenschaft Movement, 17–18, 20, 21, 23–24

"With Malice Toward None" (Max Heller), 175

Witt, Louis, 246 (n. 50)

Wolf, Horace J., 187

Wolf, Simon, 135–36, 155, 242 (n. 55)

"Woman in the World and at Home" (Max Heller), 148, 149

Woman's Journal, 148

Women, 74–76, 148–50

Woodward, C. Vann, 232 (n. 23)

World Congress of Races, 156

World War I, 164–65, 173, 175, 179

World Zionist Congress (WZC), 197, 199

Yeshivahs, 17

Young Men's Democratic Association (YMDA), 41, 50, 78

Young Men's Hebrew Association, 125–26, 140

Zangwill, Israel, 113–14, 156

Zion Congregation (Chicago), 23–25, 28, 221 (n. 7), 222 (n. 15)

Zionism, 109–38; and Balfour Declaration, 177–78, 180–86; Brandeis and, 167, 170, 175, 240 (n. 15); CCAR and, 244 (n. 21); discussed in *Jubilee Souvenir*, 195; Felsenthal and, 85; HUC and, 167–68, 237 (n. 45); James and Isaac Heller and, 192; and immigration and anti-Semitism, 121–22; and racism, 112; and Reform Judaism, 109–10, 127–29, 135, 136–37, 138, 160–62, 166–68, 175–76, 184–85, 187, 203, 234 (nn. 2, 4), 235 (n. 14), 238 (n. 60); and separation of church and state, 153; Temple Sinai and, 248 (n. 13); and U.S. anti-Semitism, 177. *See also* Palestine

"Zionism and the Mission" (Max Heller), 137

"Zionism and Our Reform Rabbinate" (Max Heller), 181

Zionist Organization of America, 184

Zionist Provisional Executive Committee, 172

Zola, Emile, 93

Zola, Gary, 235 (nn. 8, 14), 237 (n. 47)

Zollschan, Ignaz, 156

Zunz, Olivier, 227 (n. 7)

Zweig, Stefan, 5

About the Author

❦

Bobbie Malone is director, Office of School Services/State Historical Society of Wisconsin. She received her bachelor's degree from Newcomb College and her master's and doctorate from Tulane University. This is her first book.